MOOSEWOOD RESTAURANT BOOK *of* DESSERTS

OTHER BOOKS FROM
MOOSEWOOD RESTAURANT

New Recipes from Moosewood Restaurant

Sundays at Moosewood Restaurant

The Moosewood Restaurant Kitchen Garden

Moosewood Restaurant Cooks at Home

Moosewood Restaurant Cooks for a Crowd

Moosewood Restaurant Low-Fat Favorites

MOOSEWOOD RESTAURANT BOOK *of* DESSERTS

THE MOOSEWOOD COLLECTIVE

Clarkson Potter/Publishers
NEW YORK

Published by Clarkson N. Potter, Inc., 201 East 50th Street, New York, New York 10022. Member of the Crown Publishing Group.

Random House, Inc. New York, Toronto, London, Sydney, Auckland
http://www.randomhouse.com/

CLARKSON N. POTTER, POTTER, and colophon are trademarks of Clarkson N. Potter, Inc.

Printed in the United States of America

BOOK DESIGN BY SHERI G. LEE / joyfunstudio
ILLUSTRATIONS BY CATHERINE ROSE CROWTHER

Library of Congress Cataloging-in-Publication Data
Moosewood restaurant book of desserts / by the Moosewood Collective.
Includes index.
1. Desserts. 2. Moosewood Restaurant. I. Moosewood Collective.
TX773.M652 1997
641.8'6—dc21 97-1234

ISBN 0-517-70209-6 (hardcover)
ISBN 0-517-88493-3 (paperback)

10 9 8 7 6 5 4 3 2 1

First Edition

CONTENTS

RECIPES BY CHAPTER

DESSERT BEVERAGES

SAUCES AND TOPPINGS

CONFECTIONS

MOOSEWOOD CLASSICS

INTRODUCTION

DESSERT DOESN'T SEEM NECESSARY—CERTAINLY NOT A DAILY nutritional requirement. We can't help but notice, however, that many people approach dessert with excitement and anticipation. Some of our customers structure their entire meal around dessert. Some even ask us to put aside a specific treat before they've ordered their main meal. A few seem to think of dessert as something a bit sinful. And how many of us consider dessert a reward for finishing the more essential part of a meal?

Perhaps we hear familiar echoes from the past: "Finish your broccoli, if you want some ice cream." We'll leave a full discussion of the psychological aspects of the interrelationships between love, security, hunger, and dessert to the experts. But what we all know is that for whatever reasons, people love desserts.

We celebrate this impulse to make a meal, a daily ritual, finer by topping it with something sweet. We don't advocate eating sugary desserts at every meal, nor do we think it's a good idea to overdo a good thing—it is by eating sour, salty, and bitter foods that we most appreciate the sweet. It's hard to imagine a life lived without ever indulging in sweets. "Sweet" isn't just a sugary taste; it's anything agreeable, pleasurable, or gratifying, and we hope this book will add to your sweet moments.

Desserts are very popular at Moosewood Restaurant, and we've been serving a new menu of homemade desserts every day for a quarter of a century.

This cookbook includes some desserts that have remained constants at the restaurant for years as well as new ones that have made a big splash with our customers. Many are low in fat or concocted from nutritious fruits and quite naturally take a place in a healthful diet.

In our usual Moosewood fashion, we have assembled a wide range of offerings in this cookbook. There are plenty of useful, everyday desserts, chosen because they are tasty, wholesome, and light, and especially appreciated when they are simple and quick to make. Other desserts are spectacular enough to mark special occasions. Some are seasonal desserts that we might make only once or twice a year, yet we wouldn't want a year to go by without them. Summer Berry Pudding, bursting with luscious, colorful fruit, is emblematic of midsummer bounty. Pecan Pumpkin Pie, served in the autumn, reminds us of our connection to this wheeling planet as it tilts away from the sun.

OUT OF THIS PROCESS COME RECIPES WE CAN TRUST—AND SO CAN YOU.

Desserts have always comprised some of the most memorable and beloved foods of the world's diverse cultures. Panforte's centuries-old lineage can be traced to the hills of Tuscany. The distinctive combination of flavors in Jamaican Black Cake evokes that island's unique and venerable history just as Besbusa's ancient North African heritage is reflected in the use of semolina and coconut. Pizza di Grano has symbolic significance in Italian and Italian-American culture, but it tastes delicious to almost everyone. Every Sunday at the restaurant, when we concentrate on a particular ethnic or regional cuisine, we research new desserts; sometimes a Moosewood classic is born.

In many parts of the world, dessert is simply fresh fruit or occasionally something purchased from a bakery. In America, we have a tradition of everyday desserts. Maybe our abundance of wood and coal, the early nineteenth-century invention of cooking stoves, and cheap, nearby sources of sugar all contributed to our dessert-loving society.

Perhaps because desserts can be expressions of caring, many people hold close a love of the good things they ate as children. Some of our recipes were passed down from generation to generation. Desserts like Anna's Country Spice Cake, Erma Mabel's Rhubarb Cake, and Regina's Ruggelach carry the names of the mother, grandmother, or aunt associated with them. These dishes, often made as little acts of loving-kindness, can evoke the past with a taste or even just a fragrance and are a special part of many a family's tradition. Holiday baking has the very smell of warmth and sharing. The joyful tradition of honoring a child's birthday every year with a special cake, for instance, creates a feeling of being beloved. Even a cookie can soften a hard day.

One thing all the different desserts in this book have in common is that they are homestyle. The ingredients are accessible, no tricky techniques are required, and the results are reliable. At Moosewood we've never gone in for Baroque architectural construct desserts. Instead, our practical dessert makers have concentrated on making a really juicy cobbler or a buttery poundcake that never fails. We'll talk you through rolling out a pie crust if you're inexperienced, but cutting a few stars in the top is about as fancy as we get most of the time. Even desserts like our Festive Celebrations Cake, which is lovely enough for once-in-a-lifetime occasions, are a relative snap to assemble.

We're always interested in simple desserts that won't overburden a busy cook. Once a recipe is developed, we make little changes each time we prepare it, hoping to improve the procedure, flavor, or texture, until we're satisfied that we have the best recipe. Before a recipe goes into our cookbook, it is tested by several Moosewood cooks and tasted by our customers, friends, and families, who are forthright with criticism and praise. Out of this process come recipes we can trust—and so can you.

Recipes include preparation times and baking or chilling times when appropriate, but time is just one of the factors that might influence your choice of a dessert. On pages 378 to 388, you'll find special lists, including low-fat desserts, children's favorites, vegan desserts, quickly prepared desserts, and the impressive desserts list for those times when you really want to make a meal memorable. There is also a mix-and-match section (page 378) that tells you where to find all of the pie crusts, fillings, frostings, glazes, and a few extra sauces that are not recipes on their own, but are parts of other recipes. The Glossary of Ingredients (page 354) includes important ingredients commonly used in dessert making and describes items that may be unfamiliar. The Guide to Tips and Techniques (page 367) is full of helpful hints for novice cooks or for those looking for a particular bit of advice or a solution to a problem.

Why does a discussion of desserts provoke the urge to confess? Well, there was a period of time, perhaps the first year or two of work at Moosewood, when some of us (Laura Branca and Dan Branca, for example) consumed a fudge brownie à la mode after almost every shift worked. For others, it's the irresistible impulse to dive into the corner of the Double Pear Crisp, hot from the oven. We're like little kids—completely shameless in our love of great desserts. The Moosewood Collective has had to proclaim "sensible guidelines" to govern our consumption of restaurant desserts, and we have soberly sworn oaths to one another, promising to take it easy on the dessert chefs and leave some for the customers. The Moosewood dessert makers, having grown wise with time, often make "worker cakes" to appease us when incredible treats, such as Prune and Armagnac Cake, come out of the oven, filling the restaurant with an enticing aroma. Even so, Moosewood waiters can still be seen erasing Amaretto Poundcake from the blackboard menu when there's one piece left on the platter. Our customers love dessert . . . but we love it, too!

OUR CUSTOMERS LOVE DESSERT AND WE LOVE IT, TOO!

DESSERTS AT MOOSEWOOD

EVER SINCE MOOSEWOOD OPENED, WE HAVE SERVED HOMEMADE desserts. And in the beginning, Susan Harville churned them out almost singlehandedly with a flair all her own, week after week, year after year, for more than a dozen years.

Until our 1993 expansion, the restaurant was quite small (tiny even), and storage space was at a premium. The desserts were always neatly tucked away next to the Brown Cow Yogurt and San Pellegrino deliveries.

Pies were perched atop the deep stainless steel pans brimming with rice pudding, and the fudge sauce was labeled with a sketch of a skull and crossbones in a good-humored attempt to keep the staff from eating it. We crammed the day's desserts into the under-the-counter refrigerator with the beverages or onto the shelves next to the mountain of freshly baked and bagged breads.

Susan wove in and out of the kitchen (also tight quarters), dodging the paths of the other cooks on the shift—managing somehow to find an occasional free stove burner and a bit of oven space for dessert making. She would regularly work a wait shift and, in the midst of attending to her tables, pop into the kitchen to whip up an extra pan of brownies or some other dessert that was running out.

She was so skillful at her work and did it so apparently effortlessly that no one could fully appreciate how difficult it was, until she took a week's vacation and one or two of us had to fill in. Susan's desserts were homey desserts that you could really sink your teeth into. Besides the famous brownies were poundcakes, trifles, apricot fool, ricotta mousse, rice pudding, gingerbread, and very chocolate cakes. As this book goes to press, we'd like to take this opportunity to thank her for all of those years of dedication and deliciousness.

Sometime in the mid-1980s, Susan went on maternity leave and Kathleen (Kip) Wilcox stepped forward to make desserts. While Kip continued to keep many of the Moosewood favorites on the menu, she had her own style of desserts to contribute as well. Delicate, light and fancy, Continental-style desserts were added to Moosewood's offerings: linzer tortes, lattice-topped pies, heart-shaped Valentine's shortbread cookies, sabayon. For another half-dozen years Kip and Susan shared the dessert-making job, collaborating, inventing, exchanging tips and ideas, and fine-tuning the recipes. Desserts flourished. The customers were happy; the workers were happy.

In recent years since our expansion, Lisa Wichman and Jenny Wang have joined the ranks of the dessertmakers. Lisa works magic with puddings, custards, flans, luscious pies, and tender cookies (we consider three a serving—if you taste one, you eat at least three). She loves to invent vegan desserts and enjoys the adventure of trying new ethnic recipes. Jenny has a special knack for creating flavor-packed, seductive desserts: perfectly shaped cakes with impeccably smooth, glossy frostings that tempt even the most health-conscious among us to try just one bite—and then another. The talents of

these four, Susan, Kip, Lisa, and Jenny, were invaluable to the creation of this dessert book. They provided endless tips and ideas to the other fourteen of us as we all became serious dessert-makers for a year.

It has been fascinating to watch the dessert-maker's job gradually evolve into a position that rotates among several people, like almost every other job at Moosewood. Even two of our long-term employees have given it a whirl. Robin Wichman, Lisa's daughter, who absorbed Lisa's skill and ease with desserts as a natural part of growing up, took a turn during the busy summer season, and Eliza Leineweber (who seizes any opportunity to make a Celebration Cake) has shared her Hawaiian specialties with us during the past year.

Desserts will always be an important slice of life at Moosewood, and our offerings now include quite a gamut of possibilities. But we will never forget the unmistakable aroma of chocolate brownies wafting from the kitchen into the dining room during the days of Susan's wait shifts.

DESSERTS WILL ALWAYS BE AN IMPORTANT SLICE OF LIFE AT MOOSEWOOD.

ABOUT THE RECIPES

MOST OF THE RECIPES IN THIS BOOK DO NOT SPECIFY WHAT KIND of milk to use, but simply call for "milk." Whenever we say "milk," feel free to use regular whole milk or 1% or 2% milk. We tested all of the recipes using 2% milk, so you can feel confident that a low-fat milk will work fine. The only exceptions are those few cases in which we specify whole milk or skim milk because that is what is required in that particular case.

Likewise, most recipes call for "unbleached white flour" and were tested with both pastry flour and all-purpose flour. At Moosewood we prefer pastry flour for most desserts because it often produces a loftier cake and lighter pastry with a more tender crumb. However, unbleached white pastry flour is not widely available in some places, so we tested all of our recipes with all-purpose flour as well. We have specified "pastry flour" only when we thought all-purpose flour gave a significantly inferior result. If you can't get pastry flour but are dying to try one of the recipes that call for it, see the tips in the Guide (page 367) for making substitutions. Humidity can also alter the *amount* of flour needed to produce a perfect dough or batter, so be attentive to the descriptions we give in the proce-

dure as well as the quantities suggested in the ingredient list.

With baked goods, it is essential to know your oven. Always check the accuracy of the thermostat and beware of any hot spots. Please refer to the tips in the Guide (page 367) for a thorough discussion of the subject.

Following each recipe we have listed the equipment required. When we thought a recipe could be made just as easily without a piece of equipment, we designated it "optional"; when the equipment made the process much easier, quicker, or produced a slightly better result—but was not absolutely necessary—then we designated that item "preferred." Be aware that proper pan size is crucial, and pay particular attention to bundt pan sizes (see page 375).

Each recipe also gives an estimated cooking time that distinguishes the hands-on preparation time from the rising, baking, or chilling time (when you are essentially free to do something else). We hope these times will serve as helpful guidelines for you. Remember that they are based on efficient, focused cooking time *after* the ingredients are organized on the counter. They don't include interruptions by children, pets, friends, phone calls, or delivery men.

The low-fat recipes in this book have been nutritionally analyzed by CBORD Group, Inc., of Ithaca, New York, who prepared and provided the data for the nutritional bars on each of these recipes. Each bar lists the number of calories and the amounts of fat, saturated fat, monounsaturated fat, and cholesterol in one serving. In instances when a recipe suggests a range of servings, the analysis applies to the largest number of servings listed. When several choices appear in the original ingredient list, the calculations are based on the first choice that appears. In a few cases, only a recipe variation is low-fat, and the nutritional bar will indicate this. The nutritional analysis does not include optional ingredients or garnishes for which no quantity is specified.

The titles of all the low-fat recipes are highlighted in a contrasting color, and are listed alphabetically on the Guiltless Low-fat Treats list (page 383) for easy reference.

EASY FRUIT
❖ DESSERTS ❖

Easy Fruit Desserts

AS MUCH AS WE MAY VALUE HANDSOME VEGETABLES AND RELIABLE grains, fruits are the colorful crown jewels of the food world. With their natural sweetness, they are already dessert before you do a thing to them, and in many cuisines throughout the world, a piece of freshly picked, sun-ripened fruit at the end of the meal is enough. A tree-ripened orange, a cluster of plump cherries or grapes, a succulent fig, a handful of berries, a slice of juicy summer melon—all are luscious enough to fill us with delight. In this chapter, we offer simple treasures—desserts that demand little preparation and need little more than a pinch of spice, a dash of sugar or honey, or perhaps a few drops of wine. Use your senses of smell and touch when testing for the best fruit. Apples should be hard, crisp, and unblemished. Melons should be aromatic and yield a little to pressure. Cherries at their peak are firm and glistening. A ripe pineapple is yellow-orange and fragrant. Look for tight-skinned plums that seem heavy for their size. Berries must be perfect: unbruised, undented, sprightly. Serving fresh fruit along with a little chocolate or a basket of whole nuts can make it seem more like dessert. Or pair fruit with cheese. We recommend some of our favorite combinations for an effortless and sophisticated dessert. Our two cheese dips enhance fruit without overwhelming its intrinsic flavor. Serve summer cherries on their stems with Sour Cream Fruit Dip and fresh red or green grapes with thin delicate crackers and Creamy Apricot Dip. Whenever possible, select recipes that make use of fruit that is in season. Take advantage of local harvests for the freshest, most flavorful fruits. By patronizing a U-pick strawberry patch, a roadside stand advertising "our own" raspberries or peaches, or a farmers' market where you may find heirloom varieties of apples, you let the local growers know that you value and recognize food that is well grown. Next best is from your local supermarket where, with a discriminating sense of smell and touch, you can find delicious fruit year-round. When the summer draws to a close, it's time to fill the house with the warm, sweet aroma of cooked fruit. A quick way to prepare fruits is by broiling, baking, or sautéing. August Plum Toast is so simple and *trés Français*. Sautéed Apples are delicious served warm over crêpes, on ice cream, or in a baked pie shell. Luscious Broiled Figs are a very special and impressive dessert. In the middle of winter when the sun is low on the horizon and the yearning for fresh fruit is upon us, poached fresh and dried fruit is a delicious option. Cold weather keepers, such as pears and apples, are ideal for simmering in juice or wine. Some of our favorites include Jewish Holiday Compote and cardamom-scented Apricot Poached Pears. Fresh fruit salads are beautiful desserts that add sparkle to your meals any time of year. Carriacou Island Fruit Salad blends exotic tropical fruits. Midsummer Fruit in Wine, enduringly popular in Italy, is another almost effort-less way to treat fresh fruit. In several other chapters in this book, you'll find more easy desserts made with fresh fruit. It's quick work with a blender to make a dessert beverage with fruit. Amaretto Peach Parfait in the Moosewood Classics chapter (page 333) is not to be missed. The Sauces and Toppings chapter (page 301) is filled with many good ways to transform fruit into scrumptious desserts; any of the Flavored Whipped Creams served with sliced fruit make a simple and perfect dessert.

Fruit and Cheese

Fruit and cheese is a classic dessert in Europe, where an endless variety of cheeses grace the market stalls, supermarkets, and specialty cheese shops. Fruit is a natural accompaniment to cheese—the sweet side of savory and a juicy contrast to creamy or slightly crumbly and dry. Its bright colors and smooth contours complement the paleness and chunkiness of cheese.

We've listed a few of our favorite combinations of fruits with cheeses that can be found in our area. Serve the fruit with a small, sharp knife so your guests can slice the apple or pear or peach into small chunks and then cut off thin slices of cheese. There are, of course, endless partners in this category of dessert.

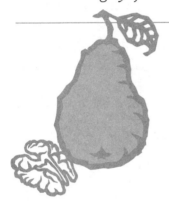

- Crisp apples, such as Mutsu, Ida Red, Cortland, or Granny Smith, with Stilton or sharp Cheddar
- Sliced Bartlett or Bosc pears with chèvre, toasted walnuts, and honey
- Assorted melons with smoked Gouda or smoked mozzarella
- Peaches and nectarines with mascarpone and Italian Sesame Cookies (page 193)
- Grapes with Camembert or Brie and water biscuits
- Comice pears with Parmesan and slices of crusty Italian bread
- Fresh berries with wheatmeal biscuits topped with creamy chèvre and thin slices of quince paste
- Sweet cherries with Sour Cream Fruit Dip (page 21)
- Oranges or tangerines with Maple Walnut Bread (page 268) and Neufchâtel
- Assorted plums with fromage blanc and Ginger Brandy Cookies (page 183)
- Comice pears with Gorgonzola and toasted hazelnuts
- Fresh pineapple with Saga blue

Fruit with Cardamom Yogurt

Cardamom is a fragrant and distinctive spice that we've combined here with orange juice and lime zest to create a refreshing chilled yogurt sauce to serve over sweet, ripe fruit. We suggest cubed melon and seedless grapes, but this sauce is also delightful with blackberries, peaches, pears, or bananas. For an interesting change in texture, try adding chopped almonds, walnuts, pecans, or shredded coconut.

IN A SMALL BOWL, whisk together the yogurt, sugar, orange juice concentrate, lime peel, cardamom, and salt. Refrigerate for at least 1 hour.

COMBINE THE MELON and grapes in a bowl. Pour the yogurt mixture over the fruit and toss gently. Serve chilled.

- **PREPARATION TIME:** 15 minutes
- **"MELDING" TIME:** 1 hour

PER 5.5 OZ SERVING: 92 CALS, 1 G TOT FAT, .2 G MONO FAT, .4 G SAT FAT, 2 MG CHOL

■ SERVES 4 TO 6

1 cup yogurt

1 tablespoon sugar

2 tablespoons frozen orange juice concentrate

½ teaspoon freshly grated lime peel

⅛ teaspoon ground cardamom

dash of salt

2 cups cubed cantaloupe or honeydew melon

2 cups green or red seedless grapes

Midsummer Fruit in Wine

New York State's Finger Lakes region is blessed with several excellent vineyards, many of them within a very short distance of Moosewood. A wine-tasting tour is a pleasant way to spend a summer's day. When we make this elegant, easily prepared dessert, we use fruit and wine produced along the shores of Cayuga and Seneca lakes.

The cherries turn the wine a rosy pink and the peaches add a fresh, bright flavor.

■ **SERVES 3 OR 4**

¼ cup sugar

1 cup white wine
  (a dry Riesling
  is nice)

1 small cinnamon stick

4 whole cloves
  (optional)

2 peaches, peeled and
  sliced

1 cup pitted sweet
  cherries

STIR THE SUGAR into the wine and add the cinnamon stick and the cloves, if desired. Add the peaches and cherries and stir well, making sure the sugar has dissolved.

REFRIGERATE FOR AT least an hour to allow the fruits to marinate in the wine. Before serving or after 2 hours—whichever comes first—remove the cinnamon stick and cloves.

SERVE IN SHALLOW bowls with a little wine spooned over the top and accompany with Cornmeal Cookies (page 181), Italian Sesame Cookies (page 193), or Pistachio Shortbread (page 196), if you like.

■ **PREPARATION TIME:** 15 minutes
■ **CHILLING TIME:** at least 1 hour

PER 6 OZ SERVING: 134 CALS, .1 G TOT FAT, 0 G MONO FAT, 0 G SAT FAT, 0 MG CHOL

Raspberry Poached Apricots

To celebrate the harvests of midsummer, choose locally grown, ripe, rosy apricots and freshly picked red raspberries for a beautiful and elegant compote that can be made with surprising ease. Keep this delicious seasonal dessert in a clear glass jar in the refrigerator, ready to be served with nonfat plain yogurt, whipped cream, or vanilla ice cream. Or serve it as a topping (after pitting the apricots) for Fluffy Sweet Biscuits (page 33) or plain cake.

IN THE SAUCEPAN, bring the sugar and water to a boil. Stir to dissolve the sugar. Cook the apricots in two batches by simmering for 2 to 4 minutes, until the fruit is soft but not mushy. Remove from the syrup and place them in a heatproof bowl. Add the raspberries to the apricots and pour the hot syrup over the fruit.

WEIGH THE FRUIT down with a plate—the apricots should be completely submerged—and chill until ready to serve. Raspberry Poached Apricots will keep tightly covered in the refrigerator for about 1 week.

- **PREPARATION TIME:** 20 to 25 minutes
- **CHILLING TIME:** about 1 hour
- **EQUIPMENT:** 2-quart nonreactive saucepan

PER 9 OZ SERVING: 202 CALS, .6 G TOT FAT, .2 G MONO FAT, 0 G SAT FAT, 0 MG CHOL

- **SERVES 6**

  1 cup sugar

  2 cups water

  1 quart whole fresh apricots

  2 cups fresh or frozen raspberries

Apricot Poached Pears

Bathed in a syrup made by reducing the poaching juice, these tender golden-brown pears harmonize beautifully with chewy, plump apricots and freshly whipped cream. For a vegan variation, replace the honey with about ⅓ cup of sugar or to taste.

- **SERVES 6**

  6 firm pears, peeled, with stems intact

  6 to 8 cups apricot or apple apricot juice

  ½ cup honey

  3 large cinnamon sticks

  3 thick slices fresh ginger root

  1 teaspoon whole cardamom seeds

  6 whole cloves

  sliced rind of 1 orange

  1 cup unsulphured dried apricots

  fresh whipped cream

  dash of ground cinnamon

PLACE THE PEARS, juice, and honey in the saucepan on medium heat. Tie the cinnamon sticks, ginger root, cardamom, cloves, and orange peel together in a small piece of cheesecloth and add to the liquid. (If you don't have any cheesecloth, just add the spices directly to the pot.) Simmer the pears for 20 to 40 minutes, stirring them occasionally, until they can be easily pierced with a sharp knife.

REMOVE EACH PEAR from the poaching liquid and set aside in a heatproof serving bowl. Boil the liquid rapidly on high heat for 10 to 15 minutes, until reduced to about 2½ cups. It will darken and begin to foam as it thickens. When reduced, pour the syrup through a strainer over the pears. Gently stir in the apricots.

COVER AND COOL to room temperature. Serve at room temperature or chill to serve later. Serve each pear on a small plate or saucer garnished with a generous amount of syrup, a few apricots, a dollop of whipped cream, and a sprinkling of cinnamon.

- **TOTAL TIME:** 45 to 60 minutes
- **EQUIPMENT:** 3- to 4-quart nonreactive saucepan

PER 6.75 OZ SERVING: 357 CALS, .8 G TOT FAT, .2 G MONO FAT, .1 G SAT FAT, 0 MG CHOL

August Plum Toast

If you could pick jam off a tree and spread it on toast, it might taste like this quick and easy seasonal dessert from the French countryside. The juiciness and tartness of fresh plums seep into the crispy, sweet bread as it bakes in the oven. August Plum Toast is a perfect brunch dish or last-minute dessert.

 PREHEAT THE OVEN to 375°.

BUTTER BOTH SIDES of each slice of challah using about 1 tablespoon of butter per slice. Place the slices on a baking sheet and set the remaining couple of tablespoons of butter aside.

IN A SMALL bowl, combine the sugar, cinnamon, and nutmeg. Sprinkle the bread slices with half of the sugar mixture and set the rest aside. Pit the plums and cut them into chunks. Arrange the plum pieces on top of the challah bread, being sure to cover each slice completely. Sprinkle on the rest of the sugar and dot the plums with the remaining butter.

BAKE FOR 25 to 30 minutes, until the edges of the bread are browned and the plums are soft and juicy. Serve immediately.

- **PREPARATION TIME:** 20 to 25 minutes
- **BAKING TIME:** 30 minutes
- **EQUIPMENT:** baking sheet

- **SERVES 4**

  - 6 tablespoons butter, softened
  - 4 slices challah or other egg bread (page 357)
  - ¼ cup sugar
  - 1 teaspoon ground cinnamon
  - ¼ teaspoon ground nutmeg
  - 8 to 12 plums

Broiled Figs

This simple rustic dessert is perfectly at home in a sophisticated menu. While an ideal finish to a meal with a French accent, it's not out of place in California cuisine, either—and then there's North African, Italian, Sephardic . . .

Serve the meltingly sweet, warm figs directly from the broiler, fanned out on a dessert plate with a dollop of sweetened yogurt, sour cream, crème fraîche, or mascarpone and garnish with orange slices or fresh raspberries. Or leave perfection alone and serve them unadorned.

■ **SERVES 4**

8 fresh figs

4 teaspoons brown sugar

¼ cup orange juice or marsala

 PREHEAT THE BROILER.

CUT EACH FIG in half lengthwise. Arrange the halves, cut side up, on the baking pan. Sprinkle with the brown sugar and drizzle on the orange juice or marsala. Broil for 5 to 7 minutes. Check the figs often and catch them at the moment the sugar begins to melt, the liquid is bubbling, and a light caramelized crust has just begun to form. Serve warm.

■ **TOTAL TIME:** 10 minutes
■ **EQUIPMENT:** broilerproof baking pan

PER 5 OZ SERVING: 119 CALS, .4 TOT FAT, .1 G MONO FAT, .1 G SAT FAT, 0 MG CHOL

A fresh fig is a teardrop of sweet, succulent fruit high in vitamins A and C, naturally low in fat, and a good source of fiber. Figs arrived in the New World via the French and Spanish in the eighteenth century, but they had been a favored fruit among the Greeks and Romans for centuries.

The figs grown in the United States, largely in California, have two growing seasons. The green-gold Calimyrna variety is available from May through June. Then from July through November the black-skinned Black Mission fig comes on the market. Halved or sliced, the salmon-pink flesh of each variety makes a stunning presentation.

A firm-ripe fig is ready for eating. An unripened fig will gradually ripen at room temperature, and once ripe, it should be chilled and eaten within a day or two. Fresh figs are quite sweet and refreshing, with a complicated texture that is at once creamy, juicy, and softly seeded. Figs harmonize well with soft, rich cheeses like mascarpone, cream cheese, and fromage blanc. They are also flattered by simple citrus- or anise-flavored sugar syrups.

Caribbean Baked Pineapple

This easily prepared, refreshing dessert provides the perfect finish for a Caribbean meal. Many supermarkets offer pre-cut fresh pineapple, which makes this an almost instant dessert. Because some pineapples are much sweeter than others, you may need to vary the amount of sugar. For extra richness, dot the pineapple with butter before baking.

4 to 5 cups fresh pineapple chunks (1 whole pineapple)

¼ cup packed brown sugar (or to taste)

¼ cup rum

½ teaspoon ground cinnamon

1 to 2 tablespoons butter (optional)

 PREHEAT THE OVEN to 400°.

COMBINE THE PINEAPPLE, brown sugar, rum, and cinnamon and mix well. Spread the mixture in the baking pan and dot with the butter, if desired. Bake until hot and bubbly, about 15 to 20 minutes.

SERVE WARM OR chilled in bowls or dessert glasses with the syrup spooned over the top.

- ■ **PREPARATION TIME:** 15 minutes
- ■ **BAKING TIME:** 15 to 20 minutes
- ■ **EQUIPMENT:** 9 × 13-inch nonreactive baking pan

PER 6.5 OZ SERVING: 124 CALS, .2 G TOT FAT, .1 G MONO FAT, .1 G SAT FAT, 0 MG CHOL

Sautéed Apples

Homey, fragrant Sautéed Apples are delicious with ice cream, frozen yogurt, whipped cream, or poundcake. Try them over pancakes for brunch or a casual supper. Or pour the sautéed apples into a baked pie shell for a French-style tart or use them as a filling for crêpes.

You may wish to add 2 tablespoons Calvados, Fra Angelico, amaretto, or your favorite liqueur for a different flavor boost.

■ **SERVES 4**

4 large, tart apples, peeled, cored, and diced into ½-inch cubes (about 4 cups)

2 tablespoons fresh lemon juice

2 tablespoons butter

1 teaspoon ground cinnamon

½ cup packed brown sugar

TOSS THE APPLE cubes with the lemon juice. Melt the butter in the skillet or saucepan on medium heat. Add the apples and sauté for 5 minutes, stirring frequently. Add the cinnamon and brown sugar and cook until the sugar melts and begins to caramelize and the apples are tender but not mushy.

SERVE WARM OR at room temperature.

■ **TOTAL TIME:** 20 minutes
■ **EQUIPMENT:** large nonreactive skillet or saucepan

Vanilla Poached Apples

Warm, soft apples in a creamy syrup—what could be sweeter? What could be more tempting?

 PREHEAT THE OVEN to 375°.

PLACE THE APPLES, cut side down, in a baking pan. Combine the juice, sugar, and vanilla bean or 1 teaspoon of the vanilla extract. Pour over the apples. Cover and bake for 45 to 50 minutes, until the apples are tender but not mushy. Transfer the apples to a shallow serving dish.

POUR THE JUICE into a saucepan or skillet and cook carefully on high heat until it is reduced by about half to a syrup. Be careful not to cook the syrup too long or it will caramelize. Remove the vanilla bean (dry for re-use in the future). If you are using vanilla extract, add the remaining teaspoon to the syrup. Pour the syrup over the apples. Serve with whipped cream and a dash of nutmeg.

- **PREPARATION TIME:** 10 minutes
- **BAKING TIME:** 45 to 50 minutes
- **COOKING TIME FOR SAUCE:** 15 minutes
- **EQUIPMENT:** 9 × 13-inch baking pan, saucepan or skillet

PER 6 OZ SERVING: 162 CALS, 1.9 G TOT FAT, .5 G MONO FAT, 1.1 G SAT FAT, 5 MG CHOL

- **SERVES 6**

3 large, firm apples, peeled, cored, and halved

2 cups unsweetened apple juice

½ cup sugar

1 vanilla bean or 2 teaspoons pure vanilla extract

fresh whipped cream

dash of freshly grated nutmeg

Strawberries and Rhubarb

In early spring, the first produce to appear at roadside stands is freshly cut rhubarb. Close on its heels come strawberries. Perhaps this is nature nudging us in the right direction—take the first offerings of the new season, mix them together, and enjoy!

Strawberries and rhubarb is a popular dessert in the northeastern United States and it's easy to make in large batches to freeze for later in the year. Serve it as a compote topped with a dollop of whipped cream or yogurt or as a topping for ice cream, Poundcake Loaf (page 123), or Fluffy Sweet Biscuits (page 33).

■ **SERVES 4**

2 cups sliced rhubarb, cut into 1-inch pieces (3 or 4 stalks)

⅓ to ½ cup sugar, to taste

2 tablespoons water

1 cup halved or quartered strawberries

 COMBINE THE RHUBARB, sugar, and water in the saucepan. Cover and simmer on medium-low heat for about 5 minutes. Add the strawberries and simmer, covered, for 5 minutes more.

SERVE WARM OR chilled.

■ **YIELD:** 1⅔ cups
■ **TOTAL TIME:** 15 minutes
■ **EQUIPMENT:** nonreactive saucepan

PER 4.25 OZ SERVING: 89 CALS, .3 G TOT FAT, 0 G MONO FAT, 0 G SAT FAT, 0 MG CHOL

Southern Compote

Here's a fruit salad with a southern accent—a deluxe holiday treat that's gorgeous to look at and ambrosial to eat. Since the sweetness of any fruit varies with its ripeness, you may wish to add a little honey or maple syrup. If you like, garnish with a few extra fresh mint leaves.

COMBINE ALL OF the ingredients in a serving bowl and chill for at least 30 minutes.

■ **TOTAL TIME:** 15 minutes

PER 10 OZ SERVING: 156 CALS, 3.2 G TOT FAT, .2 G MONO FAT, 2.1 G SAT FAT, 0 MG CHOL

■ **SERVES 4**

- 4 oranges, peeled and sectioned with juice
- 1 large or 2 small ripe plums, seeded and diced
- 6 large strawberries, sliced
- 3 tablespoons unsweetened grated coconut
- 2 tablespoons bourbon, or to taste (optional)
- 2 kiwis, peeled and diced
- ½ cantaloupe, peeled and diced
- 1 tablespoon chopped fresh mint leaves

Jewish Holiday Compote

Dried fruit compotes are homespun, simple desserts that provide a very satisfying finish to rich holiday meals.

■ **SERVES 4 TO 6**

3 cups dried mixed fruit, such as pears, pitted prunes, and pitted apricots

1 cinnamon stick or ½ teaspoon ground cinnamon

⅛ teaspoon ground cloves

1 teaspoon freshly grated orange peel

½ cup orange juice

½ cup warm water

½ cup dry white wine or white grape juice*

3 tablespoons honey or sugar

* If you use grape juice instead of wine, reduce or omit the honey, to taste.

CUT THE PEARS into 1-inch pieces; leave the prunes and apricots whole. Combine all of the ingredients in a saucepan and simmer on low heat for 15 minutes. Remove from the heat. As the compote cools, the juices will thicken to form a syrup.

SERVE WARM OR cold.

■ **TOTAL TIME:** 30 minutes
■ **EQUIPMENT:** saucepan

PER 5.5 OZ SERVING: 276 CALS, .5 G TOT FAT, .2 G MONO FAT, 0 G SAT FAT, 0 MG CHOL

Fig, Pear, and Orange Compote

Readily available winter fruits are very attractive served in concert, especially when coated with a rich, aromatic glaze.

Our favorite poaching liquid for this compote is a mixture of orange juice and wine in about equal amounts, but either can be used alone with delicious results. Red or white wine may be used. Red wine stains the pears a rosy hue.

Use Black Mission figs alone or in combination with Calimyrna figs to provide a glossy, dark contrast to the bright oranges.

STICK THE CLOVES into the strips of orange peel and combine them in the pot with the orange juice and/or wine, cinnamon stick, and sugar or honey. Bring the mixture to a boil on high heat. Add the figs, cover, reduce the heat, and simmer for about 15 minutes. Add the pears, cover, and cook on low heat until the pears are tender, about 10 to 15 minutes, depending on their ripeness.

REMOVE THE FRUIT with a slotted spoon and place it in a serving bowl. Discard the orange peel and the cinnamon stick. Heat the remaining liquid on medium heat for 5 to 10 minutes, until it is reduced by half and thickens to a syrup. Add the orange segments to the cooked fruit and pour the syrup over it all.

SERVE WARM, at room temperature, or chilled. If desired, garnish with a dollop of whipped cream, yogurt, or crème fraîche (page 359). Tightly covered and refrigerated, this compote will keep for 3 or 4 days.

- **PREPARATION TIME:** 40 minutes
- **COOKING TIME:** 40 minutes
- **EQUIPMENT:** 2-quart nonreactive pot

PER 6.5 OZ SERVING: 222 CALS, 1 G TOT FAT, .2 G MONO FAT, .1 G SAT FAT, 0 MG CHOL

- **SERVES 8**

8 whole cloves

2 three-inch strips fresh orange peel

3 cups orange juice, wine, or a combination

1 cinnamon stick

$\frac{1}{2}$ cup sugar or $\frac{1}{4}$ cup honey

$\frac{1}{2}$ pound dried figs, stemmed and cut into halves (about $1\frac{1}{2}$ cups)

2 pounds pears (4 or 5), peeled, cored, and chopped into bite-sized pieces (about 4 cups)

3 seedless oranges, peeled and sectioned or sliced into rounds (about $1\frac{1}{2}$ cups)

Carriacou Island Fruit Salad

We named this dish in memory of Audre Lorde (1934–1992), a black woman warrior poet whose family roots are from this small spice island off the coast of Grenada. Over the years her works have inspired many of us at Moosewood.

In this fresh and interesting salad, tropical fruits are dressed with intensely fruity guava paste, which is nicely balanced by the warmth of rum.

We've listed the fruits we like best for this salad, but 3 cups of almost any fruit will do. Guava paste, usually packed in attractively decorated tins, is available in well-stocked super-markets and specialty grocery stores. It keeps well in the refrigerator.

■ **SERVES 3 OR 4**

DRESSING

¼ cup guava paste

2 tablespoons rum

FRUIT

1 grapefruit, sectioned (page 372)

1 mango, cut into bite-sized pieces (page 372)

1 banana, sliced

4 to 8 strawberries, halved or quartered

COMBINE THE GUAVA paste and rum and whisk together in a bowl or whirl in a blender until smooth. Gently toss the fruit with the dressing. If you have the time, let the salad sit at room temperature for about 30 minutes to allow the fruit juices to mingle with the dressing.

SERVE CHILLED OR at room temperature.

■ **YIELD:** 3 cups
■ **TOTAL TIME:** 15 to 20 minutes

PER 6 OZ SERVING: 101 CALS, .4 G TOT FAT, .1 G MONO FAT, .1 G SAT FAT, 0 MG CHOL

California Spa Salad

Here's a cool, creamy, guiltless affair that shouldn't be kept a secret. It's light, healthful, and wholesome as well as refreshing and delicious—no pain and no gain.

For even more color, use a combination of red and green grapes or use green grapes with red plums.

IN A BOWL, combine the yogurt, sesame seeds, and dates. Gently stir in the prepared grapes, oranges, and peaches or plums.

SERVE CHILLED.

- **YIELD:** 7 cups
- **YOGURT DRAINING TIME:** 2 hours
- **PREPARATION TIME:** 30 to 35 minutes
- **CHILLING TIME:** at least 1 hour

PER 6.5 OZ SERVING: 106 CALS, .8 G TOT FAT, .2 G MONO FAT, .2 G SAT FAT, 1 MG CHOL

■ **SERVES 8**

YOGURT DRESSING

- 1 cup nonfat vanilla yogurt, drained for at least 2 hours (page 366)
- 1 tablespoon lightly toasted sesame seeds
- ¼ cup chopped whole pitted dates

FRUIT

- 2 cups seedless red grapes, sliced into halves
- 2 cups seeded sectioned orange slices (about 6 oranges) (page 372)
- 2 cups peeled sliced peaches or plums

Creamy Apricot Dip

Try this appealing dip with fresh fruits such as strawberries, cherries, peaches, apples, or pears, or on slightly sweet crackers, such as wheat biscuits, sesame crackers, or water biscuits.

Fromage blanc is a creamy, low-fat, French-style skim milk cheese available in the cheese section of large supermarkets. If you can't find it, use any plain low-fat cheese spread or plain nonfat yogurt cheese.

This recipe can be easily multiplied and made in quantity.

■ YIELDS ½ CUP

½ cup fromage blanc (page 362) or plain nonfat yogurt cheese (page 366)

¼ teaspoon freshly grated orange peel

2 tablespoons confectioners' sugar

2 tablespoons apricot fruit spread or preserves

2 tablespoons chopped toasted almonds (optional) (page 364)

MIX TOGETHER the fromage blanc, orange peel, confectioners' sugar, and fruit spread or preserves until smooth. Chill for about an hour.

SPRINKLE THE TOASTED almonds on top, if desired, and serve.

■ **PREPARATION TIME:** 5 minutes
■ **CHILLING TIME:** about 1 hour

Sour Cream Fruit Dip

Slightly tangy, but a little sweet, this sour-cream-based dip enhances the sweetness and succulence of fresh seasonal fruits. During the fleeting summer days when sweet cherries ripen, serve this dip with a fresh, plump assortment of the black, red, or rosy yellow cherries that appear at your local supermarkets or fruit stands. Or accompany this cool, citrusy, snow-white dip with other fresh fruits, such as strawberries, pears, plums, peaches, or apricots.

This recipe may be easily doubled and is lower in fat when made with yogurt cheese.

■ **YIELDS 1 CUP**

3 to 4 tablespoons
confectioners' sugar

1 cup sour cream
or yogurt cheese
(page 366)

2 to 3 teaspoons
freshly grated lemon
or orange peel

3 tablespoons chopped
dried cherries
(optional)*

2 tablespoons toasted
slivered almonds
(page 364)
sliced fruit

* Dried cherries are often available in supermarkets or health food stores.

 IN A SMALL bowl, sift the confectioners' sugar over the sour cream or yogurt cheese and stir until well mixed. Add the grated lemon or orange peel and dried cherries, if using. Chill for 1 to 2 hours before serving.

TO SERVE, MOUND the dip in a small dish or in the center of a platter and sprinkle on the almonds. Arrange the sliced fruit around the dip or on a side platter.

VARIATION Top with chopped toasted pecans and/or Candied Citrus Zest (page 330).

■ **PREPARATION TIME:** 10 minutes
■ **CHILLING TIME:** at least 1 hour

COBBLERS
CRISPS
AND THEIR
COUSINS

Cobblers, Crisps, and Their Cousins

IN THIS CHAPTER, YOU WILL FIND COBBLERS, CRISPS, CRUMBLES, dumplings, puffs, slumps, and clafoutis—funny names for wonderful things. These simple, toothsome desserts are made of fresh fruits or berries baked with sweet pastry crusts, nuts, oats, or custards. The names of these desserts describe their covering, crust, or binding. Definitions of terms vary from one region to another, and all of this is open to friendly debate. But their charming, homespun names remind us that great cooking began in the kitchens of down-to-earth people who knew how to take a basketful of ripe blueberries, bake them under golden, melt-in-your-mouth shortcake, and create an experience of happiness that endures. The recipes were seldom written down. Ingredients were measured by handfuls, pinches, and dashes and were adjusted by appearance, texture, and taste. Cobblers, slumps, and shortcakes are closely related to each other. A cobbler (cobbled together from this and that) has a deep layer of sliced fruit or berries on the bottom and a thick crust of flaky biscuit or pastry dough spread on top. The fruit and pastry bake together and the dish can be served hot or cold. The fruit is usually sweetened and forms a thick, juicy syrup, which is readily soaked up by the biscuit when served. Our colorful Strawberry Mango Cobbler is fresh, unusual, and enticingly fragrant. We also give you an old-fashioned Blueberry Slump with Orange Dumplings, with plenty of fruit and a light, cakey top.

Cobbler is like a topsy-turvy, family-sized version of old-fashioned shortcake—a hot biscuit sliced open, covered with sweetened berries and their syrup, and topped with whipped cream. Our recipe for Fluffy Sweet Biscuits is perfect for shortcake. Using individual store-bought sponge cakes for strawberry shortcake is relatively new, and while they are light and sweet, they are not traditional shortcake. The short in shortcake refers to shortening, not stature. Crisps and crumbles are kissing cousins from North America and Great Britain respectively. Their fruit is on the bottom of the baking dish and is topped with either a coarse mixture of flour, sugar, and butter or (Moosewood-style) with rolled oats, nuts, honey or maple syrup, and spices. They bake until the fruit is tender and the topping is crisp and crumbly. Be sure to try Navajo Peach Crumble with its lovely golden topping of cornmeal and pine nuts and tart-sweet Cranberry Pear Crisp. And don't miss the Double Pear Crisp in the Moosewood Classics chapter. A clafouti is a dessert of French origin in which the fruit is baked in a creamy, flavored custard. One thing we love about clafoutis is how easy they are to make. We whip up the batter in a blender and pour it over various fruits flavored with extracts, liqueurs, or juices. The classic French recipe features cherries; our versions include chocolate cherry, peach almond, and spiced plum. Sometimes clafoutis are called puffs because the egg custard becomes golden and puffy as it bakes. Our untraditional Ginger Pear Puff is spicy and aromatic. And speaking of French classics, our fresh and unexpected version of crêpes—Tropical Fruit Crêpes—is easy to make ahead to have on hand. Baked stuffed fruits have long been homey favorites. Attractive Apple Dumplings reveal hidden raspberries along their rosy pastry seams. Don't be surprised if you are begged and badgered to make these delightfully unpretentious treats again and again.

Blueberry Cobbler

Slump, cobbler, buckle, betty, pandowdy, and grunt are all terms used to describe baked desserts replete with fruit and covered with a topping that is usually, but not always, more like a biscuit than a cake. Although there seems to be no consistent definition for any of these names, there may be regional differences or preferences for certain terminology. Whatever you choose to call your dessert, this recipe guarantees any cook a delicious use of blueberries. The addition of preserves intensifies the blueberry flavor of our slump.

■ **SERVES 6 TO 8**

FRUIT LAYER

3 cups fresh or frozen blueberries (16-ounce package)

⅓ cup unsweetened blueberry preserves or jam

⅓ cup sugar

1 teaspoon freshly grated lemon peel

1 tablespoon fresh lemon juice

2 tablespoons unbleached white flour

TOPPING

1 cup unbleached white flour

1 teaspoon baking powder

¼ cup sugar

1 large egg

1 teaspoon freshly grated lemon peel

3 tablespoons butter, melted

⅔ cup milk

 PREHEAT THE OVEN to 400°. Butter the baking pan.

IN A BOWL, combine the blueberries, preserves or jam, sugar, lemon peel, lemon juice, and flour and stir gently until mixed. Spoon evenly into the prepared baking dish and set aside while you prepare the topping.

SIFT THE FLOUR, baking powder, and sugar into a bowl. In a separate bowl, lightly beat the egg and combine it with the lemon peel, melted butter, and milk. Make a depression in the dry ingredients, add the liquids, and stir just until mixed. Spread the topping evenly over the berry mixture.

BAKE FOR 40 to 50 minutes, until the top is golden brown and firm to the touch and the fruit is bubbly. Cool for 10 to 15 minutes before serving.

■ **PREPARATION TIME:** 20 minutes
■ **BAKING TIME:** 40 to 50 minutes
■ **EQUIPMENT:** nonreactive 8-inch square baking pan

Apple Raspberry Crisp

To allow the flavor of the fruit to predominate, we've added only a small amount of sugar to the crunchy almond-crumb topping. If you use particularly tart apples or raspberries, you might choose to increase the sugar a little. Mutsus are among our favorite apples to use in desserts, but any firm baking apple will do. Frozen raspberries work well when fresh ones are not available.

PREHEAT THE OVEN to 375°. Butter or oil the baking pan.

PEEL, CORE, AND slice the apples. Gently toss the apple slices and the raspberries together and place them in the prepared baking dish. Combine the flour and sugar in a mixing bowl. Using a pastry cutter or two knives, cut the butter into the flour until the butter pieces are the size of small peas. Thoroughly mix in the chopped almonds. Spread the topping evenly over the fruit.

BAKE FOR ABOUT 40 minutes, until the apples are tender and the topping is lightly browned. Serve warm or at room temperature, topped with a dollop of whipped cream, if desired.

- **PREPARATION TIME:** 25 minutes
- **BAKING TIME:** 40 minutes
- **EQUIPMENT:** 2-quart nonreactive baking pan (about 7 × 11 inches)

- **SERVES 6 TO 8**

5 large apples (about 2 pounds or 5 cups sliced)

1½ to 2 cups fresh or frozen unsweetened red raspberries (12-ounce package)

1 cup unbleached white flour

⅓ cup sugar

⅓ cup butter

⅓ cup finely chopped toasted almonds (page 364)

dollop of freshly whipped cream (optional)

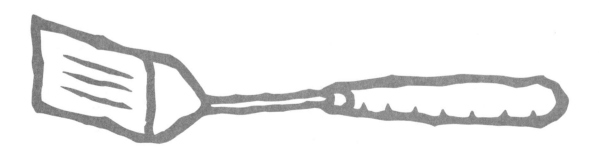

Triple Ginger Apple Crisp

Ginger preserves, a pinch of ground ginger, and gingersnaps make this apple crisp a ginger lover's dream. The apples are tossed with ginger preserves and the topping is a spiced mixture of rolled oats and crumbled gingersnaps, butter, and honey. The flavor and intensity of both ginger preserves and gingersnaps vary, so use the amount of preserves and brand of cookies that most suit your taste.

■ **SERVES 8 TO 10**

FRUIT LAYER

6 cups peeled apple slices

¼ to ½ cup ginger preserves

2 tablespoons hot water

TOPPING

½ cup butter, melted

⅓ cup honey

1 teaspoon ground cinnamon

½ teaspoon ground nutmeg

½ teaspoon ground ginger

2 cups rolled oats

1 cup gingersnap cookie crumbs (about 15 cookies; see Note)

 PREHEAT THE OVEN to 350°.

PLACE THE APPLE slices in the unoiled baking pan. In a small bowl, stir together the ginger preserves and hot water. Pour over the apple slices and toss to coat them evenly.

IN A BOWL, combine the butter, honey, cinnamon, nutmeg, and ginger and mix well. Stir in the oats and gingersnap cookie crumbs until well blended. Spread the oat mixture evenly over the apple slices, tamp down, and bake for 35 to 45 minutes, until the apples are tender and the topping is crisp.

SERVE AT ROOM temperature.

NOTE Make cookie crumbs by crushing gingersnaps between two pieces of wax paper or in a plastic bag, using a rolling pin, or by whirling them in the bowl of a food processor. We recommend Archway brand.

■ **PREPARATION TIME:** 25 to 30 minutes
■ **BAKING TIME:** 35 to 45 minutes
■ **EQUIPMENT:** 9 × 12-inch baking pan

Cranberry Pear Crisp

Here is a warming wintertime dessert that will excite the senses with its tart, sweet, crunchy, and juicy tastes and textures. Bosc pears work very nicely in this easy crisp, and you can adjust the amount of maple syrup to allow for your sweet tooth or the ripeness of the pears. The rich aroma of toasted oats and cinnamon and the lovely spangle of rubylike berries make it a bring-to-the-table-right-away centerpiece.

 PREHEAT THE OVEN to 350°.

PEEL AND CORE the pears and slice them into eighths. Combine the sliced pears with the cranberries and maple syrup to taste in the baking pan. In a small cup, dissolve the cornstarch in half of the juice or cider, then add it to the fruit with the rest of the juice and the nutmeg and toss to mix.

COMBINE THE TOPPING ingredients in a bowl and sprinkle over the fruit. Cover and bake for 30 minutes, then uncover and bake for 20 to 25 minutes more, until the fruit is tender but firm and the topping is crisp and golden.

SERVE WARM, AT room temperature, or chilled.

- **PREPARATION TIME:** 30 minutes
- **BAKING TIME:** 50 to 55 minutes
- **EQUIPMENT:** 2½-quart baking pan

■ **SERVES 8 TO 10**

- 6 medium to large pears
- 2 cups fresh cranberries, rinsed and picked over
- ⅓ to ⅔ cup pure maple syrup
- 1 tablespoon cornstarch
- ⅔ cup apple or pear juice or apple cider
- ½ to ¾ teaspoon freshly grated nutmeg

TOPPING

- 2 cups rolled oats
- ⅓ cup packed brown sugar
- ⅓ cup butter, melted
- 1 teaspoon ground cinnamon

Navajo Peach Crumble

In some high desert canyons of Arizona, Navajo people tend their prized peach orchards. We were surprised that peaches could grow in such a harsh climate of extremes, but they thrive next to the hot rock walls of the canyon. This recipe adds cornmeal and pine nuts, staples of the southwestern United States, for a luscious, easily prepared crumble.

This dish is also excellent made with blueberries or thinly sliced apples, in which case you may wish to forgo the pine nuts. The topping can be made ahead of time; just cover and chill it until ready to bake.

■ **SERVES 4**

TOPPING

½ cup unbleached white flour

⅓ cup cornmeal

⅓ cup sugar

⅛ teaspoon salt

⅓ cup butter

1 tablespoon toasted pine nuts, (optional) (page 364)

FRUIT

3 cups peeled and sliced fresh peaches (1 pound frozen)

⅓ cup sugar

1 tablespoon fresh lemon juice

½ teaspoon ground cinnamon

 PREHEAT THE OVEN to 375°.

IN A BOWL, combine the flour, cornmeal, sugar, and salt. Cut the butter into the mixture with two knives or by rubbing the mixture between your thumbs and fingers until coarse crumbs form. Stir in the pine nuts, if using, and set aside.

COMBINE THE PEACHES, sugar, lemon juice, and cinnamon and spread in the unoiled pie pan. Sprinkle the topping mixture evenly over the fruit. Bake until the fruit is bubbling and the topping is golden, about 30 minutes. Allow to sit for a few minutes before serving fresh and warm from the oven, or serve at room temperature or chilled. Store refrigerated.

■ **PREPARATION TIME:** 20 minutes
■ **BAKING TIME:** 30 minutes
■ **EQUIPMENT:** 9- or 10-inch pie pan

Cherry Almond Crumble

This dessert exemplifies all the virtues of a homespun crumble. The warm crust has a wonderful almond aroma, and cherries and almonds go together like hugs and kisses. Whether you use fresh or frozen fruit, this crumble tastes luscious and looks great. If you have frozen sweet cherries on hand, this is a very easy and fast dessert to prepare, perfect for a busy day or when guests arrive unexpectedly.

 PREHEAT THE OVEN to 350°.

POUR THE CHERRIES into the unoiled pie pan and set aside.

COARSELY CHOP the almonds in the bowl of a food processor. Add the flour, brown sugar, butter, and almond extract and process until crumbly and well combined. Sprinkle the topping evenly over the cherries and bake until the fruit is bubbly and the topping golden, about 35 to 45 minutes.

SERVE WARM OR cold. Top with vanilla ice cream or frozen yogurt, if desired.

- **PREPARATION TIME:** 10 minutes with frozen cherries, 20 minutes with fresh
- **BAKING TIME:** 35 to 45 minutes
- **EQUIPMENT:** food processor, nonreactive 9-inch pie pan

- **SERVES 6 TO 8**

2 12-ounce packages unsweetened frozen sweet cherries (4 to 5 cups pitted fresh sweet cherries)

½ cup almonds

½ cup unbleached white flour

½ cup packed brown sugar

¼ cup butter

½ teaspoon pure almond extract

vanilla ice cream or frozen yogurt (optional)

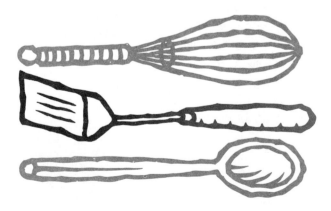

Strawberry Mango Cobbler

This delightful, rosy-hued cobbler is packed with mangoes and strawberries and topped with golden brown, flaky biscuits. The baking time and the amount of sugar necessary will vary depending upon the ripeness of the mangoes.

■ **SERVES 6**

FRUIT LAYER

2 mangoes*

1½ pints fresh strawberries (or 16-ounce frozen package)

½ cup packed brown sugar

½ teaspoon ground cinnamon

¼ teaspoon ground cardamom

3 tablespoon unbleached white flour

TOPPING

1 cup unbleached white flour

1 teaspoon baking powder

¼ teaspoon baking soda

¼ cup sugar

1 large egg

½ teaspoon pure vanilla extract

¼ cup butter, melted

⅓ cup buttermilk

* *When combined, the prepared mangoes and strawberries should equal about 6 cups.*

 PREHEAT THE OVEN to 375°.

PEEL THE MANGOES and cut them into bite-sized pieces (page 372). Cut the strawberries into halves or quarters, depending on their size. In a bowl, gently mix the fruit with the brown sugar, cinnamon, cardamom, and flour. Place this mixture in the baking pan and set aside.

SIFT TOGETHER the flour, baking powder, baking soda, and sugar. In a separate bowl, lightly beat the egg and combine it with the vanilla, melted butter, and buttermilk. Make a depression in the dry ingredients and add the buttermilk mixture all at once. Stir just until combined; the dough will be slightly stiff. Drop the batter by large spoonfuls into 6 slightly flattened mounds that are evenly spaced over the fruit.

BAKE FOR 30 to 40 minutes, until the fruit is bubbling and the dough is golden brown and firm to the touch. Cool for at least 20 minutes before serving warm or at room temperature.

■ **PREPARATION TIME:** 35 minutes, using fresh berries
■ **BAKING TIME:** 30 to 40 minutes
■ **COOLING TIME:** 20 minutes
■ **EQUIPMENT:** nonreactive 7 × 11-inch baking pan

Fluffy Sweet Biscuits

These biscuits complement almost any fresh fruit. They can easily be split in half, smothered with fruit, and topped with whipped cream, ice cream, or one of our Low-fat Creamy Toppings (page 319). Try them with strawberries, blackberries, or mangoes, or experiment with fruit combinations. In the winter months, pair these biscuits with some of our sauces, such as Chunky Winter Fruit Sauce (page 305) or Cherry Sauce (page 304).

 PREHEAT THE OVEN to 400°.

SIFT TOGETHER the flour, sugar, baking powder, baking soda, and salt into a large bowl. Using a pastry cutter or two knives, cut in the butter until the mixture is crumbly and resembles coarse meal.

IN A SEPARATE, small bowl, lightly beat the egg and combine it with the buttermilk and vanilla. Make a well in the center of the dry ingredients and pour the liquid ingredients into it, stirring quickly just until combined.

TURN THE DOUGH out onto a lightly floured surface and knead gently, folding the dough over four or five times. Lightly flour the surface again, if necessary, and flatten the dough to about a ½-inch thickness with the palms of your hands or a rolling pin. Cut with a knife into squares or cut into rounds with a biscuit cutter or a glass, dipping the glass or cutter in flour as needed to prevent sticking. Place the biscuits on an unoiled baking sheet.

BAKE FOR 10 to 15 minutes, until golden brown.

- **PREPARATION TIME:** 15 to 20 minutes
- **BAKING TIME:** 10 to 15 minutes
- **EQUIPMENT:** baking sheet, biscuit cutter (optional)

■ **YIELDS 12**

2 cups unbleached white flour

⅓ cup sugar

2 teaspoons baking powder

½ teaspoon baking soda

¼ teaspoon salt

½ cup butter*

1 large egg

⅔ cup buttermilk

1 teaspoon pure vanilla extract

* For the flakiest biscuits, use very cold butter.

Apple Dumplings

This is a lovely, elegant dessert—apples stuffed with a raspberry filling that delicately colors some of the flaky pastry that surrounds each dumpling.

■ **SERVES 4**

FILLING

1 cup fresh or frozen red raspberries

¼ cup seedless raspberry preserves or fruit spread

1 tablespoon sugar, or to taste

4 medium baking apples, such as Crispin, Northern Spy, or Jonagold

1 recipe Best All-Purpose Pie Crust (page 64)*

* When you make the pie dough, add 3 tablespoons of sugar to the flour in the recipe before cutting in the butter. Divide the dough into four equal balls and refrigerate.

 PREHEAT THE OVEN to 375°. Butter the baking pan.

IN A SMALL bowl, combine the raspberries, preserves or fruit spread, and sugar. Mix well and set aside. Peel the apples. Carefully core them, leaving the bottom intact and making a generous cavity. Spoon the filling into the apples.

ON A LIGHTLY floured surface, roll out ¼ of the pie dough. (Especially in hot or humid weather, keep the unrolled balls of dough refrigerated until you are ready to roll them out.) Place a filled apple in the center of the piece of dough and, using your hands, lift the dough and mold it around the apple. Pinch the dough together to seal it well. Place the dumplings, sealed side down and about an inch apart, in the prepared pan. Keep them refrigerated until all four are ready for the oven. Bake the dumplings for 45 to 50 minutes, until the pastry is golden and the apple is tender.

VARIATION For Puff Pastry Apple Dumplings, peel, core, and halve 2 large apples and mound the filling on the four halves. Cut one thawed sheet of puff pastry into four equal pieces. On a lightly floured surface, roll out each piece large enough to fully enclose an apple half. Sprinkle each piece with a teaspoon of sugar. Place a filled apple on the center of a pastry square and brush the edges of the pastry with water or egg white. Fold each corner to the center and twist them together to form a little topknot. Pinch the side seams together to seal the pastry. Place in a buttered baking pan and bake at 400° for about 30 minutes, until the apples are tender.

■ **PREPARATION TIME:** 40 minutes (variation: 25 minutes)
■ **BAKING TIME:** 45 to 50 minutes
■ **EQUIPMENT:** rolling pin, 9 × 13-inch nonreactive baking pan

Ginger Pear Puff

Clafouti is a French dessert with a custard base that is classically made with cherries. In this lovely and elegant variation, sliced gingered pears are baked in a creamy custard and topped with a lively glaze of ginger, cinnamon, and Framboise. We recommend that you use ripened pears or thinly slice firmer pears to ensure that they bake fully.

 PREHEAT THE OVEN to 375°.

PEEL, QUARTER, AND core the pears. Slice each pear section into ¼-inch-thick slices and toss them with the ginger and lemon juice in the pie pan. Whisk together the eggs, milk, flour, sugar, vanilla, and melted butter until smooth (see Note). Pour this mixture over the pears and bake for 35 to 40 minutes, until the custard is just firm and set.

WHILE THE PUFF is baking, combine all of the glaze ingredients in a saucepan and simmer on low heat for about 5 minutes. Cool the puff for a few minutes before spreading the warm glaze over the top. Serve warm or at room temperature.

NOTE If the milk and eggs are cold, the butter may congeal into small lumps, so the batter will not be completely smooth. Don't worry; the lumps will disappear during the baking.

- **PREPARATION TIME:** 15 minutes
- **BAKING TIME:** 35 to 40 minutes
- **EQUIPMENT:** nonreactive 10-inch pie pan, small saucepan

- **SERVES 8**

3 large pears

2 teaspoons grated, peeled fresh ginger root

1 tablespoon fresh lemon juice

3 eggs

1 cup milk

½ cup unbleached white flour

⅔ cup sugar

2 teaspoons pure vanilla extract

3 tablespoons butter, melted

SPICED SPIKED GLAZE

¼ cup ginger preserves*

½ teaspoon ground cinnamon

2 tablespoons raspberry-flavored liqueur, or other fruit liqueur

1 tablespoon butter

Available in well-stocked supermarkets or specialty food stores, usually found with the jams and jellies.

Chocolate Cherry Clafouti

According to Julia Child, clafouti originated in eastern France near Limoges. It is a soft, puffy, crêpe-like omelet—almost like a pancake, almost like a pudding—and the silky custard is almost always combined with fruit.

Clafouti looks best and has the finest texture when served within hours after baking, but it still tastes good the next day. It can be made with a wide range of fresh, canned, or frozen fruits. Create your own favorite clafouti by choosing our basic or low-fat batter and adding the fruit and flavorings you have at hand. Baking times will vary depending on the fruit; see our variations to spur your imagination.

Serve with a dusting of confectioners' sugar or garnish with whipped cream.

■ **SERVES 6 TO 8**

3 cups pitted sweet cherries, fresh, frozen, or canned in water

½ cup chocolate chips

BASIC CLAFOUTI BATTER

4 eggs

1 cup milk

¾ cup unbleached white flour

1 teaspoon pure vanilla extract or ½ teaspoon pure almond extract

½ cup sugar

¼ teaspoon ground cinnamon

1 tablespoon butter

 PREHEAT THE OVEN to 350°. Lightly butter the baking pan.

ARRANGE THE CHERRIES and chocolate chips in the bottom of the baking dish. In a blender, combine the ingredients for the basic or low-fat batter and whirl until smooth. Pour the batter over the cherries and bake for 55 to 65 minutes, until the clafouti is puffed and golden and a knife inserted in the center comes out clean.

COOL FOR AT least 15 minutes before serving warm or at room temperature.

 VARIATIONS For Spiced Plum Clafouti, use 3 cups of sliced pitted plums with ½ teaspoon of freshly grated lemon peel, 1 to 2 tablespoons of brandy, and ¼ teaspoon of ground nutmeg. Bake for about 50 minutes.

FOR PEACH AND ALMOND Clafouti, use 3 cups of sliced pitted peaches flavored with 1 to 2 tablespoons of amaretto and top with ¼ cup of crumbled amaretti cookies and ¼ cup cup of chopped almonds. Bake for about 40 minutes.

FOR APPLE CLAFOUTI, use 3 cups tart sliced baking apples flavored with ½ teaspoon ground cinnamon or cardamom and ½ teaspoon freshly grated orange or lemon peel. Bake for about 50 minutes.

- **PREPARATION TIME:** 15 minutes
- **BAKING TIME:** about 1 hour
- **EQUIPMENT:** nonreactive 10-inch pie pan or 9-inch square baking pan

PER 6 OZ LOW-FAT VARIATION SERVING: 219 CALS, 5.2 G TOT FAT, 1.8 G MONO FAT, 2.5 G SAT FAT, 67 MG CHOL

LOW-FAT CLAFOUTI BATTER

- 2 eggs
- 2 egg whites
- 1 cup buttermilk
- ¾ cup unbleached white flour
- 1 teaspoon pure vanilla extract or ½ teaspoon pure almond extract
- ½ cup sugar
- ¼ teaspoon ground cinnamon

Blackberry Slump with Orange Dumplings

Dating back to the days of early American settlements and open-hearth cooking, slumps, also known as grunts, are similar to cobblers, except the dough is covered and steamed rather than baked. The fruit can be simmered on the stovetop or baked. In this recipe, a deep layer of blackberries is topped with puffy, orange-flavored dumplings.

Blackberry picking used to be a common summer pastime. Gingerly reaching into blackberry bushes prickly with thorns and surrounded by drunken bees out in the broiling sun was a chore brightened only by the glad anticipation of the tangy tart-sweet taste of a blackberry dessert. If you don't find them fresh at the farmers' market or growing somewhere beside the road, blackberries can be purchased frozen.

The topping is optional. As well as adding a slight note of spice, it gives the otherwise pale dumplings a speckled brownness that we find attractive.

■ **SERVES 6 TO 8**

FRUIT LAYER

4½ cups fresh blackberries or 2 pounds frozen unsweetened blackberries

¾ cup sugar

½ cup fresh orange juice

DUMPLINGS

1 cup unbleached white flour

¼ teaspoon salt

1 teaspoon baking powder

½ teaspoon baking soda

¼ teaspoon ground nutmeg

COMBINE THE BLACKBERRIES, sugar, and orange juice in the skillet or flameproof baking pan (see Variation). Cover with a tight-fitting lid or aluminum foil and set aside.

STIR TOGETHER THE flour, salt, baking powder, baking soda, and nutmeg. Stir in the orange peel, if using, until well distributed. Add the melted butter and the buttermilk and stir only until the liquid is absorbed; mixing the soft, sticky dough just barely enough will make the lightest dumplings.

IF MAKING THE topping, mix together the sugar, cinnamon, nutmeg, and pepper in a small cup and set aside.

BRING THE BLACKBERRY mixture to a boil and then reduce the heat. Drop large spoonfuls of the dumpling batter on top of the simmering fruit until all of the batter is used. Sprinkle the sugar topping over the dumplings. Cover tightly and simmer gently for 20 minutes, until the dumplings are puffed and set and feel dry to the touch on top but are not browned. Don't remove the lid until the end of the cooking time or the steaming dumplings will deflate and toughen.

TO COOL, UNCOVER the slump and set it on a rack for about 15 minutes before serving. Serve warm, spooned into individual serving bowls and topped with whipped cream or ice cream, if desired.

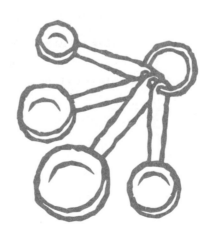 VARIATION If you do not have a nonreactive skillet or flameproof casserole dish, use the "oven steam" method. Preheat the oven to 400°. Bring the blackberry mixture to a boil on the stovetop in a nonreactive saucepan and then pour it into a 2½-quart glass baking dish. After dropping on the dumpling batter, cover tightly with a lid or aluminum foil and place in the oven for 20 minutes, until the dumplings are done.

- **PREPARATION TIME:** 25 minutes
- **COOKING TIME:** 25 minutes
- **EQUIPMENT:** 8- to 10-inch nonreactive skillet or flameproof baking pan (or a nonreactive saucepan and a 2½-quart glass baking dish—see Variation)

1 tablespoon freshly grated orange peel (optional)

2 tablespoons butter, melted

½ cup buttermilk

TOPPING (OPTIONAL)

1 tablespoon sugar

¼ teaspoon ground cinnamon

pinch of ground nutmeg

pinch of ground black pepper

fresh whipped cream or ice cream (optional)

Maple Walnut Baked Apples

The hills around Ithaca are dotted with apple orchards, providing us with bushels of crisp, carefully cultivated apples. Every week of autumn brings a beautiful, newly ripe variety to enjoy. We celebrate the bounty with this simple, old-time recipe, an enduring favorite.

■ **SERVES 4**

4 large cooking apples, such as Mutsu, Greening, or Rome Beauty

½ cup chopped toasted walnuts (page 364)

2 tablespoons packed brown sugar

1 teaspoon ground cinnamon

¼ teaspoon ground nutmeg

¼ cup pure maple syrup

½ cup unsweetened apple juice

 PREHEAT THE OVEN to 375°.

WASH AND CORE the apples, leaving the bottoms intact. Partially peel each apple in horizontal rings or vertical stripes. In a bowl, combine the walnuts, brown sugar, cinnamon, nutmeg, and 2 tablespoons of the maple syrup. Stuff the hollowed-out center of each apple with the nut mixture.

PLACE THE APPLES upright and close together in the pan. Combine the apple juice with the remaining 2 tablespoons of maple syrup and pour around the apples. Cover the baking pan with aluminum foil and bake for about 45 minutes, until the apples are tender.

SERVE HOT OR cold with vanilla frozen yogurt, whipped cream, Rum Custard Sauce (page 317), or one of the Low-fat Creamy Toppings (page 319).

■ **PREPARATION TIME:** 15 minutes
■ **BAKING TIME:** 45 minutes
■ **EQUIPMENT:** nonreactive 9-inch baking pan or pie pan

Baked Almond-Stuffed Pears

At Moosewood one way we enjoy summer peaches is baked in marsala. Pears, which are available for a longer season, are a delicious variation on this classic Italian dessert. Accompany these tender pears and their crisp streusel topping with a little whipped cream or a drizzle of bittersweet chocolate.

PREHEAT THE OVEN to 350°.

PEEL, HALVE, AND core the pears, leaving the stems on. Arrange the pear halves, cut side down, in the baking pan. Pour the marsala over the pears, cover, and bake for 20 to 30 minutes, until crisp-tender.

MEANWHILE, USING YOUR fingertips, combine the almonds, butter, brown sugar, cinnamon, and flour in a small bowl until the crumbs cling together. Sprinkle the almond extract over the streusel and mix. Turn the baked pears cut side up and, using your fingers, press the streusel into the hollow cores of the pears.

BAKE THE PEARS another 30 minutes, basting with the marsala after 15 minutes. Serve plain or with vanilla ice cream, if desired.

- **PREPARATION TIME:** 30 minutes
- **BAKING TIME:** 50 to 60 minutes
- **EQUIPMENT:** 9 × 13-inch nonreactive baking pan

- **SERVES 6**

6 large, firm Bosc, Bartlett, or red D'Anjou pears

1½ cups marsala, preferably sweet

½ cup coarsely ground almonds

1 tablespoon butter, softened

1½ tablespoons packed brown sugar

½ teaspoon ground cinnamon

2 teaspoons unbleached white flour

1 teaspoon pure almond extract

vanilla ice cream (optional)

Tropical Fruit Crêpes

Crêpes are a light and pleasing wrapper for all manner of fillings. Here we fill the traditional French wrapper with tropical flavors native to some of France's former colonies. For a Southeast Asian ethnic night at Moosewood, we serve them filled with bite-sized pineapple and banana pieces and topped with either peanut sauce or Fresh Mango Sauce (page 308).

While the crêpe batter rests, there is time to prepare both the filling and the topping sauce. Our Peanut Coconut Lime Sauce couldn't be simpler to make—and with some additional salt and hot pepper this sauce can double as a great satay sauce for Indonesian kebabs some other night.

Unfilled crêpes can be made in advance and stored, well wrapped, in the refrigerator for up to 3 days, or frozen for a couple of months. Freezing just enough crêpes for a single meal in separate plastic packages saves time and prevents waste. Thaw them, wrapped, overnight in the refrigerator or thaw in a microwave oven.

■ SERVES 4 OR 5

2 large eggs, beaten
1 tablespoon vegetable oil
¾ cup unbleached white flour
⅔ cup milk
⅔ cup water
pinch of salt
1 teaspoon pure vanilla extract
1 tablespoon sugar

WITH A WHISK, blender, or food processor, combine the eggs, oil, flour, milk, water, salt, vanilla, and sugar until smooth. Let the batter rest for about 20 minutes.

MEANWHILE, PREPARE THE sauce by whisking together the peanut butter, coconut milk, lime juice, brown sugar, and salt, if desired. If you prefer a slightly thinner sauce, whisk in an additional ⅛ cup of either coconut milk or water. The finished sauce should be smooth, thick, and creamy. Set aside.

HEAT THE SKILLET or crêpe pan on medium-high heat and very lightly brush it with oil or butter. When the skillet is well heated, pour in a scant ¼ cup of batter and swirl it around to just coat the bottom. Cook the crêpe until the edges are light brown and lacy and the top looks dry, about ½ minute. Flip it with a spatula and cook the second side for about 15 seconds, until lightly browned. Transfer the crêpe to a plate. (You should have 10 crêpes.) If the crêpes begin to stick during cooking, lightly brush the pan with oil.

FILL THE CRÊPES with the cubed fruit, roll them up, and top each with about 2 tablespoons of sauce. Serve immediately.

 VARIATIONS   Other filling possibilities include Strawberries and Rhubarb (page 14), Sautéed Apples (page 12), Caribbean Baked Pineapple (page 11), Fruit Ricotta Mousse (page 341), and Chocolate Ricotta Mousse (page 340). Other toppings can be one of our Low-fat Creamy Toppings (page 319) or Flavored Whipped Creams (page 318).

- **YIELD:** 10 crêpes
- **PREPARATION TIME:** 20 to 25 minutes
- **COOKING TIME:** 10 minutes
- **EQUIPMENT:** 7- or 8-inch crêpe pan or nonstick skillet

PEANUT COCONUT LIME SAUCE

½ cup peanut butter, preferably smooth

½ cup unsweetened coconut milk

3 tablespoons fresh lime juice, or to taste

3 tablespoons packed brown sugar

pinch of salt (optional)

FILLING

2½ cups cubed pineapple

2½ cups cubed bananas

PIES, TARTS AND FILO PASTRIES

Apple Pie with Orange

Blueberry Cherry Pie

Butterscotch Banana Cream Pie

Chocolate Meringue Pie

Coconut Custard Pie ▪ Lemon Chess Pie

Green Tomato Mincemeat Pie

Mango Pie ▪ Pecan Pumpkin Pie

Peach Pie in a Gingerbread Crust

Scandinavian Berry Pie

Strawberry Cream Pie ▪ Three Nut Tart

Lime Tart ▪ Pear Meringue Tart

Best All-Purpose Pie Crust

Sweet Pastry Crust

Caramel Apple Tarte Tatin

Chocolate Date Walnut Baklava

Chocolate Fruit Purses

Filo Pastry Cups ▪ Greek Custard Pastry

Nut and Fruit Filled Filo Pastry

Orange Meringues

Plum Strudel ▪ Winter Fruit Strudel

Pies, Tarts, and Filo Pastries

IF YOU ARE FORTUNATE, YOU'VE KNOWN A GREAT PIE MAKER. IF YOU are really fortunate, they've baked you delicious pies year after year. Our customers often choose freshly baked, homemade pie over any other dessert. They say it's hard to find good pies made from scratch. Gone are the days when every roadside eatery had a made-on-the-spot, simple-but-fresh apple pie. Although pies and tarts are often lumped together as they are here, they are really very different. Tarts are showy works of edible art, sweet giant cookies with delectable toppings. The crust is baked, often separately from its toppings, in a straight-sided pan with a crimped rim. It is usually removed from the pan before serving. Characteristic toppings are fruit, nuts, and/or a thin layer of rich, flavorful custard. Eat tarts soon after assembling, before their freshness and sparkle fade. Pies, made in pans with sloping sides, are sturdier pastries with crusts that protect their moist fillings. There are many variations of pie crusts. In general, pies are better keepers than tarts, may be reheated, and store well in the freezer. Paper-thin sheets of filo produce desserts with a distinctive crispness. Filo pastry is readily available in well-stocked supermarkets. We use it to surround fruits, nuts, or custard with a delicate, buttery crust to make desserts that look impressive but require no rolling out of dough. Our Chocolate Date Walnut Baklava shares the multilayered crunchiness of the well-known pastry but adds creamy chocolate and chewy dates. Filo Pastry Cups are versatile, edible containers for a host of fillings. Chocolate Fruit Purses use a ready-made puff pastry dough to enclose the delectable filling. Lively and low-fat Orange Meringues, based on a simple combination of beaten egg whites and sugar, form a light crust to cradle the luscious fruit topping. For many of us, mastering the art of making pie crust is a sign of the accomplished cook. With attention to our simple instructions, even novice bakers can approach pie crust making with confidence. Standard ingredients are flour, butter, a pinch of salt, a little sugar for sweetening, and a tablespoon or two of water. We recommend pastry flour for the most tender crusts and all-purpose flour for a less fragile, more elastic product. Pastry flour is made from a higher ratio of soft wheat. Because it has less gluten, it makes a lighter crust than all-purpose flour. The key to a flaky crust is a light touch and minimal handling. The crumbs of the unbaked dough should just barely hold together. For rolling out the dough, some cooks favor a marble slab, others prefer pastry cloth or wax paper, and many of us just sprinkle flour on an available flat surface. Decorative crimping, cut-outs, and slashes are touches that can make a pie distinctive. For a shiny patina, try brushing the crust with milk or an egg wash, and for a little glitter, sprinkle with sugar. When you've developed the knack for making pastry dough, try hand building a rectangular crust for Three Nut Tart. Or make little individual tarts by cutting out cookie shapes and topping them with fresh fruit. Make several tart crusts in aluminum foil pans and freeze them for a later date. Whether you like to casually toss together a hearty filling or artfully arrange freshly picked summer fruits on a crust, homemade pies and tarts are bound to please.

Apple Pie with Orange

Is there any better dessert than a well-made, home-baked apple pie? Probably not. Apple pie is at the top of almost everyone's list of best desserts.

Creating simple and straightforward dishes, yet always with a certain elegance and finesse, is the hallmark of dessert chef Kip Wilcox. She loves to give a quirky little tweak to a recipe. The added tang of orange here gives an interesting twist to this time-honored, beloved classic.

■ **SERVES 8**

double 10-inch pie crust (page 64)

FILLING

- 8 cups peeled, thinly sliced baking apples (about 6 medium apples)
- 1 tablespoon orange juice
- ½ cup sugar
- 2 tablespoons unbleached white flour
- 1 teaspoon ground cinnamon
- 1 teaspoon freshly grated orange peel
- 2 tablespoons milk

fresh whipped cream, vanilla frozen yogurt, or ice cream

 PREHEAT THE OVEN to 375°.

ROLL OUT HALF of the pie dough, fit it into the pie pan, and set aside. Cover and set aside the other half of the dough.

IN A LARGE mixing bowl, toss the apple slices with the orange juice, sugar, flour, cinnamon, and grated orange peel until the apples are well coated. Pour the filling into the pie shell.

ROLL OUT THE remaining dough into a large circle and place it on top of the filling. Tuck and crimp the edges of the dough. Cut a few decorative slits in the top crust to allow steam to escape during baking. Brush the crust with milk to coat evenly.

BAKE FOR ABOUT 1 hour, until the juices bubble and the apples are tender when pierced with a sharp knife. If you are using a glass pie pan, check the bottom of the crust to be sure that it is thoroughly baked. Cool slightly before serving. Serve warm or cold with a dollop of whipped cream, vanilla frozen yogurt, or ice cream.

■ **PREPARATION TIME:** 35 minutes
■ **BAKING TIME:** about 1 hour
■ **EQUIPMENT:** rolling pin, 10-inch pie pan

Blueberry Cherry Pie

Fruit pies are always in demand at Moosewood. Blueberries and cherries make a great combo and are nicely complemented by the almond flavoring and fresh lemon juice in the filling. If you are feeling whimsical, replace the usual "steam-release" slits in the top crust with cut-out stars or moons to make a perfect Fourth of July or midnight soiree pie.

There is, of course, no equal to just-picked fresh fruit in season, but high-quality, unsweetened frozen fruits are readily available year-round in most supermarkets, so you can make this pie anytime. Using frozen cherries, which are already pitted, will save you about 15 minutes of preparation time. To be most efficient, prepare the pie dough while the filling sits.

 PREHEAT THE OVEN to 375°.

ROLL OUT HALF of the pie dough, fit it into the pie pan, and set aside. Cover and set aside the other half of the dough.

COMBINE THE BLUEBERRIES, cherries, sugar, lemon juice, almond extract, and tapioca and set aside for at least 10 minutes. If you are using frozen fruit, combine it with the sugar and lemon juice and set it aside to thaw; then add the almond extract and tapioca. Spoon the filling into the pie crust.

ROLL OUT THE remaining dough and place it on top of the filling. Seal and crimp the edges. Cut slits in the top crust to let steam escape from the pie as it cooks. Bake for 50 to 60 minutes, until the crust is golden brown and the fruit is bubbling. Cool on a rack for at least 20 minutes before serving.

- **PREPARATION TIME:** 45 minutes, including pitting cherries
- **BAKING TIME:** 50 to 60 minutes
- **COOLING TIME:** about 20 minutes
- **EQUIPMENT:** rolling pin, 10-inch pie pan

- **SERVES 8 TO 10**

double 10-inch pie crust (page 64)

FILLING

- 4 cups fresh blueberries (16 ounces frozen unsweetened blueberries)
- 2 cups pitted fresh sweet cherries (12 ounces frozen sweet cherries)
- ¾ cup sugar
- 1 tablespoon fresh lemon juice
- 1 teaspoon pure almond extract
- 3 tablespoons quick-cooking tapioca

Butterscotch Banana Cream Pie

When Moosewood's Lisa Wichman helped her mother make cream pies, her job was to stir the custard until it thickened. That seemed to her to take an eternity back then, but in actuality, our Butterscotch Banana Cream Pie is quite simple and fast to make, especially if you have a prebaked pie crust in your freezer.

■ **SERVES 8**

10-inch prebaked pie shell (page 64), cooled to room temperature

FILLING

¼ cup cornstarch

½ cup packed brown sugar

2 cups milk

3 large egg yolks, lightly beaten

2 tablespoons butter

1 teaspoon pure vanilla extract

3 or 4 bananas, sliced

IN THE SAUCEPAN, combine the cornstarch and brown sugar. Slowly add enough milk, a little at a time, to make a smooth paste. Add the rest of the milk and the egg yolks and whisk until smooth. Cook on medium heat, stirring constantly, until the mixture becomes thick, about 10 to 15 minutes. If it starts to become lumpy, reduce the heat slightly and stir more vigorously. Remove from the heat and stir in the butter until it melts. Add the vanilla and the bananas and stir well. Pour the filling into the prebaked pie shell and refrigerate until cold, about 2 hours.

VARIATION Use a sweet pastry crust instead of the pie shell, such as Sweet Pastry Crust (page 66) or Sweet Lemon Crust (page 65).

■ **PREPARATION TIME:** 30 minutes for filling
■ **CHILLING TIME:** 2 hours
■ **EQUIPMENT:** heavy saucepan

Chocolate Meringue Pie

Many of us at Moosewood have fond memories of chocolate meringue pie, an American classic widely available in diners and roadside restaurants. Our recipe uses cornstarch, a perfect thickener for a creamy, smooth filling. And because the starch stabilizes the filling, the egg yolks can be simply mixed with everything else instead of carefully added at the end!

Unsweetened chocolate gives the pie an intense chocolate flavor that is not too sweet. For a quicker version of this pie, top it with whipped cream instead of meringue.

IN THE SAUCEPAN off the heat, combine the cornstarch, sugar, and salt. Slowly add the milk, stirring to make a paste. Stir in the remaining milk and whisk in the egg yolks. Break the chocolate into pieces and add to the milk. Place the saucepan on medium heat and cook, stirring constantly, for 10 to 15 minutes, until the custard thickens and the chocolate melts. (Have patience—just when you're sure the chocolate will be a speckled mess forever, it reaches the right temperature and instantly becomes silky and smooth.) Remove from the heat, stir in the vanilla, and pour into the prebaked pie shell. Set aside.

PREHEAT THE OVEN to 350°.

WITH AN ELECTRIC mixer, whip the egg whites and cream of tartar on high speed until soft peaks form. Add the vanilla and sugar and beat until glossy, stiff peaks form. Spread the meringue over the chocolate filling, making certain it touches the edges of the crust all around. (The baked meringue will shrink if it is not spread out to the crust's edge.) Bake for 12 to 15 minutes, until the meringue is golden brown. Cool to room temperature, then chill before serving.

- **PREPARATION TIME:** 25 minutes for filling, 5 minutes for meringue
- **BAKING TIME:** 12 to 15 minutes for meringue
- **CHILLING TIME:** 2 hours
- **EQUIPMENT:** heavy saucepan, electric mixer

- **SERVES 8**

10-inch prebaked pie shell (page 64), cooled to room temperature

FILLING

¼ cup cornstarch

¾ cup sugar

¼ teaspoon salt

2½ cups milk

3 large egg yolks, lightly beaten

4 ounces unsweetened chocolate

2 teaspoons pure vanilla extract

MERINGUE

3 large egg whites

¼ teaspoon cream of tartar

½ teaspoon pure vanilla extract

⅓ cup sugar

Coconut Custard Pie

In our grandmothers' generation, many a homemaker's reputation for cooking prowess rested comfortably on a generous coconut custard pie. Since then, this pie has become more of a diner classic than a home favorite, alas. Our creamy, rich version is easy to make, however, and may help revive a tradition. It's the perfect finish for a Caribbean- or southern-style meal and is always wecome at a summer picnic or barbecue.

■ **SERVES 8**

10-inch prebaked pie shell (page 64), cooled to room temperature

FILLING

6 eggs

⅔ cup packed brown sugar

pinch of salt

1½ cups milk

1 cup half-and-half

1 teaspoon pure vanilla extract

1 teaspoon coconut extract or an additional teaspoon pure vanilla extract (optional)

2 tablespoons unbleached white flour

1 cup unsweetened grated coconut

 PREHEAT THE OVEN to 350°.

IN A BLENDER, combine the eggs, brown sugar, salt, milk, half-and-half, vanilla, coconut extract, and flour and blend until smooth. Spread the grated coconut on a baking sheet or toaster oven tray and lightly toast at 350° for about 5 minutes, until golden. Stir the coconut into the custard mixture. Pour the filling into the prebaked pie shell.

BAKE AT 350° for 50 minutes, until a knife inserted in the center comes out clean. Cool for at least 20 minutes. Serve warm or chilled.

■ **PREPARATION TIME:** 15 minutes for filling
■ **BAKING TIME:** 50 minutes
■ **COOLING TIME:** 20 minutes
■ **EQUIPMENT:** blender, baking sheet

Lemon Chess Pie

A few generations ago, chess pie was a popular southern dessert because it was not only simple and thrifty, but also delicious. This version has a surprisingly smooth, light, creamy custard that goes perfectly with our crumbly Sweet Pastry Crust.

 PREHEAT THE OVEN to 325°.

WHIRL ALL OF the filling ingredients in a blender until smooth. Pour the custard into the baked pie crust and bake for about 35 minutes, until the custard is firm and set. Cool somewhat before serving.

- **PREPARATION TIME:** 5 to 8 minutes for filling
- **BAKING TIME:** 35 minutes
- **EQUIPMENT:** blender

- **SERVES 6**

9-inch prebaked Sweet Pastry Crust (page 66), cooled to room temperature

FILLING
- ¾ cup buttermilk
- 2 large eggs
- 2 egg whites
- ½ cup sugar
- ½ teaspoon freshly grated lemon peel
- 2 tablespoons fresh lemon juice
- 2 tablespoons unbleached white flour
- ½ teaspoon pure vanilla extract

Green Tomato Mincemeat Pie

A delicious, fruity mincemeat can be made by combining green tomatoes with apples, nuts, and spices. In this recipe, the pie is baked "country style": the bottom crust is rolled out larger than the pie plate and its outer edges are wrapped over the top of the filling to make a package—a perfect gift and no crimping. A bit of orange peel makes the buttery, flaky crust unusual and delicious.

We suggest using half green tomatoes, half apples; however, you may vary the ratio 3:2 or 2:3 according to the amount of fruit you have on hand. Be sure to chop the tomatoes and apples so they are equal in size and shape, about ½-inch pieces.

Serve with whipped cream, vanilla ice cream, or frozen yogurt.

PREHEAT THE OVEN to 375°.

IN A SMALL saucepan, bring the water and salt to a rolling boil and add the tomatoes. Blanch for 3 minutes, or until the water returns to a boil. Drain the tomatoes and place them in a large bowl.

ADD THE APPLES, lemon juice, pecans, raisins, brown sugar, cinnamon, cloves, ginger, and lemon peel. Drizzle the molasses over the filling and stir. Sprinkle the flour over the ingredients and toss gently until uniformly coated. You should have about 6 cups of filling.

ROLL OUT THE dough until it is 3 to 4 inches larger in diameter than the pie pan. Transfer the dough to the pie pan. This may be made easier by loosely folding the dough in half or in fourths, so that it looks like a fan. Then lift the dough, center it in the pie pan, and unfold it.

POUR THE FILLING into the crust. Gently fold the excess dough over the filling. The dough will be uneven and rough at the edges with some filling peeking out of the middle, giving the pie an unpretentious, down-home look.

BAKE FOR 45 to 55 minutes, until the crust is golden and the filling bubbles. (Place a baking sheet on the rack below to catch any bubbled-over juices.) Cool on a rack for an hour before serving.

- **PREPARATION TIME:** 35 minutes
- **BAKING TIME:** 45 to 55 minutes
- **COOLING TIME:** 1 hour
- **EQUIPMENT:** 9-inch pie pan, rolling pin

■ **SERVES 6 TO 8**

1 recipe Best All-Purpose Pie Crust (page 64), flavored with the freshly grated peel of 1 orange, and chilled

FILLING

1 cup water

1 teaspoon salt

2½ cups chopped green tomatoes (about 3 medium tomatoes)

2½ cups peeled and chopped apples (about 3 medium apples)

2 tablespoons fresh lemon juice

1 cup coarsely chopped toasted pecans (page 364)

1 cup raisins

¾ cup packed brown sugar

½ teaspoon ground cinnamon

½ teaspoon ground cloves

½ teaspoon ground ginger

freshly grated peel of 1 lemon

1 tablespoon molasses

¼ cup unbleached white flour

Mango Pie

Mangoes used to be an exotic luxury in much of the world. Today mangoes, a major crop of the Caribbean, are readily available all year. Mangoes range in color from red to green. Choose firm fruit, whatever their color. In this recipe, unripe mangoes will yield a texture similar to that of apple pie, and ripe mangoes cook up more like peach pie.

Serve this succulent pie plain or topped with a scoop of rum raisin or cinnamon ice cream or with pineapple or lime sherbet.

■ **SERVES 8**

1 double 9-inch pie crust (page 64)

FILLING

4½ cups mango cubes (about 4 pounds or 4 medium mangoes)*

1 teaspoon freshly grated lime peel

2 tablespoons fresh lime juice

1 cup sugar

½ teaspoon ground cinnamon

½ teaspoon ground nutmeg

3 tablespoons cornstarch

* For cutting, pitting, and peeling mangoes, see page 372.

 PREHEAT THE OVEN to 375°.

ON A DRY, lightly floured surface, roll out half of the pie crust dough to about a ⅛-inch thickness. Arrange in the pie pan and trim the edges with scissors or a sharp knife.

COMBINE ALL OF the filling ingredients in a large bowl. Toss to coat the fruit evenly. Fill the pie shell with the fruit mixture. Roll out the remaining dough and place on top of the filling. Trim the top crust and then crimp and flute the edges. With the tip of a paring knife, cut small slits in the top crust to allow steam to escape.

BAKE FOR 45 to 60 minutes, until the filling is bubbling and the pie is lightly browned.

■ **PREPARATION TIME:** 45 minutes
■ **BAKING TIME:** 45 to 60 minutes
■ **EQUIPMENT:** rolling pin, 9-inch pie pan

Pecan Pumpkin Pie

This Thanksgiving, serve the pie that solves your guests' dilemma of whether to choose pumpkin or pecan pie for dessert—pumpkin pie with a surprise pecan layer. You can always keep controversy alive by offering a choice of whipped cream or vanilla ice cream.

PREHEAT THE OVEN to 400°. Prepare the pie crust by rolling it out and crimping the edge to form a high-standing rim.

FOR THE PECAN filling, whisk the eggs in a bowl until foamy. Stir in the corn syrup or maple syrup, brown sugar, vanilla, salt, and pecans. Spread the pecan filling over the bottom of the pie crust. Bake for about 20 minutes, until the filling is set and slightly puffed.

MEANWHILE, WHISK THE eggs for the pumpkin filling and stir in the pumpkin purée, milk, brown sugar, cinnamon, ginger, salt, and vanilla until well blended.

WHEN THE PECAN filling has set, remove it from the oven. Pour the pumpkin filling over the pecan layer and bake for about 40 minutes, until the pumpkin layer is set in the middle.

DECORATE BY PRESSING toasted pecan halves around the outside edge of the pie. Cool for at least 20 minutes before cutting. Serve warm or at room temperature.

- **PREPARATION TIME:** 35 minutes
- **BAKING TIME:** 40 minutes
- **COOLING TIME:** 20 minutes
- **EQUIPMENT:** rolling pin, 10-inch pie pan

This recipe works with whole, reduced fat, or skim milk, light cream, half-and-half, or evaporated whole or skim milk.

- **SERVES 8**

10-inch pie crust
(page 64)

PECAN FILLING

2 large eggs

½ cup corn syrup or pure maple syrup

½ cup packed brown sugar

½ teaspoon pure vanilla extract

¼ teaspoon salt

1 cup coarsely chopped toasted pecans (page 364)

PUMPKIN FILLING

3 eggs

1¾ cups cooked pumpkin purée (15-ounce can)

1 cup milk

¾ cup packed brown sugar

1½ teaspoons ground cinnamon

1½ teaspoons ground ginger

½ teaspoon salt

1 teaspoon pure vanilla extract

toasted pecan halves

Peach Pie in a Gingerbread Crust

When peaches, lemon, and ginger team up, the effect is bright, hot, sweet, and positively delightful. This pie has a spicy cookie crust filled with sweet and tangy peaches.

■ **SERVES 8**

GINGERBREAD CRUST

1½ cups unbleached white flour

½ cup packed brown sugar

1 teaspoon ground ginger

1 teaspoon ground cinnamon

¼ teaspoon ground allspice

½ teaspoon salt

1 teaspoon baking powder

½ cup chilled butter, cut into pieces

1 tablespoon unsulphured molasses

2 tablespoons cold water

FILLING

6 cups peach slices

½ cup packed brown sugar

1 tablespoon peeled grated fresh ginger root

1½ tablespoons cornstarch

2 tablespoons fresh lemon juice

 PREHEAT THE OVEN to 375°.

IN A MEDIUM bowl, sift together the flour, brown sugar, ginger, cinnamon, allspice, salt, and baking powder. Cut the butter into the dry ingredients with your fingertips or a pastry cutter until the mixture is crumbly and resembles cornmeal. Drizzle the molasses and water over the dough, mixing with your fingertips until the crumbs of dough begin to cling together.

SET ASIDE ½ cup of the dough. Gather the rest of the dough together and knead it into a ball. Press it evenly into the bottom and sides of the pie pan and bake for 10 to 15 minutes.

IN A BOWL, toss the peaches with the brown sugar and fresh ginger root. Dissolve the cornstarch in the lemon juice, sprinkle it over the peaches, and mix lightly.

WHEN THE CRUST is baked, pour the peaches into the pie pan. Crumble the remaining dough over the peaches. Bake the pie on the upper rack of the oven for 40 to 55 minutes, checking the pie after 30 minutes. If the crust has browned, place a foil collar around the exposed edge of the crust to protect it for the rest of the baking time. When the peaches are tender and bubbly and the crust is brown, remove the pie from the oven and cool for several minutes before serving.

■ **PREPARATION TIME:** 25 to 30 minutes
■ **BAKING TIME:** 10 to 15 minutes for crust; 40 to 55 minutes for filled pie
■ **EQUIPMENT:** 10-inch pie pan

With frozen peaches, use two 1-pound packages, thawed and drained. The pie may need to bake slightly longer.

Scandinavian Berry Pie

This big, beautiful, festive pie has a deep, wine-red color and tart-sweet taste. This is a good pie for any time of year, and it is quickly becoming a winter holiday favorite with us.

The natural acids in sour cream make the lofty crust exceptionally tender. Weaving the top pie crust into a lattice is well worth the extra bit of effort for an impressive pie.

COMBINE THE FILLING ingredients in the saucepan. Stir frequently on high heat for about 5 minutes (15 minutes for frozen berries), until boiling and thickened. The cranberries will begin to pop. Set aside to cool. Combine the flour, baking powder, and salt in a large mixing bowl. Using a pastry cutter or two knives, cut in the butter just enough to achieve an evenly textured crumbly mix. Stir in the sour cream, working quickly to form a soft dough. Dust the dough with flour and gently knead for 1 to 2 minutes until it forms into a ball.

PREHEAT THE OVEN to 375°.

ON A HEAVILY floured board, roll out about ⅔ of the pie dough to fit the pie pan. Trim the edges with scissors. Fill the crust with the berry mixture and set aside.

ROLL OUT THE remaining dough about ¼ inch thick and cut into eight strips about 1 inch wide. Weave them into a lattice over the filling, using four vertical strips and four horizontal strips. Place the strips about 1½ inches apart. Fold the ends under the bottom crust, pinch the edges together, and flute. Lightly brush the top of the lattice with the cream or milk, taking care not to push the strips into the filling. Dust with the sugar.

PLACE THE PIE on the baking sheet and bake for 35 to 40 minutes, until the crust is puffed and golden.

- **PREPARATION TIME:** about 1 hour
- **BAKING TIME:** 35 to 40 minutes
- **EQUIPMENT:** large heavy nonreactive saucepan, rolling pin, 10-inch pie pan, rimmed baking sheet

- **SERVES 8 TO 10**

FILLING

- 12 ounces fresh or frozen cranberries
- 4 cups fresh or frozen blueberries (about 1½ pounds)
- 1 tablespoon freshly grated orange peel
- ¼ cup orange juice
- 1½ cups sugar
- ¼ cup cornstarch

SOUR CREAM CRUST

- 2½ cups unbleached white flour
- 2 teaspoons baking powder
- ¼ teaspoon salt
- 1 cup butter
- 1 cup sour cream
- ¼ cup flour for dusting the dough

GLAZE

- 1 tablespoon heavy cream or milk
- 1 tablespoon sugar

Strawberry Cream Pie

For an intense strawberry flavor make this pie when the fruit is at its peak. We've added a minimal amount of sugar to allow the fresh fruit flavor to predominate.

■ **SERVES 8**

10-inch prebaked pie shell (page 64), cooled to room temperature

FRUIT

4 cups sliced or quartered fresh strawberries (2 pints whole)

¼ cup sugar, or to taste

1 tablespoon cornstarch dissolved in 1 tablespoon water

CUSTARD

¼ cup cornstarch

½ cup sugar

¼ teaspoon salt

2 cups milk

3 large egg yolks, lightly beaten

2 teaspoons pure vanilla extract

fresh whipped cream (optional)

COMBINE THE STRAWBERRIES and sugar in the saucepan and place on medium heat. Bring to a simmer, stirring gently. Stir the dissolved cornstarch into the simmering berries. Cook just until thickened and translucent and set aside.

FOR THE CUSTARD, combine the cornstarch, sugar, and salt in a heavy saucepan. Gradually add a little milk to make a paste and then whisk in the rest of the milk and the egg yolks until smooth. Cook on medium heat, stirring constantly, until the mixture thickens, about 7 or 8 minutes. Lower the heat, if necessary, to prevent the custard from sticking or becoming lumpy. Remove from the heat and stir in the vanilla.

STIR THE COOKED strawberries into the custard and pour the mixture into the prebaked pie shell. Refrigerate for about 2 hours, until thoroughly chilled. Serve with whipped cream, if desired.

■ **PREPARATION TIME:** 30 minutes for filling
■ **CHILLING TIME:** about 2 hours
■ **EQUIPMENT:** heavy saucepan

Three Nut Tart

This tart combines the distinctive flavors and characters of three nuts—pecans, almonds, and pine nuts—in a sweet cookie-like crust. Slice it into bars for eating out of hand, or serve the tart garnished with vanilla ice cream and fresh fruit for a more elegant offering.

If you don't have a proper tart pan, make the crust into a free-form rectangle in a baking dish, flattening and shaping the crust with your hands, and then pinching the edges into a little ridge around its perimeter or building the crust ½ inch up the sides of the pan. It can be as plain or as decorative as you like.

 PREHEAT THE OVEN to 375°.

TOSS TOGETHER THE toasted pecans, almonds, and pine nuts in a medium bowl and set aside.

IN THE SAUCEPAN, simmer the butter, sugar, and water for about 5 minutes, until reduced to a thin syrup that coats a spoon. Remove from the heat and stir in the cream, orange peel, and liqueur. Add the nuts to the syrup and stir until evenly coated.

ARRANGE THE NUTS evenly over the chilled crust and bake for 25 to 35 minutes, or until the nuts are toasted and the crust is lightly browned. Cool before slicing.

- **PREPARATION TIME:** 25 minutes for filling
- **BAKING TIME:** 25 to 35 minutes
- **EQUIPMENT:** 10-inch tart pan with a removable bottom or a 9-inch square baking dish, heavy nonreactive saucepan

- **SERVES 8**

10-inch Sweet Pastry Crust (page 66), shaped to fit the pan and chilled for 1 hour in the freezer

FILLING

1¾ cups toasted pecans

¾ cup toasted almonds

3 tablespoons toasted pine nuts (page 364)

1 tablespoon butter

½ cup sugar

¼ cup water

2 tablespoons heavy cream

¼ teaspoon freshly grated orange peel

2 tablespoons orange-flavored liqueur, such as Grand Marnier (optional)

Lime Tart

We usually associate citrus fruit with Florida or California; however, New Mexico, Arizona, and Texas all grow limes, lemons, grapefruits, and oranges. This not too sweet lime tart goes well with the spicy hot dishes indigenous to the Southwest.

■ SERVES 8

LIME CRUST

- 1 cup unbleached white flour
- 1 tablespoon sugar
- ½ teaspoon freshly grated lime peel
- pinch of salt
- ⅓ cup butter
- 1 teaspoon pure vanilla extract
- 1½ to 4 tablespoons ice water

FILLING

- ¼ cup fresh lime juice (2 or 3 limes)
- 1 teaspoon freshly grated lime peel
- ½ cup sugar
- 1 tablespoon unbleached white flour
- ¾ cup plain nonfat yogurt
- 3 ounces Neufchâtel or cream cheese
- 3 eggs

 PREHEAT THE OVEN to 350°.

COMBINE THE FLOUR, sugar, lime peel, and salt and mix well. Cut the butter into the flour until the mixture resembles coarse cornmeal. Mix in the vanilla. Sprinkle on just enough ice water to form a dough and gently knead until it forms a ball.

ON A FLOURED surface, gently roll out the dough and place it in the pan, crimping the edges to form a high rim. With a fork, prick the crust all over, including the sides. Line the crust with aluminum foil, fill it with pie weights (see Note, page 65), and bake for 25 minutes. Then remove the foil and pie weights and return the crust to the oven to bake 5 minutes longer. Set the crust aside (but don't turn off the oven).

FOR THE FILLING, combine the lime juice, lime peel, sugar, flour, yogurt, Neufchâtel or cream cheese, and eggs in a blender and whirl until smooth. Pour the filling into the baked pie crust and bake for about 35 minutes, until set.

COOL TO ROOM temperature and then cover and refrigerate for about 2 hours, until well chilled. Remove the tart from the pan and serve.

- ■ **PREPARATION TIME:** 30 minutes
- ■ **BAKING TIME:** 30 minutes for crust, 35 minutes for filled tart
- ■ **CHILLING TIME:** 2 hours
- ■ **EQUIPMENT:** rolling pin, 9-inch pie pan or tart pan with removable bottom, blender or food processor

Pear Meringue Tart

Lightly spiced, sautéed pears complement a delicate, melt-in-your-mouth almond meringue crust in a dessert that is scrumptious yet low in fat and calories. Decorate with shaved chocolate and/or a few toasted slivered almonds, if you like. Use a sharp knife to cut this tart.

PREHEAT THE OVEN to 250°. Line the baking sheet with parchment or wax paper.

IN A LARGE bowl, whip the egg whites at low speed until foamy. Add the cream of tartar and salt and beat at medium speed until soft peaks form. Gradually add the sugar and beat on high speed until the whites are satiny and very stiff, about 5 minutes. Gently fold in the ground almonds and nutmeg.

ON THE PREPARED baking sheet, smooth the meringue into a 10-inch circle. Bake in the upper half of the oven for 1¼ hours, until firm and hollow sounding when tapped. Turn off the oven and let the meringue sit in the warm oven for 45 minutes. Peel off the parchment paper. Cool the meringue crust on a wire rack. Store in plastic wrap until ready to serve.

PEEL, CORE, AND and slice each pear lengthwise into about 12 slices and toss with the lemon juice. Transfer to a skillet and add the apple or pear juice, butter, cloves, and nutmeg. Sauté on medium-high heat for about 15 minutes, until the pears are lightly caramelized. Remove the cloves and cool.

JUST BEFORE SERVING, assemble the tart by spooning the pears evenly over the crust, leaving a small border of meringue. Once assembled, this tart will keep for only a day.

- **PREPARATION TIME:** 35 minutes
- **BAKING TIME:** 1¼ hours
- **SITTING TIME:** 45 minutes
- **EQUIPMENT:** baking sheet, parchment or wax paper, electric mixer, skillet (preferably nonstick)

PER 4.25 OZ SERVING: 175 CALS, 4.7 G TOT FAT, 2.5 G MONO FAT, 1.1 G SAT FAT, 3 MG CHOL

■ **SERVES 8 TO 10**

MERINGUE CRUST

- 3 large egg whites
- ⅛ teaspoon cream of tartar
- ⅛ teaspoon salt
- ¾ to 1 cup sugar
- ½ cup lightly toasted finely ground almonds (page 364)
- ¼ teaspoon ground nutmeg

FRUIT

- 6 large pears (about 6 cups sliced pears)
- 2 tablespoons fresh lemon juice
- 1 cup unsweetened apple or pear juice
- 1 tablespoon butter
- 5 whole cloves
- ½ teaspoon ground or freshly grated nutmeg

Best All-Purpose Pie Crust

This crust may be made in the food processor or by hand. Either way, it is critical to work quickly to avoid developing the gluten and to preserve a tender, melt-in-your-mouth texture.

It's great to have a rolled-out and crimped pie crust ready and waiting in the freezer. Well sealed in a freezer bag, the crust will keep for up to a month. When ready to use, just pop it into a preheated oven as if you had just prepared it. For a two-crust pie, double the ingredients.

■ YIELDS 1 CRUST

1½ cups unbleached white flour

½ teaspoon salt

2 tablespoons sugar (optional)

½ cup chilled butter

3 to 4 tablespoons ice water

TO MAKE BY hand, combine the flour, salt, and sugar, if using, in a large bowl. Work the butter into the flour with a knife, pastry cutter, or your fingers until the mixture resembles coarse meal. Sprinkle the ice water onto the crumbly dough and, with your hands, push the dough from the sides to the middle of the bowl to form a ball that holds together. Transfer to a work surface. Cut the dough in half, place half on top of the other, and press down. Repeat the cutting and pressing steps three or four times until all of the water is incorporated into the dough and it clings together.

ON A FLOURED surface, gently flatten the ball of dough with a rolling pin. Starting from the center, roll the dough into a circle about an inch larger than the diameter of the pie pan. Lift the dough into the pan. Fold the edges under and crimp with your fingers or a fork.

TO MAKE IN a food processor, cut the butter into 1-inch pieces and place them in the bowl of the food processor. Add the flour, salt, and sugar. Process until all of the ingredients are incorporated. With the processor on, add the water a tablespoon at a time until the dough begins to clump but is still crumbly. Continue to drizzle a little water and pulse the food processor, stopping to test the dough with your fingertips to see if it is moist enough to hold together.

WHEN YOU CAN gather the dough into a ball, remove it from the processor, place it on a lightly floured surface, and roll out and fit into the pan as above.

TO MAKE A prebaked pie shell, preheat the oven to 375°. Prick the prepared crust in several places with a fork. Line the crust with aluminum foil and a layer of dried beans to weight it down (see Note). Bake for 15 to 20 minutes, until the crimped edge is lightly toasted. Remove the beans and foil and continue to bake for about 10 minutes, until the shell is golden brown and the bottom is no longer moist—if you use a glass pie pan, you can look at the bottom of the pan to check that all moisture has baked out of the crust. Cool before filling.

NOTE You can use dried beans or rice for pie weights. The added weight prevents air bubbles from forming in the crust and also supports the sides of the crust.

This recipe yields enough dough to make one 9- or 10-inch single pie crust. For a two-crust pie, double the quantities.

VARIATIONS For Cream Cheese Crust, add 2 ounces of cream cheese along with the butter.

For Sweet Lemon Crust, use 2 tablespoons of water and 2 tablespoons of lemon juice in place of the 4 tablespoons of water. Mix 1 teaspoon of grated lemon peel and the optional sugar into the dry ingredients.

- **YIELD:** one 9- or 10-inch single pie crust
- **PREPARATION TIME:** 10 to 15 minutes
- **BAKING TIME (PREBAKED PIE SHELL):** 25 to 30 mintues
- **EQUIPMENT:** rolling pin, 9- or 10-inch pie pan, food processor (optional)

Sweet Pastry Crust

This crust resembles a shortbread cookie: crumbly, rich, and sweet. We offer two methods which work equally well—by hand or with a food processor. Experiment to discover which you prefer.

■ YIELDS I CRUST

¼ cup sugar

2 teaspoons freshly grated orange or lemon peel (optional)

½ cup chilled butter, cut into small chunks

¼ teaspoon salt

1½ cups unbleached white pastry flour (page 361)

1 large egg yolk

1 teaspoon pure vanilla extract (optional)

1 to 2 tablespoons cold water, if necessary

TO MAKE BY hand, in a bowl, stir together the sugar and the citrus peel, if using, until thoroughly blended. Add the butter, salt, and flour. Working quickly with your fingers, rub together the ingredients until the mixture is crumbly. Work in the egg yolk until the dough is light yellow. Sprinkle the vanilla, if using, and water, if needed, over the dough and mix with your hands until the dough begins to hold together. Form the dough into a ball, cover with plastic wrap, and chill for at least 30 minutes.

TO PREPARE IN the food processor, whirl together the sugar and citrus peel, if using, until well blended. Add the butter, salt, and flour and pulse until crumbly. Add the egg yolk and pulse a few seconds. Sprinkle in the water and the vanilla, if using, and pulse until the dough forms larger clumps. Push the dough together with your hands and if it doesn't hold together, add a few more drops of cold water and pulse again. When it holds together, cover with plastic wrap, and chill for at least 30 minutes before rolling out.

ON A LIGHTLY floured surface, roll out the dough into a circle and fit into your pie pan. Chill until ready to use. Or shape the dough into any desired shape on a baking sheet. Chill before baking so that the dough will hold its shape.

■ **YIELD:** one 9- or 10-inch single pie crust
■ **PREPARATION TIME:** about 15 minutes
■ **EQUIPMENT:** food processor (optional), rolling pin

Caramel Apple Tarte Tatin

We make this classic French apple tart with none of the usual apple pie spices, which allows the full bouquet of apple flavors to really stand out. Commercial frozen puff pastry dough adds simplicity to the preparation and elegance to the presentation of this tart.

 PREHEAT THE OVEN to 400°.

DISSOLVE THE SUGAR and water in a saucepan on medium heat, stirring constantly until the mixture is clear, about 6 to 8 minutes. Turn the heat to high and cook without stirring until the caramel turns a honey-brown color, about 5 more minutes. Remove from the heat immediately and cool while you prepare the apples.

PEEL, CORE, AND quarter the apples. Melt the butter in the skillet. Arrange a fan of apple slices in a circle around the perimeter and fill in the center with the remaining slices. Cover and cook on medium heat for 8 to 10 minutes, until the apples begin to soften. While the apples cook, carefully stir the sour cream into the cooled caramel (it may sputter if the caramel is still very hot). When the apples are becoming tender, sprinkle on the lemon juice and salt and pour the caramel evenly over the apples.

TRIM THE CORNERS from the pastry to make a rough circle about 10 inches in diameter. Fit the dough over the apples, tucking in the edges around the inside of the pan. Bake for 30 minutes, until the pastry is puffed and golden. Remove from the oven and let stand for 5 minutes. Cover with a plate larger than the skillet and invert very carefully to unmold the tart onto the plate. Serve warm.

■ **PREPARATION TIME:** 20 to 30 minutes
■ **BAKING TIME:** 30 minutes
■ **EQUIPMENT:** 10-inch well-seasoned cast-iron pan or other ovenproof nonstick skillet

■ **SERVES 8**

- 1 cup sugar
- ⅓ cup water
- 5 medium, firm apples, such as Mutsu and Crispin (about 1¾ pounds)
- 2 tablespoons butter
- ½ cup sour cream
- 1½ tablespoons fresh lemon juice
- ¼ teaspoon salt
- 1 sheet prepared puff pastry, defrosted (about ½ pound) (page 365)

Chocolate Date Walnut Baklava

Homemade baklava is an impressive dessert. This unusual version is intensely flavored with chocolate and chewy dates, but it is not overly sweet. It is quite striking when you've drizzled and spattered chocolate on the top in your best Jackson Pollock manner.

Filo dough is wonderfully convenient and not difficult to work with. If you have everything handy for quick assembly, the thin sheets will stay moist and flexible as you work.

Baklava is a good make-ahead dessert because it keeps well without refrigeration. In keeping with its Middle Eastern origins, serve Chocolate Date Walnut Baklava with a small cup of strong espresso or mint tea.

■ **SERVES 18**

¾ to 1 cup semi-sweet chocolate chips

2 cups chopped walnuts (about ½ pound)

2 cups chopped pitted dates (about ½ pound)

1½ teaspoons ground cinnamon

⅔ cup butter

¾ to 1 cup fresh whole wheat bread crumbs

12 sheets packaged filo dough (about ½ pound)

½ cup honey

1 ounce semi-sweet or sweet chocolate (optional)

1 to 2 tablespoons water (optional)

a few fresh orange slices

 PREHEAT THE OVEN to 375°.

FIND A WORKING surface large enough to accommodate the unfolded stack of filo leaves and the baking pan side by side. Don't unwrap the filo until you're ready to assemble the baklava.

IN A BOWL, combine the chocolate chips, walnuts, dates, and cinnamon and set aside. Melt the butter in the saucepan on medium-low heat. Have the bread crumbs handy.

UNWRAP AND UNFOLD the filo and place the stack next to the baking pan. With a pastry brush, coat the pan with butter. Working quickly, lay 1 filo sheet folded in half crosswise on the pan, brush with butter, and sprinkle with bread crumbs. Repeat three times. Spread half of the date mixture evenly over the top, leaving ¼ inch uncovered on all four edges. Layer 4 more doubled sheets of the filo, buttering and sprinkling bread crumbs on each layer. Spread on the remaining date mixture and layer the remaining filo sheets as before. Brush the top with butter.

WITH A SHARP knife, score the top few filo leaves into a pattern of 18 rectangular pieces by making two lengthwise cuts and five crosswise cuts (see Note). Bake for about 35 minutes, until golden brown. While the baklava is still hot, cut all the way through the scoring. Drizzle the baklava with honey, pouring a little honey into the cracks between the pieces.

IF YOU WANT to decorate the top, combine the ounce of chocolate with the water in a double boiler (page 370) and melt on medium-high heat for 3 to 5 minutes. Stir until just thin enough to drizzle and hold a line. Randomly drizzle the chocolate over the top of the baklava. Serve at room temperature, garnished with fresh orange slices.

 NOTE If you prefer, score the baklava in the traditional diamond-shaped pattern.

- **PREPARATION TIME:** 50 minutes
- **BAKING TIME:** 35 minutes
- **EQUIPMENT:** saucepan, 9 × 13-inch baking pan, pastry brush

Chocolate Fruit Purses

How can something so easy to prepare look so impressive? Using minimal ingredients to maximum effect, these little pastries require only five items often found in a well-stocked kitchen.

The purses can be made with fresh fruit when it is available, but they are equally delicious filled with frozen fruit. Puff pastry and frozen fruit are available in the freezer section of most large supermarkets, and once you've tried this dessert, you'll want to have them on hand as staples in your freezer. The recipe is easily doubled and makes an elegant dessert to serve at parties or get-togethers.

■ SERVES 4

1 cup lightly packed
    fresh or frozen red
    raspberries or pitted
    sweet cherries

2 tablespoons sugar

1 tablespoon
    cornstarch

½ cup semi-sweet
    chocolate chips

1 sheet commercially
    prepared puff pastry,
    defrosted*

* Remove the puff pastry from your freezer before doing anything else; it takes at least 20 minutes to thaw.

PREHEAT THE OVEN to 400°. Lightly butter a baking sheet or large baking dish.

COMBINE THE FRUIT, sugar, and cornstarch in the saucepan. Cook on low heat, stirring often, until the mixture thickens, about 5 minutes. Remove from the heat and stir in the chocolate chips.

ON A LIGHTLY floured surface, unfold the defrosted puff pastry. Stretch it slightly to form a square, then cut it in quarters to form four squares. Mound ¼ of the filling in the center of each square. Brush the edges with water, lift the four corners of each square up and over the filling, and twist them together to form a small topknot. Pinch each side seam together to seal the pastries.

PLACE ON THE prepared baking sheet, leaving an inch or so of space between the pastries. Bake until puffed and golden, about 20 minutes. These pastries are best served warm.

■ **PREPARATION TIME:** 15 to 20 minutes
■ **BAKING TIME:** 20 minutes
■ **EQUIPMENT:** baking sheet, small heavy saucepan

Filo Pastry Cups

These crisp, versatile pastry cups make an elegant foundation for a variety of fillings, including Summer Berry Sauce (page 309), Sautéed Apples (page 12), White Chocolate and Raspberry Fool (page 228), Blueberry Peach Sauce (page 303), Chocolate Ricotta Mousse (page 340), and frozen yogurt or ice cream. For an added touch, brush melted semi-sweet chocolate on the bottom of each cooled baked pastry cup.

PREHEAT THE OVEN to 400°. Lightly oil the muffin tins or custard cups.

IN THE SAUCEPAN, melt the butter and set aside. On a clean surface, lay out 3 stacked filo sheets. Brush the top sheet with the melted butter and sprinkle on half of the sugar. With a sharp knife, cut the stacked sheets in half lengthwise and into thirds crosswise to make six equal squares.

MAKE THREE PASTRY stars from the six squares by laying one 3-layered square on top of a second one and then rotating the top one 45° so that the two 3-layered squares form an 8-pointed star. Gently press the middle of each filo star down into a muffin or custard cup and mold it to the shape of the cup. Either leave the points up like a lily or fold them over the rim of the muffin or custard cup. Fill only 3 cups of each 6-cup muffin tin, alternating so that the filo cups don't touch one another. If using custard cups, arrange them on a baking sheet.

REPEAT THIS PROCEDURE with the remaining 3 sheets of filo. Bake at 400° for 15 to 20 minutes, until the pastry is crisp and golden. Remove and cool before filling. Pastry cups can be made several hours or a day in advance of filling and serving. Store in the muffin tins or custard cups wrapped in plastic.

- **PREPARATION TIME:** 10 minutes
- **BAKING TIME:** 10 to 15 minutes
- **EQUIPMENT:** I-cup capacity muffin tins or six 8-ounce custard cups, small saucepan

■ **SERVES 6**

- 2 tablespoons butter
- 6 sheets filo pastry*
- 1 tablespoon sugar

* When working with filo pastry, it is important not to let the dough become dry and brittle. Keep the unused sheets of dough covered with a damp cloth as you work.

Greek Custard Pastry

Like baklava, this flaky pastry is made with sheets of filo dough; however, in this case, it's filled with a baked custard rather than ground nuts. Delicately spiced with cinnamon, lemon peel, and vanilla, the custard is thickened with farina. The result is creamy but not heavy. The buttery filo becomes golden and crisp in the oven and is drizzled with a lemony sugar syrup after baking.

■ **SERVES 9**

CUSTARD

2 cups milk

½ cup sugar

2 tablespoons farina (cream of wheat)

2 eggs

1 teaspoon freshly grated lemon peel

¼ teaspoon ground cinnamon

2 tablespoons butter, at room temperature

½ teaspoon pure vanilla extract

¼ teaspoon salt

½ cup packed chopped dates (optional)*

* If using the dates when making the syrup, reduce the amount of sugar to ⅓ cup and reduce the water to ¼ cup.

IN THE SAUCEPAN, heat the milk on medium heat until steaming but not boiling. While the milk heats, whisk together the sugar, farina, eggs, lemon peel, and cinnamon in a bowl. When the milk is hot, whisk it into the egg mixture. Return the mixture to the saucepan and cook, stirring constantly until thick, 8 to 10 minutes. Remove from the heat and stir in the softened butter, vanilla, and salt. Fold in the chopped dates, if using. Set aside at room temperature, stirring once in a while, for about 1 hour.

WHEN READY TO assembly the pastry, preheat the oven to 350°.

BRUSH THE BAKING pan with some of the melted butter. Place 2 sheets of filo in the pan, allowing the long edges to hand over the sides. Brush butter on the top sheet. Lay down 2 more sheets, perpendicular to the first ones, so that the long edges hang over the other sides of the pan. Butter the top sheet. Top with another 4 sheets, 2 aligned each way, and butter the top sheets.

POUR THE COOLED custard into the filo-lined pan. Fold the overhanging edges up and over and butter the tops. Cut the remaining 4 filo sheets in half. Lay them on top, buttering every other one and tucking in the edges. Bake for 35 to 40 minutes, until the top is golden.

WHILE THE PASTRY bakes, make the syrup. In a small sauce-pan, dissolve the sugar in the water and lemon juice. Cook on medium heat until clear and slightly thick, 5 to 8 minutes. When the baked pastry has cooled for 15 minutes, cut it into nine equal squares and pour the syrup over it.

SERVE AT ROOM temperature or chilled. Store refrigerated.

- **PREPARATION TIME:** 40 minutes
- **SITTING TIME:** 1 hour
- **BAKING TIME:** 35 to 40 minutes
- **COOLING TIME:** 15 minutes
- **EQUIPMENT:** saucepan, 8-inch square baking pan, pastry brush

PASTRY

⅓ cup butter, melted

12 filo sheets

SYRUP

¾ cup sugar

½ cup water

1 teaspoon fresh lemon juice

Nut and Fruit Filled Filo Pastry

There is just enough buttery filo to contain the sweet nutty filling in this interesting spiral-shaped pastry. Serve narrow wedges with coffee or Greek-style with mint tea.

■ **SERVES 8 TO 10**

1½ cups whole almonds

8 ounces dried apricots (about 1 cup)

2 tablespoons packed brown sugar

3 tablespoons honey

2 teaspoons ground cinnamon

8 sheets filo pastry

¼ cup butter, melted

SYRUP

peel from 1 orange, cut into strips

¼ cup fresh orange juice

½ cup sugar

TOAST THE ALMONDS in a 350° oven for about 10 minutes. Cool for several minutes, then finely chop the nuts. If you are using a food processor, add the apricots, brown sugar, honey, and cinnamon and process until the mixture if finely chopped. Otherwise, mince the apricots and stir them together with the sugar, honey, cinnamon, and nuts.

ON A DRY flat surface, stack 2 sheets of filo and brush the top sheet with melted butter. In a thin, even line about 1 inch from a long edge of the buttered filo, spread a generous ¾ cup of the filling. Roll up the filo to form a long thin roll. Carefully lift the roll into the pie pan and curve it to fit along the perimeter of the pan. Lightly brush the roll with butter. Repeat the above procedure to make 3 more rolls, coiling each into the pie pan to form a one-layer, spiraled pastry. Butter each roll as you go. Nestled close together, all four rolls should neatly fit into the pie pan, with the end of the last roll finishing in the center. Bake for 30 to 35 minutes, until the pastry is crisp and lightly browned.

WHILE THE PASTRY bakes, make the syrup. Combine the orange peel, orange juice, and sugar in a small saucepan and bring to a boil on high heat. Reduce the heat and simmer gently for 10 minutes. Remove from the heat and strain.

POUR THE SYRUP over the pastry as soon as it comes out of the oven, then cool. Serve at room temperature, cut into narrow wedges.

■ **PREPARATION TIME:** 30 minutes
■ **BAKING TIME:** 30 to 35 minutes
■ **EQUIPMENT:** food processor (optional), pastry brush, 10-inch pie pan

Orange Meringues

These sweet, airy puffs, scented with citrus, are easily prepared and totally fat-free.

Serve Orange Meringues plain or filled with fresh fruit. Or top them with Orange Sauce (page 306) or Pineapple Orange Sauce (page 306), Raspberry Sauce (page 310), or Summer Berry Sauce (page 309) and be careful not to swoon.

Stored in a sealed container, meringues keep for up to a week. If they become soft, reheat them for 5 minutes in a 200° oven, turn off the heat, and let them cool in the oven until dry.

PREHEAT THE OVEN to 225°. Line a baking sheet with parchment paper or butter it and lightly dust with flour.

IN A LARGE bowl, beat the egg whites and cream of tartar with an electric mixer at high speed until soft peaks form. Gradually sprinkle in the sugar, continuing to beat until stiff peaks form. The whites should be glossy but not dry. Gently fold in the orange peel.

DROP LARGE SPOONFULS of the batter onto the prepared sheet. With the back of the spoon, spread each dollop of batter into a 3- to 4-inch circle with a slight hollow in the center. You should have 12 meringues.

BAKE FOR 1½ hours, then turn off the oven and let the meringues gradually cool in the warm oven for 1 hour.

- **YIELD:** 12 meringues
- **PREPARATION TIME:** 20 to 25 minutes
- **BAKING TIME:** 1½ hours
- **COOLING TIME:** 1 hour
- **EQUIPMENT:** baking sheet, electric mixer

PER 1.25 OZ SERVING: 76 CALS, 0 G TOT FAT, 0 G MONO FAT, 0 G SAT FAT, 0 MG CHOL

- **SERVES 6**

3 large egg whites, at room temperature (about ½ cup)*

¼ teaspoon cream of tartar

½ cup sugar

1 teaspoon freshly grated orange peel

As for an angelfood cake, the egg whites for meringues must be completely free of yolk and at room temperature in order to whip up to their full volume.

Plum Strudel

The season for plums grown in the United States is mid-May through September, but plums grown in the southern hemisphere are often available in midwinter. Prune-type plums are best for holding color and shape when cooked, but any variety of plum will do.

This luscious, easy-to-prepare strudel contains only ¼ cup of butter for 8 to 10 servings.

■ **SERVES 8 TO 10**

2 pounds plums, pitted and chopped into bite-sized pieces (about 4 cups)

3 tablespoons quick-cooking tapioca

⅓ cup plus ½ cup packed brown sugar

1 tablespoon fresh lemon juice

½ to 1 teaspoon ground ginger

pinch of salt

½ cup bread crumbs

½ teaspoon ground cinnamon

½ pound filo pastry* (about 10 sheets)

¼ cup butter, melted

* Work quickly so that the filo dough will not dry out and become brittle.

 PREHEAT THE OVEN to 400°. Butter the baking sheet.

IN A BOWL, combine the plums, tapioca, ⅓ cup brown sugar, lemon juice, ginger, and salt. In another bowl, combine the bread crumbs, ½ cup brown sugar, and cinnamon. Set aside.

UNROLL THE FILO dough on a clean, dry surface. Place 2 filo sheets on a clean, dry towel, brush the top lightly with butter, and sprinkle with a little of the bread crumb mixture. Continue layering in this way, ending with a filo sheet and reserving a tablespoon of bread crumbs and 1 to 2 teaspoons of butter.

TURN THE TOWEL so that the long edge of the filo is facing you. Mound the plum mixture onto the filo stack into a rectangle positioned 3 inches from one of the long edges and about 2 inches from each of the short edges. Fold the short ends of the stack up and over and then tightly roll up the strudel lengthwise, like a jelly roll. Carefully place the strudel, seam side down, on the baking sheet. Brush the top with the remaining butter and sprinkle it with the reserved bread crumbs.

BAKE FOR 25 to 30 minutes, until the strudel is crisp and golden. Carefully remove it to a serving platter.

SERVE WARM OR at room temperature. Slice the strudel with a long serrated knife, using a sawing motion.

■ **PREPARATION TIME:** 35 to 40 minutes
■ **BAKING TIME:** 25 to 30 minutes
■ **EQUIPMENT:** baking sheet, dry kitchen towel, pastry brush

PER 5.25 OZ SERVING: 274 CALS, 6.1 G TOT FAT, 1.8 MONO FAT, 3.0 G SAT FAT, 12 MG CHOL

Winter Fruit Strudel

This sweet-tart, moist, dense, and chewy fruit filling is in delicious contrast to the light, flaky crust. The dried fruits absorb the juices from the pears and cranberries, making a firm pastry that slices easily for holiday parties. Serve plain or with whipped cream or vanilla ice cream.

 PREHEAT THE OVEN to 350°. Butter the baking sheet.

IN A MEDIUM-SIZED bowl, mix together all of the filling ingredients and set aside. Working quickly in a draft-free spot to prevent the filo from becoming brittle, lay 2 sheets of filo flat on the counter and brush the top sheet with melted butter. Repeat this four times, stacking the filo leaves on top of one another, until you have used all of the filo. Be sure to butter the top layer.

SPREAD THE FILLING evenly over the filo, leaving a 2-inch margin around the edges. Fold the two shorter side margins over the filling; then start at a long side and carefully roll the filo into a log. Transfer the strudel roll to the prepared baking sheet and brush with the remaining butter.

BAKE THE STRUDEL for 35 to 45 minutes, until golden brown. Allow the strudel to cool for 30 minutes. Slice the warm strudel with a serrated knife and serve.

- **PREPARATION TIME:** 20 minutes
- **BAKING TIME:** 35 to 45 minutes
- **COOLING TIME:** 30 minutes
- **EQUIPMENT:** baking sheet, pastry brush

PER 4.25 OZ SERVING: 214 CALS, 6.3 G TOT FAT, 1.8 G MONO FAT, 3.6 G SAT FAT, 16 MG CHOL

■ SERVES 6 TO 8

FILLING

- 2 firm pears, peeled, cored, and coarsely chopped
- 1 cup fresh cranberries
- ¼ cup golden raisins
- ½ cup chopped dried prunes
- ¼ cup currants
- ½ cup chopped dried apricots
- 3 tablespoons packed brown sugar
- ½ teaspoon ground cinnamon
- ¼ teaspoon ground allspice
- ¼ teaspoon ground cardamom
- ¼ teaspoon ground nutmeg

FILO

- 10 14 × 18-inch sheets filo dough
- ¼ cup butter, melted

LAYERED OR FILLED CAKES

Buttercream Frosting

Big Banana Bourbon Cake

Buttermilk Spice Cake

Cassata

Chocolate Cherry Angelfood Cake

Coconut Lemon Layer Cake

Festive Celebrations Cake

Frosted Orange Layer Cake

Texas Italian Cream Cake

Irish Oatmeal Cake

Maple Cake

Chocolate Espresso Roll

Lemon Jelly Roll

Hazelnut Torte

Mocha Walnut Torte

Dark Chocolate Layer Cake

Chocolate Almond Meringue Torte

Zuccotto

Layered or Filled Cakes

IT MIGHT BE DISAPPOINTING TO BLOW OUT THE BIRTHDAY CANDLES on a plate full of bran muffins. Could the bride and groom feed each other bread pudding with the same panache as wedding cake? Some occasions cry out for a lavish, impressive cake. (Of course, the cakes here needn't be saved for landmark celebrations; enjoy them anytime.) Layered cakes contrast a moist, springy cake with the smooth, sweet creaminess of a filling or frosting—a nice counterpoint. Fillings and frostings can make the difference between a plain cake and an elegant ensemble. We encourage you to mix and match different frostings and fillings with cakes. Hazelnut Torte could be filled with Chocolate Ganache, the Irish Oatmeal Cake would be well paired with Maple Butter-cream Frosting, and Big Banana Bourbon Cake would be in good company with Chocolate Vegan Glaze. Also note that the flavors of fruit can be brighter and fresher in fillings than when baked into the cake. Coconut Lemon Layer Cake, airy Chocolate Cherry Angelfood

Cake, Cassata, and Frosted Orange Layer Cake demonstrate this point. A chocolate layer cake, one wedge cut out to seductively reveal the sumptuous interior, is perhaps the most familiar image of the classic cake. Our dreamy, buttery Dark Chocolate Layer Cake is the epitome of this American-style ideal. European tortes, like Mocha Walnut Torte, take a somewhat different direction: Made with less flour and butter, they rely upon eggs for levity and ground nuts for rich flavor. A filled cake with true architectural stature is the dome-shaped Zuccotto, which is filled with nuts, chocolate, and cream. Angelfood cakes move into the lofty celestial spheres, using a generous amount of whipped egg whites to create a very light cake. Angelfood cake is fat-free, and even frosted or filled, it is lower in fat than most standard layer cakes. And when the occasion arises for a large-scale, multitiered cake, the recipe for the Festive Celebrations Cake can be multiplied without altering its excellent taste, texture, and structure. Successful cake baking is an exacting process. Although we usually tinker with other recipes, we have learned to follow the specifics of ingredients, measurements, pan sizes, and oven temperatures given in cake recipes. Please check our Guide to Tips and Techniques (pages 367 to 375) for instructions and tips on cake making and decorating. For other good decorating ideas, see the section that immediately follows. The easiest way to cut a standard layer cake is with a sharp, thin knife. Angelfood and jelly roll cakes cut best with a long serrated knife. In general, a frosted cake is most cleanly cut by dipping the knife in hot water and then wiping it with a damp paper towel before each cut.

Here is a host of tips for creating fancy cakes that work. We think you'll especially like the section on decorating cakes with pizazz but without a lot of special equipment. A few more simple decorating ideas as well as directions for making a good homemade substitute for a pastry bag can be found on page 368.

Home-style Layer Cakes

When making a home-style, two-layer cake, turn both cake layers out onto racks to cool. Use the cake layer with the flattest top as the bottom layer and transfer it to a serving plate upside down (original top side down). Frost the middle. Place the second cake layer right side up so that the flat surfaces meet with the frosting between them to form a level two-layer cake. Frost first the sides and then the top of the cake. For easy spreading and to smooth the top of the frosted cake, dip the knife in hot water from time to time.

The best layers for a layer cake are perfectly flat. But life (and baking) isn't *always* perfect. To help prevent domed layers, spread the batter slightly up the sides of the pan and make a small depression in the center to offset the higher rising in the middle. But should both cake layers *still* end up very domed and unsuitable for a bottom layer (which ideally has two flat sides), level one of the domed cake layers by cutting off the top with fishing line, heavy thread, or dental floss, using the top of the pan as a guide.

If the top of the cake layer has puffed up and out over the top edge of the cake pan, be sure to trim this edge before turning the cake layer out of the pan.

To keep the edges of a serving plate frosting-free, slide thin strips of wax paper under the outer edge of the bottom layer before frosting.

Fancy Filled Layer Cakes

When creating layers by slicing a cake in half (or thirds) horizontally, a lazy Susan or cake decorating turntable is helpful but not necessary. You can also use a cake stand or large flat plate. Use a serrated knife with a blade longer than the cake's diameter, if available.

If you have a turntable, press the blade of the knife horizontally against the side of the cake where you intend to cut and then turn the cake to score it evenly all around. If you have no lazy Susan, find guides for the knife that measure half (or a third) the cake's height. Place long, narrow objects (such as thick dowels, bundles of chopsticks, or domino boxes) on either side of the cake and then rest the blade of the knife on them as you slice through horizontally. Use a sawing motion and follow the scoring or the guides as you cut the cake into layers. Before separating the layers, make a small vertical mark on the side of the cake (through all of the layers). That way, if your layers are uneven, you can realign them after frosting the middle and the end result will lie flat.

Lift off each layer and set it aside. Frost or fill the top of each layer in turn, starting with the bottom layer. Use the vertical mark to align the layers as you restack them to build the layer cake. Frost or glaze the outside of the cake, if desired.

Building a Tiered Cake

Assembling a tiered cake is not that hard. The secret is that the lower tiers themselves never support the upper ones. Hidden cardboard circles and plastic drinking straws form a support structure.

Using the cake pans as templates, draw 12-, 9-, and 6-inch circles on stiff, clean cardboard, cut them out, and set them aside.

Level the top and sides of each tier, if necessary

(*see opposite*). Make a small vertical mark on the side of each tier through both the top and bottom layers to help align the layers later. Cut each tier in half horizontally to make 2 layers. Place the bottom layers cut side up on their matching cardboard circles, sprinkle any sugar flavorings you wish to use over the cut sides, and spread with filling or frosting. Use the vertical mark to align the layers of each tier. Finish by frosting first the sides and then the tops of each tier with an even ¼-inch of frosting.

Insert a straw in the center of the 12-inch tier, mark where it is just level with the frosting, pull it out, and use it to measure at least 7 more straw pieces of equal length. If you don't have sturdy straws, cut more for extra support. Measure and cut out 6 straw pieces for the 9-inch tier. Mark a circle on the 12-inch tier where the perimeter of the 9-inch tier will be when it is centered and placed on the larger tier. Insert the straw pieces vertically into the bottom tier just inside the marked circle, spacing them evenly around the perimeter. Repeat, marking and inserting straw pieces in the 9-inch tier to support the 6-inch tier. With the straws in place, the tiers can be assembled with confidence. To hide the edges of the cardboard circles, pipe frosting around the perimeters where the tiers meet. It's often easiest to do these final steps at the site of the special occasion.

Decorating a Fancy or Tiered Cake

Traditionally, fancier cakes are encased in a very smooth, thin layer of frosting, which becomes a canvas for all kinds of piped designs. If you are proficient with a pastry bag and decoration tubes, then you can pipe rosettes or other designs to your heart's content. Repeating patterns tend to be the most successful and any mistakes can be scraped off and redone or hidden by fresh flowers. On the other hand, a quite elegant presentation can be made with very little piping and a few artfully placed blooms. Some that can be eaten safely are alyssum, chrysanthemums, daisies, day lilies, dianthus, geraniums, hollyhocks, jasmine, lavender, lilacs, marigolds, nasturtiums, pansies, roses, sunflower petals, and violets. (Choose homegrown or organically raised flowers to minimize the danger of ingesting harmful pesticides).

Leaves made of chocolate can be a very elegant addition, especially if you are decorating with real flowers. We recommend using rose leaves as molds because they're easy to find and have intricate, detailed veins. Rinse and dry several leaves. Paint the undersides with about an ⅛-inch-thick layer of melted chocolate and then place in the freezer just until firm. Peel the leaf away from the chocolate. If you are gentle and the leaves are resilient, you should be able to paint each leaf several times. Store the finished chocolate leaves in the refrigerator or freezer until ready to use. The warmth of your hands will melt the chocolate leaves almost instantly, so transfer them to the cake with a knife or spatula.

One of the most elegant pastry shop cake decorations is also the easiest. All you need is a gallon-sized plastic bag, a toothpick, and a small amount of colored icing, such as fruit purée or chocolate melted with a tablespoon of butter. Fill the bag with the icing and cut off a very small tip from one corner of the bag. Squeeze out some icing to test how thickly and quickly it comes out and make the opening larger if necessary.

Pipe a spiral of 6 or 7 concentric circles beginning near the edge of the cake and ending in the center. There should be 1 to 1½ inches between each coil. Draw a toothpick through the coils from the center to the edge of the cake in a straight line. Continue as if you were dividing the cake into 8, 9, or 12 servings. You should end up with a design reminiscent of a spider web. Refrigerate the frosted cake to set the frosting.

Buttercream Frosting

Why would anyone take the time and effort to collect more than a dozen egg yolks and cook a sugar syrup to exactly 239° just to embellish a cake? Let's face it, most people would simply whip together some butter, confectioners' sugar, and flavoring and be done with it. However, that kind of frosting is often sickeningly sweet. A classic buttercream frosting is infinitely smoother, silkier, and far more subtly sweet. It is simply the correct choice for a festive celebrations cake.

At Moosewood, we prefer vanilla buttercream to all the rest, but other possibilities abound. Instant coffee granules dissolved in a spoonful of water will turn the ivory-colored buttercream a rich shade of café au lait. Raspberry purée makes the basic buttercream a vivid pink. Puréed apricots or mangoes tint it gold.

The unused egg yolks from our Festive Celebrations Cake batter (page 96) yield just enough buttercream to fill and frost the cake. This is a very rich frosting, so a thin layer is more than enough. Halve the recipe to frost a 2-layer, 12-inch cake or the equivalent. Should you want to spread the frosting more lavishly, you'll have to fill the cake with something else or else break out more egg yolks and make more frosting.

■ **YIELDS 6 CUPS**

15 egg yolks

2 cups sugar

1 cup water

4 cups unsalted butter, at room temperature

2 tablespoons pure vanilla extract (optional)

BEAT THE EGG yolks with an electric mixer on high speed for 2 to 3 minutes until they lighten; set aside. Combine the sugar and water in the saucepan and place on medium-high heat. Boil until the sugar dissolves, 3 to 4 minutes. Increase the heat to high and boil the syrup another 4 to 5 minutes, until a candy thermometer registers 239°. Immediately remove from the heat.

WITH THE MIXER on high speed, beat the egg yolks, gradually adding the syrup a few tablespoons at a time. Avoid pouring the syrup on the beaters or it will end up on the sides of the bowl instead of in the eggs. Continue beating the egg and syrup mixture until it is no longer hot to the touch, about 5 minutes. Add the softened butter a few tablespoons at a time, beating well after each addition. The consistency will not be frosting-like until the last few tablespoons of butter are added. When finally thick and creamy, beat in the vanilla, if using, and any other flavorings (see Variations). Set aside in a cool place until ready to use.

 NOTE If possible, use Buttercream Frosting soon after it is made. If stored in the refrigerator, always let it return to room temperature before spreading, because cold buttercream is very likely to curdle and become grainy when beaten. Adding 1 or 2 tablespoons of melted butter may help restore its original satiny texture.

VARIATIONS
To 3 cups of buttercream (½ recipe), add:

■ up to 6 ounces of bittersweet, semi-sweet, or white chocolate, melted completely and cooled to room temperature.

■ up to 2 tablespoons of instant coffee granules dissolved in 2 teaspoons of hot water.

■ up to 2 tablespoons of freshly grated orange peel and ¼ cup of orange juice in place of the vanilla.

■ ½ cup of raspberry purée or other fruit purée in place of the vanilla.

■ up to ¼ cup of liqueur, with or without the vanilla, as desired.

■ **TOTAL TIME:** 25 to 30 minutes
■ **EQUIPMENT:** electric mixer, small heavy saucepan

Big Banana Bourbon Cake

With a spirited presence as sweet and generous as southern hospitality, this impressive cake charms most everyone. The golden caramelized banana slices on top lose their attractive color after several hours, so plan to assemble the cake not too long before presenting it.

■ **SERVES 8 TO 10**

CAKE

½ cup butter, at room temperature

1 cup sugar

3 eggs

5 ripe bananas, mashed (about 1½ cups)

2 teaspoons pure vanilla extract

2 cups unbleached white flour

1 teaspoon baking soda

1 teaspoon baking powder

1 teaspoon salt

BOURBON WHIPPED CREAM FROSTING

1 cup heavy cream

3 tablespoons confectioners' sugar

1 tablespoon bourbon

1 teaspoon pure vanilla extract

PREHEAT THE OVEN to 350°. Lightly butter or oil the cake pans.

CREAM THE BUTTER and sugar together until smooth and creamy. Add the eggs one at a time, beating well after each addition. Beat in the mashed bananas and vanilla. Sift together the flour, baking soda, baking powder, and salt. Fold the dry ingredients into the banana mixture.

POUR HALF OF the batter into each of the prepared pans. Bake until the cakes are golden brown and a knife inserted in the center comes out clean, 20 to 25 minutes. Cool the cakes in the pans for 15 to 20 minutes. Gently remove them from the pans and place on a rack to cool completely.

TO PREPARE THE frosting, combine the heavy cream, confectioners' sugar, bourbon, and vanilla in a chilled bowl. Beat with an electric mixer and chilled beaters until stiff. Refrigerate until you are ready to assemble the cake.

TO PREPARE THE banana glaze, slice the bananas into rounds. In the saucepan, melt the butter. Add the bananas, lemon juice, brown sugar, and bourbon. Cook on medium-low heat for 3 to 5 minutes, stirring gently to avoid mashing the bananas, until they are cooked and the glaze is lightly caramelized. Set aside.

TO ASSEMBLE THE layer cake, frost the top of one of the cakes with the whipped cream frosting and pour on about ⅓ of the banana mixture. Place the second cake atop the bottom layer and frost the sides and top of the cake with the remaining whipped cream frosting. Pour the remaining banana mixture over the top and allow the glaze to drip down the sides, if desired. Serve immediately.

ANY LEFTOVER CAKE should be covered and refrigerated.

- **PREPARATION TIME:** 25 minutes
- **BAKING TIME:** 20 to 25 minutes
- **EQUIPMENT:** two 9-inch round cake pans, electric mixer, chilled bowl and beaters, nonreactive saucepan

BANANA GLAZE

- 3 large ripe bananas
- 2 tablespoons butter
- 2 tablespoons fresh lemon juice
- 3 tablespoons packed brown sugar
- ½ cup bourbon

Buttermilk Spice Cake

This delicious, old-fashioned birthday cake kind of cake has a wonderful aroma. Ice with our tasty Cream Cheese Frosting (see Note) or bake as a sheet cake in a 9 × 13 × 2-inch or 8½ × 11 × 2-inch pan and frost or dust the top with confectioners' sugar.

■ SERVES 16

DRY INGREDIENTS

3 cups unbleached pastry flour (page 361)

2 teaspoons ground cinnamon

1 teaspoon ground allspice

½ teaspoon ground cloves

¼ teaspoon ground ginger

1½ teaspoons baking powder

1½ teaspoons baking soda

½ teaspoon salt

1 cup dried currants or raisins

WET INGREDIENTS

¾ cup butter

½ cup sugar

1 cup packed brown sugar

2 eggs, lightly beaten

1½ cups buttermilk

1 teaspoon pure vanilla extract

PREHEAT THE OVEN to 350°. Butter or oil the cake pans and dust them with flour.

COMBINE THE DRY ingredients, stirring the raisins or currants in after the rest of the dry ingredients are mixed together. In a separate bowl, cream the butter, sugar, and brown sugar until smooth and light. Add the eggs, buttermilk, and vanilla. Cream until smooth. Stir the dry ingredients into the wet ingredients and beat well.

POUR THE BATTER into the cake pans and bake for 35 to 40 minutes, until a toothpick inserted in the center comes out clean. Cool the cakes in the pans for 5 minutes. Run a knife around the outer edges of the cakes and turn them out onto a rack to cool for about 30 minutes.

FOR THE FROSTING, cream the butter and Neufchâtel or cream cheese together with a food processor or an electric mixer until blended and light. Beat in the vanilla and gradually add the confectioners' sugar until the frosting is a good consistency for spreading. If it's too stiff, add a little milk. If it's too soft, add more confectioners' sugar. Add the extract, is using.

ASSEMBLE THE LAYER cake (page 82), spreading the frosting between the two layers and then on the top and sides of the cake.

NOTE This smooth, no-nonsense frosting is perfect on spice cake, carrot cake, zucchini cake, and banana cake. For a buffet or party, serve a platter of chilled ripe strawberries and pineapple chunks on toothpicks and dip first into Cream Cheese Frosting at room temperature and then into toasted coconut, chocolate shavings, finely chopped nuts, or other crunchy coatings.

THE RECIPE CAN BE halved for frosting single-layer cakes such as Red Devil Cake (page 135).

- **PREPARATION TIME:** 25 minutes
- **BAKING TIME:** 35 to 40 minutes
- **COOLING TIME:** 30 minutes
- **FROSTING TIME:** 15 minutes
- **EQUIPMENT:** two 9-inch round cake pans, electric mixer or food processor

CREAM CHEESE FROSTING

- ¼ cup butter, at room temperature
- 6 ounces Neufchâtel or cream cheese, at room temperature
- 1 teaspoon pure vanilla extract
- 3 cups confectioners' sugar
- ½ teaspoon pure almond, lemon, or orange extract (optional)

Cassata

A traditional Sicilian holiday cake, Cassata is an impressive dessert for any important festivity. Happily, it is not difficult to make. It is a fairly substantial concoction and is most welcome as the sweet ending to a light Mediterranean meal. It is also a perfect choice for an occasion when dessert alone is served.

Cassata can be served after chilling for only about 40 minutes, but it is easier to slice into neat servings when it is chilled for at least 2 hours. Garnish with fresh strawberries, cherries, or orange slices and serve with strong hot coffee.

■ **SERVES 16 TO 20**

RICOTTA CHEESE FILLING

- 2 cups ricotta cheese
- 1 teaspoon pure vanilla extract
- ½ cup raspberry fruit spread or ½ cup confectioners' sugar
- freshly grated peel of 1 orange
- ¼ cup chopped toasted almonds (page 364)
- 2 cups chopped dried fruit (a combination of prunes, figs, pears, apricots, raisins, or cherries)

TO MAKE THE filling, whip the ricotta cheese with an electric mixer on high speed until very smooth and somewhat fluffed up, about 5 minutes. Mix in the vanilla and fruit spread or confectioners' sugar. With a spoon, fold in the orange peel, almonds, and dried fruit. Cover and refrigerate until ready to assemble the cake.

CAREFULLY CUT BOTH layers of the cake in half horizontally using a long serrated bread knife and a gentle sawing motion. Place a cake layer on a serving plate, sprinkle with 1 tablespoon of orange liqueur, and spoon on ⅓ of the ricotta filling. Repeat twice, layering the cake, liqueur, and filling until all of the filling is used. Use the smooth rounded side of a cake layer—not a cut side for the top of the cake and sprinkle it with the remaining tablespoon of liqueur.

COMBINE THE CHOCOLATE and water in the double boiler and heat, stirring constantly, until the chocolate is melted and smooth. Spread the glaze evenly over the top of the cake, allowing it to drip over the sides.

IF YOU WISH to decorate the cassata, gently press small pieces of dried fruit into the chocolate glaze while it is still warm.

REFRIGERATE THE CASSATA for at least 40 minutes before serving.

VARIATION When time is short, you can substitute a purchased cake, such as a plain poundcake, spongecake, or angelfood cake. Our favorite of the already made cakes for cassata is panettone, an Italian sweet bread that is very popular at Easter time and for the winter holidays, when you should be able to find it at Italian bakeries or imported from Italy at most well-stocked supermarkets. Panettone freezes very well, so we like to stock up whenever it is available. This recipe makes the right amount of filling and glaze for a large 2-pound panettone or two smaller 1-pound panettones.

TO ASSEMBLE A panettone cassata, carefully remove the paper collar from the panettone. Cut off the domed top and a 1 inch slice from the bottom of the cake and set these two layers aside. Score a circle in the top of the middle layer 1-inch from the outer edge. Using the scoring as a guide, cut out the inner cylindrical core and remove it, leaving the outer ring intact. Now slice the inner core horizontally into four round slices. Sprinkle the liqueur over the cut surfaces of three of the slices.

TO REASSEMBLE THE panettone, place the outer ring of the middle layer back on the bottom layer. Fill the outer ring by alternating the filling with the three liqueured inner core slices, beginning and ending with filling. (There will be one plain core slice left over). Reposition the rounded top layer and brush the outside with the chocolate glaze. Chill before serving.

- **PREPARATION TIME:** 50 minutes
- **BAKING TIME:** 30 to 35 minutes
- **CHILLING TIME:** at least 40 minutes
- **EQUIPMENT:** electric mixer, double boiler (page 370)

1 recipe (2 layers) Frosted Orange Layer Cake (page 98), thoroughly cooled and not frosted

¼ cup orange-flavored liqueur, such as Grand Marnier

4 ounces semi-sweet chocolate, broken into pieces

3 tablespoons water

a few colorful pieces of dried fruit (optional)

Chocolate Cherry Angelfood Cake

This heavenly combination of light, cloudlike cake, creamy cherry filling, and smooth, rich chocolate glaze is perfect for special occasions and celebrations. It is best to assemble it just before serving. If you have never made an angelfood cake before, read the helpful information in the note on page 141.

■ **SERVES 12**

CAKE

¾ cup unbleached white pastry or cake flour (page 361)

¼ cup unsweetened cocoa powder

¼ teaspoon salt

1½ cups sugar

1¾ cups egg whites, at room temperature (about 12 large eggs)

1 teaspoon cream of tartar

1 teaspoon pure vanilla extract

½ teaspoon pure almond extract

CHERRY CREAM CHEESE FILLING

1 cup Neufchâtel or cream cheese, or at room temperature

⅓ cup confectioners' sugar

¼ teaspoon pure almond extract

12-ounce package frozen sweet cherries, thawed and drained, juice reserved (two 15-ounce cans, drained)

 PREHEAT THE OVEN to 350°.

COMBINE THE FLOUR, cocoa, salt, and ¾ cup of the sugar and sift together three times. Set aside. In a large bowl, beat the egg whites and cream of tartar with an electric mixer on medium speed until soft peaks form. Increase the speed to high and gradually add the remaining ¾ cup sugar. Beat until stiff, glossy peaks form. At this point, when the bowl is tilted at a 30- to 45-degree angle, the egg whites should not slide. Take care not to overbeat.

SPRINKLE THE VANILLA and almond extracts over the whites and fold in with a rubber spatula. Sprinkle about ⅓ cup of the flour mixture over the whites and gently fold in. Continue to sprinkle and fold in more flour, ⅓ cup at a time, until all of the flour mixture has been incorporated.

POUR THE BATTER into the unoiled tube pan. Run a knife through the batter in a zigzag pattern to puncture any large air pockets. Bake until the cake springs back when lightly touched, 40 to 50 minutes. Invert the pan on its feet or over a long-necked bottle and cool completely, about 2 hours. Loosen the cake by running a knife around the edges. To take the cake out of the tube pan, remove the center cylinder section, then carefully lift the cake with spatulas from the base and transfer it to a serving platter.

FOR THE FILLING, combine the Neufchâtel or cream cheese, confectioners' sugar, and almond extract and beat until smooth. Add the drained cherries, stirring just until mixed. Set aside.

SHORTLY BEFORE ASSEMBLING the cake, prepare the glaze. In a small, heavy pan on very low heat, melt the chocolate. Whisk in the cherry juice.

TO ASSEMBLE THIS masterpiece, carefully cut the cake in half horizontally with a serrated knife, using a sawing motion so as not to flatten it. Spread the bottom half with the filling. Replace the top half of the cake and drizzle the glaze over the top and down the sides. Refrigerate until ready to serve.

- **PREPARATION TIME:** 35 minutes
- **BAKING TIME:** 40 to 50 minutes
- **COOLING TIME:** 2 hours
- **EQUIPMENT:** electric mixer, 10-inch tube pan, small, heavy saucepan

CHOCOLATE CHERRY GLAZE

4 ounces semi-sweet chocolate

¼ cup cherry juice, reserved from drained cherries

Coconut Lemon Layer Cake

Here is a layer cake that can be made as 2 separate layers or as a 10-inch bundt cake and cut into 2 or 3 layers. Sandwich the layers with tangy lemon curd and frost the cake with velvety lemon cream. Coconut milk gives a subtle coconut flavor to the cake, while the crunchy-chewy toasted coconut topping provides more than a hint of this tropical fruit.

■ **SERVES 12 TO 16**

CAKE

- 1 cup butter, at room temperature
- 2 cups sugar
- 1 cup coconut milk (reduced-fat works fine, page 358) or 1 cup milk plus 1 teaspoon pure coconut extract
- 2 teaspoons pure vanilla extract
- 2½ cups unbleached white flour
- 1 tablespoon baking powder
- ½ teaspoon salt
- 6 egg whites

PREHEAT THE OVEN to 350°. Butter and flour the cake pans or bundt pan.

WITH AN ELECTRIC mixer, cream the butter and sugar until light and fluffy. In a separate bowl, mix together the coconut milk and vanilla. Add half of the milk mixture to the butter and sugar mixture and beat until well blended. Into another bowl, sift together the flour, baking powder, and salt. Add the sifted mixture to the butter mixture and stir well. Thoroughly mix in the remaining milk mixture. The batter will be very heavy.

USING AN ELECTRIC mixer with clean, dry beaters and a clean bowl, beat the egg whites until stiff peaks form. Fold the beaten whites into the batter until no trace of white remains—be diligent. Pour the batter into the prepared pan(s) and bake until the tip of a knife inserted in the center of the cake comes out clean, about 40 minutes for layer cakes, 1 hour for a bundt cake. Cool on a rack.

WHILE THE CAKE is baking, make the lemon curd. In the saucepan, whisk together the lemon peel, juice, sugar, and eggs. On medium heat, cook the mixture, whisking constantly until the curd thickens, about 5 to 7 minutes. Remove from the heat. For a perfectly smooth curd, pour the curd through a fine-mesh strainer to remove the lemon peel and any bits of egg. Whisk in the butter a little at a time. Refrigerate the curd until well chilled, about 1 hour.

WHEN THE CAKE has baked and cooled, prepare it for filling and frosting. For a bundt cake, use a long serrated knife to cut it horizontally into halves or thirds. With either type of cake, spread about half of the chilled curd between its layers.

WHIP THE CREAM until stiff and stir in the remaining lemon curd. Spread the whipped lemon cream over the cake and chill well. Serve sprinkled with toasted coconut flakes.

- **PREPARATION TIME:** 20 minutes for cake, 25 minutes for curd while cake bakes
- **BAKING TIME:** 40 minutes for layer cakes, about 1 hour for bundt cakes
- **COOLING TIME:** 40 minutes for cake
- **CHILLING TIME:** 1 hour for lemon curd filling
- **EQUIPMENT:** two 9-inch round cake pans or one 10-inch bundt pan, electric mixer, small nonreactive saucepan

LEMON CURD FILLING

- 1 tablespoon freshly grated lemon peel
- 1/3 cup fresh lemon juice
- 3/4 cup sugar
- 3 eggs
- 1/2 cup butter, at room temperature
- 1 cup heavy cream
- 1/2 cup toasted coconut flakes (page 358)

Festive Celebrations Cake

The sight of a foot-tall, three-tiered wedding cake is often cause for awe and amazement. All too often, though, the cake is dry and the decorative frosting is 90 percent eye appeal, 10 percent jaw breaker. For a festive cake really to succeed, it must succeed on all levels: from holding up in warm weather to eliciting oohs *and* ahs *for presentation—and taste.*

Fancy cakes can be intimidating and, granted, they do require time and attention. But the thought of making one needn't cause fear and trembling. This recipe makes a three-tiered cake. Half of the batter is used for one 12-inch cake that forms the bottom tier and the other half of the batter is divided to make both a 9-inch and a 6-inch cake—these become the upper two tiers. The tiers are each about 2½ inches high, so they can be easily cut in half horizontally to make 2-layer filled tiers. The cake uses only egg whites and the frosting is made with the leftover egg yolks. Sprinkling the cut cake layers with a flavored sugar syrup prevents the cake from becoming dry, and you can add a subtle distinctiveness to each layer by using different flavors.

If you don't have a handheld mixer and/or a bowl large enough to hold all of the cake batter, make it in two batches. Use 4 teaspoons of the baking powder in the batch for the 12-inch cake and the remaining 5 teaspoons in the batch for the 9-inch and 6-inch cakes. Divide all of the other ingredients equally between the two batches.

Here are some other cake configurations that can be made using this recipe.

For a robust 6-layer, 9-inch cake about 7½ inches tall:

* Make three 9-inch cakes; each will be about 2½ inches tall. Cut each cake in half to make six layers. This requires three deep cake pans.
* Make six 9-inch cakes; each will be about 1¼ inches tall. This requires six 1½-inch-deep cake pans rather than three 3-inch-deep ones.

And look what you can make if you cut the original recipe in half:

* A 12-inch cake about 2½ inches tall that can be cut in half to make a 2-layer cake.
* A 2-tiered cake with a 9-inch bottom layer and a 6-inch top layer. For this configuration, use 5 teaspoons of baking powder in the recipe. Cut each of the two cakes in half to make two 2-layer filled tiers.

PREHEAT THE OVEN to 350°. Butter the bottoms of the cake pans, fit each with a circle of wax or parchment paper, and butter and flour the paper and sides of the pans.

IN A LARGE mixing bowl, combine the sugar, flour, baking powder, and salt. With an electric mixer on low speed, beat the butter into the flour mixture. Add 1 cup of the milk and continue beating for another minute or so. In a medium bowl, lightly whisk together the rest of the milk, the egg whites, vanilla, and almond extract, if using. Pour ⅓ of the milk mixture at a time into the butter mixture, beating well and scraping down the sides of the bowl after each addition.

POUR THE BATTER into the three prepared pans, smooth the tops, and bake until the tip of a knife inserted in the center comes out clean, 1 to 1¼ hours. When the cakes are ready, let them rest in the pans on racks for 10 minutes. Then invert each onto a rack, turn right side up, and let cool completely.

WHILE THE CAKES cool, make the flavoring of your choice (or half batch of each). For either flavoring, combine the sugar and water in a saucepan, bring to a boil on medium heat, and cook for several minutes, until the sugar has completely dissolved. Remove from the heat. Stir in either the liqueur or the citrus juice and peel and set aside to cool. Strain the citrus flavoring to remove the peel just before using.

SLICE EACH CAKE tier in half horizontally (page 82) and sprinkle about 2½ tablespoons of flavoring(s) on the cut side of each layer. Fill and frost the cake tiers with a thin layer of Buttercream Frosting. Assemble the tiers and decorate the cake following the directions on pages 82 to 83.

- **PREPARATION TIME:** 20 minutes for cake
- **BAKING TIME:** 1 to 1¼ hours
- **COOLING TIME:** about 30 minutes
- **ASSEMBLY TIME:** 30 to 45 minutes
- **EQUIPMENT:** a 6-inch, a 9-inch, and a 12-inch round cake pan—all at least 3 inches deep, wax or parchment paper, electric mixer, nonreactive saucepan

■ **SERVES ABOUT 50**

CAKE

- 5 cups sugar
- 8 cups unbleached white flour
- 3 tablespoons baking powder
- 2 teaspoons salt
- 3 cups butter, at room temperature
- 3 cups milk
- 2 cups egg whites (about 15 whites— reserve the yolks for the frosting)
- 2 tablespoons pure vanilla extract
- 1 teaspoon pure almond extract (optional)

LIQUEUR FLAVORING

- ¼ cup sugar
- ⅔ cup water
- 3 tablespoons liqueur*

* We suggest Framboise, Fra Angelico, Kahlúa, or brandy. Take a trip to a well-stocked liquor store and you will find a world of fruit-, nut-, herb-, and spice-flavored liqueurs.

CITRUS FLAVORING

- 6 tablespoons sugar
- ½ cup water
- 2 tablespoons fresh lemon or lime juice
- 1 tablespoon freshly grated lemon or lime peel
- 6 cups Buttercream Frosting (page 84)

Frosted Orange Layer Cake

With a pale frosting flecked with orange, this lovely cake is appropriate for a birthday celebration or other festivity. Everyone loves its full-bodied orange flavor.

Decorate the top with edible flowers, such as nasturtiums, or sprinkle with Candied Citrus Zest (page 330).

■ **SERVES 10 TO 12**

CAKE

2⅔ cups unbleached white flour

2½ teaspoons baking powder

½ teaspoon salt

1 cup butter, at room temperature

2 cups sugar

4 eggs, separated

2 teaspoons pure vanilla extract

1 teaspoon pure orange extract or 1 tablespoon orange juice concentrate

1 tablespoon freshly grated orange peel

1 cup orange juice

ORANGE FROSTING

½ cup butter, at room temperature

3 cups confectioners' sugar

3 to 4 tablespoons fresh orange juice

1 tablespoon freshly grated orange peel

PREHEAT THE OVEN to 350°. Lightly oil the cake pans and dust them with flour.

SIFT TOGETHER THE flour, baking powder, and salt. In a large bowl, cream the butter and sugar until smooth and light. Add the egg yolks one at a time, beating well after each addition. Add the vanilla, orange extract or juice concentrate, and grated orange peel and beat well. Beat in the flour and orange juice alternately in thirds. In a separate bowl, beat the egg whites until stiff but not dry. Gently fold them into the batter.

SPOON THE BATTER evenly into the prepared pans and bake for 30 to 35 minutes, until the edges pull away from the sides of the pan and the top springs back when touched. Cool the cake in the pans on a rack for 5 or 10 minutes. Run a knife around the outer edges of the cakes and invert them onto a rack to cool completely.

TO PREPARE THE frosting, beat the butter until light. Add the confectioners' sugar ½ cup at a time, beating well after each addition. Add the orange juice and grated orange peel and beat well. If the frosting is too stiff, beat in more orange juice. If it's too soft or if it curdles, beat in more sugar.

FROST THE CAKE when it is completely cool.

■ **PREPARATION TIME:** 25 to 30 minutes
■ **BAKING TIME:** 30 to 35 minutes
■ **COOLING TIME:** at least 20 minutes
■ **EQUIPMENT:** two 9-inch round cake pans, electric mixer

Texas Italian Cream Cake

Filled with coconut and pecans and frosted with fluffy cream cheese, this foolproof cake bakes up big for a dramatic presentation. By all indications, this cake, popular throughout the southern United States, has its origins in Texas, where, for some mysterious reason, it is always called Italian Cream Cake.

PREHEAT THE OVEN to 350°. Butter the cake pans and lightly dust them with flour.

IN A BOWL, sift together the flour, baking soda, and salt. Add the grated coconut and mix well. Set aside.

IN A LARGE bowl with an electric mixer, cream the butter and sugar. Add the eggs one at a time, beating well after each addition. Stir in the vanilla and coconut extracts. Alternate adding the buttermilk and the flour mixture to the creamed mixture, beating well after each addition to form a smooth batter. Stir in the toasted pecans.

DIVIDE THE BATTER evenly between the two prepared pans. Bake until the cake begins to pull away from the edges of the pan and a knife inserted in the center comes out clean, about 30 minutes. Cool the layers in the pans for about 5 minutes and then turn them out onto a rack to cool completely.

FROST WITH Cream Cheese Frosting.

- **PREPARATION TIME:** 20 minutes
- **BAKING TIME:** 30 minutes
- **EQUIPMENT:** two 9-inch round cake pans, electric mixer

■ **SERVES 12**

2 cups unbleached white flour

1¼ teaspoons baking soda

¼ teaspoon salt

½ cup unsweetened grated coconut

1 cup butter, at room temperature

2 cups sugar

4 large eggs

1 teaspoon pure vanilla extract

1 teaspoon pure coconut extract

1 cup buttermilk

1 cup lightly toasted chopped pecans (page 364)

1 recipe Cream Cheese Frosting (page 89)

Irish Oatmeal Cake

Moosewood's Maureen Vivino is a dynamo of activity, exhibiting feats of memory, miracles of scheduling, and endless stamina that the rest of us can only marvel at. Maureen attributes her energy to zazen, t'ai chi, Irish step dancing, and her daily morning bowl of oatmeal.

Oatmeal is a powerful food. The moistness and mild sweetness of oats lend a special touch to this very delectable cake.

■ **SERVES 12 TO 16**

CAKE

2 cups unbleached white flour

¼ teaspoon salt

1 teaspoon baking powder

1¼ teaspoons baking soda

1 cup rolled oats

¾ cup butter, softened

1 cup packed brown sugar

2 large eggs

2 teaspoons pure vanilla extract

1½ cups buttermilk

BUTTERSCOTCH FROSTING

6 tablespoons unsalted butter

1 cup packed brown sugar

1 cup confectioners' sugar

1 teaspoon pure vanilla extract

2 tablespoons milk

 PREHEAT THE OVEN to 350°. Butter and flour the pans.

SIFT TOGETHER THE flour, salt, baking powder, and baking soda. In a blender, whirl the oats to the consistency of cornmeal. Stir them into the flour mixture and set aside.

WITH AN ELECTRIC mixer, cream the butter and brown sugar until light. Add the eggs one at a time, beating well after each addition. Combine the vanilla and buttermilk and add alternately with the flour mixture. Mix until well blended.

POUR THE BATTER into the prepared pans and bake for about 30 minutes, until a knife tests clean and the cake begins to pull away from the sides of the pan. Cool in the pans for about 5 minutes and then turn out onto racks to cool completely.

FOR THE FROSTING, melt the butter in the saucepan. Add the brown sugar and simmer on very low heat for at least 10 minutes, stirring occasionally. (Cooking the brown sugar creates a smoother frosting, so don't cheat on the time.)

TRANSFER THE BUTTER–brown sugar mixture to a bowl. With an electric mixer, beat in the confectioners' sugar and vanilla. Add the milk a little at a time until the frosting is smooth and creamy. While the frosting is still warm, fill and frost the cake.

■ **PREPARATION TIME:** 30 minutes for cake, 15 minutes for frosting
■ **BAKING TIME:** 30 minutes
■ **EQUIPMENT:** two 9-inch cake pans, blender, electric mixer, saucepan

Maple Cake

This handsome moist cake is quick and easy to prepare. We often add a little natural maple flavoring to both the cake and the frosting to give it a more intense and aromatic essence. Decorate the frosted cake with toasted walnut halves or fresh strawberries.

Maple Buttercream Frosting is also great with Buttermilk Spice Cake (page 88), Frosted Apple Spice Cupcakes (page 276), or Banana Muffins (page 274).

PREHEAT THE OVEN to 350°. Butter or oil the cake pans. Lightly dust the pans with flour.

SIFT TOGETHER THE flour, baking powder, baking soda, and salt and set aside. In a separate bowl, use an electric mixer to cream the butter and brown sugar until light. Add the eggs one at a time, beating well after each addition. Add the maple syrup and vanilla. Beat well. Thoroughly mix in the applesauce, then gently fold in the dry ingredients just until combined.

POUR THE BATTER into the prepared pans and bake for 20 to 25 minutes, until a knife inserted in the center comes out clean. Cool completely on a rack.

FOR THE FROSTING, beat the butter with an electric mixer or food processor until creamy. Add the confectioners' sugar ½ cup at a time, beating well after each addition. Add the vanilla and maple syrup and mix well. Spread the frosting on the thoroughly cooled cake.

- **PREPARATION TIME:** 25 minutes for frosted cake
- **BAKING TIME:** 20 to 25 minutes
- **EQUIPMENT:** two 9-inch round cake pans, electric mixer, food processor (optional)

■ **SERVES 12**

CAKE

2½ cups unbleached white flour

1 teaspoon baking powder

1 teaspoon baking soda

½ teaspoon salt

½ cup butter

½ cup packed brown sugar

3 eggs

½ cup pure maple syrup

1 teaspoon pure vanilla extract

1 cup unsweetened applesauce

MAPLE BUTTERCREAM FROSTING

½ cup butter, softened

2½ cups confectioners' sugar

1 teaspoon pure vanilla extract

¼ cup pure maple syrup

Chocolate Espresso Roll

Now you can drink your double latte macciato and eat it, too! This is a great dinner party dessert. It's lovely with a light dusting of confectioners' sugar, but chocolate lovers should try coating the finished cake with Chocolate Glaze (page 185).

■ **SERVES 8**

CAKE

½ cup unbleached white flour

½ cup unsweetened cocoa powder

6 large egg whites, at room temperature

¼ teaspoon cream of tartar

¼ teaspoon salt

6 large egg yolks, at room temperature

1 teaspoon pure vanilla extract

¾ cup sugar

PREHEAT THE OVEN to 350°. Lightly oil a jelly roll pan and line it with wax paper or parchment paper.

SIFT TOGETHER THE flour and cocoa and set aside. In a large bowl, beat the egg whites until foamy. Add the cream of tartar and salt and continue to whip until stiff peaks form. Set aside.

WITHOUT WASHING THE beaters, whip the egg yolks and vanilla in another bowl until the yolks are pale yellow. Gradually add the sugar and beat, stopping occasionally to scrape down the beaters and bowl, until the mixture thickens and forms ribbons of batter as it drips off the beaters. Using a rubber spatula, fold the egg whites and the cocoa mixture alternately into the yolk mixture by thirds. The batter will be light and airy.

SPREAD THE BATTER evenly out to the edges of the prepared pan. Bake for 10 to 13 minutes, until the edges begin to pull away from the sides of the pan and the middle springs back when lightly touched.

LAY THE TOWEL flat on a dry surface. Sprinkle the towel lightly with confectioners' sugar. Invert the cake onto the towel. Peel off the paper and trim ½ inch from each edge of the cake. Fold the towel over a short end of the cake and roll up loosely. Place the towel-covered cake roll seam side down and cool for about 30 minutes.

MEANWHILE, MAKE THE filling. Pour the cream, coffee or espresso granules, and confectioners' sugar into a medium bowl with deep sides. With an electric mixer, beat the cream until stiff and set aside. Carefully unroll the cake (it will not be absolutely flat) and spread on the whipped cream. Gently peeling the cake away from the towel, roll the filled cake back up, place it seam side down on a plate, cover with plastic wrap, and refrigerate.

DUST WITH CONFECTIONERS' sugar (sifted through a sieve) just before serving.

 VARIATIONS Use any of our Flavored Whipped Creams (page 318) as alternative fillings.

- **PREPARATION TIME:** 40 minutes
- **BAKING TIME:** 10 to 13 minutes
- **COOLING TIME:** 30 minutes for cake
- **EQUIPMENT:** 15 × 10-inch jelly roll pan, wax or parchment paper, electric mixer, a napless linen towel slightly larger than the jelly roll pan

COFFEE WHIPPED CREAM FILLING

1 cup heavy cream

2 teaspoons instant coffee granules or espresso powder

3 tablespoons confectioners' sugar

sprinkling of confectioners' sugar

Lemon Jelly Roll

A spiral of lemony sponge cake encloses creamy lime custard in this unusual, very special dessert. The key to making a successful jelly roll is handling the cake very, very gently. For a finishing touch, dust the Lemon Jelly Roll with confectioners' sugar sifted through a sieve and garnish it with fresh berries and flowers. It's a perfect ending for a sunset supper in the country.

■ **SERVES 6 TO 8**

LIME CURD FILLING

3 large eggs

6 tablespoons fresh lime juice

1 tablespoon freshly grated lime peel

½ cup sugar

½ cup butter, melted

LEMON SPONGE CAKE

3 large eggs, separated

½ cup sugar

grated peel of ½ lemon

1½ tablespoons freshly squeezed lemon juice

pinch of salt

¼ teaspoon cream of tartar

2 tablespoons cornstarch

½ cup unbleached white flour

confectioners' sugar

berries and fresh whipped cream (optional)

TO PREPARE THE custard, whisk together the eggs, lime juice, lime peel, and sugar in a saucepan. Cook on medium heat, continuing to whisk until the custard thickens. Remove from the heat and whisk in the butter a little at a time. Chill.

PREHEAT THE OVEN to 350°. Lightly butter the jelly roll pan and smooth parchment or wax paper over the buttered surface. Lightly butter the paper lining, dust it with flour, and set aside.

WITH AN ELECTRIC mixer, beat the egg yolks at high speed until they turn pale yellow. Add ¼ cup of the sugar a little at a time, beating at high speed until the mixture is thick and forms a smooth ribbon when the beater is lifted from the bowl. Beat in the lemon peel and lemon juice. With a rubber spatula, transfer the egg mixture to another bowl.

WASH AND DRY the beaters and mixer bowl. Beat the egg whites, salt, and cream of tartar at high speed until soft peaks form. Gradually add the remaining ¼ cup of sugar while continuing to beat at high speed until the egg whites are stiff. Set aside.

SIFT THE CORNSTARCH and half of the flour over the egg and lemon mixture and fold gently until well mixed but still streaky. Fold in half of the egg whites, then the remaining flour, and finally the rest of the egg whites.

WITH A RUBBER spatula, spread the batter evenly out to the edges of the prepared pan and smooth the top. Put the pan in the center of the oven. Bake for 12 to 15 minutes, until the edges are light brown and begin to pull away from the sides of the pan.

SPREAD THE TOWEL on the counter and sprinkle it with confectioners' sugar. Remove the cake from the oven and immediately invert it onto the towel. Lift off the pan and gently peel away the paper. With a sharp knife trim the crisp edges. Fold the towel over a short end of the cake, roll the towel and cake up into a loose spiral, and cool. This will help the cake keep a rolled shape when filled.

WHEN THE CUSTARD is thoroughly chilled, unroll the cooled cake very carefully. It will curl at one end. Spread the custard evenly over the surface of the cake. Beginning at the curled end, gently reroll the cake. With a serrated knife, cut a thin slice from each end. Transfer the cake to a platter. Sprinkle a few tablespoons of confectioners' sugar through a sieve over the cake. Chill until ready to serve.

IT IS EASIEST to slice this cake with a serrated knife. Garnish with berries and whipped cream, if desired.

- **PREPARATION TIME:** 1 hour
- **BAKING TIME:** 12 to 15 minutes
- **COOLING TIME:** at least 30 minutes
- **EQUIPMENT:** nonreactive saucepan, 10 × 15-inch jelly roll pan, parchment or wax paper trimmed to fit the baking pan, electric mixer, a napless linen towel slightly larger than the jelly roll pan

Hazelnut Torte

Our European-style nut torte relies upon fragrant hazelnuts and hazelnut liqueur for flavor and a generous amount of eggs for lightness and delicacy. It makes an elegant birthday or special occasion cake when frosted and filled with any number of frostings, glazes, or flavored whipped creams.

Try it filled and frosted with our Basic Vanilla or Mocha Flavored Whipped Cream (page 318), Coffee Frosting (page 109), or Buttercream Frosting (page 84). Or fill it with about ⅔ cup of one of the flavored whipped creams and ice it with Chocolate Cream Glaze (page 198).

■ **SERVES 10**

CAKE

1½ cups whole hazelnuts

7 large eggs, separated

1¼ cups sugar

¼ cup butter, melted and slightly cooled

1 teaspoon pure vanilla extract

¾ cup unbleached white flour

2 tablespoons cornstarch

½ teaspoon salt

SUGAR SYRUP

2 tablespoons sugar

1 tablespoon water

3 tablespoons hazelnut-flavored liqueur, such as Fra Angelico

 PREHEAT THE OVEN to 350°.

SPREAD THE HAZELNUTS on an unoiled baking sheet and toast for 10 minutes. Allow the nuts to cool for a few minutes and keep the oven at 350° for baking the cake. While the nuts cool, lightly butter the cake pans. Using the outline of a pan as a guide, cut two circles of parchment paper and place one in each buttered pan. Lightly butter the parchment paper.

RUB THE HAZELNUTS in a clean, dry cloth to remove most of the skins. Chop the nuts to a fine texture in the bowl of a food processor or in small batches in a blender and set aside.

WITH AN ELECTRIC mixer, beat the egg yolks for about a minute, until the color lightens. Add the sugar and continue to beat for a couple of minutes. Beat in the butter and vanilla. On low speed, mix in the flour, cornstarch, and salt. Stir in the hazelnuts. In a separate bowl with clean, dry beaters (see Note), whip the egg whites until stiff peaks form. Stir ⅓ of the whipped egg whites into the cake batter, then gently fold in the remaining whites in two batches.

POUR THE BATTER into the prepared pans and bake until the cake pulls away from the sides of the pan and the top is set and springy, about 30 minutes. Remove the cake from the oven and cool in the pans on a rack.

MEANWHILE, MAKE THE syrup. In a small saucepan, heat the sugar and water just until the sugar dissolves. Remove from the heat and add the hazelnut liqueur. When the cake layers have cooled for at least 15 minutes, turn them out of their pans and cool for another 5 to 10 minutes on the rack. Drizzle half of the syrup on each layer. After about 20 minutes, when the cakes are completely cool to the touch, frost or fill as desired.

NOTES Wax paper can be used in place of parchment paper, but it must be peeled off while still warm to prevent sticking. It is also possible to generously butter and flour the pans and dispense with the paper completely.

Fats or water will prevent the egg whites from stiffening.

- **PREPARATION TIME:** 45 minutes
- **BAKING TIME:** 30 minutes
- **COOLING TIME:** 20 to 25 minutes
- **EQUIPMENT:** baking sheet, two 9-inch round cake pans, parchment paper (see Note), food processor or blender, an electric mixer

Mocha Walnut Torte

Walnuts, coffee, and chocolate are sublime in this elegant torte. A simple whipped cream frosting is a fitting counterpoint to the highly flavored cake. Garnish with colorful candied violets or fresh fruits such as strawberries, kiwi, or raspberries.

■ **SERVES 12**

CAKE

1½ cups walnuts

6 eggs, separated

1⅓ cups sugar

2 tablespoons instant coffee granules or espresso powder

¼ cup very hot water

¼ cup unbleached white flour

¼ cup cornstarch

½ teaspoon salt

½ cup unsweetened cocoa powder

WHIPPED CREAM FROSTING

1½ cups heavy cream

1 teaspoon pure vanilla extract

⅓ cup confectioners' sugar

PREHEAT THE OVEN to 350°. Line the bottom of two cake pans with 9-inch parchment circles. Butter and flour the bottoms and sides of the lined pans.

IN A FOOD processor or in small batches in a blender, whirl the walnuts until ground or finely chopped but not a paste. Set aside. Using an electric mixer, beat the egg yolks for 3 or 4 minutes, until light in color. Add the sugar and beat until smooth. Dissolve the coffee in the hot water. With the mixer on medium speed, resume beating the egg yolks and add the coffee in a slow, steady stream. Sift the flour, cornstarch, salt, and cocoa into the batter and stir until well blended.

IN A SEPARATE bowl, beat the egg whites until stiff peaks form. Stir ⅓ of the whites into the batter and then gently fold in the rest in two equal batches. Fold in the ground nuts.

CAREFULLY POUR THE batter into the prepared pans and bake for about 35 minutes, until the cakes are firm and pull away from the sides of the pans. Cool the cakes in the pans for 15 minutes before inverting onto a rack and removing from the pans.

WHEN THE CAKES have cooled, prepare the frosting. With a whisk or an electric mixer, beat the cream until frothy and beginning to thicken. Add the vanilla and sift in the confectioners' sugar. Continue to beat until soft peaks form. Frost the cake and store it in the refrigerator until ready to serve. The frosted torte will keep for 3 or 4 days. Chill any leftovers.

■ **PREPARATION TIME:** 20 to 30 minutes
■ **BAKING TIME:** 35 minutes
■ **EQUIPMENT:** two 9-inch layer cake pans, food processor or blender, electric mixer

Dark Chocolate Layer Cake

There must be almost as many chocolate cake recipes as there are bakers, each one swearing by cocoa or baking chocolate, sour cream or milk or water, oil or butter, brown sugar or white. We're partial to cocoa, water, butter, and brown sugar. This recipe has just the right amount of sweetness, richness, and "chocolaty-ness."

This cake is especially pretty drizzled with 1 ounce of melted semi-sweet chocolate thinned with a little strong coffee. Chocolate lovers might prefer this cake with Chocolate Ganache (page 314) and raspberry jam between the layers.

IN A MIXING bowl, gradually add a bit of the boiling water to the cocoa, whisking to make a paste, then whisk in the rest of the water. Set aside to cool.

PREHEAT THE OVEN to 350°. Butter the cake pans and lightly dust them with flour.

SIFT TOGETHER THE flour, baking soda, and salt and set aside. With an electric mixer, cream the butter and brown sugar. Add the eggs one at a time, beating well after each addition. Mix in the vanilla extract. Add the flour mixture alternately with the cooled cocoa mixture, beating after each addition.

DIVIDE THE BATTER evenly between the two prepared pans. Bake for 25 to 30 minutes, until a knife inserted into the center comes out clean. Cool the layers in the pans for about 5 minutes, then turn them out onto racks to cool completely.

FOR THE FROSTING, cream the butter and confectioners' sugar with an electric mixer. Gradually add the coffee and Kahlúa, if desired, beating well until the frosting is a good consistency for spreading.

- **PREPARATION TIME:** 25 minutes
- **BAKING TIME:** 25 to 30 minutes
- **FROSTING TIME:** 15 minutes
- **EQUIPMENT:** electric mixer, two 9-inch round cake pans

■ **SERVES 16**

CAKE

1½ cups boiling water

¾ cup unsweetened cocoa powder

2 cups unbleached white flour

1¼ teaspoons baking soda

⅛ teaspoon salt

1 cup butter, at room temperature

1⅓ cups packed brown sugar

2 large eggs

2 teaspoons pure vanilla extract

COFFEE FROSTING

½ cup butter, at room temperature

3½ cups confectioners' sugar

4 to 5 tablespoons strong coffee

1 tablespoon Kahlúa (optional)

Chocolate Almond Meringue Torte

Here's another fine creation from Linda Dickinson, one of Moosewood's finest chefs. Layers of crisp, airy meringue filled with a rich chocolate whipped cream and topped with a glossy chocolate frosting add up to an unusual, gorgeous, and tempting dessert that wows guests every time. As impressive as it looks, it's not at all difficult to make.

■ **SERVES 10**

MERINGUE

⅓ cup toasted almonds
(page 364)

⅓ cup semi-sweet
chocolate chips
(or 2 ounces semi-
sweet chocolate,
broken into pieces)

2 tablespoons
unsweetened cocoa
powder

⅔ cup sugar

4 egg whites

¼ teaspoon cream
of tartar

½ teaspoon pure
almond extract

**CHOCOLATE
ALMOND FILLING
AND FROSTING**

1 cup semi-sweet
chocolate chips (or
about 6 ounces semi-
sweet chocolate)

1½ cups heavy cream

¼ teaspoon pure
almond extract

¼ cup chopped toasted
almonds

PREHEAT THE OVEN to 275°. Prepare the baking sheet either by lining it with parchment paper or lightly buttering it and dusting with flour. Set aside.

IN A FOOD processor, whirl the almonds and chocolate together until finely crumbled. Add the cocoa and ⅓ cup of the sugar and whirl again until well combined. Set aside.

IN A LARGE bowl, beat the egg whites and cream of tartar until soft peaks form. Continuing to beat, gradually add the remaining ⅓ cup of sugar and the almond extract. The whites should hold stiff peaks and look glossy but not dry. Gently fold in the chocolate-almond mixture in several batches. When finished, the mixture will not be a uniform color but will have specks of chocolate throughout.

IF YOU LINED the baking sheet with parchment, use a pen to trace around the cake pan, making two circles at least an inch apart, and flip it over. For a buttered and floured baking sheet, trace the 8-inch circles with a chopstick, a knife, or your fingertip. With a spatula, spread the meringue batter evenly inside the two circles on the prepared baking sheet.

BAKE IN THE center of the oven for 45 to 60 minutes, until the meringue is dry to the touch but still soft in the middle. Turn off the heat and leave the meringue in the warm oven for about 30 minutes. Remove from the oven and cool completely.

WHEN COOL, ASSEMBLE the torte or store the meringues in an airtight container to assemble the next day.

TO ASSEMBLE, PREPARE the Chocolate Almond Filling and Frosting. Melt the chocolate and set it aside. Whip 1 cup of the cream until stiff. Fold in 2 tablespoons of melted chocolate and add the almond extract. Place one meringue circle on a serving plate, top it with the whipped cream, and place the second meringue circle on top. Add the rest of the heavy cream to the remaining melted chocolate and reheat briefly, stirring to form a smooth sauce. Let it cool for a minute or two, then spread it over the top, letting some drizzle artistically down the sides. Sprinkle the top with the chopped almonds.

REFRIGERATE UNTIL READY to serve. Use a serrated knife and a sawing motion to cut the torte. It is best if eaten the same day as assembled, but it will keep for 2 or 3 days.

- **PREPARATION TIME:** 45 minutes
- **BAKING TIME:** 45 to 60 minutes
- **SITTING TIME:** 30 minutes
- **COOLING TIME:** 30 minutes
- **EQUIPMENT:** baking sheet, food processor, 8-inch round cake pan, electric mixer

Zuccotto

Zuccotto is a sumptuous Florentine dessert that echoes in shape the famous cathedral dome which dominates the skyline of that glorious Renaissance city. Making an impressive presentation, this confection combines rich poundcake, chocolate, nuts, cream, and aromatic liqueurs like a fine mosaic.

The domed surface of the Zuccotto can be strikingly decorated with dustings of cocoa and confectioners' sugar in alternating brown and white triangles. Or go wild with embellishments, the way Moosewood's Ned Asta likes to do. She lavishes piped whipped cream, whole nuts, drizzled chocolate, cherries, and perhaps raspberries in baroque splendor. Ned explains that her ancestry is Sicilian, not Tuscan, so maybe she didn't get the genes for tasteful restraint. Her DNA is apparently programmed for beautiful excess.

■ **SERVES 10 TO 12**

½ cup whole hazelnuts, toasted (page 364)

½ cup whole almonds, toasted

5 ounces semi-sweet chocolate

1½ cups heavy cream

½ cup confectioners' sugar

1 teaspoon pure vanilla extract

1 Poundcake Loaf (page 123)

3 tablespoons coffee-flavored liqueur, such as Kahlúa

3 tablespoons hazelnut-flavored liqueur, such as Fra Angelico

FINELY CHOP THE hazelnuts and almonds. Coarsely chop 2 ounces of the chocolate and set aside. Gently melt the remaining 3 ounces of chocolate in the top of a double boiler or in a microwave. Combine the nuts and chopped chocolate and divide equally between two mixing bowls. Whip the cream, confectioners' sugar, and vanilla until stiff, being careful not to overbeat. Divide the whipped cream between the two bowls and fold in. Slowly add the melted chocolate to one of the bowls and stir gently until well blended.

LINE THE SERVING bowl with plastic wrap, allowing a couple of inches to hang over the rim. Cut the poundcake into ¼- to ⅜-inch slices. Cut these diagonally in half to create triangular pieces. Line the bottom and sides of the bowl with a single layer of cake pieces, fitting them together as closely as possible. Reserve the remaining pieces. Combine the liqueurs in a mixing cup. Use a spoon or a baster to drizzle about ⅔ of the liqueur over the cake slices as evenly as possible.

USING A RUBBER spatula, spoon the lighter colored cream into the cake-lined bowl, spreading it over the cake surface. Fill the remaining cavity with the chocolate cream. Use as many of the reserved cake pieces as necessary to cover the top of the bowl. Drizzle the top with the remaining liqueur. Cover snugly with plastic wrap and place a plate and a weight on top to compress the cake. Refrigerate overnight or for 24 hours.

WHEN READY TO serve, remove the weight, plate, and top piece of plastic wrap. Place an attractive serving dish over the bowl and invert. Lift the bowl off the cake and carefully peel off the plastic wrap.

IF DESIRED, make a decorative design with cocoa powder and confectioners' sugar: Cut a large circle from a piece of parchment or other lightweight paper. (The circle should be large enough to cover the dome of the Zuccotto.) Fold the circle in half three times to form a wedge that is ⅛ of the circle. Unfold the paper and cut out four alternating wedges, leaving the other four wedges connected in the center. Drape this stencil over the Zuccotto and dust with confectioners' sugar. Carefully remove the stencil and rotate it to cover the confectioners' sugar design. Dust with cocoa and remove the stencil. You will have a pattern of alternating light and dark wedges.

SERVE CHILLED AND store in the refrigerator.

- ■ **PREPARATION TIME:** 40 minutes plus chilling overnight
- ■ **EQUIPMENT:** double boiler (page 370), round 1½-quart serving bowl for molding, parchment paper (optional)

POUNDCAKES
AND OTHER CAKES

Poundcakes and Other Cakes

YOU MAY FIND THIS CHAPTER A VALUABLE RESOURCE FOR HOME entertaining, cake sales, or other social events. It contains a broad selection of impressive poundcakes, bundt cakes, chiffon cakes, upside-down cakes, and other distinctive cakes, some of which are surprisingly simple to prepare. Dictionaries will tell you that poundcake is a rich, finely textured yellow cake whose prototype supposedly called for one pound each of flour, butter, and sugar with eggs added. Sounds simple enough! Those of us trusting and foolhardy enough to have tried this formula found that it won't work. Maybe the name "poundcake" was nothing but a ploy to confound rival bakers and keep a secret recipe under wraps. Other possible explanations are that nobody really measured anything in the old days or that a pound ain't what it used to be. Poundcakes are dense, with less air whipped into them than layer cakes. But "dense" should never be confused with heavy, coarse, tough, or dry. The cake should be moist and tender, long-keeping, and not gooey-sweet. Really good poundcake is like a little slice of heaven. Pound-cakes are our standard, everyday cake at Moosewood. There are many wonderful recipes and variations that are worth following faithfully. Be sure to look in the Moosewood Classics chapter for Our Favorite Poundcake—the grandmother of the many varieties we've developed over the years, such as Pecan Cardamom Poundcake and Chocolate Hazelnut Orange Poundcake, both found in this chapter. Bundt cakes were the fanciest cakes on the block in the '50s and '60s. "Bundt" is derived from the German word for a group meeting together, which makes sense—our bundt cakes generously serve 12 to 16 people. The finished cake looks festive and elegant because the batter is poured into a deep, fluted, ring-shaped pan that creates peaks and valleys. Once inverted onto a platter, it can be dressed up with confectioners' sugar or a pretty glaze. Poundcakes and bundt cakes are rich enough to be completely satisfying and their simplicity makes them extremely versatile. Because they are dense and finely textured, they can support additions such as raisins and chopped or ground nuts without falling apart when sliced. They hold their shape well even when laced with whiskey, brandy, or a liqueur, and are good with a variety of toppings such as whipped cream, glazes, sauces, and, of course, ice cream. Leftover poundcake is the foundation for other desserts such as Savannah Banana Pudding and Fresh Fruit Trifle. And now, those mysterious "other cakes!" The chiffon cake was invented in 1927 to showcase a brand new product called "vegetable oil." Its airy, ethereal texture is achieved by folding stiffly beaten egg whites into the batter using a simple "two bowl" method. There are many flavor options, but we've chosen fruit combinations: peach and raspberry, strawberry and lemon, and orange and pineapple. We've included a number of cakes that are quickly prepared any time: Black Mocha Cake, upside-down cakes, and Greek Walnut Yogurt Cake. Chocolate aficionados will appreciate the half dozen cakes that feature their favorite flavor. Low-fat cakes that everyone will enjoy include Gingerbread with Pears, Fat-Free Carrot Cake, Orange Coconut Angelfood Cake, and Olive Oil and Citrus Cake. We suspect that adding vegetables to cake recipes was the invention of creative and thrifty American farmwives. While Zucchini Spice Cake and Fat-Free Carrot Cake may be familiar by now, less usual is our naughty Red Devil Cake with chocolate and red beets and Anna's Country Spice Cake, which blends the sweetness of parsnips with tart dried cranberries.  Fruitcakes needn't be the dreaded, leaden confection that nobody wants at holiday time. Our Irish Whiskey Cake and Italian Fruitcake have rich, complex flavors, and we've developed an unusual quick version of traditional fruitcake called Jamaican Black Cake, with dried tropical fruit, rum, and dark beer, baked with molasses and spice. Take Plum Upside-Down Cake to a reunion party. Bake "Pretty in Pink" Chiffon Cake for a sweet sixteen party. And if you want a deep and lasting relationship with someone, Chocolate Grand Marnier Cake has been known to work some powerful magic.

Brandied Raisin Sour Cream Poundcake

When raisins are plumped in brandy and folded into a rich sour cream batter, the result is a cake reminiscent of fine old European baking. This new addition to our repertoire is fast becoming one of Moosewood's most beloved poundcakes. It is smooth and rich, and every bite of raisin bursts with brandy.

PREHEAT THE OVEN to 325°. Oil and flour the bundt pan. Combine the raisins and brandy in a small bowl and set aside while you prepare the cake batter.

WITH AN ELECTRIC mixer, cream the butter with the sugar until light, 3 to 5 minutes. Add the eggs one at a time, beating well after each addition. In a separate bowl, sift together the flour, baking powder, and salt and set aside. Drain the raisins, reserving the brandy. Combine the vanilla, sour cream, and reserved brandy and mix until blended.

ADD THE FLOUR mixture and the sour cream mixture alternately to the butter-egg mixture, beating well after each addition. Stir in the plumped raisins. Pour the batter into the prepared pan and bake for about 1¼ hours, until a knife inserted in the cake comes out clean. Allow to cool for 10 minutes, then invert onto a serving plate.

- **PREPARATION TIME:** 15 minutes
- **BAKING TIME:** 1¼ hours
- **COOLING TIME:** 10 minutes
- **EQUIPMENT:** 10-inch bundt pan, electric mixer

■ **SERVES 16**

1½ cups raisins
3 tablespoons brandy
1½ cups butter
2⅔ cups sugar
4 eggs
3 cups unbleached white flour
1½ teaspoons baking powder
½ teaspoon salt
2 teaspoons pure vanilla extract
¾ cup sour cream

Chocolate Hazelnut Orange Poundcake

Here is a poundcake that indulges all of the senses — the visual effect of speckled dark chocolate, the aroma of orange zest, the flavor of toasted hazelnuts, and then the music of umms *and* ahhs—*irresistible.*

■ **SERVES 12 TO 16**

2 cups butter, at room temperature

2½ cups sugar

6 eggs, lightly beaten

2 teaspoons pure vanilla extract

freshly grated peel of 1 orange

4 cups unbleached white flour

2 teaspoons baking powder

½ cup orange juice

½ cup milk

1 cup ground toasted hazelnuts (page 364)

1 cup coarsely chopped semi-sweet chocolate

PREHEAT THE OVEN to 350°. Lightly butter the bundt pan and dust it with flour.

IN A LARGE bowl, cream together the butter and sugar until light. Thoroughly beat in the eggs, vanilla, and orange peel. In a separate bowl, combine the flour and baking powder. Add the flour mixture by thirds, alternating first with the orange juice and then with the milk, and beat well after each addition. Stir in the nuts and chocolate by hand.

POUR THE BATTER into the prepared pan and bake for 1¼ to 1½ hours, until a knife inserted in the center comes out clean. Cool the cake in the pan for 10 minutes; then turn it out and transfer to a wire rack to cool completely.

■ **PREPARATION TIME:** 50 minutes
■ **BAKING TIME:** 1¼ to 1½ hours
■ **COOLING TIME:** at least 10 minutes
■ **EQUIPMENT:** 10-inch bundt pan

Pecan Cardamom Poundcake

Nutty and spicy, with a hint of black pepper, this recipe borrows some of the traditional spices of Indian cuisine to give our usual, ever-popular poundcake an unusual flavor.

PREHEAT THE OVEN to 350°. Lightly butter the bundt pan and dust it with flour.

IN A LARGE mixing bowl, cream together the butter and brown sugar until light and blended. With an electric mixer, beat in the eggs and vanilla. In a separate bowl, sift together the flour, cardamom, cinnamon, allspice, black pepper, and baking powder. Beat half of the flour mixture into the egg mixture. Add the coffee and beat until smooth. Beat in the remaining flour mixture and then beat in the milk. Stir in the pecans by hand.

POUR THE BATTER into the prepared pan and bake for 1¼ to 1½ hours, until a knife inserted in the center comes out clean. Let the cake rest for 10 minutes before removing it from the pan. Cool on a wire rack.

FOR THE GLAZE, whirl the coffee and confectioners' sugar in a blender until smooth. Brush on the still warm cake for a shiny finish.

- **PREPARATION TIME:** 35 to 40 minutes
- **BAKING TIME:** about 1½ hours
- **COOLING TIME:** 10 minutes
- **EQUIPMENT:** 10-inch bundt pan, large mixing bowl, electric mixer, blender

■ SERVES 12 TO 16

- 2 cups butter, at room temperature
- 3 cups packed brown sugar
- 6 eggs
- 2 teaspoons pure vanilla extract
- 4 cups unbleached white flour
- 2 teaspoons ground cardamom
- 1½ teaspoons ground cinnamon
- ½ teaspoon ground allspice
- ½ teaspoon ground black pepper
- 2 teaspoons baking powder
- ½ cup strong coffee or decaffeinated coffee, cooled
- ½ cup milk
- 1 cup chopped toasted pecans (page 364)

COFFEE GLAZE

- ½ cup freshly brewed regular or decaffeinated coffee
- 3 cups confectioners' sugar

Polenta Poundcake

Moist, dense, and rich, Polenta Poundcake is our version of a simple and sophisticated Italian classic. It makes the most of the golden color, natural sweetness, and pleasantly crumbly texture of cornmeal.

- **SERVES 16 TO 24**

1 pound butter, at room temperature

3 cups sugar

6 eggs

2 teaspoons pure vanilla extract

3 cups unbleached white pastry flour (page 361)

2 teaspoons baking powder

½ cup milk

1 cup cornmeal (a combination of fine and coarse grind is nice)

confectioners' sugar (optional)

PREHEAT THE OVEN to 350°. Butter the bundt pan and dust it with flour (see Note).

USING AN ELECTRIC mixer, cream the butter and sugar until light. Add the eggs and vanilla and beat until fluffy. Stir in the flour and baking powder and mix until smoothly blended. Add the milk and mix until smooth. Thoroughly mix in the cornmeal.

SCRAPE THE BATTER into the prepared pan and bake for about 1¼ hours.

CHECK THE CAKE after an hour, being careful not to jar the pan. When the cake is golden brown, firm, and pulling slightly away from the pan, remove it from the oven. Cool upright for 10 minutes and then invert onto a serving plate, leaving the baking pan in place for 10 minutes before removing it. If needed, tap the sides of the bundt pan with the handle of a butter knife or the back of a wooden spoon to help loosen the cake from the pan. Dust with confectioners' sugar, if you wish.

SERVE POLENTA POUNDCAKE warm, 30 minutes from the oven, or at room temperature. When the poundcake is well cooled, wrap it in a plastic bag. It will keep, refrigerated or at room temperature, for up to a week.

NOTE To remove excess flour from the sides of the pan, tap the pan several times on the counter (or bang it once with determination) and discard the flour that falls out.

- **PREPARATION TIME:** 25 minutes
- **BAKING TIME:** 1¼ hours
- **COOLING TIME:** 20 minutes
- **EQUIPMENT:** 10-inch bundt pan, electric mixer

Poundcake Loaf

A buttery cake perfect for eating on its own, poundcake is also an important component of elegant dessert creations. We use this poundcake in our Savannah Banana Pudding (page 214), in Fresh Fruit Trifle (page 338), and in Zuccotto (page 112), where it is soaked with Fra Angelico liqueur and encases two cream fillings. For these recipes, this loaf is more than enough, so you can still enjoy eating it unadorned, or with some berries, or glazed with chocolate, or spread with jam, or topped with ice cream . . .

 PREHEAT THE OVEN to 350°. Butter and flour the loaf pan.

WITH AN ELECTRIC mixer, cream the butter until light. Add the sugar and cream until fluffy. Add the eggs one at a time, beating well after each addition. Add the vanilla, baking powder, and salt and beat well. Reduce the mixer speed to low and add the flour, mixing until well incorporated. Add the milk and beat until well blended, another minute or so.

POUR THE BATTER into the prepared pan and bake until a knife inserted in the center comes out clean, about 1¼ hours. Cool in the pan on a rack before serving.

- **PREPARATION TIME:** 15 minutes
- **BAKING TIME:** 1¼ hours
- **EQUIPMENT:** 9 × 5-inch loaf pan, electric mixer

■ **SERVES 8 TO 10**

- 1 cup butter, at room temperature
- 1⅓ cups sugar
- 4 eggs
- 2 teaspoons pure vanilla extract
- ½ teaspoon baking powder
- ¼ teaspoon salt
- 1¾ cups unbleached white flour
- ⅓ cup milk

Pumpkin Raisin Poundcake

Poundcake lends itself to seemingly endless variation. Here, the warm, familiar flavors of pumpkin pie spices enhance the sweet tang of plump raisins soaked in orange juice. Pumpkin contributes a delicate taste and a soft, moist texture that make this a cake that flips right out of the pan and keeps well for a long time.

■ **SERVES 16**

1 cup raisins

½ cup orange juice

1 cup butter

1¼ cups sugar

½ cup packed
 brown sugar

1¾ cups cooked
 pumpkin purée
 (28-ounce can)

4 eggs

½ cup buttermilk

3 cups unbleached
 white flour

1 teaspoon baking soda

2 teaspoons
 baking powder

½ teaspoon salt

½ teaspoon
 ground ginger

½ teaspoon
 ground allspice

½ teaspoon
 ground nutmeg

2 teaspoons
 ground cinnamon

COMBINE THE RAISINS and orange juice in a the saucepan, cover, and simmer for about 10 minutes. Uncover and set aside.

PREHEAT THE OVEN to 350°. Butter and flour the bundt pan.

WITH AN ELECTRIC mixer, cream the butter until light. Gradually add the sugar and brown sugar, beating well after each addition. Beat in the pumpkin purée and then the eggs, one at a time. Add the buttermilk and blend well. Stir the raisins and juice into the batter. Sift together the flour, baking soda, baking powder, salt, ginger, allspice, nutmeg, and cinnamon. Add the dry ingredients to the batter, stirring just until moistened.

POUR THE BATTER into the prepared bundt pan and bake for about 1¼ hours, until the cake pulls away from the sides of the pan and a knife inserted in the center comes out clean. Cool the cake in the pan on a rack for 15 minutes; then invert the cake onto a serving plate and cool completely.

■ **PREPARATION TIME:** 40 minutes
■ **BAKING TIME:** about 1¼ hours
■ **COOLING TIME:** 15 minutes
■ **EQUIPMENT:** small saucepan, 10-inch bundt pan, electric mixer

Old-Fashioned Fresh Apple Cake

This cake is simple, juicy, and homey with the flavor of unadorned chunks of fresh apple. It makes a simple and straightforward dessert or snack. Dust the cooled cake with a little confectioners' sugar or serve with freshly whipped cream or whipped cream cheese.

PREHEAT THE OVEN to 350°. Oil or butter the baking pan.

COMBINE THE MELTED butter and brown sugar, beating well by hand or using an electric mixer. Add the vanilla, then beat in the eggs one at a time. Sift together the flour, baking soda, baking powder, and salt. Fold the flour mixture into the butter mixture—the batter will be stiff. Fold in the chopped apples, lemon juice, and lemon peel.

POUR THE BATTER into the prepared baking pan and bake for 45 to 50 minutes, until the cake is golden and a knife inserted in the center comes out clean.

SERVE WARM OR at room temperature.

- **PREPARATION TIME:** 30 minutes
- **BAKING TIME:** 45 to 50 minutes
- **EQUIPMENT:** 9-inch square nonreactive baking pan, electric mixer (optional)

- **SERVES 9**

½ cup butter, melted

1 cup packed brown sugar

1 teaspoon pure vanilla extract

2 eggs

1½ cups unbleached white flour

1 teaspoon baking soda

1 teaspoon baking powder

½ teaspoon salt

2 cups peeled chopped apples, such as Mutsu, Macintosh, Rome, or Granny Smith

2 tablespoons fresh lemon juice

¼ teaspoon freshly grated lemon peel

"Pretty in Pink" Chiffon Cake

In the mood for some retro fun? Think pink. Think chiffon. You can make an unforgettable strawberry lemon chiffon cake from the '40s that is airy, delicious, and back in style again. Put on your snood and your white anklets and be sure the eggs are at room temperature.

Stiffly beaten egg white is the secret to chiffon cake. No peeking in the oven, no jitterbugging in the kitchen. When the gang comes over to cut a rug, top each piece with Strawberry Sauce and whipped cream, and you'll make the company jump. See ya later, Alligator.

■ SERVES 10

CAKE

1½ cups unbleached
    white flour

1 cup sugar

2 teaspoons
    baking powder

½ teaspoon salt

½ cup vegetable oil

2 large egg yolks

7 large egg whites

½ teaspoon cream
    of tartar

2 tablespoons
    confectioners' sugar

½ cup strained puréed
    fresh or frozen
    strawberries*

3 tablespoons fresh
    lemon juice

2 teaspoons freshly
    grated lemon peel

* Use a strainer to drain any excess liquid from the purée for a thick, smooth sauce.

PREHEAT THE OVEN to 325°. Oil and lightly dust the tube pan with flour.

SIFT TOGETHER THE flour, sugar, baking powder, and salt into a large bowl. Make a well in the center of the dry ingredients and add the oil and egg yolks—but don't mix yet.

IN ANOTHER LARGE bowl, beat the egg whites until soft and foamy. Add the cream of tartar and confectioners' sugar and continue to beat until stiff but not dry. Without washing the beaters, beat the flour and oil mixture at low speed. Gradually add the puréed strawberries, lemon juice, and lemon peel, beating just until blended.

WITH A RUBBER spatula, gently fold a small portion of the egg white mixture into the batter. Then, in five or six additions, fold the batter into the egg whites. The batter will be light and bubbly, with some egg whites showing.

POUR THE BATTER into the prepared pan and bake for 25 minutes. Increase the oven temperature to 350° and continue to bake for another 20 to 25 minutes, or until the cake is well risen and a cake tester inserted into the center comes out clean.

WHILE THE CAKE bakes, combine the strawberries, lemon juice, and sugar for the sauce in a small bowl and set aside. Allow the sauce to sit at room temperature for at least 30 minutes before serving, but store it in the refrigerator.

WHEN THE CAKE is baked, remove it from the oven and cool it upright in the pan for about 10 minutes, then turn it out onto a rack. When the cake is cool to the touch, gently lift it onto a serving plate and cool completely.

CUT THE CAKE into wedges with a serrated knife and serve each piece topped with a generous ¼ cup of Strawberry Sauce and, if you like, whipped cream.

 NOTE Allow this cake the luxury of an oven all to itself and don't open the oven door while it bakes. Safe from drafts, it will rise to its fullest height. And don't be surprised when the very pink batter cooks to a cake that has only the slightest hint of pink about it.

VARIATION For a Peach Melba Chiffon Cake, simply reduce the lemon juice to 2 tablespoons and replace the strawberries with raspberries that have been forced through a sieve or food mill to remove the seeds. To make about 3 cups of Peach Melba Sauce, combine 1½ cups of chopped peeled peaches, 1½ cups of fresh raspberries, 2 tablespoons of Framboise, 1 tablespoon of fresh lemon juice, and sugar to taste in a small bowl. Mix thoroughly. Thawed frozen fruit will work, but the sauce is most flavorful served at room temperature, so be sure to allow enough time for it to warm up. The full-bodied fruit flavor of Peach Melba Sauce is versatile and can be delicious on poundcake, nonfat frozen yogurt, or ice cream.

IF USING FROZEN raspberries, a 12-ounce package will yield enough raspberry purée for both the cake batter and the sauce; unsweetened Stilwell Select Red Raspberries is a brand we like.

- **PREPARATION TIME:** 30 to 40 minutes
- **BAKING TIME:** 45 to 50 minutes
- **COOLING TIME:** 10 minutes
- **EQUIPMENT:** 9-inch tube pan, electric mixer

STRAWBERRY SAUCE

- 2 cups sliced fresh or frozen strawberries
- 1 tablespoon fresh lemon juice

sugar to taste

fresh whipped cream (optional)

Hawaiian Chiffon Cake

The chiffon cake was invented in 1927 to showcase a brand new product called "vegetable oil." The recipe development of our chiffon cake seemed more like a chemistry lesson than a creative cooking project, but the ease and magic of making a chiffon cake was a pleasant surprise. Its airy, ethereal texture and versatile flavor possibilities are well worth the "two bowl" effort.

This cake, like Greta Garbo, "wants to be alone" in the oven. Opening and closing the oven door during baking may cause the cake to fall. Be gentle!

■ **SERVES 10 TO 12**

CAKE

2 cups unbleached white flour

½ cup sugar

½ cup packed brown sugar

2 teaspoons baking powder

½ teaspoon salt

3 large egg yolks, at room temperature

½ cup vegetable oil

½ cup drained crushed pineapple, juice reserved for glaze

2 tablespoons freshly grated orange peel

7 large egg whites, at room temperature

2 tablespoons confectioners' sugar

½ teaspoon cream of tartar

½ cup fresh orange juice

PREHEAT THE OVEN to 325°. Oil and lightly dust with flour a 9-inch tube pan.

SIFT TOGETHER THE flour, sugar, brown sugar, baking powder, and salt into a large mixing bowl. Make a well in the center of the dry ingredients and add—but do not mix in—the egg yolks, oil, crushed pineapple, and orange peel.

IN ANOTHER LARGE mixing bowl, beat the egg whites with the electric mixer until they are soft and foamy. Add the confectioners' sugar and cream of tartar, and continue beating until the egg whites are stiff but not dry. Without washing the beaters, beat the flour and oil mixture at low speed until everything is well mixed. Add the orange juice and continue beating just until blended.

USING A RUBBER spatula, fold a small portion of egg whites into the flour mixture. Then, in five or six additions, gently fold the flour mixture into the egg whites. The batter will be light and bubbly, with some egg whites showing.

POUR THE BATTER into the prepared pan and bake for 25 minutes. Increase the oven temperature to 350° and bake for another 20 to 25 minutes, or until the cake is well risen and a tester inserted in the center comes out clean.

COOL THE CAKE upright for 10 minutes then invert onto a cooling rack. While the cake cools, combine all of the glaze ingredients and whisk until smooth. When the cake drops out of the pan and is cool to the touch, gently transfer it to a serving plate. Glaze the cake immediately and decorate with mandarin orange sections, if desired. When completely cool, cut with a serrated knife, using a sawing motion.

VARIATION For a Banana Pineapple Chiffon Cake, replace the orange juice with pineapple juice and add 1 teaspoon of pure vanilla extract and 1 tablespoon of natural banana flavoring. If desired, garnish with banana slices tossed in a tablespoon of freshly squeezed lemon or lime juice.

FOR A LOVELY Pineapple Glaze, combine 1½ cups of sifted confectioners' sugar, 2 tablespoons of pineapple juice, 1 tablespoon of freshly squeezed lemon juice, and 2 teaspoons of freshly grated lemon peel and beat until smooth. Spoon or brush over the warm cake, allowing the glaze to drizzle down the sides.

- **PREPARATION TIME:** 40 minutes
- **BAKING TIME:** 45 to 50 minutes
- **COOLING TIME:** 20 to 30 minutes
- **EQUIPMENT:** 10-inch tube pan, electric mixer

ORANGE GLAZE

- 2 cups sifted confectioners' sugar
- 2 tablespoons fresh orange juice
- 2 tablespoons pineapple juice
- 1 tablespoon fresh lemon juice
- 2 teaspoons freshly grated orange peel

mandarin orange sections (optional)

Pineapple Banana Upside-Down Cake

Pineapple upside-down cake endures as a nostalgic favorite because in childhood its home-style richness seemed so festive and special. In this version, bananas are added to the pineapple batter to scent the cake and to reduce the amount of fat usually called for in standard recipes. And what a lovely tropical pair they make with their complementary flavors and textures.

■ **SERVES 6 TO 8**

TOPPING

20-ounce can unsweetened sliced pineapple, undrained

¼ cup butter

½ cup sugar

CAKE BATTER

2 eggs

¾ cup packed brown sugar

½ cup buttermilk

½ cup mashed ripe bananas

3 tablespoons vegetable oil

1 teaspoon pure vanilla extract

½ teaspoon ground cinnamon

¼ teaspoon ground nutmeg

½ teaspoon baking soda

½ teaspoon baking powder

½ teaspoon salt

1¼ cups unbleached white flour

 PREHEAT THE OVEN to 350°.

DRAIN THE PINEAPPLE, reserving ⅓ cup of the juice. In the skillet, melt the butter on medium heat. Add the sugar and cook, stirring constantly. When the sugar starts to turn brown, after about 3 minutes, remove it from the heat and continue stirring to prevent the residual skillet heat from browning the sugar unevenly.

CAREFULLY ADD THE drained pineapple juice; the mixture will sputter somewhat. Return the pan to low heat and stir to combine the juice and the caramelized sugar. When the sugar has melted again and the mixture is smooth, remove from the heat. Arrange the pineapple slices close together in a decorative layer on the bottom of the skillet; reserve any remaining pineapple.

FOR THE CAKE batter, whisk together the eggs, brown sugar, buttermilk, bananas, oil, and vanilla. Sift together the cinnamon, nutmeg, baking soda, baking powder, salt, and flour. Add the dry ingredients to the wet and stir until smooth.

POUR THE BATTER over the pineapple slices and top with any reserved slices. Bake for 30 to 40 minutes, until a knife inserted in the center comes out clean. Cool the cake in the skillet for 10 minutes, then invert it onto a serving plate. Serve warm or cool to room temperature.

■ **PREPARATION TIME:** 20 minutes
■ **BAKING TIME:** 30 to 40 minutes
■ **COOLING TIME:** 10 minutes
■ **EQUIPMENT:** 10-inch cast-iron or other ovenproof skillet

Plum Upside-Down Cake

This is sweet and satisfying, like a fruit cobbler turned upside down to show off a moist buttery cake studded with sugar-glazed plums.

PREHEAT THE OVEN to 350°. Lightly spray, oil, or butter the baking pan.

STIR TOGETHER THE melted butter and brown sugar for the fruit layer until the sugar dissolves. Cut each plum into 6 to 8 wedges. Arrange the plum wedges in the prepared pan and top them with the butter and sugar mixture.

TO MAKE THE cake batter, cream the softened butter and brown sugar together with an electric mixer. Beat in the eggs and buttermilk or yogurt. In a separate bowl, combine the flour, cornmeal, baking powder, cinnamon, and salt. Fold the dry ingredients into the creamed mixture. Fold in the vanilla. Spread the cake batter evenly over the fruit.

BAKE FOR 30 to 35 minutes, until a knife inserted in the center comes out clean.

COOL IN THE pan. When cool, run a knife around the edge of the pan and invert the cake onto a platter. If necessary, loosen the cake with a spatula.

- **PREPARATION TIME:** 20 to 25 minutes
- **BAKING TIME:** 30 to 35 minutes
- **EQUIPMENT:** 7 × 11-inch baking pan, electric mixer

■ **SERVES 8**

FRUIT LAYER

- ½ cup butter, melted
- ½ cup packed brown sugar
- 5 or 6 red or purple plums

CAKE BATTER

- ½ cup butter, softened
- ¾ cup packed brown sugar
- 2 eggs
- ¼ cup buttermilk or yogurt
- 1 cup unbleached white flour
- ¼ cup cornmeal
- 1½ teaspoons baking powder
- ½ teaspoon ground cinnamon
- ½ teaspoon salt
- 2 teaspoons pure vanilla extract

Date Orange Cake

This wonderful version of a Middle Eastern-style, syrup-soaked cake is packed with nuts and morsels of sweet dates and is fragrant with a fresh orange scent. It can be offered as an authentic finish to a Middle Eastern-style meal, served with demitasse of Turkish coffee or mint tea. It is also an excellent cake for fancy brunches, lunch boxes, or afternoon teas.

■ **SERVES 12**

CAKE

3 cups unbleached white flour

1 teaspoon salt

1 teaspoon baking soda

1 cup butter, at room temperature

1½ cups sugar

3 eggs

1 cup buttermilk

⅔ cup finely chopped pitted dates

⅔ cup chopped walnuts or pecans

2 tablespoons freshly grated orange peel

1 teaspoon pure vanilla extract

ZESTY ORANGE SAUCE

½ cup fresh orange juice

2 tablespoons freshly grated orange peel

½ cup sugar

¼ teaspoon pure vanilla extract

PREHEAT THE OVEN to 350°. Butter or oil the cake pan and lightly dust it with flour.

SIFT TOGETHER THE flour, salt, and baking soda. In a separate bowl, cream together the butter and sugar until light. Alternate adding the dry ingredients and the buttermilk to the butter mixture, adding about a third of the dry ingredients at a time and about half of the buttermilk, and beating well after each addition. Stir in the dates, nuts, orange peel, and vanilla. Pour the batter into the prepared pan and bake for 35 to 45 minutes, until a knife inserted in the center comes out clean.

WHILE THE CAKE is baking, prepare the Zesty Orange Sauce. Combine the orange juice, orange peel, sugar, and vanilla in a bowl. Stir until the sugar dissolves and set aside. When the cake is baked, remove it from the oven and poke little holes in the top with a pick. Briskly stir the Zesty Orange Sauce and pour it over the cake; the sauce should go down the holes and soak into the cake.

SERVE WARM OR cool.

■ **PREPARATION TIME:** 40 minutes
■ **BAKING TIME:** 35 to 45 minutes
■ **EQUIPMENT:** 9 × 13-inch cake pan, electric mixer

Erma Mabel's Rhubarb Cake

Rhubarb is one of those welcome, reliable, carefree perennials that herald the spring in gardens throughout the whole eastern United States, and out West, too. The beautiful ruby stalks make great pies, cakes, and sauces. They cook up soft and have a tangy fruit flavor. Thankfully, rhubarb stalks are available seasonally in markets everywhere. The leaves of the plant are always discarded because they are inedible and poisonous.

Here is a recipe that originated many generations ago in the hills and hollows of north central West Virginia. It made its way to Ithaca, New York, and onto the Moosewood menu via Erma Mabel's granddaughter, Lisa Wichman, and great granddaughter, Robin Wichman—both dessert chefs at the restaurant.

■ **SERVES 8**

½ cup butter,
   at room temperature

1 cup sugar

3 large eggs

1½ cups unbleached
   white flour

3 teaspoons
   baking powder

¼ teaspoon salt

½ cup milk

1 teaspoon pure
   vanilla extract

2½ cups chopped
   rhubarb*
   (about 4 stalks)

** Cut the rhubarb into
¾- to 1-inch pieces.*

 PREHEAT THE OVEN to 350°. Butter the baking dish and lightly dust it with flour.

WITH AN ELECTRIC mixer, cream the butter and sugar until light. Add the eggs one at a time, beating well after each addition. In a separate bowl, sift together the flour, baking powder, and salt. Combine the milk and vanilla in a small bowl or cup. Alternate adding the dry and the wet ingredients to the butter mixture, beating well after each addition.

SPREAD ABOUT ⅔ of the batter into the prepared pan. Sprinkle it with all of the rhubarb pieces. Top with the rest of the batter, spreading it as evenly as possible but with a light touch—try not to push the rhubarb pieces into the bottom layer of batter. Bake for 35 to 40 minutes, until a knife inserted into the center comes out clean and the cake is golden brown.

VARIATION Replace the rhubarb with 2½ cups of fresh blackberries.

■ **PREPARATION TIME:** 30 minutes
■ **BAKING TIME:** 35 to 40 minutes
■ **EQUIPMENT:** 7 × 11-inch nonreactive baking dish, electric mixer

Fat-Free Carrot Cake

No eggs, no oil! Many old recipes that evolved from the limited availability of perishable ingredients are perfectly suited to contemporary low-fat and dairyless diets. This cake was inspired by a pioneer recipe and requires neither eggs nor butter or oil of any kind.

The texture of the cake improves if you have time to let the cooked carrot mixture sit and absorb the liquid before you prepare the cake batter. Plan ahead so you can let it sit overnight.

■ **SERVES 12**

2 cups packed finely grated carrots

1½ cups packed brown sugar

1¾ cups water

1 cup raisins or other chopped dried fruit

1 teaspoon pure vanilla extract

3 cups unbleached white flour

1 teaspoon ground cinnamon

¼ teaspoon ground cloves

½ teaspoon freshly grated nutmeg

½ teaspoon ground ginger

1 teaspooon salt

1 teaspoon baking soda

2 teaspoons baking powder

confectioners' sugar or Lemon Glaze (page 266)

IN THE SAUCEPAN, combine the carrots, brown sugar, water, raisins or dried fruit, and vanilla. Bring to a boil and simmer for 5 minutes, then remove from the heat, cover, and let sit for at least an hour. In a large bowl, combine the flour, cinnamon, cloves, nutmeg, ginger, salt, baking soda, and baking powder. Whisk or stir to combine thoroughly and set aside.

PREHEAT THE OVEN to 300° about 15 minutes before you are ready mix the batter. Generously oil and flour the bundt pan.

STIR THE COOLED carrot mixture into the dry ingredients just until no trace of flour is left. Pour the batter into the prepared bundt pan and bake until the cake feels firm to the touch and a knife inserted into the cake comes out clean, about 1 hour. Cool in the pan for 10 minutes on a rack, then invert onto a serving plate. Dust with confectioners' sugar or top with our simple Lemon Glaze.

 VARIATIONS Add 1 cup of chopped nuts and/or ½ cup of unsweetened shredded coconut to the batter.

■ **PREPARATION TIME:** 15 minutes
■ **STEEPING TIME:** at least 1 hour
■ **BAKING TIME:** about 1 hour
■ **COOLING TIME:** 10 minutes
■ **EQUIPMENT:** saucepan, 10-inch bundt pan

PER 4.5 OZ SERVING: 261 CALS, .4 G TOT FAT, 0 G MONO FAT, .1 G SAT FAT, 0 MG CHOL

Red Devil Cake

Here is an easy-to-make and very pleasant devil's food cake. A surprise ingredient is the secret to this cake's rich flavor and barely discernible rosy hue. You'll never guess what it is without peeking at the ingredient list, but then it's obvious—beets! We promise you'll be able to slip these nutritious beets into the cake and none of your friends or family will be the wiser as they indulge in their dessert.

PREHEAT THE OVEN to 350°. Generously oil the baking pan.

DRAIN THE BEETS, reserving ½ cup of the juice. In a blender, purée the beets with the reserved juice to make about 1¼ cups of purée. Set aside.

IN A LARGE bowl, beat the eggs well. Thoroughly whisk in the sugar, oil, vanilla, salt, and beet purée until very smooth. In a separate bowl, sift together the flour, cocoa, and baking soda. Add the dry ingredients to the wet ingredients a little at a time, whisking until smooth.

POUR THE BATTER into the prepared pan and bake for 45 to 50 minutes, until a knife inserted in the center comes out clean. Cool in the pan. Serve topped with confectioners' sugar, whipped cream, Chocolate Buttercream Frosting (page 84), or Cream Cheese Frosting (page 89).

- **PREPARATION TIME:** 20 minutes
- **BAKING TIME:** 45 to 50 minutes
- **EQUIPMENT:** 9-inch square or round baking pan, blender

■ **SERVES 9**

15-ounce can sliced beets

3 eggs

1½ cups sugar

½ cup vegetable oil

1 teaspoon pure vanilla extract

½ teaspoon salt

1½ cups unbleached white flour

¾ cup unsweetened cocoa powder

1½ teaspoons baking soda

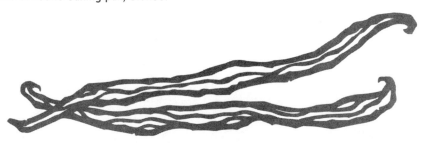

Zucchini Spice Cake

This slightly sweet spice cake is an ideal selection for a breakfast banquet or brunch, or a choice accompaniment to a midafternoon tea. Dowse with brandy for a more spirited dessert or dress it up with Lemon Cream Cheese Frosting (page 277).

■ **SERVES 16**

½ cup butter

1½ cups packed brown sugar

3 eggs

1½ cups unbleached white pastry flour (page 361)

2 teaspoons baking powder

½ teaspoon salt

2 teaspoons ground ginger

2 teaspoons ground cinnamon

½ teaspoon ground nutmeg

½ teaspoon ground cardamom

2 teaspoons pure vanilla extract

1½ cups grated zucchini

1 cup chopped toasted nuts, such as almonds, pecans, or walnuts (page 364)

½ cup currants or raisins

sprinkling of confectioners' sugar

PREHEAT THE OVEN to 350°. Generously butter or oil the bundt pan.

IN A LARGE bowl with an electric mixer, cream together the butter and brown sugar until light. Beat in the eggs and mix well. In a separate bowl, combine the flour, baking powder, salt, ginger, cinnamon, nutmeg, and cardamom. Fold the dry ingredients into the creamed mixture. Fold in the vanilla, zucchini, nuts, and raisins.

POUR THE BATTER evenly into the prepared pan and bake for 40 to 45 minutes, until the cake is golden and a knife inserted in the center comes out clean. Cool in the pan for 10 minutes and then invert the cake onto a plate—tap the bottom of the pan to help release the cake, if needed.

SPRINKLE WITH CONFECTIONERS' sugar and serve warm or at room temperature.

■ **PREPARATION TIME:** 40 minutes
■ **BAKING TIME:** 40 to 45 minutes
■ **COOLING TIME:** 10 minutes
■ **EQUIPMENT:** 10-inch bundt pan, electric mixer

Gingerbread with Pears

"HAD I BUT ONE PENNY IN THE WORLD, THOU SHOULDST HAVE IT FOR GINGERBREAD."
William Shakespeare

Pears and ginger have an affinity for one another. The chunks of sweet pear add moisture and a delicate fruity flavor to this gingery childhood favorite. Gingerbread with Pears is versatile, low-fat, and easy to make—an everyday sort of dessert. Serve it plain, dusted with confectioners' sugar, beside a scoop of frozen yogurt, or topped with Fresh Mango Sauce (page 308).

Here, at the end of the twentieth century, we calculate that each serving costs about 21 cents, so . . . had I but twenty-one pennies in the world . . .

 PREHEAT THE OVEN to 350°. Lightly oil the baking pan.

COMBINE ALL OF the dry ingredients in a mixing bowl. In a separate bowl, combine the wet ingredients. Pour the wet ingredients into the dry ingredients and stir just until combined—don't overmix. Stir in the pears. Pour the batter into the prepared pan and bake for 35 to 45 minutes, until a knife inserted into the center of the cake comes out clean.

CUT IN SQUARES and serve warm and fragrant straight from the oven or cool to room temperature.

- **PREPARATION TIME:** 20 minutes
- **BAKING TIME:** 35 to 45 minutes
- **EQUIPMENT:** 8- or 9-inch square baking pan

PER SERVING: 250 CALS, .5 G TOT FAT, .1 G MONO FAT, .1 G SAT FAT, 0 MG CHOL

> Because baking soda begins working as soon as it contacts acidic liquids, be sure to have the pears prepared before combining the wet and dry ingredients.

- **SERVES 9**

DRY INGREDIENTS
- 2 cups unbleached white flour
- 1 cup sugar
- 2 teaspoons ground ginger
- 1 teaspoon ground cinnamon
- ½ teaspoon salt
- 1½ teaspoons baking soda, sifted

WET INGREDIENTS
- ½ cup unsulphured molasses
- 2 egg whites, lightly beaten
- ½ cup buttermilk
- 2 tablespoons fresh lemon juice
- 2 fresh pears, peeled, cored, and chopped into small pieces

Olive Oil and Citrus Cake

The pleasant fruitiness of olive oil, especially that of a strong, green, extra-virgin oil, adds an intriguing, hard-to-identify flavor to this light, citrusy cake.

■ **SERVES 8 TO 10**

5 large eggs
⅓ cup olive oil
1½ cups sugar
½ teaspoon salt
2 teaspoons ground cinnamon
1 teaspoon pure vanilla, lemon, or orange extract
grated peel and juice of 1 orange
grated peel and juice of 1 lemon
2 cups unbleached white pastry flour (page 361)
1 teaspoon baking powder

confectioners' sugar for dusting (optional)

PREHEAT THE OVEN to 325°. Oil the springform pan and dust it with flour.

SEPARATE THE EGGS. Set the yolks aside and, using an electric mixer, whip the egg whites until stiff but not dry. Set them aside.

USING AN ELECTRIC mixer, cream together the oil and the sugar. Beat in the reserved egg yolks. Add the salt, cinnamon, extract, and grated citrus peels and juices and beat until smooth. Add the flour and baking powder and mix until thoroughly combined. With a spatula, carefully fold in the whipped egg whites.

POUR THE BATTER into the prepared pan and bake for about 45 minutes, until the cake is golden, firm in the center, and pulling away from the sides of the pan. Remove from the oven and cool on a rack for 10 to 15 minutes.

RUN A KNIFE around the outside of the cake and remove the outer ring of the springform pan. Use a spatula or wide knife to loosen the cake from the bottom of the pan and transfer it to a serving plate. Dust with confectioners' sugar, if desired.

■ **PREPARATION TIME:** 25 minutes
■ **BAKING TIME:** 45 minutes
■ **COOLING TIME:** 10 to 15 minutes
■ **EQUIPMENT:** 10-inch springform pan, electric mixer

Honey Cake

Honey cakes are traditionally baked at Rosh Hashanah, the Jewish New Year, to ensure a sweet year. This favorite family recipe is from Davina Stein, poet, Latin scholar, a sweet lady, and Moosewood's Wynelle Stein's mother. It will fill your home with the autumnal aroma of honey and spice.

PREHEAT THE OVEN to 350°. Lightly oil the tube pan or bundt pan.

CREAM THE SUGAR and oil with an electric mixer until well blended. Beat in the honey and eggs. In a separate bowl, sift the flour, baking powder, baking soda, salt, ginger, cinnamon, allspice, and cloves. Add the dry ingredients to the honey mixture with the coffee and liqueur, if using, and mix well.

POUR THE BATTER into the prepared pan and bake for 50 to 60 minutes, until the cake pulls away from the sides of the pan and a knife inserted in the center comes out clean. Cool the cake in the pan on a rack for 15 minutes. Invert onto a serving plate and dust with confectioners' sugar, if desired. The moist, dense nature of this cake gives it a tendency to fall somewhat as it cools.

- **PREPARATION TIME:** 20 minutes
- **BAKING TIME:** 50 to 60 minutes
- **COOLING TIME:** 15 minutes
- **EQUIPMENT:** 10-inch tube pan or bundt pan, electric mixer

- **SERVES 12 TO 16**

1 cup sugar

½ cup vegetable oil

1½ cups honey (1 pound)

3 eggs

3 cups unbleached white flour

½ teaspoon baking powder

½ teaspoon baking soda

½ teaspoon salt

1 teaspoon ground ginger

2 teaspoons ground cinnamon

½ teaspoon ground allspice

⅛ teaspoon ground cloves

1 cup strong black coffee, cooled

1 tablespoon coffee-flavored liqueur, such as Kahlúa (optional)

sprinkling of confectioners' sugar (optional)

Orange Coconut Angelfood Cake

Many of us at Moosewood grew up in awe of our mothers' magical creations known as angelfood cakes. While searching for low-fat recipes to serve at the restaurant and at home, we recently "rediscovered" this family of light, wispy cakes and reawakened those childhood memories. If you have never made an angelfood cake before, read our helpful tips in the note at the end of the recipe.

This airy, fat-free cake is full of tropical flavor. Slice the cake with a serrated knife, using a sawing motion to avoid flattening the cake. Serve unadorned or topped with Pineapple Orange Sauce (page 306) or fresh mango slices.

■ **SERVES 12**

1 cup unbleached white pastry or cake flour (page 361)

¼ teaspoon salt

1½ cups sugar

1 tablespoon freshly grated orange peel

1½ cups egg whites, at room temperature (about 10 large eggs)

1 teaspoon cream of tartar

2 teaspoons pure coconut extract

 PREHEAT THE OVEN to 350°.

SIFT TOGETHER THE flour, salt, and ¾ cup of the sugar. Sift twice more. Stir in the orange peel and set aside.

IN A LARGE bowl, beat the egg whites and cream of tartar with an electric mixer on medium speed until soft peaks form. Increase the speed to high and gradually add the remaining ¾ cup sugar, a tablespoon or two at a time. Beat until stiff, glossy peaks are formed. At this point, the whites will not slide when the bowl is tilted. Be careful not to overbeat.

SPRINKLE THE COCONUT extract over the whites and fold it in with a rubber spatula. Sprinkle about ⅓ cup of the flour mixture over the whites and gently fold it in. Repeat until all of the flour has been incorporated into the whites.

POUR THE BATTER into the unoiled tube pan and run a knife through it in a zigzag pattern to deflate any large air pockets. Bake until the cake is puffed and golden and springs back to the touch, about 45 minutes.

INVERT THE PAN on its feet or on a long-necked bottle and cool completely, 1½ to 2 hours. When cool, loosen the cake by carefully running a knife around the edges, then remove to a serving platter.

NOTE To ensure a high, light cake, all equipment and utensils must be completely oil-free. The egg whites must not contain even a speck of yolk. Eggs separate more easily when cold, so keep them refrigerated until you are ready to use them. The whites, however, beat better at room temperature, so place the bowl of whites in a pan of warm water while you prepare the other ingredients.

- **PREPARATION TIME:** 25 to 30 minutes
- **BAKING TIME:** 45 minutes
- **COOLING TIME:** 1½ to 2 hours
- **EQUIPMENT:** electric mixer; 10-inch tube pan, preferably with removable bottom

PER 2.25 OZ SERVING: 148 CALS, .1 G TOT FAT, 0 G MONO FAT, 0 G SAT FAT, 0 MG CHOL

Anna's Country Spice Cake

No, we haven't lost our minds—parsnips do add a sweet moistness to this golden autumn harvest cake. Dried cranberries are becoming more available in larger supermarkets and can be a nice touch, but raisins or currants work just as well. Grated carrots can substitute for the parsnips, if you prefer, but don't knock the parsnips until you've tried them!

- **SERVES 9**

½ cup vegetable oil

¾ cup packed
brown sugar

2 eggs

1½ cups peeled grated
parsnips

1 teaspoon freshly
grated orange peel

½ cup drained crushed
pineapple

¾ cup unbleached
white flour

¾ cup whole wheat
pastry flour
(page 361)

2 teaspoons
baking powder

1 teaspoon baking soda

½ teaspoon salt

1½ teaspoons
ground cinnamon

¼ teaspoon
ground cloves

½ cup raisins, currants,
or dried cranberries

½ cup chopped pecans,
walnuts, or almonds
(optional)

PREHEAT THE OVEN to 325°. Oil the baking pan and dust it with flour.

IN A LARGE mixing bowl, beat together the oil, brown sugar, and eggs until thoroughly combined. Stir in the grated parsnips, orange peel, and crushed pineapple. Set aside.

SIFT TOGETHER THE flours, baking powder, baking soda, salt, cinnamon, and cloves. Stir the flour mixture into the wet ingredients in two or three batches until well mixed. Fold in the dried fruit and the nuts, if using.

POUR THE BATTER into the prepared pan and bake until the top feels firm and a knife inserted in the center comes out clean, about 1 hour.

- **PREPARATION TIME:** 40 minutes
- **BAKING TIME:** 1 hour
- **EQUIPMENT:** 8-inch square nonreactive baking pan

Chocolate Ginger Cake

Chocolate and ginger bring such wonderfully distinctive flavors to this cake that it doesn't need much added fat to provide richness. Think of it as a Caribbean-Mexican hybrid that can enliven southern-style or tropical menus.

Top each slice with some Fresh Mango Sauce (page 308) if you like, or if fat content is not a concern, try it with one of our Flavored Whipped Creams (page 318).

PREHEAT THE OVEN to 350°. Butter the cake pan and dust it with cocoa.

IN A LARGE mixing bowl, whisk together the brown sugar, buttermilk, applesauce, oil, eggs, and vanilla. In another bowl, combine the flour, cocoa, baking soda, baking powder, salt, and cinnamon. Sift the flour mixture into the applesauce mixture and blend until smooth. Stir in the grated ginger.

POUR THE BATTER into the prepared pan and bake until a knife inserted in the center of the cake comes out clean, 30 to 45 minutes.

- **PREPARATION TIME:** 15 minutes
- **BAKING TIME:** 30 to 45 minutes
- **EQUIPMENT:** 9-inch round cake pan

■ **SERVES 8 TO 10**

1¼ cups packed brown sugar

⅔ cup buttermilk

⅓ cup unsweetened applesauce

¼ cup vegetable oil

2 eggs

1 teaspoon pure vanilla extract

1 cup unbleached white flour

⅔ cup unsweetened cocoa powder

1 teaspoon baking soda

½ teaspoon baking powder

½ teaspoon salt

1 teaspoon ground cinnamon

1 tablespoon freshly grated ginger root

Chocolate Grand Marnier Cake

This is a dark, handsome cake with a glossy glaze that keeps well and travels well. Orange slices arranged on the serving plate in a ring around the cake are all the embellishment needed; however, you may wish to serve whipped cream, sweetened with confectioners' sugar and flavored with a little Grand Marnier on the side to go with the strong coffee you'll surely want.

■ **SERVES 16**

CAKE

1 cup butter

5 ounces unsweetened chocolate

1¾ cups orange juice

¼ cup orange-flavored liqueur, such as Grand Marnier

2 cups sugar

¼ teaspoon salt

2 cups unbleached white flour

1 teaspoon baking soda

2 eggs, lightly beaten

CHOCOLATE ORANGE GLAZE

3 ounces semi-sweet chocolate

2 tablespoons orange juice or orange-flavored liqueur, such as Grand Marnier

PREHEAT THE OVEN to 275° (yes, that really is 275°). Generously butter the bundt pan and coat it with cocoa powder or flour.

GENTLY HEAT THE butter, chocolate, and orange juice in the saucepan for about 15 minutes, stirring occasionally. Add the Grand Marnier and sugar and beat with an electric mixer until smooth. Set aside to cool for 5 minutes. Add the salt, flour, and baking soda and beat until smooth. Add the eggs and beat well.

POUR THE BATTER into the prepared bundt pan. Bake for about 1½ hours, until the cake pulls away from the sides of the pan and springs back when touched in the middle. Remove the cake from the oven and allow to cool for 10 minutes. Place a plate on top of the bundt pan and invert the cake onto the plate with one smooth movement. When the pan is cool enough to touch, about 15 to 20 minutes, remove the bundt pan.

WHEN THE CAKE is almost cool, prepare the glaze. Combine the chocolate and orange juice or liqueur and gently heat in a double boiler or on a heat diffuser for about 10 to 15 minutes. When the chocolate has melted, stir the glaze until smooth. Use a pastry brush to coat the surface of the cake evenly with the glaze.

■ **PREPARATION TIME:** 45 minutes
■ **BAKING TIME:** about 1½ hours
■ **COOLING TIME:** 15 to 20 minutes
■ **EQUIPMENT:** 10-inch bundt pan, large heavy saucepan, electric mixer, double boiler (page 370) or heat diffuser, pastry brush

Irish Whiskey Cake

This rich poundcake is studded with fruit and subtly flavored with good Irish whiskey. The combination of dried fruit is up to you, but we suggest fruits in a variety of colors to make the cake look festive. Ah, 'tis a fine thing, indeed it is!

COMBINE THE DICED fruit and ⅔ cup of whiskey in the saucepan. Simmer on low heat for about 10 minutes, until the fruit has softened. Set aside to cool.

PREHEAT THE OVEN to 325°. Butter the bundt pan and lightly dust it with flour.

USING AN ELECTRIC mixer, beat the butter and sugar in a large bowl until light. Add the eggs one at a time, beating until light. Add the orange peel, lemon peel, almond extract, and salt. Sift together the flour and baking powder and add to the butter mixture in several additions, beating well after each. Fold the dried fruit and the almonds into the batter by hand.

POUR THE BATTER into the prepared pan and bake for 1¼ to 1½ hours, or until a knife inserted in the center comes out clean. Allow the cake to cool in the pan for about 10 minutes, then invert it onto a serving plate and cool for an additional 10 minutes. Remove the pan and cool completely. For a more pronounced whiskey flavor, brush the warm cake with the optional 2 to 3 tablespoons of whiskey. Lightly dust the cake with confectioners' sugar before serving.

VARIATION Reduce the butter to 1¼ cups and the sugar to 2 cups, omit the almond extract, and add ¼ cup of almond paste.

- **PREPARATION TIME:** 40 minutes
- **BAKING TIME:** 1¼ to 1½ hours
- **COOLING TIME:** 20 minutes
- **EQUIPMENT:** small heavy saucepan, 10-inch bundt pan, electric mixer

■ SERVES 16

2½ cups diced dried fruit*

⅔ cup Irish whiskey, plus an optional 2 to 3 tablespoons

1½ cups butter, at room temperature

2¼ cups sugar

6 large eggs

2 teaspoons freshly grated orange peel

2 teaspoons freshly grated lemon peel

2 teaspoons pure almond extract

¼ teaspoon salt

3 cups unbleached white pastry flour (page 361)

1 teaspoon baking powder

1 cup toasted chopped almonds (page 364)

2 to 3 tablespoons confectioners' sugar

Try a mixture of 3 or 4 of the following: apricots, peaches, cherries, cranberries, raisins, prunes, or dates.

Black Mocha Cake

This is the kind of cake everyone should have in their repertoire because it is delicious, moist and springy, easy to make, extremely reliable, and quite versatile. It's an all-purpose chocolate cake that can be made in various shapes and sizes—as a bundt cake, sheet cake, layer cake, or cupcakes.

Black Mocha Cake is flavorful enough to serve plain, but you can make this dark, chocolaty cake special and decorative with just a dusting of confectioners' sugar, a dollop of whipped cream or Strawberry Sauce (page 127), or an arrangement of sliced fresh fruit. Here we offer it with a boiled coconut-and-pecan frosting that usually defines a German Chocolate Cake. The frosting is chewy, crunchy, and satisfying. Use only the freshest unsweetened coconut and lightly toast the pecans, if you like, for a finishing touch. For variety, try it iced with Cream Cheese Frosting (page 89). •

■ SERVES 12 TO 16

CAKE

¾ cup unsweetened
   cocoa powder

2 cups sugar

1¾ cups unbleached
   white flour

1 teaspoon
   baking powder

1 teaspoon baking soda

1 teaspoon salt

½ cup vegetable oil

1 cup fresh strong
   coffee, at room
   temperature

1 cup milk, buttermilk,
   or yogurt

2 eggs

1 teaspoon pure
   vanilla extract

PREHEAT THE OVEN to 350°. Lightly butter or spray the cake pan or place paper liners in the muffin tins, if making cupcakes.

IN A LARGE bowl, sift together the cocoa, sugar, flour, baking powder, baking soda, and salt. In another bowl with a whisk or electric mixer, lightly beat together the oil, coffee, milk (or buttermilk or yogurt), eggs, and vanilla. Pour half of the wet ingredients into the dry ingredients and mix until smooth. Add the remaining wet ingredients and stir until incorporated.

POUR THE BATTER into the prepared pan(s). Bake for 20 to 40 minutes (see Note), until a knife inserted in the center comes out clean. Cool in the pan(s) before frosting.

TO MAKE THE optional frosting, combine the sugar, evaporated milk, egg yolks, and butter in the saucepan. Bring the mixture to a boil, stirring constantly, then reduce the heat to medium and cook until thick, about 12 to 15 minutes. Remove from the heat and stir in the vanilla, coconut, and pecans. The frosting is easiest to spread while it's still somewhat warm.

Traditionally, it is spread only between the layers and on top of the cake but not on the sides.

NOTE The baking time for the cake depends upon the pan you decide to use. Here's a good guide for the different sizes and shapes:

- 9 × 13-inch pan: 25 to 30 minutes
- 10-inch bundt pan: 30 to 35 minutes
- two 9-inch round pans: 35 to 40 minutes
- two standard 12-cup muffin tins: about 20 minutes

- YIELD: 1 cake or 24 cupcakes
- PREPARATION TIME: 20 minutes, plus 15 minutes for frosting
- BAKING TIME: 20 to 40 minutes (see Note)
- EQUIPMENT: any of the following baking pans: 10-inch bundt pan, 9 × 13-inch pan, two 9-inch round cake pans, or two standard 12-cup muffin tins; whisk or electric mixer; small saucepan

GERMAN CHOCOLATE CAKE FROSTING (OPTIONAL)

⅔ cup sugar

⅔ cup evaporated milk

2 egg yolks

⅓ cup butter

1 teaspoon pure vanilla extract

1 cup plus 2 tablespoons toasted unsweetened grated coconut (page 358)

1 cup toasted chopped pecans (page 364)

Flourless Chocolate Cake

Less dense than most flourless cakes, this one has a drier, mousse-like texture. It is difficult to believe that there is no flour, starch, or ground nuts to provide structure—it's all in the eggs. This cake is perfect for a meatless Passover meal.

■ **SERVES 8**

½ cup butter

6 ounces semi-sweet chocolate

2 ounces unsweetened chocolate

8 eggs

½ cup sugar

1 teaspoon pure vanilla extract

¼ teaspoon salt

 PREHEAT THE OVEN to 275°.

IN A SAUCEPAN on low heat, melt the butter with the semi-sweet and unsweetened chocolates, stirring constantly to facilitate melting and prevent scorching. Set aside and let cool to room temperature.

WHILE THE CHOCOLATE is cooling, butter and flour the springform pan.

SEPARATE THE EGG whites and yolks into two bowls. Using an electric mixer with clean and dry beaters, beat the egg whites until soft peaks form. Gradually add the sugar and continue beating until stiff peaks form. Set aside.

WHEN THE CHOCOLATE has cooled, stir it into the egg yolks along with the vanilla and salt and mix thoroughly. Fold in the egg whites until no trace of the whites remain. Pour the batter into the prepared pan and bake until the center is set, about 1 hour. Cool in the springform pan before removing to a serving dish—the cake may fall somewhat as it cools.

■ **PREPARATION TIME:** 20 to 25 minutes
■ **BAKING TIME:** 1 hour
■ **EQUIPMENT:** small saucepan, 9-inch springform pan, electric mixer

Greek Walnut Yogurt Cake

This moist, dense cake is quite tart-sweet and a small piece will satisfy. Garnish the cake with colorful orange slices and serve with tea, coffee, dessert wine, or a strong cup of Greek coffee or demitasse.

PREHEAT THE OVEN to 350°. Butter the nonreactive baking pan.

TOAST THE WALNUTS until fragrant (page 364), chop finely, and set aside.

IN A LARGE mixing bowl, use an electric mixer to cream together the butter and sugar. Add the egg and yogurt and beat until smooth. Add the grated citrus peels, cinnamon, salt, and flour. Sift in the baking powder and baking soda. Mix until the dry ingredients are evenly moistened and then stir in the chopped walnuts.

POUR THE BATTER into the prepared pan and bake for about 25 minutes, until the cake is brown and a knife inserted into the center comes out clean. Remove from the oven and cool on a rack for 5 minutes.

WHILE THE CAKE cools, place all of the syrup ingredients in the saucepan. Bring to a boil, reduce the heat, and simmer for 5 to 10 minutes, until slightly thickened.

WITH A SKEWER, pierce the still warm cake through to the bottom in several places and pour the hot syrup slowly over it, allowing the syrup to soak into the cake. Serve the cake directly from the pan or transfer it to a serving plate once it has absorbed the syrup.

- **PREPARATION TIME:** 25 minutes
- **BAKING TIME:** 25 minutes
- **COOLING TIME:** 5 minutes
- **EQUIPMENT:** 8-inch square or 9-inch round nonreactive baking pan, electric mixer, small saucepan, skewer

■ SERVES 8 OR 9

CAKE

- ¾ cup whole walnuts
- ¼ cup butter, at room temperature
- ½ cup sugar
- 1 large egg
- ¾ cup plain yogurt
  freshly grated peel of 1 lemon (about 1 tablespoon)
- 1 tablespoon freshly grated orange peel
- ½ teaspoon ground cinnamon
  pinch of salt
- 1 cup unbleached white flour
- 1 teaspoon baking powder
- ½ teaspoon baking soda

SYRUP

- juice of 1 lemon
  juice of 1 orange
- ½ cup sugar
  1-inch cinnamon stick

Besbusa

Besbusa is a sweet cake that is popular in the Middle East and parts of North Africa. It uses semolina, a flour prepared from durum wheat, that is available in the United States in large supermarkets and specialty groceries. Most besbusa is made with coconut, topped with almonds, and soaked with a sweet syrup. We have replaced the traditional sugar or honey syrup with maple syrup, which adds a special flavor. Our Moosewood version of this delicious dessert is surprisingly easy and quick to make, too.

■ **SERVES 16**

CAKE

¾ cup vegetable oil, preferably canola

1 cup sugar

1 large egg

4 large egg whites

1 teaspoon pure vanilla extract

1 cup semolina

½ cup unsweetened grated coconut

SYRUP

¼ cup pure maple syrup

1 tablespoon water

16 whole almonds, toasted (page 364)

 PREHEAT THE OVEN to 350°. Butter the baking pan.

WITH AN ELECTRIC mixer, beat the oil and sugar until well blended. Add the egg and the egg whites one at a time, beating well after each addition. Add the vanilla, semolina, and coconut, beating until smooth. Pour the batter into the prepared baking dish.

BAKE FOR ABOUT 25 minutes, until the cake is golden brown and a tester inserted in the center comes out clean.

MEANWHILE, COMBINE THE maple syrup and water (see Note). As soon as the cake is done, drizzle the syrup over the top as evenly as possible. Cut the besbusa in half lengthwise and in fourths across its width. Cut each of these eight squares on the diagonal to make sixteen triangles. Place a toasted almond in the center of each triangle. Cool before serving.

 NOTE If you prefer a simple sugar syrup, combine ¼ cup of sugar and 2 tablelspoons of water.

■ **PREPARATION TIME:** 20 minutes
■ **BAKING TIME:** 25 minutes
■ **EQUIPMENT:** 7 × 11-inch baking pan, electric mixer

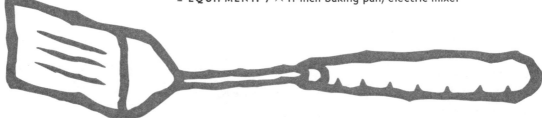

Jamaican Black Cake

This Caribbean version of the classic English fruitcake is flavored with dark rum, stout, and exotic dried fruits. We have taken some liberties with the traditional recipes.

The result is admittedly a dark brown—not black—cake, with a chewy fruit bottom and a moist and tender top. It may not be strictly traditional, but we think you'll enjoy this taste of the Tropics.

■ **SERVES 9**

 IN THE SAUCEPAN, combine all of the dried fruit, the stout, and the rum and simmer on low heat, stirring occasionally, until the fruit has softened, about 10 or 15 minutes. Set aside to cool.

PREHEAT THE OVEN to 325°. Butter the baking pan.

IN A LARGE bowl, cream together the butter and brown sugar (by hand works fine). Stir in the molasses and then beat in the eggs one at a time. Add the vanilla, allspice, nutmeg, and ginger. Sift together the flour, baking powder, and cocoa and add to the batter, alternating with the cooked dried fruit mixture and beating well after each addition.

POUR THE BATTER—it will be rather thin—into the prepared pan and bake until a knife inserted into the center comes out clean, 40 to 60 minutes, depending upon the size of the pan. Cool the cake in the pan.

SERVE AT ONCE or wrap tightly and store. It will keep for at least a week.

NOTE   Choose a mixture of 2 or 3 of your favorite dried fruits from the following: papaya, mango, dates, raisins, or currants.

- ■ **PREPARATION TIME:** 45 minutes
- ■ **BAKING TIME:** 40 to 60 minutes
- ■ **EQUIPMENT:** 1-quart nonreactive saucepan, nonreactive 8-inch square or 7 × 11-inch baking pan

1 cup diced dried
   pineapple

1 cup diced mixed dried
   fruit (see Note)

¾ cup Guinness Stout
   or other dark beer

½ cup dark rum

¾ cup butter,
   at room temperature

½ cup packed
   brown sugar

¼ cup unsulphured
   molasses

3 large eggs

1 teaspoon pure
   vanilla extract

¼ teaspoon
   ground allspice

¼ teaspoon
   ground nutmeg

¼ teaspoon
   ground ginger

1 cup unbleached
   white flour

1 teaspoon
   baking powder

2 tablespoons
   unsweetened cocoa
   powder

Italian Fruitcake

Descended from a centuries-old tradition of celebrating the abundance of another year, this substantial cake is crammed with good things. Our favorite combination of dried fruit is figs, cherries, raisins, and coarsely chopped apricots. The cake can be baked and served the same day, but it also keeps well for a couple of weeks, tightly wrapped and refrigerated, to serve at holiday time.

Garnish this robust cake with orange or pear slices. Because it is so dense and rich, serve Italian Fruitcake in small slices with Spumonte or other Italian dessert wine.

BUTTER THE SPRINGFORM pan or bundt pan and dust with cocoa, if desired.

IN THE SAUCEPAN, combine the figs and other dried fruit with the marsala or sherry. Bring to a boil, then lower the heat and simmer for 3 or 4 minutes. Remove from the heat and stir in the olive oil or butter, honey, and orange peel. Cover the pan and set aside.

PREHEAT THE OVEN to 350°.

IN A LARGE mixing bowl, stir together the almonds, walnuts, chocolate chips, flour, bread crumbs, brown sugar, cinnamon, nutmeg, salt, pepper, and baking soda. Add the eggs and the fruit mixture and stir until all of the dry ingredients are moistened.

POUR THE BATTER into the prepared pan and bake for 1 hour to 1 hour and 10 minutes, until the cake begins to pull away from the sides of the pan and a knife inserted in the center tests clean. Cool on a rack for about 15 minutes before removing the sides of the springform pan or inverting the bundt cake onto a serving plate.

- **PREPARATION TIME:** 20 to 30 minutes
- **BAKING TIME:** 1 hour to 1 hour and 10 minutes
- **COOLING TIME:** 15 minutes
- **EQUIPMENT:** 10-inch springform pan or bundt cake pan, medium nonreactive saucepan

- **SERVES 16 TO 24**

WET INGREDIENTS

1½ cups dried figs, stemmed and coarsely chopped

1½ cups other dried fruit

¾ cup marsala or sherry

3 tablespoons olive oil or butter

½ cup honey

2 tablespoons freshly grated orange peel

DRY INGREDIENTS

½ cup whole almonds, toasted and coarsely chopped

½ cup whole walnuts, toasted and coarsely chopped (page 364)

½ cup semi-sweet chocolate chips

2 cups unbleached white pastry flour (page 361)

1 cup toasted bread crumbs

1 cup packed brown sugar

1 teaspoon ground cinnamon

½ teaspoon ground nutmeg

½ teaspoon salt

pinch of ground black pepper

2 teaspoons baking soda

2 eggs, lightly beaten

CHEESE CAKES CHEESE PIES AND PARFAITS

Cappuccino Cheesecake

Pumpkin Cheesecake

Raspberry Chocolate Cheesecake

Tangerine Cheesecake

Very Low-fat Vanilla Cheesecake

Tropical Tofu "Cheesecake"

Torta di Ricotta

Creamy Apricot Tart

Pizza di Grano

Yogurt Cream Cheese Parfaits

Banana Sour Cream Parfait

Cheesecakes, Cheese Pies, and Parfaits

WHOEVER INVENTED THE FIRST CHEESECAKE WAS CLEARLY A PERSON of culinary brilliance. This fortuitous combination of ingredients in all its variations has become synonymous with sensual pleasure. Our recipes include a range of cheesecakes from the traditional to the dairyless Tropical Tofu "Cheesecake" and a Very Low-Fat Vanilla Cheesecake. All share the smooth, velvety texture one expects and some have flavorings you may not have encountered in a cheesecake before: tangerine, pumpkin, cappuccino, and raspberry-chocolate. In this chapter, we also include a few other dairy-based desserts: no-bake Banana Sour Cream Parfait; reduced-fat Creamy Apricot Tart; sweet Pizza di Grano which is a traditional Italian Easter dessert; and Torta di Ricotta, an interesting hybrid between a cheesecake and conventional cake. A well-wrapped cheesecake can be kept for several days, and if you're cooking for a crowd, cheese-cakes can go a long way, since even small portions of this rich dessert are generous. Although it may be gilding the lily, cheesecakes can be accompanied with a dollop of any of the fruit sauces found on pages 303 to 311. We use low oven temperatures to achieve cheesecakes with smooth, creamy textures. So be sure to plan ahead so the cheesecake can have the oven all to itself. And remember that cheesecakes demand proper chilling before serving; eight hours or overnight is best.

Cappuccino Cheesecake

A luxuriously rich cheesecake that uses only reduced-fat dairy products! The long, slow baking time ensures a smooth, creamy texture. Trust us, your patience will be rewarded.

 COMBINE ALL OF the crust ingredients and press into the bottom of the springform pan. Preheat the oven to 300°.

USING AN ELECTRIC mixer, beat the Neufchâtel until it is whipped and fluffy. Beat in the cottage cheese, sour cream, sugar, egg, egg whites, cocoa, cinnamon, coffee granules, vanilla, salt, cornstarch, and liqueur, if using, until the batter is smooth.

POUR INTO THE prepared crust and bake until the cheesecake is set and the edges have pulled away from the pan (the center may still jiggle slightly), about 1 hour and 50 minutes. Chill thoroughly before serving.

VARIATIONS Substitute one of our other cheesecake crusts (pages 159, 160, 162).

FOR A VANILLA CHEESECAKE, omit the cocoa, cinnamon, coffee granules, and coffee liqueur; increase the vanilla to 2 teaspoons; and add 1 teaspoon of freshly grated lemon peel. We like to serve Vanilla Cheesecake with a fruit topping such as Cherry Sauce (page 304), Raspberry Sauce (page 310), Summer Berry Sauce (page 309), or Peach Melba Sauce (page 127).

- **PREPARATION TIME:** 20 minutes
- **BAKING TIME:** 1 hour and 50 minutes
- **CHILLING TIME:** about 1 hour
- **EQUIPMENT:** 9- or 10-inch springform pan, electric mixer

■ **SERVES 12**

SHREDDED WHEAT CRUST

- ¾ cup crumbled shredded wheat
- ¼ cup ground nuts
- 1 tablespoon sugar
- 1 tablespoon vegetable oil

CHEESECAKE

- 16 ounces Neufchâtel
- 2 cups 1% or 2% cottage cheese
- 1 cup reduced-fat sour cream
- 1⅓ cups sugar
- 1 egg
- 2 egg whites
- 3 tablespoons unsweetened cocoa powder
- ½ teaspoon ground cinnamon
- 3 tablespoons instant coffee granules
- 1 teaspoon pure vanilla extract
- ¼ teaspoon salt
- ¼ cup cornstarch
- 2 tablespoons coffee-flavored liqueur, such as Kahlúa (optional)

Pumpkin Cheesecake

Here is a rich and creamy pastel-colored confection with a ginger cookie crust. This cheesecake works equally well with cream cheese or Neufchâtel, but use regular sour cream, not reduced-fat, for best results.

■ **SERVES 12**

2 ounces ginger wafers (about 10) or 7 gingersnaps

1½ pounds cream cheese or Neufchâtel, at room temperature

1½ cups packed brown sugar

3 eggs

2 cups cooked pumpkin purée (15-ounce can)

1 cup sour cream

1 teaspoon ground cinnamon

½ teaspoon ground ginger

½ teaspoon ground nutmeg

½ teaspoon salt

1 teaspoon pure vanilla extract

 PREHEAT THE OVEN to 350°.

USING A ROLLING pin, finely crush the ginger wafers in a plastic bag or between two pieces of wax paper, or whirl them in a food processor until fine. Butter or oil the sides and bottom of the springform pan and dust it with the ginger cookie crumbs, allowing loose crumbs to settle on the bottom.

CREAM TOGETHER THE cream cheese or Neufchâtel and brown sugar until smooth. Add the eggs one at a time, beating well and scraping the sides of the bowl after each addition. Add the pumpkin, sour cream, cinnamon, ginger, nutmeg, salt, and vanilla and beat until well blended.

POUR THE FILLING into the pan and bake for about 1 hour, until the edge is firm and the center still jiggles. Allow to cool at room temperature and then chill well. Remove the sides of the springform pan just before serving.

■ **PREPARATION TIME:** 20 minutes
■ **BAKING TIME:** 1 hour
■ **CHILLING TIME:** at least 1 hour
■ **EQUIPMENT:** rolling pin, 9-inch springform pan, electric mixer

Raspberry Chocolate Cheesecake

Here we use frozen raspberry concentrate in place of the fresh fruit (dodging the pesky raspberry seed problem) and combine it with chocolate to make a cheesecake filling that is delightful with our almond crust. Cherry juice concentrates would also work well in this luscious cheesecake.

 PREHEAT THE OVEN to 300°. Oil the springform pan.

CRUSH THE AMARETTI in a food processor, or a few at a time in a blender, or with a rolling pin. Thoroughly combine the crumbs with the ground nuts and butter and pat into the bottom of the prepared pan.

IN A SMALL bowl, combine the juice concentrate and cornstarch. In a large bowl, beat the cream cheese with an electric mixer until softened and creamy. Add the sugar, eggs, sour cream, salt, and vanilla and beat until the batter is smooth. Stir 1 cup of the cheesecake batter into the dissolved cornstarch mixture. To the remaining cheesecake batter add the melted chocolate and blend well.

POUR THE CHOCOLATE batter into the springform pan. Next pour the raspberry-flavored batter in a circular pattern onto the batter in the pan. Use the spatula to swirl or slightly mix the raspberry batter into the cheesecake by making small, curving strokes. Mix only slightly for a marbled pattern.

BAKE FOR 1½ hours, or until the cheesecake has separated from the sides of the pan and the center is nearly set. Cool for 15 minutes, then drizzle on the melted chocolate glaze. Chill completely before serving. Run a knife dipped in water around the cake's outer edge to help release it from the pan.

- **PREPARATION TIME:** 20 minutes
- **BAKING TIME:** 1½ to 1¾ hours
- **CHILLING TIME:** at least 2 hours
- **EQUIPMENT:** 9 or 10-inch springform pan; food processor, blender, or rolling pin; electric mixer; small rubber spatula

- **SERVES 12**

AMARETTI CRUST

- 16 amaretti (page 354)
- ⅓ cup ground nuts, such as almonds, walnuts, or hazelnuts
- 3 tablespoons butter, at room temperature

FILLING

- ½ cup frozen raspberry or mixed berry juice concentrate, thawed
- 2 tablespoons cornstarch
- 24 ounces cream cheese
- 1 cup sugar
- 3 eggs
- 2 cups sour cream
- ½ teaspoon salt
- 1 teaspoon pure vanilla extract
- 3 ounces semi-sweet chocolate, melted

GLAZE (OPTIONAL)

- 1 ounce semi-sweet chocolate, melted

Tangerine Cheesecake

Tangerine peel and tangerine juice concentrate pack this cheesecake with vibrant flavor and imbue it with a golden orange tint. The brown sugar, oats, and nuts make a crust with just enough butter to hold it together—a welcome alternative to the usual graham cracker crust.

■ **SERVES 12**

NUTTY OAT CRUST

¼ cup packed brown sugar

2 tablespoons butter, melted

½ cup oats

½ cup nuts, such as almonds, walnuts, or pecans

FILLING

1½ pounds Neufchâtel or cream cheese, at room temperature

1 cup sugar

3 eggs

2 cups sour cream

2 teaspoons freshly grated tangerine or orange peel

1 cup tangerine juice concentrate (page 363)

2 teaspoons ground ginger

½ teaspoon salt

PREHEAT THE OVEN to 325°. Butter or oil the spring-form pan.

USING A FOOD processor or blender, whirl the crust ingredients until finely textured and crumbly. Evenly spread the mixture on the bottom of the pan.

BEAT THE NEUFCHÂTEL or cream cheese with an electric mixer or in a food processor until light and creamy, about 5 minutes. Add the sugar and continue to beat, stopping to scrape the sides of the bowl. Add the eggs one at a time, beating well after each addition. Add the sour cream, grated citrus peel, juice concentrate, ginger, and salt and beat until well blended.

POUR THE FILLING into the prepared pan. Bake for about 1½ hours, until the edges are firm, the top lightly browned, and the center begins to puff up. Chill completely before removing from the pan. Run a knife dipped in water around the cake's outer edge to help ensure a clean release from the pan.

VARIATIONS For Lime Cheesecake, replace the grated tangerine peel with lime peel and substitute ⅔ cup of limeade concentrate for the cup of tangerine juice concentrate.

FOR A VANILLA CHEESECAKE, omit the grated tangerine peel, tangerine juice concentrate, and ground ginger. Add 1 tablespoon of pure vanilla extract.

■ **PREPARATION TIME:** 20 to 25 minutes
■ **BAKING TIME:** about 1½ hours
■ **CHILLING TIME:** at least 6 hours or preferably overnight
■ **EQUIPMENT:** 9- or 10-inch springform pan, food processor or blender, electric mixer

Very Low-fat Vanilla Cheesecake

There are only 2 grams of fat in each serving of this sumptuous cheesecake. The secret is nonfat yogurt cheese, which is traditionally drained for 12 to 24 hours in advance. In case you can't wait a day for your cheesecake, the Quick Yogurt Cheese Method works fine in this recipe. The remaining preparation is really a snap. Garnish the cake with fresh berries, if you like.

PREHEAT THE OVEN to 300°. Butter or oil the spring-form pan.

USING A ROLLING pin, crush the graham crackers between two pieces of wax paper or in a plastic bag. Dust the pan with the crumbs, spreading any loose crumbs evenly over the bottom.

BRISKLY STIR THE yogurt cheese, flour, salt, vanilla, lemon peel, sugar, and eggs until well blended. Pour the batter into the pan and bake for about 1 hour and 20 minutes, until the edges are firm and the center jiggles slightly. Remove the cheesecake from the oven and chill well. Remove the sides of the springform pan just before serving.

- **PREPARATION TIME:** 20 minutes once the yogurt cheese is ready
- **BAKING TIME:** 1 hour and 20 minutes
- **CHILLING TIME:** at least 1 hour
- **EQUIPMENT:** 8- or 9-inch springform pan, rolling pin

PER 6.75 OZ SERVING: 198 CALS, 1.5 G TOT FAT, .9 G MONO FAT, .9 G SAT FAT, 91 MG CHOL

- **SERVES 10 TO 12**

2 whole graham crackers

3 to 4 cups nonfat vanilla-flavored yogurt cheese (page 366)*

¼ cup unbleached white flour

1 teaspoon salt

1 tablespoon pure vanilla extract

1 tablespoon freshly grated lemon peel (optional)

1 cup sugar

4 eggs, beaten

* If you make this cheesecake with plain nonfat yogurt, an additional ¼ cup of sugar will boost the flavor.

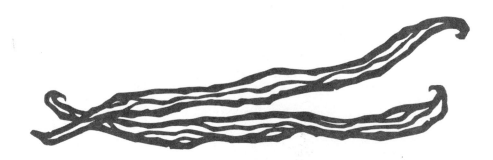

Tropical Tofu "Cheesecake"

Linda Dickinson has graced Moosewood since 1973 and is universally acknowledged as a superlative cook with a sure creative hand and a discriminating touch with flavorings. So the rest of us decided that LD (as we call her) should be the one to take on the daunting task of developing a really tasty tofu "cheesecake."

Even the most critical Moosewood taste testers and cheese lovers among us had to say that, for a tofu "cheesecake," this is mighty good. Silken tofu and coconut milk give this dairy-less cake a smooth, creamy texture. Bright with the tropical flavors of banana, pineapple, and lemon, the cake is a sure success.

To make this recipe with a blender rather than a food processor, you may need to work in small batches. For a vegan variation, simply replace the eggs in the filling with 3 tablespoons of cornstarch.

■ **SERVES 8 TO 12**

GRAHAM CRACKER COCONUT CRUST

- 6 whole graham crackers
- ¾ cup rolled oats
- ½ cup unsweetened grated coconut
- 2 tablespoons vegetable oil
- 2 tablespoons packed brown sugar
- ½ teaspoon freshly grated lemon peel
- 3 cups unsweetened crushed pineapple in juice (20-ounce can)

 PREHEAT THE OVEN to 350°.

COARSELY CRUMBLE THE graham crackers and combine them in a food processor or blender with the oats and coconut. Pulse to create fine crumbs. Add the oil, brown sugar, lemon peel, and 3 tablespoons of juice from the canned pineapple and process until thoroughly combined. The mixture should be moist enough to hold together when pressed. Drain the crushed pineapple and reserve it and the remaining juice separately. Lightly oil the springform pan and press the crust mixture evenly over the bottom. Bake for 15 minutes, until fragrant and golden. Set aside.

WHILE THE CRUST bakes, prepare the filling. Drain the silken tofu and discard the liquid. Combine all of the filling ingredients in the bowl of a food processor or in batches in a blender and whirl until smooth and creamy.

POUR THE FILLING evenly over the crust and bake for 50 to 60 minutes, until the center is fairly firm to the touch. A knife inserted in the center will *not* come out clean. Set the cake aside to cool.

FOR THE TOPPING, combine the cornstarch with 2 tablespoons of the reserved pineapple juice in the saucepan and stir to dissolve. Add the reserved crushed pineapple to the cornstarch mixture and bring to a boil, stirring frequently. Lower the heat and cook gently for a minute or two, until thickened. Remove from the heat and stir in sugar to taste. Set aside to cool.

WHEN BOTH THE cake and the topping are cool, spread the pineapple over the top of the "cheesecake." If desired, garnish with the toasted grated coconut. Chill for at least 3 hours before serving and overnight for the best flavor.

- PREPARATION TIME: 35 minutes
- BAKING TIME: 50 to 60 minutes
- CHILLING TIME: at least 3 hours
- EQUIPMENT: food processor (preferably) or blender, 9- or 10-inch springform pan, small nonreactive saucepan

FILLING

2 10-ounce cakes firm silken tofu*

2 ripe bananas (about ¾ cup mashed)

3 large eggs

1 cup unsweetened coconut milk (page 358)**

½ cup sugar

1 teaspoon pure vanilla extract

¼ teaspoon pure lemon extract

¼ teaspoon salt

1 teaspoon freshly grated lemon peel

TOPPING

1 tablespoon cornstarch

1 to 2 tablespoons sugar, or to taste

2 to 3 tablespoons toasted unsweetened grated coconut (optional) (page 358)

* *Mori-Nu brand silken tofu has a texture and mild flavor particularly suitable for this dessert.*

** *Reduced-fat coconut milk works fine here and will make the dish considerably lower in fat.*

Torta di Ricotta

Although this sturdy cake contains a significant amount of ricotta cheese, it is only distantly related to cheesecake and is not nearly as dense. The sides and bottom brown beautifully as the cake bakes, so a crust would be entirely out of place here.

■ **SERVES 10**

2 pounds ricotta cheese

1 cup sugar

4 eggs

1 tablespoon freshly grated lemon peel

1 cup unbleached white flour

½ teaspoon salt

1 teaspoon baking powder

1 cup raisins

 PREHEAT THE OVEN to 350°. Butter and flour the cake pan.

IN A FOOD processor, whirl the ricotta, sugar, eggs, and lemon peel until smooth, about 1 minute. Transfer the ricotta mixture to a bowl and stir in the flour, salt, and baking powder until well blended. Fold in the raisins.

POUR THE BATTER into the prepared pan and bake for 1 hour and 5 minutes, or until a knife inserted in the center comes out clean. Cool the cake in the pan for 10 minutes and then turn out onto a serving plate—or serve directly from the pan when completely cool.

■ **PREPARATION TIME:** 10 minutes
■ **BAKING TIME:** about 1 hour and 5 minutes
■ **COOLING TIME:** 10 minutes
■ **EQUIPMENT:** 9-inch round cake pan, food processor

Creamy Apricot Tart

This unusual hybrid of a recipe—not quite a tart, not quite a cheesecake—combines the richness of cheesecake with the creamy lightness of yogurt and oatmeal. Puréed canned apricots infuse it with a pale gold color and a hint of tartness.

If you make it in a food processor, this is a one bowl recipe.

 PREHEAT THE OVEN to 350°.

BREAK UP THE graham crackers or whole wheat crackers and place them in the food processor. Process to a fine crumb. Add the butter, sugar, and cinnamon and process for another 30 seconds. The mixture should clump when a small amount is pinched together. Press the crust evenly and firmly on the bottom and up the sides of the tart pan. Set aside.

IN THE FOOD processor, process the oats to the consistency of coarse flour. With the processor on, pour in the boiling water. The mixture will be very thick. Add the apricots, Neufchâtel or cream cheese, yogurt, sugar, and eggs and process until well blended. The batter will be somewhat thin. Pour it into the prepared crust and bake for 45 to 55 minutes, until the edges are set and the center jiggles only slightly.

WHILE THE TART cools, heat the apricot preserves, stirring constantly until thin enough to spread. Glaze the top of the tart with the heated preserves. Serve at room temperature or chilled.

- **PREPARATION TIME:** 20 minutes
- **BAKING TIME:** 45 to 55 minutes
- **EQUIPMENT:** food processor, 9-inch pie or tart pan (preferably with fluted edges)

- **SERVES 8**

GRAHAM CRACKER BUTTER CRUST

- 6 graham crackers (about 1 cup graham cracker crumbs) or 12 whole wheat crackers*
- 2 tablespoons butter, softened or melted
- 1 tablespoon sugar
- pinch of ground cinnamon

FILLING

- 1/3 to 1/2 cup oats
- 1/2 cup boiling water
- 1 cup drained canned apricots
- 8 ounces Neufchâtel or cream cheese
- 1/2 cup nonfat vanilla yogurt
- 1/2 cup sugar
- 2 eggs
- 1/4 cup apricot preserves

* We recommend Carr's whole wheat crackers, which are sweet, tasty, and have no preservatives or hydrogenated oils.

Pizza di Grano

For centuries, special dishes containing grains, seeds, or eggs, symbolizing fertility, rebirth, and renewal, have been prepared in the springtime. One of the most beloved of these is Pizza di Grano, also known as Pastiera or Easter Pie, a marvelous citrus-flavored ricotta pie, nubbly with grain.

This dessert, which originated in Naples, is also baked every year in Brooklyn, Providence, and many other Italian-American settlements. In Moosewood cook Tony Del Plato's old neighborhood, it was an annual rivalry to see which of the women on the block could produce the very best Easter pie. Giuseppa Del Plato, Tony's mom, always made his favorite.

Commercially prepared hulled soft wheat, called Gran Pastiera, is available in cans at Italian groceries and it is seasonally available in many large supermarkets. This is a nice convenience, as it saves you the time of an overnight soaking of the wheat; however, it is not at all difficult to soak the grain yourself. Soft, white-hulled winter wheatberries, sometimes called shelled wheat, are usually available in health food stores. The soaked grain freezes well, so we often prepare extra to be used another time.

Serve Pizza di Grano in small wedges with coffee or an Italian dessert wine. Garnish, if desired, with a tangy fresh fruit, such as green grapes. Store refrigerated, but return to room temperature before serving.

■ **SERVES AT LEAST 12**

WHEATBERRIES

16 ounces canned Gran Pastiera or 2 cups soaked wheatberries (see Note)

1 cup milk

¼ cup sugar

pinch of ground cinnamon

2 strips of fresh lemon peel (½ inch wide)

COMBINE THE GRAN Pastiera or soaked wheatberries with the milk, sugar, cinnamon, and strips of lemon peel in a saucepan. Bring to a boil, lower the heat, and simmer, stirring frequently, for 20 to 30 minutes, until most of the milk has been absorbed and the grain is tender. Remove and discard the lemon peel strips and refrigerate the cooked wheatberries.

WHILE THE GRAIN cooks, prepare the pastry. Combine the flour, sugar, and salt in a bowl and cut in the butter with a pastry cutter or two knives until the mixture resembles coarse meal. Separate one of the eggs and set aside the yolk. In a separate bowl, lightly beat the whole egg, the egg white, and the ice water or milk. With a fork, stir the egg mixture into the flour until the dough holds together. Shape into two balls, one a bit larger than the other. Cover and refrigerate.

WITH AN ELECTRIC mixer or blender, whip the ricotta, sugar, eggs, lemon peel, orange peel, salt, cinnamon, orange flavoring, and vanilla until smooth. When the cooked wheatberry mixture has cooled, stir it into the whipped ricotta mixture.

TO ASSEMBLE THE pie, preheat the oven to 350°. On a lightly floured surface, roll the larger ball of dough into a circle that is a bit larger than the pie pan. Fit the dough into the pan and trim the excess. Pour in the filling. Roll the remaining ball of dough into a 10-inch circle and cut it into wide strips. Arrange the strips in a lattice over the filling and crimp the outside edge of the pastry. Gently brush with the reserved egg yolk.

BAKE FOR 45 to 55 minutes, until the pastry is golden and the filling is set. Cool on a rack and serve at room temperature.

NOTE To soak enough dry hulled, soft, white wheat-berries for one pie, place ½ cup of the berries in a large heatproof bowl and add 2 cups of boiling water. Cover and set aside overnight at room temperature. Drain and rinse with fresh water.

VARIATION To make a version with rice, soak ½ cup of white rice in 2 cups of water overnight. Cover and simmer the rice for 20 minutes following the instructions for wheatberries above. This should yield 2 cups of cooked rice.

- PREPARATION TIME: 1¼ hours
- BAKING TIME: 45 to 55 minutes
- EQUIPMENT: saucepan, electric mixer or blender, 10-inch pie pan

PASTRY

2 cups unbleached white pastry flour (page 361)

½ cup sugar

pinch of salt

½ cup butter

2 eggs

1 tablespoon ice water or milk

FILLING

16 ounces ricotta cheese

1 cup sugar

4 eggs

freshly grated peel of 2 lemons

freshly grated peel of 1 orange

½ teaspoon salt

pinch of ground cinnamon

2 tablespoons orange-flavored liqueur or orange flower water, or 1 teaspoon pure orange extract

1 teaspoon pure vanilla extract

Yogurt Cream Cheese Parfaits

This is a wonderful, no-bake summer dessert to make when fresh fruits and berries are abundant, although frozen or canned fruit will also work. The parfaits are like little individual cheesecakes, with layers of graham cracker crumbs, sweetened yogurt cheese and cream cheese, and a fruit glaze. They should be served thoroughly chilled and garnished with fresh fruit.

■ **SERVES 6**

YOGURT CHEESE LAYER

2 cups yogurt cheese (page 366)

8 ounces Neufchâtel or cream cheese, at room temperature

1 tablespoon pure vanilla extract

¼ cup sugar

FRUIT GLAZE LAYER

2 cups prepared fruit (see Note)

½ cup sugar

2 tablespoons cornstarch dissolved in ⅓ cup fruit juice or water

GRAHAM CRACKER CRUMB LAYER

½ cup crushed graham crackers (about 6 crackers)

2 tablespoons butter, melted

1 tablespoon pure maple syrup or honey, or to taste

FOR THE YOGURT cheese layer, whirl the yogurt cheese, Neufchâtel or cream cheese, vanilla, and sugar in a food processor or a blender, or beat by hand or with an electric mixer, until the mixture is creamy and free of lumps. Set aside.

TO PREPARE THE fruit glaze, combine the prepared fruit, sugar, and cornstarch dissolved in fruit juice or water in the saucepan. Bring to a boil, then lower the heat and simmer, stirring constantly, until the sauce becomes thick and clear. Set aside.

COMBINE THE CRUSHED graham crackers, melted butter, and maple syrup or honey in a small bowl and mix well.

TO ASSEMBLE THE parfaits, divide the graham cracker mixture equally among the parfait glasses, custard cups, or wine glasses. Distribute half of the yogurt cheese mixture among the glasses. Spoon half of the fruit mixture into the glasses. Repeat the yogurt cheese and fruit layers. Chill thoroughly, for about 4 hours or overnight.

SERVE CHILLED.

NOTE By prepared fruit we mean washed, picked over, peeled, seeded, and/or sliced. We suggest peaches, strawberries, plums, blueberries, blackberries, and/or raspberries.

■ **PREPARATION TIME:** 30 minutes with prepared yogurt cheese
■ **CHILLING TIME:** 4 hours
■ **EQUIPMENT:** food processor, blender, or electric mixer; heavy nonreactive saucepan; six 8-ounce parfait glasses, custard cups, or wine glasses

Banana Sour Cream Parfait

For those who are fond of bananas and sour cream, this rich and elegant inspiration goes a few giant steps further. The creamy, slightly tart banana "pudding" complements the sweet vanilla cookie crumb layers for an easy-to-assemble dessert.

 COMBINE THE COOKIE crumbs with the melted butter and honey or maple syrup. Set aside 2 tablespoons of the crumb mixture and divide the rest equally among the glasses or custard cups.

USING AN ELECTRIC mixer, beat the Neufchâtel until fluffy. Add the sour cream, vanilla, mashed bananas, sugar, and lemon juice and beat until smooth (see Note). Spoon evenly into the prepared custard cups. Sprinkle the reserved crumb mixture over the parfaits. Cover with plastic wrap and chill for at least 3 hours. Garnish with sliced bananas just before serving.

 NOTE You can also purée all of the parfait filling ingredients in the bowl of a food processor, if you prefer.

VARIATION Layer sliced strawberries in the middle of the parfait and garnish with strawberry and banana slices.

- **PREPARATION TIME:** 15 minutes
- **CHILLING TIME:** 3 hours
- **EQUIPMENT:** rolling pin, 6 parfait glasses or 8-ounce custard cups, electric mixer or food processor

■ **SERVES 6**

CRUMB LAYER

½ cup vanilla wafer crumbs*

2 tablespoons butter, melted

1 tablespoon honey or pure maple syrup

PARFAIT FILLING

8 ounces Neufchâtel

2 cups nonfat sour cream

1 teaspoon pure vanilla extract

2 ripe bananas, mashed (about 1 cup)

½ cup sugar

1 tablespoon fresh lemon juice

a few banana slices

* *We recommend Frookie brand, which is made with natural ingredients. To make crumbs neatly and easily, place the vanilla wafers in a resealable plastic bag and crush them with a rolling pin.*

COOKIES AND BARS

Cookies and Bars

COOKIES AND BARS ARE PERHAPS MORE APPRECIATED ON AN EVERYDAY basis than any other dessert. Who wouldn't want a cookie? We can easily imagine starting a day with Italian Sesame Cookies dunked in morning coffee, enjoying a Chocolate Cranberry Crunch for a nice afternoon snack, and finishing an evening meal with fresh fruit served with Pistachio Shortbread. Cookies are very much an American culinary institution. The word "cookie" derives from the Dutch *Koekje,* meaning "little cake," and was first seen in print during the 1700s in New York City, formerly a Dutch colony. While other countries' culinary traditions certainly encompass cookies, biscuits, and similar treats, North Americans have become passionate cookie lovers, supporting gourmet cookie shops and long supermarket aisles filled with packaged cookies. Of course there's no contest between homemade cookies and store-bought fare. Flavor, aroma, texture, and delicacy are always compromised with time, packaging, and low-quality ingredients. Many commercially produced cookies are loaded with ingredients that seem to require a chemistry degree to interpret. For many of us, helping to make cookies or brownies is a memorable childhood kitchen experience, and it is always a sure bet for engaging children in creative activity. Our recipes include drop, bar, rolled-out, twice-baked, and hand-formed cookies. Drop cookies are made with a soft dough that is "dropped" by spoonfuls onto baking sheets. Their quick and easy preparation make them perfect for those who are time-pressed or impatient. Macaroons and meringues are simple and gratifying drop cookies, as are Cowboy Cookies—our favorite version of chocolate chip cookies. Bar cookies are easy to prepare and require no juggling of multiple baking sheets in and out of the oven. We have unusual Spiced Pumpkin Squares, sumptuous Lime Pecan Bars that could be served at a dinner party, and two delicious brownies—Hazelnut Brownies and Black and White Brownies. (Our recipe for beloved Moosewood Fudge Brownies is in the Moosewood Classics chapter.) Rolled-out cookies are worth the extra time and effort because of their distinctively crisp yet delicate texture and their buttery taste. Cut into fanciful shapes and forms, Chocolate Sugar Cookies and Gingerbread Cookies can be as much fun to make as they are to eat. Jammy Cake Shortbread and Regina's Ruggelach are rolled cookies that we usually make in quantity to have on hand in the cookie jar or to give as presents. We offer three variations of our basic butter cookie, a quintessentially rich, delicately flavored cookie whose dough is chilled for ease in handling. Small chunks of the dough can be rolled between the palms and easily made into Jam Drops, or the dough can be formed into a jelly roll and sliced into Butternut Cookies (a simple refrigerator cookie made with nuts) or the fancier two-tone Pinwheel Cookies (made with a combo of plain and chocolate doughs). Other cookies can also be hand-formed or pressed into shape, like our crisp Shortbreads, Cornmeal Cookies, and buttery 110th Street Walnut Crescents. Guava Pinwheels are unusual, picturesque, and really fast to make. Biscotti are twice-baked cookies that are delightfully crunchy and quite a bit lower in fat than most other cookies. They are good keepers and are nice served with coffee, tea, or dessert wine—handy treats when unexpected visitors arrive. Savvy cooks make extra dough or batches of baked cookies and bars to keep in the freezer. Baked cookies or raw dough can be frozen for up to 9 months. Unwrap frozen baked cookies or bars and thaw at room temperature for about 10 minutes, or heat briefly in a 300° oven. Frozen cookie dough for drop cookies or bars needs to be thawed only until it is soft enough to be spooned out. For easy handling of rolled cookie dough, thaw it overnight in the refrigerator. Cookies and bars are portable—good for lunch boxes, picnic baskets, and snacks when traveling. Holiday or gift cookies sent through the mail should be carefully packed in tins or boxes surrounded with materials to cushion the cookies.

Butterscotch Oatmeal Lace Crisps

These crisp wafer cookies with lacy, delicate edges must be made small and be removed from the baking sheet promptly. Bake them one sheet at a time. If they stay on the sheet too long, they'll crumble when you try to remove them. Clean any accumulated caramelized sugar and butter from your spatula as you go to ensure a clean sweep under these delicate little cookies.

■ **YIELDS 48**

½ cup butter,
    at room temperature

½ cup packed
    brown sugar

1 egg

1 teaspoon pure
    vanilla extract

¼ teaspoon salt

1 tablespoon
    cornstarch

1½ cups rolled oats

PREHEAT THE OVEN to 350°. Butter or oil the baking sheets.

IN A BOWL, cream together the butter and brown sugar until light. Add the egg and beat well. Stir in the vanilla, salt, and cornstarch. Add the oats and mix well. The batter will be moist.

DROP BATTER ONTO a baking sheet by teaspoonfuls about 3 inches apart. Bake for 6 to 10 minutes, until the cookies are golden. Let the cookies cool on the sheet for 2 or 3 minutes, then with the spatula, carefully remove them to a dry, smooth, flat surface or wax paper to cool completely. While the first batch bakes, prepare the second baking sheet, so it's ready to put into the oven when the first batch comes out. This recipe makes four batches of 2-inch cookies.

STORE COOLED COOKIES in layers separated by wax paper in an airtight container.

VARIATIONS Add 1 teaspoon of ground cinnamon and ⅓ cup of finely chopped dried cranberries, dried tart cherries, currants, or raisins.

ADD ½ CUP of finely ground almonds, ½ teaspoon of pure almond extract, and an additional ¼ teaspoon of salt.

- **PREPARATION TIME:** 10 minutes
- **BAKING TIME:** 6 to 10 minutes per batch
- **EQUIPMENT:** baking sheets, thin-bladed spatula

110th Street Walnut Crescents

To omorfo fegari! *Even in its most subtle and sly shape, the moon is a fascinating object. These Greek-style cookies mirror that country's love affair with the heavenly bodies.*

Moosewood's Penny Condon has named these treats for 110th Street in New York City, where she visits her friend Gavrielle Levine—and the pastry shop across the street.

■ **YIELDS 60**

1 cup butter, softened

1 cup packed finely ground walnuts

1 teaspoon pure vanilla extract

1 cup confectioners' sugar

pinch of salt

2 cups unbleached white flour, plus extra flour for rolling

confectioners' sugar for dusting

 WITH AN ELECTRIC mixer, cream together the butter and ground walnuts. Beat in the vanilla. On low speed, slowly add the confectioners' sugar, salt, and flour and beat until well blended. Scrape the dough onto a sheet of wax paper or plastic wrap, flatten, cover, and chill until firm, about 3 hours.

WHEN YOU'RE READY to bake the crescents, preheat the oven to 350° and lightly butter two baking sheets.

DIVIDE THE DOUGH into two parts. Because this dough softens quickly as it warms, keep the part you're not using in the refrigerator until you're ready to roll it out. Roll each half of the dough between two pieces of wax paper into a 9 × 15-inch rectangle. Cut the rectangle into fifteen 3-inch squares and cut each square diagonally into two triangles. Roll and pinch each triangle into a crescent shape. Place each crescent on a baking sheet.

BAKE THE CRESCENTS for 10 to 12 minutes, until the edges are golden brown. Cool. Using a sieve, dust the crescents liberally with confectioners' sugar. Store in a tightly covered container.

NOTE If you like, instead of rolling out the dough, simply make ¾-inch balls and form them into crescents.

■ **PREPARATION TIME:** 10 minutes
■ **BAKING TIME:** 10 to 12 minutes per batch
■ **CHILLING TIME:** 3 hours
■ **EQUIPMENT:** electric mixer, wax paper or plastic wrap, 2 baking sheets, rolling pin

Guava Pinwheels

These pretty pastries filled with guava paste (see Note) are delicate, easily prepared, and not too sweet. Served with hot coffee or tea, they are a perfect little something with which to end a meal. Stored in a covered container, Guava Pinwheels will keep for about a week.

PREHEAT THE OVEN to 400°.

WORKING GENTLY BUT quickly, unfold the puff pastry sheet. If you don't handle it too much and your counter is dry, you can ignore the recommendations on the box and dispense with the floured board and the rolling pin. Spread the guava paste evenly on the pastry sheet.

CURL THE TWO longer edges up and roll them inward like jelly rolls to meet in the middle. Dip your fingers in water and lightly dampen the pastry between the two rolls; then gently but firmly press the two rolls together along the seam. Using a sharp, thin knife, cut the joined rolls crosswise into ½-inch-thick heart-shaped slices.

ARRANGE THE SLICES cut side down on the unoiled baking sheet and bake for about 20 minutes, until the pastries are puffed and golden. Using a spatula, transfer the pinwheels to a plate to cool.

NOTE Guava paste is an intensely flavored Latin American concoction, denser and more flavorful than jam or jelly. We especially like Goya brand guava paste, which is made in Brazil. Guava paste served with cream cheese on crackers is a classic Mexican dessert. We substitute guava paste for jelly in peanut butter-and-jelly sandwiches and also enjoy it on bread for breakfast.

- **PREPARATION TIME:** 20 minutes
- **BAKING TIME:** 20 minutes
- **EQUIPMENT:** baking sheet

■ **SERVES 8**

1 eight-ounce sheet commercially prepared puff pastry (page 365), defrosted*

½ cup guava paste (4 ounces), at room temperature

* Frozen puff pastry defrosts in about 20 minutes. Open the box and separate the two sheets.

Butter Cookies Three Ways

A simple butter cookie recipe can be the starting point for many delightful creations. Ours have a light, delicate texture and the unmistakable richness of butter.

The basic cookie dough is great baked just as it is or topped with a whole or half nut, a few chocolate chips, or sprinkling of sugar just before baking. However, we have provided directions for three of our favorite variations: Butternut Cookies, Jam Drops, and Pinwheel Cookies.

The dough can be refrigerated for up to 3 days. Keep some of it on hand in the freezer; it will keep for up to 6 months. Thaw frozen dough in the refrigerator for a day before using.

■ **YIELDS 60 TO 72**

BASIC COOKIE DOUGH

1½ cups unsalted butter, at room temperature*

1 cup sugar

2 egg yolks

2 teaspoons pure vanilla extract

3 cups unbleached white flour

½ teaspoon salt

* Good, fresh butter has a delicate but noticeably delicious fragrance. We use sweet unsalted butter for the finest flavor. Try a few brands to find the best one in your area. It's good to soften the butter at room temperature for a couple of hours before beginning the recipe—especially if you plan to mix by hand.

WITH A WOODEN spoon or an electric mixer, cream the butter until light. Beat in the sugar, adding a little at a time, until well blended. Beat in the egg yolks one at a time, then add the vanilla and beat until smooth. Gradually add the flour and salt, mixing just until the dough is uniformly smooth. The dough is now ready to chill, shape, and bake or freeze or flavor for one of the three variations below.

FOR BUTTERNUT COOKIES, stir the chopped nuts into the dough. Form the dough into two 6-inch-long cylindrical logs about 2 inches in diameter. Wrap the logs in plastic and chill for at least 2 hours. The dough needs to be firm enough to hold its shape when sliced.

AT THE END of the chilling time, preheat the oven to 350°.

USING A SHARP knife, slice the logs into ¼-inch-thick cookies and place them about an inch apart on unoiled baking sheets. Bake for 15 to 20 minutes, until the edges of the cookies are lightly golden. Cool on the baking sheets for a few minutes, then transfer to racks to finish cooling.

FOR JAM DROPS, cover and refrigerate the dough for 1 hour. When it is firm, preheat the oven to 350°.

GENTLY ROLL TEASPOONFULS of the dough between your palms to form 1-inch balls. It is best not to overhandle the dough. Place the balls about 1½ inches apart on lightly oiled baking sheets. With your fingertip, make an indentation in the center of each ball. Fill each hollow with a scant ¼ teaspoon of fruit preserves. Bake the cookies for 15 to 20 minutes, until the edges are lightly golden. Cool on the baking sheets for a few minutes, then transfer to racks to cool completely.

FOR PINWHEEL COOKIES, gently melt the chocolate with the sugar and cinnamon in a double boiler. Remove half of the dough from the bowl and set aside. Add the melted chocolate to the bowl and stir to make an evenly colored brown dough. Cut both the dark (chocolate) and the light (vanilla) balls of dough into halves. Wrap each piece in plastic and flatten into a ½-inch-thick disk. Chill for at least 1 hour.

ON FOUR LIGHTLY floured pieces of wax paper, roll the disks into 12-inch squares. Flip each dark square onto a light square, peel off the wax paper, and press lightly with the rolling pin to seal the two dough layers together. You will have two double-layered 12-inch squares. (If the dough is already soft and sticky, refrigerate it for 10 minutes.) Roll up each square of dough, jelly roll fashion, to form two logs, removing the wax paper as you roll. Wrap in plastic and chill for at least 1½ hours, until the dough is firm enough to hold its shape when sliced.

WHEN THE DOUGH is firm, preheat the oven to 350°.

USING A SHARP knife, slice the logs into ¼-inch-thick cookies and place them an inch apart on lightly oiled baking sheets. Bake until the edges of the cookies are lightly golden, about 15 minutes. Cool on the baking sheets for a few minutes, then transfer to racks to cool completely.

- **PREPARATION TIME:** 15 to 20 minutes
- **BAKING TIME:** 15 to 20 minutes per batch
- **CHILLING TIME:** about 1 to 2 hours
- **EQUIPMENT:** electric mixer (optional), double boiler (page 370), baking sheets

BUTTERNUT COOKIES
½ cup finely chopped nuts

JAM DROPS
½ cup preserves or fruit spread

PINWHEEL COOKIES
2 ounces unsweetened baking chocolate

¼ cup sugar

½ teaspoon ground cinnamon

Chocolate Sugar Cookies

These crisp chocolate wafers may be rolled out and cut into shapes suitable for any festivity. Try using them to make ice cream sandwiches (page 260). The dough may be prepared a few days in advance and then baked at the last minute. Store the cookies in a tin with a tight-fitting lid to keep them fresh.

■ **YIELDS 18**

½ cup butter, softened

¾ cup sugar

1 large egg

1 teaspoon pure vanilla extract

1½ cups unbleached white pastry flour (page 361)

⅓ cup unsweetened cocoa powder

½ teaspoon baking powder

¼ teaspoon salt

confectioners' sugar for sprinkling

IN A MEDIUM bowl, cream the butter and sugar together until smooth. Beat in the egg and vanilla until light. Sift together the flour, cocoa, baking powder, and salt. Stir the dry ingredients into the butter mixture and form into a thick dough. If the dough is soft, wrap it in plastic and chill for ½ hour.

PREHEAT THE OVEN to 375° and butter the baking sheet.

ON A LIGHTLY floured surface, roll out the dough to about a ¼-inch thickness and cut into shapes. Place the cookies on the prepared baking sheet, sprinkle with confectioners' sugar, and bake for 15 to 20 minutes, until the centers of the cookies are firm. With a spatula, transfer the cookies to a cooling rack.

■ **PREPARATION TIME:** 20 minutes
■ **BAKING TIME:** 15 to 20 minutes per batch
■ **EQUIPMENT:** baking sheet, rolling pin, cookie cutters, spatula

Cornmeal Cookies

We developed this plain, crumbly cookie with the golden warmth of sweet corn for a celebration at the American Indian Program at Cornell University. Either pastry flour or all-purpose flour can be used. Pastry flour yields a thinner, crisper cookie and all-purpose flour a denser one. Any type of cornmeal will do, but we especially like to combine a finely ground yellow cornmeal, for color, with a coarsely ground cornmeal, for crunch.

 PREHEAT THE OVEN to 325°.

USING AN ELECTRIC mixer, cream together the butter and sugar. Add the salt, vanilla, egg, and lemon peel and beat well. Add the flour and cornmeal, and mix until smooth.

IN A FLAT-BOTTOMED bowl or on a plate, combine the topping ingredients and set aside. Roll the dough into 1-inch balls and place them on unoiled baking sheets about 2 inches apart. When the sheets are filled, dip a flat-bottomed glass in the topping mixture and press down on each ball of dough, flattening it slightly, to about 1½ inches in diameter (dip the glass in the topping mixture each time).

BAKE FOR ABOUT 20 minutes, until the cookies are lightly browned around the edges. Transfer the cookies to a wire rack to cool. Store in an airtight container.

 VARIATIONS Stir 1 cup of dried cranberries into the dough before forming into balls.

To make larger, crisp cookies for ice cream sandwiches, form the dough into 1½-inch balls and flatten them to about 3 inches in diameter. The resulting 4-inch cookies are good filled with a tart sorbet or frozen yogurt, such as raspberry or lemon.

- **PREPARATION TIME:** 20 to 25 minutes
- **BAKING TIME:** 20 minutes per batch
- **EQUIPMENT:** electric mixer, baking sheets

- **YIELDS 54 TO 60**

COOKIE DOUGH

- 1 cup butter, at room temperature
- 1 cup sugar
- ½ teaspoon salt
- 1 teaspoon pure vanilla extract
- 1 egg
- finely grated peel of 1 lemon (about 1 tablespoon)
- 1½ cups unbleached white flour
- 1½ cups cornmeal

TOPPING

- 3 to 4 tablespoons cornmeal
- 3 to 4 tablespoons sugar

Cowboy Cookies

We're not sure why these are called Cowboy Cookies—perhaps for their homespun, sturdy, trail-mix qualities—but they may just be the best of the chocolate chip cookie genre. Moosewood sisters Susan Harville and Nancy Lazarus have made them since childhood to rave reviews and have given out the recipe over the years like a pyramiding chain letter. You may have it already. If not, you'll be glad you do now.

Cowboy Cookies appeal to a wide range of people. We sent an enormous box of them to Moosewood cook Tony Del Plato while he was working with Navajo and Hopi people in Big Mountain, Arizona. By return post we received a brief and to-the-point message: "Send more cowboys, please. We love to eat them up. Signed, the Indians."

■ **YIELDS ABOUT 84**

- 1 cup butter, at room temperature
- ½ cup sugar
- ½ cup packed brown sugar
- 2 large eggs
- 1 teaspoon pure vanilla extract
- 2 cups unbleached white pastry flour (page 361)
- ½ teaspoon salt
- 1 teaspoon baking soda
- ½ teaspoon baking powder
- 2 cups rolled oats
- 12 ounces semi-sweet chocolate chips (about 1½ cups)

 PREHEAT THE OVEN to 350°.

IN A LARGE bowl, thoroughly cream the butter, sugar, and brown sugar with an electric mixer. Add the eggs and vanilla and beat well. In a separate bowl, combine the flour, salt, baking soda, and baking powder. Add the dry ingredients to the butter and sugar mixture and blend well. Mix in the oats. Using a large spoon or your hands, fold in the chocolate chips, and the raisins and walnuts, if using. The dough will be fairly stiff.

ON UNOILED BAKING sheets, drop generous rounded teaspoonfuls of dough about 4 inches apart. Bake for about 12 minutes, until golden. Cool completely before storing in a sealed container.

 VARIATION Add 1 cup of raisins and/or ½ cup of coarsely chopped toasted walnuts.

■ **PREPARATION TIME: 20 to 25 minutes**
■ **BAKING TIME: about 12 minutes per batch**
■ **EQUIPMENT: electric mixer, baking sheets**

Ginger Brandy Cookies

This is a wonderful, snappy holiday cookie—like an old-fashioned sugar cookie all jazzed up.

WITH AN ELECTRIC mixer or food processor, cream together the butter and ⅔ cup of the sugar until light and well blended. Add the molasses and egg and beat well. In a separate bowl, sift together the flour, salt, baking soda, ginger, cinnamon, and cloves. Alternate adding the dry ingredients and the brandy to the wet ingredients, stirring well after each addition. Form the dough into a ball and chill for 30 minutes.

PREHEAT THE OVEN to 350°. Spray or oil the baking sheets.

SPREAD THE TOPPING sugar on a plate. Shape the dough into 1-inch balls, roll each ball in sugar, and place on the baking sheets. Bake for about 12 minutes, until just firm and a bit crisp around the edges. Remove the cookies to a rack and let cool.

- **PREPARATION TIME:** 20 minutes
- **BAKING TIME:** about 12 minutes
- **CHILLING TIME:** 30 minutes
- **EQUIPMENT:** electric mixer or food processor, baking sheets

■ **YIELDS 48**

DOUGH

- ½ cup butter, at room temperature
- ⅔ cup sugar
- ¼ cup unsulphured molasses
- 1 egg
- 2 cups unbleached white flour
- pinch of salt
- 1 teaspoon baking soda
- 1 tablespoon ground ginger
- 2 teaspoons ground cinnamon
- ¼ teaspoon ground cloves
- 2 tablespoons brandy

TOPPING

- 3 tablespoons confectioners' sugar

Gingerbread Cookies

To visit Moosewood's Sara Robbins at her home, you travel through a lovely rural landscape, down a narrow dirt road, past a field of contented cows and a little round pond, until you come to a pretty cottage surrounded by hollyhocks. As you open the door, you are likely to be greeted by wonderful baking aromas.

You may doubt it's as easy as Sara makes it look to whip up cookies in minutes without a second thought, but, in fact, her unfussy recipes are always sturdy and reliable. This dark, spicy dough makes perfect gingerbread boys and girls (or bears and ghouls!) or, rolled out thinly, great gingersnaps. Note that the cayenne may be a tad too spicy for some junior palates.

■ YIELDS 24 TO 36

2½ cups unbleached white flour

1 tablespoon unsweetened cocoa powder

pinch of salt

½ teaspoon baking soda

4 teaspoons ground ginger

2 teaspoons ground cinnamon

1 teaspoon ground allspice

1 teaspoon ground nutmeg

1 teaspoon ground cloves

pinch of cayenne

½ cup butter, softened

½ cup sugar

½ cup unsulphured molasses

1 egg

SIFT TOGETHER THE flour, cocoa, salt, baking soda, ginger, cinnamon, allspice, nutmeg, cloves, and cayenne. In a separate bowl, cream together the butter and sugar with an electric mixer until light. Beat in the molasses and egg. Stir in the dry ingredients. With floured hands, push the dough from the sides to the middle of the bowl to form a ball that holds together. Cut the dough in half. Place one half on top of the other and push down. Repeat three or four times until all of the flour mixture is incorporated and the dough forms a ball. Wrap the dough in plastic and chill for 30 minutes.

PREHEAT THE OVEN to 350°. Spray or oil the baking sheets.

ON A LIGHTLY floured surface, roll out the dough ¼ inch thick. Using cookie cutters or the rim of a glass, cut out the cookies. Use a spatula to transfer the cookies to the baking sheets. Bake for 10 to 12 minutes, until set and lightly browned at the edges. Cool on a rack and serve.

■ **PREPARATION TIME:** 20 minutes
■ **BAKING TIME:** 10 to 12 minutes per batch
■ **CHILLING TIME:** 30 minutes
■ **EQUIPMENT:** baking sheets, electric mixer, rolling pin, cookie cutters

Katie's Orange Cookies

A light orange flavor and a glossy chocolate glaze make these butter cookies very appealing. Whether you brush the dark glaze artfully over each cookie to create a crescent moon shape or quickly swipe the glaze straight over half of each one, they are quite smart-looking.

Pastry flour yields a crisper, more delicate cookie, while all-purpose flour makes for a slightly heavier, sturdier one. Use pastry flour for cookies you'll serve that afternoon at a tea party and all-purpose flour for cookies you expect to pack into lunch boxes or send in the mail to a lucky someone. Well wrapped in plastic, these cookies will keep for at least a week.

 PREHEAT THE OVEN to 350°.

USING AN ELECTRIC mixer, cream together the butter and sugar until light. Add the vanilla or orange extract, egg, salt, and grated orange peel and mix well. Sprinkle in the baking powder and flour and beat on low speed until thoroughly blended. At this point, if you like, the dough can be refrigerated and then later shaped into cookies and baked.

FORM THE DOUGH into 1-inch balls and place them about 3 inches apart on unoiled baking sheets. For each ball of dough, dip a flat-bottomed glass into the confectioners' sugar and press the dough into a flat, ¼-inch-thick wafer.

BAKE FOR 10 to 15 minutes, until the edges of the cookies are golden brown. Remove with a spatula and cool on racks.

FOR THE GLAZE, combine the butter, corn syrup, and chocolate in the saucepan. Cook on low heat, stirring until melted and smooth. Remove from the heat. Using a pastry brush, coat about half of the top of each cookie with the chocolate glaze. Cool until the glaze has hardened, about 20 minutes.

- **PREPARATION TIME:** 20 minutes
- **BAKING TIME:** 10 to 15 minutes per batch
- **COOLING TIME:** 20 minutes
- **EQUIPMENT:** electric mixer, baking sheets, small saucepan, pastry brush

■ **YIELDS 40**

¾ cup butter, at room temperature

1 cup sugar

1 teaspoon pure vanilla or orange extract

1 large egg

½ teaspoon salt

2 tablespoons freshly grated orange peel

1 teaspoon baking powder

2 cups unbleached white flour

2 tablespoons confectioners' sugar for topping

CHOCOLATE GLAZE

2 tablespoons butter

1 tablespoon light corn syrup

3 ounces semi-sweet chocolate

Peanut Butter Cookies

A throwback to the '50s and a perennial favorite with all ages, these cookies are versatile and chewy—perfect for lunch boxes, snacks, late-night treats, and a host of variations. Peanut Butter Cookies are also a good choice for ice cream sandwiches (page 260).

■ **YIELDS 48**

1 cup peanut butter

1 cup butter, at room temperature

2 cups packed brown sugar

2 eggs

2 teaspoons pure vanilla extract

3 cups unbleached white flour

½ teaspoon salt

1 teaspoon baking soda

1 teaspoon baking powder

PREHEAT THE OVEN to 350°. Lightly oil or spray the baking sheets.

USING AN ELECTRIC mixer or a food processor, cream the peanut butter, butter, and brown sugar until light and well blended. Beat in the eggs one at a time. Stir in the vanilla. Sift together the flour, salt, baking soda, and baking powder. Gently fold the dry ingredients into the wet ingredients.

ROLL TABLESPOONFULS OF dough between your palms to form 2-inch balls and place them about 2 inches apart on the baking sheets. Press each cookie with the tines of a fork to create a crisscross pattern. Bake for 10 minutes. Transfer the cookies to a rack to cool.

VARIATIONS For Chocolate Chip Peanut Butter Cookies, fold 1 cup of chocolate chips into the dough, form into balls, and bake as above.

For Peanutty Peanut Butter Cookies, place about 1 cup of chopped peanuts in a shallow bowl and roll each ball of dough in the peanuts to evenly coat the outside. Then bake as above.

For Peanut Butter and Jelly Gems, make a depression in the center of each ball of dough with your thumb and fill the hollow with ¼ teaspoon of jam or fruit preserves. Bake as above.

■ **PREPARATION TIME:** 15 minutes
■ **BAKING TIME:** 10 minutes per batch
■ **EQUIPMENT:** baking sheets, electric mixer or food processor

Nut Macaroons

This exceedingly simple recipe yields a crunchy, richly flavored cookie. You can use any kind of nut, but our favorite in this recipe is pecans—they're a perfect match for brown sugar.

PREHEAT THE OVEN to 300°. Lightly oil a large baking sheet.

MIX TOGETHER ALL of the ingredients until well blended. Roll teaspoonfuls of the dough between your palms into 1-inch balls. Place the balls about 2 inches apart on the baking sheet.

BAKE UNTIL FIRM, set, and lightly browned, about 35 minutes. Cool the cookies on the baking sheet for 5 minutes before transferring them to racks for further cooling.

- **PREPARATION TIME:** 10 minutes
- **BAKING TIME:** 30 minutes
- **COOLING TIME:** 10 to 15 minutes
- **EQUIPMENT:** baking sheet

- **YIELDS 16**

1 egg white, unbeaten

1¼ cups finely ground nuts, such as pecans, almonds, hazelnuts, or walnuts (1½ cups whole nuts)

¾ cup packed brown sugar

1 teaspoon pure vanilla extract (optional)

¼ teaspoon ground cinnamon (optional)

Chocolate Crispy Rice Macaroons

This cookie is all about texture. Egg whites, sugar, and almonds are the basis of classic macaroons. This version omits the nuts but includes the chewiness of coconut—an ingredient considered essential to macaroons by some—plus the added crunchiness of crispy rice.

■ **YIELDS ABOUT 36**

3 ounces semi-sweet chocolate

2 egg whites
pinch of salt

¾ cup sugar

1 teaspoon pure vanilla extract

1½ cups unsweetened grated coconut

1½ cups crisped rice cereal

PREHEAT THE OVEN to 350°. Generously oil the baking sheets or line them with parchment paper.

MELT THE CHOCOLATE in a double boiler, microwave, or small pan on medium heat, stirring continuously. Set aside to cool slightly. Meanwhile, with a whisk or an electric mixer, whip together the egg whites and the salt until soft peaks form. Gradually beat in the sugar until completely incorporated into the whites. The mixture should be glossy. In another bowl, combine the melted chocolate, vanilla, coconut, and crispy rice. Fold in the beaten egg whites until the mixture is evenly colored.

WITH A TABLESPOON, drop spoonfuls of dough onto the prepared baking sheets, spacing them at least 1 inch apart. Each cookie should be about 1½ inches in diameter. Bake until the macaroons are firm and dry on the surface, about 15 to 20 minutes. Remove them from the tray and transfer to a rack to cool.

■ **PREPARATION TIME:** 15 minutes
■ **BAKING TIME:** 15 to 20 minutes per batch
■ **EQUIPMENT:** 2 baking sheets, parchment paper (optional), double boiler (page 370)

PER .5 OZ SERVING: 53 CALS, 2.5 G TOT FAT, .3 G MONO FAT, 2 G SAT FAT, 0 MG CHOL

Chocolate Meringue Cookies

Moosewood cook Joan Adler, who also works as a patient advocate and health counselor, likes discovering and inventing recipes that fulfill special dietary needs. So here is a wheat-free cookie that is low-fat, too! These cookies with their crisp, satisfying crunch and rich chocolate flavor are like little, sweet kisses of chocolate.

PREHEAT THE OVEN to 250°. Line the baking sheets with parchment paper or with a brown paper bag cut to fit the baking sheet. Spray with cooking spray.

SIFT TOGETHER THE cocoa and cornstarch and set aside. Combine the egg whites, salt, and cream of tartar in a large bowl and, using an electric mixer at medium speed, beat until foamy. Gradually add the confectioners' sugar 1 tablespoon at a time. Continue to beat for at least 3 minutes, until thick and glossy and stiff peaks form. Beat in the vanilla. Gently fold in the sifted cocoa and cornstarch; it's okay if the batter is somewhat marbled.

DROP BY SMALL teaspoons onto the prepared baking sheets; 25 small cookies will fit on each sheet. Bake for 1½ hours, until the cookies are hard and crisp. Turn the oven off and leave the cookies in it—without opening the door to snitch any—for a few hours or overnight.

WITH A SPATULA, carefully remove the cookies to an airtight container.

- **PREPARATION TIME:** 1½ hours
- **BAKING TIME:** 1½ hours
- **COOLING TIME:** at least a few hours or overnight
- **EQUIPMENT:** 2 baking sheets, parchment paper or heavy brown paper bags cut to fit the baking sheets, electric mixer

PER .2 OZ SERVING: 13 CALS, .1 G TOT FAT, 0 G MONO FAT, .1 G SAT FAT, 0 MG CHOL

- **YIELDS ABOUT 48**

6 tablespoons unsweetened cocoa powder

3 tablespoons cornstarch

3 egg whites, at room temperature

¼ teaspoon salt

¼ teaspoon cream of tartar

¾ cup confectioners' sugar

1 teaspoon pure vanilla extract

Anise Almond Biscotti

Bring Little Italy into your home with our fragrant and exotic biscotti. These twice-baked toasts are twice the treat since they are both low-fat and easy to make.

■ YIELDS 24

⅔ cup whole almonds

2 eggs

1 egg white

1 tablespoon anise seeds

½ teaspoon pure almond extract

½ teaspoon ground black pepper

1 cup sugar

2 cups unbleached white flour

1 teaspoon baking powder

¼ teaspoon salt

PREHEAT THE OVEN to 325°. Spread the almonds on an unoiled baking sheet and bake for about 10 minutes, or until fragrant. Transfer to a bowl and set aside to cool.

INCREASE THE OVEN temperature to 350°. Lightly oil the baking sheet.

BEAT THE EGGS and egg white in a large bowl until pale yellow. Stir in the anise seeds, almond extract, pepper, and sugar. Sift in the flour, baking powder, and salt and mix until well blended. Coarsely chop the nuts and stir them into the dough by hand. Using lightly floured hands or two rubber spatulas, transfer the dough to the baking sheet and form it into two logs about 3 inches in diameter. Pat the logs to an even thickness.

BAKE FOR 35 to 40 minutes, until the logs are set and firm. Cool the logs on a rack for about 10 minutes. Reduce the oven temperature to 325°. Using a sharp knife, slice the logs diagonally crosswise into ½-inch pieces. Place the biscotti cut side down on the baking sheet and bake for 20 to 25 minutes, just until lightly browned. The biscotti will become firmer as they cool.

STORED IN AN airtight container, they will keep for a few weeks.

■ PREPARATION TIME: 25 minutes
■ BAKING TIME: total of about 1 hour
■ EQUIPMENT: baking sheet

PER 1 OZ SERVING: 98 CALS, 2.5 G TOT FAT, 1.4 G MONO FAT, .4 G SAT FAT, 22 MG CHOL

Date Hazelnut Chocolate Biscotti

Biscotti have become widely popular in this country as companions to espresso, cappuccino, and latté; in Italy, they frequently accompany dessert wines. Traditional biscotti are firm, crisp biscuits, lightly sweetened and delicately flavored with anise or almond, but there are many more richly indulgent varieties. Boasting hazelnuts, dates, chocolate chips, and liqueur, these biscotti are admittedly somewhat decadent.

■ YIELDS ABOUT 24

½ cup whole hazelnuts

¼ cup butter, at room temperature

⅔ cup sugar

2 eggs

1 tablespoon brandy, chocolate liqueur, or hazelnut-flavored liqueur, such as Fra Angelico

1 teaspoon pure vanilla extract

1 teaspoon baking powder

½ teaspoon salt

2 cups unbleached white flour

½ cup chopped pitted dates

½ cup semi-sweet chocolate chips

 PREHEAT THE OVEN to 325°.

SPREAD THE HAZELNUTS on a baking sheet and toast in the oven for about 10 minutes, until fragrant. Allow the nuts to cool for a few minutes and then rub them in a dry towel to remove most of the skins. Coarsely chop the nuts and set them aside. Turn the oven up to 350°. Lightly oil the baking sheet.

CREAM THE BUTTER and sugar until light and blended. Beat in the eggs, liqueur, and vanilla. Sift in the baking powder, salt, and flour and mix well. Stir in the chopped nuts, dates, and chocolate chips. Using lightly floured hands or two rubber spatulas and working directly on the baking sheet, form the dough into two logs about 3 inches in diameter. Pat the logs to an even thickness.

BAKE FOR 30 to 35 minutes, until the logs are set and firm. Cool the logs on a rack for about 10 minutes. Reduce the oven temperature to 325°. Using a sharp knife and cutting on the diagonal, slice the logs into pieces about ½ inch thick. Place the biscotti cut side down on the baking sheet and bake for another 25 to 30 minutes, until they are firm and lightly browned.

STORE IN AN airtight container.

- **PREPARATION TIME:** 30 minutes
- **BAKING TIME:** total of about 1 hour
- **EQUIPMENT:** baking sheet

Pecan Currant Biscotti

Cornmeal, currants, and spices are appealing components of these imaginative twice-baked biscuits. They are outstanding partners for a cup of espresso or cappuccino, Spiced Ethiopian-style Coffee (page 297), or one of the other coffee variations.

■ **YIELDS ABOUT 36**

⅔ cup pecan halves

2 eggs, lightly beaten

1 egg white

½ teaspoon
   ground cinnamon

⅛ teaspoon
   ground nutmeg

1 teaspoon pure
   vanilla extract

2½ cups sugar

⅓ cup packed
   brown sugar

1½ cups unbleached
   white flour

½ cup cornmeal

1 teaspoon
   baking powder

¼ teaspoon salt

¾ cup currants

PREHEAT THE OVEN to 325°. Spread the pecans on a baking sheet and bake for about 10 minutes, until lightly browned and fragrant. When the nuts have cooled, coarsely chop them and set aside. Increase the oven temperature to 350°. Lightly oil a baking sheet.

BEAT THE EGGS and egg white in a large bowl until light. Stir in the cinnamon, nutmeg, vanilla, sugar, and brown sugar. Add the flour, cornmeal, baking powder, and salt and mix until well blended. Stir in the toasted nuts and currants. Using lightly floured hands or two rubber spatulas and working directly on the baking sheet, form the dough into two logs about 12 inches long and 3 inches in diameter. Place the logs at least 3 inches apart on the baking sheet and pat to an even thickness.

BAKE FOR 25 to 30 minutes, until the logs are set and firm. Cool on a rack for about 10 minutes. Reduce the oven temperature to 325°. Using a sharp knife, slice the logs on a severe diagonal into ½-inch pieces. Place the biscotti cut side down on the baking sheet and bake for about 15 minutes, until lightly browned. The biscotti will become firmer as they cool. Cool on the baking sheets. Store in an airtight container.

■ **PREPARATION TIME:** 30 to 35 minutes
■ **BAKING TIME:** total of 40 to 45 minutes
■ **EQUIPMENT:** baking sheet

PER 1.25 OZ SERVING: 120 CALS, 2.2 G TOT FAT, 1.3 G MONO FAT, .3 G SAT FAT, 15 MG CHOL

Italian Sesame Cookies

Plain and simple, Italian Sesame Cookies are the kind of satisfying accompaniment to tea or coffee that you could find yourself enjoying on a very regular basis. These biscuits will be familiar to anyone who frequents Italian-American bakeries.

PREHEAT THE OVEN to 350°. Lightly butter or oil the baking sheets.

SIFT THE FLOUR, sugar, baking powder, and salt into the bowl of a food processor or into a mixing bowl. Cut the butter into ½-inch cubes and work it into the dry ingredients until just crumbly. Combine the vanilla and the beaten eggs and add to the flour mixture. Process, pulsing, or beat until the dough is just moistened and uniform.

PLACE THE SESAME seeds in a shallow bowl or plate. On a lightly floured surface, divide the dough into four equal parts and shape each part into a very thin log—about 18 inches long and ½ inch in diameter. Moisten each log with water using a pastry brush, cut the log into 10 cylindrical cookies, and roll the edges of each cookie in the sesame seeds. Place them 1 inch apart on the prepared baking sheet and bake until golden and firm, about 30 minutes. Remove to a rack to cool.

THESE COOKIES WILL keep for up to 2 weeks in an airtight container.

NOTE Rotate the cookie sheets from top to bottom and front to back of your oven about halfway through the baking time to ensure even baking.

- **PREPARATION TIME:** 20 to 25 minutes
- **BAKING TIME:** 30 minutes per batch
- **EQUIPMENT:** 2 baking sheets, food processor (optional), pastry brush

- **YIELDS ABOUT 40**

3 cups unbleached white flour

1 cup sugar

1½ teaspoons baking powder

½ teaspoon salt

¾ cup cold butter

2 teaspoons pure vanilla extract

3 eggs, lightly beaten

½ cup sesame seeds

Regina's Ruggelach

These fruit-filled spiral cookies, a variation on a classic pastry from the European Jewish tradition, were inspired by a recipe from Regina Goldin, Penny Condon's mother.

■ **YIELDS 40**

DOUGH

- 1 cup butter, at room temperature
- 1 tablespoon sugar
- ¾ teaspoon salt
- 2½ cups unbleached white flour, sifted
- 1 cup sour cream

FILLING

- 6 ounces apricot or raspberry fruit spread or jam
- 6 ounces orange marmalade
- 1 tablespoon freshly grated lemon peel
- 2 teaspoons fresh lemon juice
- ½ cup packed brown sugar
- 1 cup finely chopped walnuts
- 1 cup golden raisins
- 1 teaspoon ground cinnamon

confectioners' sugar

USING AN ELECTRIC mixer, blend the butter, sugar, and salt. Add the flour slowly, mixing well. Mix in the sour cream and form the dough into a soft ball. Transfer it to a sheet of wax paper and shape it into a rough rectangle. Wrap and refrigerate for at least an hour or up to one week.

WHEN THE DOUGH has chilled, make the filling. Simmer the jams, lemon peel, and lemon juice until the jams begin to melt. Stir in the brown sugar until dissolved. Add the nuts, raisins, and cinnamon. Remove from the heat and set aside to cool.

PREHEAT THE OVEN to 350°. Oil the baking sheet and set aside.

DIVIDE THE RECTANGLE of dough into four equal parts. Return three parts to the refrigerator while you work with the first one. Using a floured surface and rolling pin, roll the dough into a 6 × 12-inch rectangle. Spread ¼ of the filling over the surface of the dough. Roll it up jelly roll fashion to make a 12-inch log. Pinch the ends together with your fingers to seal the log and carefully transfer it to the baking sheet.

REPEAT WITH THE other three parts of the dough. Slice each log on the diagonal into 10 pieces. Arrange the cookies on the baking sheet with a little space between them. Bake for 40 minutes, until golden brown. (Or bake the logs whole for 55 minutes, and then slice.)

COOL WELL. DUST with confectioners' sugar. Store the cookies in a sealed container.

■ **PREPARATION TIME:** 45 minutes
■ **BAKING TIME:** 40 minutes for sliced cookies, 55 minutes for whole logs
■ **CHILLING TIME:** at least 1 hour
■ **EQUIPMENT:** electric mixer, large baking sheet, rolling pin

Jammy Cake Shortbread

This is an elegant high tea type of shortbread that melts in your mouth and is reminiscent of little jam tarts.

IN A LARGE bowl, stir together the sugar and lemon peel to produce a fragrant lemon-scented sugar. Add the butter and beat with an electric mixer or by hand for about 1 minute, until light and creamy. In a small bowl or cup, whisk together the egg yolk, lemon juice, and vanilla and blend them into the butter mixture. Stir in the flour to make a dough.

DIVIDE THE DOUGH into four equal parts. Flatten each portion into a disk, cover with plastic wrap, and refrigerate for at least 2 hours.

PREHEAT THE OVEN to 350°.

IN A SMALL bowl, mix together the fruit preserves and confectioners' sugar and set aside. Lightly flour a smooth, dry surface and roll out each disk of dough into a ¼-inch-thick circle about 6 inches across. Transfer two of the circles to an unoiled baking sheet. Spread both circles evenly with the fruit filling, leaving a ½-inch border uncovered, and top each with one of the remaining circles of dough to form a sandwich. Pinch or flute the edges.

BAKE FOR 25 to 30 minutes, until the edges are golden and the center is firm. Remove the shortbreads from the oven and, while still warm, cut each into 12 wedges. Transfer to a rack to cool. When the shortbread wedges are cool, dust them with confectioners' sugar.

- **PREPARATION TIME:** 25 to 30 minutes
- **CHILLING TIME:** 2 hours
- **BAKING TIME:** 25 to 30 minutes
- **EQUIPMENT:** electric mixer, baking sheet, rolling pin

■ YIELDS 24

DOUGH

½ cup sugar

1 teaspoon freshly grated lemon peel

1 cup butter, at room temperature

1 large egg yolk

1 tablespoon fresh lemon juice

1 teaspoon pure vanilla extract

2 cups unbleached white flour

FILLING

⅔ cup fruit preserves, such as raspberry, apricot, or a combination

1 tablespoon confectioners' sugar

sprinkling of confectioners' sugar

Pistachio Shortbread

Imagine yourself in the Latin Quarter in Paris, enjoying this luscious nutty shortbread with a little scoop of lime sorbet and a demitasse. Or perhaps on Moosewood's shaded patio with a mug of spearmint tea?

■ **YIELDS 24**

½ cup shelled natural pistachios

⅔ cup confectioners' sugar

2 teaspoons pure vanilla extract

1 teaspoon pure orange extract

1 cup butter

2 cups unbleached white flour

24 whole shelled pistachios for decorating

TOAST THE ½ cup of pistachios in a 350° oven for about 15 minutes, stirring once or twice, until lightly browned. Remove from the oven and cool completely.

IN A FOOD processor, process the nuts until finely ground. Add the sugar, vanilla, and orange extract and continue processing until well mixed. Add the butter a few tablespoons at a time, processing until completely blended. Add the flour and pulse until just incorporated.

WITH A RUBBER spatula, turn out the dough and divide it into fourths. Flatten each piece into a disk, cover with plastic wrap, and refrigerate for about 1 hour.

PREHEAT THE OVEN to 350°. Line the baking sheets with parchment paper to absorb any excess butter.

PLACE EACH DISK on a well-floured surface and roll it out into a circle about 4 to 5 inches in diameter and ¼ inch thick. Slide each shortbread disk onto the baking sheet and score into 6 wedges. Decorate each wedge with a single pistachio.

BAKE FOR 20 to 25 minutes in the top third of the oven. Rotate the cookie sheet once midway through baking. Remove the cookies from the oven and, while warm, cut each disk into 6 wedges. Cool completely before storing in a tightly covered container.

■ **PREPARATION TIME:** 35 minutes
■ **CHILLING TIME:** 1 hour
■ **BAKING TIME:** 20 to 25 minutes per batch
■ **EQUIPMENT:** food processor, 2 baking sheets lined with parchment paper, rolling pin

Black and White Brownies

Not even Bette Yip, Moosewood's reigning chocoholic queen, could have packed any more chocolate into this unapologetically indulgent dessert. Pure white chocolate swirls its way through a dense, rich mocha brownie that becomes even more glorious when topped with its bittersweet chocolate glaze.

PREHEAT THE OVEN to 350°. Lightly butter the baking pan and dust it with flour.

BREAK UP THE white chocolate and melt it in a double boiler. Stir and set aside. Meanwhile, combine the unsweetened chocolate, butter, and coffee granules and heat in a double boiler, stirring until melted. Set aside to cool for about 5 minutes.

WITH AN ELECTRIC mixer or whisk, beat the eggs, sugar, and vanilla until light and creamy. Add the chocolate-coffee mixture, beating until well mixed. Beat in the flour just until evenly distributed.

POUR THE BATTER into the prepared pan. Drop the melted white chocolate by spoonfuls into the batter. With a knife, swirl the white chocolate through the batter for a marbled effect. Bake 30 to 40 minutes, until the center is firm and begins to puff slightly. Cool thoroughly.

WHILE THE BROWNIES cool, prepare the glaze. Combine the chocolate and the cream in a double boiler and cook on medium heat, stirring often, until the chocolate melts. Set aside to cool, stirring occasionally, until a warm, velvety glaze results. Pour the glaze over the brownies. Allow to cool completely before cutting.

- **PREPARATION TIME:** 30 minutes
- **BAKING TIME:** 30 to 40 minutes
- **EQUIPMENT:** 8-inch square baking pan, 2 double boilers (page 370) or the equivalent, electric mixer

■ YIELDS 16

BROWNIES

- 8 ounces white chocolate
- 3 ounces unsweetened chocolate
- ¾ cup butter
- 2 teaspoons instant coffee granules or espresso powder
- 2 eggs
- ¾ cup sugar
- 2 teaspoons pure vanilla extract
- ½ cup unbleached white flour

BITTERSWEET CHOCOLATE GLAZE

- ⅓ cup chopped bittersweet chocolate or semisweet chocolate morsels
- ¼ cup heavy cream

Hazelnut Brownies

This luscious, deep-chocolate brownie is baked atop a crust of toasted, ground hazelnuts and iced with a glaze of dark bittersweet chocolate and cream.

■ **YIELDS 16**

BROWNIES

- 1 cup whole hazelnuts
- 2 ounces unsweetened chocolate
- 6 tablespoons butter
- 2 large eggs
- ¾ cup sugar
- 1 teaspoon pure vanilla extract
- ½ cup unbleached white flour

CHOCOLATE CREAM GLAZE

- ¾ cup chopped semi-sweet chocolate or chocolate chips
- ⅓ cup heavy cream

PREHEAT THE OVEN to 350°. Lightly butter the baking pan and dust it with flour.

SPREAD THE HAZELNUTS on a baking sheet and toast for 10 minutes, until fragrant. Meanwhile, melt the unsweetened chocolate and the butter in a double boiler. Set aside to cool for 5 minutes.

REMOVE THE NUTS from the oven and rub them in a clean, dry cloth to partially remove the skins. Grind the nuts in a food processor or blender until very fine—the ground nuts should almost clump together like chunky nut butter. Press the nut mixture into the prepared pan and set aside.

USING AN ELECTRIC mixer or a wire whisk, beat the eggs, sugar, and vanilla until creamy. Then beat in the melted chocolate mixture until creamy. Add the flour and beat until well mixed.

POUR THE BATTER over the nut layer in the pan and bake for 30 to 35 minutes, until the center is firm to the touch and just beginning to puff. Remove the brownies from the oven and cool for at least 45 minutes.

WHILE THE BROWNIES cool, prepare the glaze. Melt the chocolate and cream in a double boiler. Stir well and set aside to cool. Occasionally stir the chocolate as it cools to a warm, velvety glaze. Pour the glaze over the brownies. Cool completely. Cut into 16 squares or 32 miniature triangles just before serving.

- ■ **PREPARATION TIME:** 30 minutes
- ■ **BAKING TIME:** 30 to 35 minutes
- ■ **COOLING TIME:** 45 minutes
- ■ **EQUIPMENT:** 8-inch square baking pan, baking sheet, double boiler (page 370), electric mixer, food processor or blender

Chocolate Cranberry Crunch

Cranberries and chocolate are a surprisingly delicious combination of flavors as well as an attractive contrast of colors.

TOPPING

2 cups fresh or unthawed frozen cranberries

1 cup semi-sweet chocolate chips

½ cup sugar

1 teaspoon ground cinnamon

BATTER

3 cups rolled oats

1½ cups unbleached white flour

1½ teaspoons baking powder

1 cup packed brown sugar

2 large eggs

1 cup butter, melted

 PREHEAT THE OVEN to 375°. Butter the baking pan.

WHIRL THE CRANBERRIES in a blender or food processor for a minute until well chopped. In a mixing bowl, combine the chopped cranberries, chocolate, sugar, and cinnamon. Set aside.

IN A SEPARATE mixing bowl, thoroughly combine the oats, flour, baking powder, and brown sugar. Lightly beat the eggs and combine them with the melted butter. Add the eggs all at once to the flour mixture and stir just until mixed. Press the batter into the bottom and up the sides of the prepared baking pan. Spread the cranberry-chocolate mixture over the oat batter.

BAKE FOR ABOUT 35 minutes, until a knife inserted in the center comes out clean. Allow to cool before cutting.

- **PREPARATION TIME:** 30 to 40 minutes
- **BAKING TIME:** 35 minutes
- **EQUIPMENT:** 7½ × 11½-inch baking pan, blender or food processor

Date Coconut Bars

This easy-to-make bar cookie is tailor-made for coconut lovers. It will conjure up visions of date and coconut palms warmed by the breezes of a North African oasis.

A word of caution about coconut— we use only unsweetened, grated coconut without preservatives, which is readily available in health food stores and in the bulk food sections of large supermarkets. Unfortunately, it is seldom refrigerated for retail sale, and without preservatives or sweetening, it can easily become stale and rancid. The wise shopper should sample a little before purchasing it, if possible. It should be mild, sweet, chewy, and delicate in flavor.

■ **YIELDS 15**

2 cups lightly packed chopped pitted dates

¾ cup water

1 teaspoon freshly grated lemon peel

¼ cup sugar

2 cups unbleached white flour

1 teaspoon baking powder

1 cup unsweetened grated coconut

¾ cup packed brown sugar

½ cup butter, melted

½ teaspoon pure lemon extract

¼ cup milk

 PREHEAT THE OVEN to 350°. Butter the baking pan.

COMBINE THE DATES, water, and lemon peel in a the saucepan. Bring the mixture to a boil, cover, and cook on low heat until the dates are soft and the water has been absorbed, about 15 minutes. Stir occasionally and add more water if necessary to prevent sticking. Add the sugar and stir until dissolved. Remove from the heat and set aside.

SIFT THE FLOUR and baking powder into a mixing bowl. Add the coconut and brown sugar and mix until thoroughly blended. In a separate bowl, combine the melted butter, lemon extract, and milk. Add to the dry ingredients and stir until just mixed; the dough will be quite stiff.

PRESS ABOUT ⅔ of the dough into the prepared baking pan. Spread the cooked dates evenly over it. Crumble the remaining dough over the dates, pressing lightly. Bake for about 30 minutes, until golden brown. Allow the bars to cool—the filling will become firm as it cools. Cut into 15 bars (5 columns by 3 rows).

■ **PREPARATION TIME:** 45 minutes
■ **BAKING TIME:** about 30 minutes
■ **EQUIPMENT:** 7 × 11-inch baking pan, medium saucepan

Lime Pecan Bars

These bars are a very popular treat at Moosewood. They have a chewy cookie crust topped with a sweet lime custard. Only freshly squeezed lime juice will provide zing without bitterness. If you can't resist the flavor of limes, you will definitely want to use the optional lime peel, although these bars are excellent without it.

Wash and finely grate the peels of 3 or 4 large limes before juicing them. If the limes are hard, soften them before peeling by rolling them on a counter with the heel of your hand, tossing them in a game of catch with your children, or throwing them on the floor. No kidding! They'll yield more juice.

■ YIELDS 12

 PREHEAT THE OVEN to 325°. Butter the baking pan.

IN THE BOWL of a food processor or by hand, finely chop the pecans. Add the melted butter, flour, and brown sugar and process or blend with your fingers to form a crumbly mixture. Press the crust into the prepared pan and bake until golden brown, about 25 to 30 minutes.

WHILE THE CRUST is baking, whisk together the eggs and sugar. Stir in the lime juice, flour, and the lime peel, if using, and mix well until smooth.

WHEN THE CRUST is baked, pour the lime custard into it and return the pan to the oven. Bake for about 20 minutes, until the topping is firm to the touch. Cool in the pan for about 1 hour. Cut into 12 pieces and gently press a pecan half into the center of each piece, if desired. Remove the bars with a spatula to a serving plate or storage container.

CRUST

½ cup pecans

¼ cup butter, melted

¾ cup unbleached white flour

⅓ cup packed brown sugar

TOPPING

3 large eggs

1 cup sugar

½ cup fresh lime juice

⅓ cup unbleached white flour

2 teaspoons finely grated lime peel (optional)

12 pecan halves, toasted (optional)

- ■ **TOTAL PREPARATION TIME:** 1 hour
- ■ **BAKING TIME:** 25 to 30 minutes for crust, plus 20 minutes for finished bars
- ■ **COOLING TIME:** 1 hour
- ■ **EQUIPMENT:** nonreactive 8-inch square baking pan, food processor (optional)

Nut Butter Granola Bars

An alternative to expensive commercial granola bars, these dessert treats are an excellent "on the go" food for after-school snacks or car trips. Store extra granola bars in the freezer and thaw them just before serving.

BARS

¼ cup vegetable oil

¾ cup peanut or almond butter

½ cup packed brown sugar

1 large egg

¼ cup water

2 teaspoons pure vanilla extract

½ cup unbleached white pastry flour (page 361)

2½ cups prepared granola

½ cup chopped almonds, pecans, or walnuts (optional)

¼ cup raisins or currants (optional)

½ cup semi-sweet chocolate chips (optional)

GLAZE (OPTIONAL)

⅔ cup pure maple syrup

 PREHEAT THE OVEN to 350°. Lightly oil the baking pan.

IN A BOWL, cream the oil and peanut butter together. Beat in the brown sugar, egg, water, and vanilla until smooth. Mix in the flour. Stir in the granola and, if using, the nuts, raisins or currants, and chocolate chips.

SPREAD THE BATTER evenly in the prepared baking pan and bake for 25 to 30 minutes, until light brown and firm. Set aside to cool.

TO MAKE THE optional glaze, heat the maple syrup in the saucepan until it simmers. Cook uncovered on low heat for about 10 minutes, until the syrup has reduced to just over ⅓ cup and is very sticky on the tip of a spoon. Watch the syrup carefully to prevent it from scorching. Spread the syrup in a thin layer over the top of the uncut granola bars. As the syrup cools, it will crystallize into maple sugar.

CUT INTO 12 or 16 bars and serve. Store leftover bars in an airtight container or freeze for up to 1 month.

■ **PREPARATION TIME:** 35 minutes, including glaze
■ **BAKING TIME:** 25 to 30 minutes
■ **EQUIPMENT:** 8-inch square baking pan, small nonreactive saucepan

Spiced Pumpkin Squares

Moist and chewy, these brownies are a lovely autumn dessert, either served plain or adorned with your favorite topping. The recipe is perfect for making with children—easy to prepare, easy to eat, and yummy, too.

■ YIELDS 9

PUMPKIN MIXTURE

- ½ cup butter
- 1 cup packed brown sugar
- 1 egg
- 1 teaspoon pure vanilla extract
- ¾ cup cooked pumpkin purée

DRY INGREDIENTS

- 1 cup unbleached white flour
- 1 teaspoon baking powder
- 1 teaspoon ground cinnamon
- ¼ teaspoon salt
- ¼ teaspoon ground ginger
- ¼ teaspoon ground allspice
- ½ cup chopped walnuts

PREHEAT THE OVEN to 350°. Butter the baking pan and dust it with flour.

WITH AN ELECTRIC mixer, cream together the butter and brown sugar until light and well blended. Beat in the egg. Add the vanilla and the pumpkin purée and continue to beat until thoroughly mixed. Sift together the flour, baking powder, cinnamon, salt, ginger, and allspice and stir them into the pumpkin mixture to form a smooth batter. Fold in the chopped walnuts by hand.

POUR THE BATTER into the prepared pan and bake until a knife inserted into the center comes out clean, about 40 minutes. Cool for about 15 minutes before cutting into squares.

- **PREPARATION TIME:** 20 minutes
- **BAKING TIME:** 40 minutes
- **COOLING TIME:** 15 minutes
- **EQUIPMENT:** 8-inch square baking pan, electric mixer

PuDDINGS AND CUSTARDS

Puddings and Custards

FROM SIMPLE STOVETOP PUDDINGS AND OVEN-BAKED BREAD PUDDINGS to rich pots de crème and elaborate trifle-like layered puddings, these desserts are comforting pleasures that hint at sensuous decadence. Silky Dark Chocolate Pudding with Bananas is a chocoholic's dream, yet it is low in fat and cooks in minutes. Magical pudding cakes go into the oven as liquid and emerge as little towers of cake perched on their creamy custard foundations. Savannah Banana Pudding achieved the status of a Moosewood favorite by the time we had all tasted it. Sometimes a hearty pudding with a nubbly texture is just what we want; Indian Pudding, Carrot Pudding, or Low-fat Sweet Potato Pudding are perfect for fall or winter desserts. Flans and baked custards, prized for their velvety texture and delicate taste, require gentle treatment. A custard should shiver as it breaks apart and its smoothness should be absolute. Our Crème Brûlée meets every expectation for this luxurious classic. Flan de Piña y Lima and Lemon Raspberry Flan are new takes on the original, enlivened by the freshness of citrus. Always use a protective water bath when baking flans and bake until the top is golden and the center is firm. If porous, pockmarked, or watery, chances are the flan was overbaked. For more tips on making successful custards, see page 370. Bread puddings were invented to use up leftover bread, but the delicious bread puddings in this chapter will prompt you to buy bread just for them. Warm and enticing Peach Bread Pudding is a revered Creole sweet. Simply prepared Summer Berry Pudding, bursting with brilliantly colored fruits, is a luscious and impressive dessert. Other bread puddings in this chapter are loaded with apple chunks, streaked with lemon curd, or thickened with molten chocolate. They are wonderful, homey treats, but there's nothing plain or ordinary about them. Rice puddings are such perennial favorites at Moosewood that we regularly dream up new variations. Creamy Rice Pudding requires little maintenance during the long, slow baking that ensures an exceptionally smooth pudding. Budini di Riso, studded with dried cherries, is baked as individual servings. Everyday Rice Pudding, quickly prepared on the stovetop, transforms leftover rice into a nourishing and pleasing dessert. Use low heat and continuous stirring for all stovetop puddings. A few puddings are not cooked at all. Thick, smooth Mango Mousse is practically nothing more than creamy drained yogurt combined with puréed mango. Heart-shaped Coeur à la Crème is a pretty red-and-white dessert—rich and not too sweet. You can whip up White Chocolate and Raspberry Fool in minutes, but you'll want to enjoy it at leisure, treasuring every soft fluffy mouthful.

Butterscotch Tapioca

Here is a comforting childhood favorite improved by the rich warm flavor of butterscotch. The tapioca is especially good made with raspberries, which add gems of color and their own distinctive tart-sweetness.

■ **SERVES 4**

3 tablespoons quick-cooking tapioca

2 cups milk

⅓ cup packed brown sugar

⅛ teaspoon salt

2 egg yolks

1 tablespoon butter

½ teaspoon pure vanilla extract

½ cup fresh or frozen red raspberries (optional)

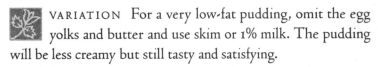 IN THE SAUCEPAN, combine the tapioca and milk and set aside for 5 minutes.

ADD THE BROWN sugar, salt, and egg yolks and mix well. Cook on low heat, stirring often, for 15 to 20 minutes, until the mixture begins to bubble and thicken. The tiny pearls of tapioca will become more visible as they cook.

REMOVE FROM THE heat and stir in the butter until it melts. Add the vanilla. The pudding will continue to thicken as it cools. Pour equal amounts into four serving cups and top with the raspberries, if desired. Chill for about an hour, until cold.

VARIATION For a very low-fat pudding, omit the egg yolks and butter and use skim or 1% milk. The pudding will be less creamy but still tasty and satisfying.

■ **YIELD:** 3½ cups
■ **PREPARATION TIME:** 10 to 15 minutes
■ **CHILLING TIME:** about 1 hour
■ **EQUIPMENT:** heavy saucepan

PER 5 OZ SERVING (VARIATION ONLY): 149 CALS, .7 G TOT FAT, .1 G MONO FAT, .1 G SAT FAT, 2 MG CHOL

Dark Chocolate Pudding with Bananas

This is an adult sort of chocolate pudding. In our experience, most children see the banana layer as an unexpected interruption of an otherwise perfectly fine chocolate treat, but adults see it as a welcome embellishment. Sautéing brings out the sweetness and full flavor of the bananas, which contrast beautifully with the bittersweet chocolate pudding. The chocolate, banana, and cinnamon make this a perfect finish for any African, Caribbean, or Brazilian meal.

PEEL THE BANANAS and slice them lengthwise into halves. In the skillet, melt the butter on medium heat. Cook the bananas for 3 to 4 minutes on each side, until golden and just beginning to brown. Transfer the bananas to a bowl and lightly mash them. Stir together the cinnamon and sugar, sprinkle over the bananas, and set aside.

IN THE SAUCEPAN, combine the cocoa, sugar, cornstarch, and salt. On medium heat, gradually add the milk, stirring briskly until the cocoa has dissolved. Cook, stirring constantly, for about 10 minutes, until the pudding is boiling, thickened, and smooth. Remove from the heat and stir in the vanilla.

TO ASSEMBLE INDIVIDUAL servings, pour about ¼ cup of the pudding into the bottom of each of the dessert cups, spoon in ¼ of the mashed bananas and cover evenly with the remaining pudding. To present the dessert in a serving bowl, layer half of the pudding in the bottom of the bowl, evenly spread on all of the bananas, and top with the rest of the pudding. Serve chilled.

 VARIATIONS For plain chocolate pudding, make this recipe without the cooked banana layer.

For a quick variation, layer the pudding with sliced raw bananas (sprinkled with cinnamon and sugar, if you like).

- **PREPARATION TIME:** 25 to 30 minutes
- **CHILLING TIME:** I hour
- **EQUIPMENT:** heavy skillet, saucepan, four 6-ounce dessert cups or a I-quart serving bowl

■ **SERVES 4**

BANANA LAYER
- 2 ripe bananas
- I tablespoon butter
- ½ teaspoon ground cinnamon
- I tablespoon sugar

PUDDING
- ⅓ cup unsweetened cocoa powder
- ⅓ cup sugar
- 3 tablespoons cornstarch
- dash of salt
- 2 cups milk*
- I teaspoon pure vanilla extract

When made with skim milk, a 7-ounce serving has only 239 calories and 4.8 grams of fat.

Carrot Pudding

This heart-healthy dessert is like a moist mini-carrot cake. Garnish with a curl of lemon peel or a dollop of nonfat vanilla yogurt.

■ SERVES 4

- 1 cup peeled and chopped carrots
- 1 cup water
- ½ cup packed brown sugar
- 2 tablespoons fresh lemon juice
- ¼ teaspoon freshly grated lemon peel
- 1 egg white
- ½ cup unbleached white flour
- 1 teaspoon baking powder
- ½ teaspoon ground cinnamon
- ¼ teaspoon ground ginger
- ¼ teaspoon ground nutmeg
- ¼ cup currants

PREHEAT THE OVEN to 350°. Lightly butter, oil, or spray four 8-ounce custard cups.

COMBINE THE CARROTS and water in the saucepan, cover, and gently simmer on medium-high heat until tender, 6 to 8 minutes. In a blender or food processor, purée the carrots with their cooking liquid and set aside in a large bowl until cool.

BEAT THE CARROT purée with the brown sugar, lemon juice, lemon peel, and egg white. Mix well. Sift together the flour, baking powder, cinnamon, ginger, and nutmeg. Fold the flour mixture into the carrot mixture. Gently stir in the currants.

DIVIDE THE BATTER evenly among the custard cups. Place the filled cups in a baking pan and add boiling water to the pan to reach halfway up the sides of the cups. Bake for about 35 minutes, until a knife inserted in the center of a pudding comes out clean. Remove the cups from the pan and cool.

SERVE WARM OR chilled.

- ■ **PREPARATION TIME:** 30 minutes
- ■ **BAKING TIME:** about 35 minutes
- ■ **EQUIPMENT:** four 8-ounce ovenproof custard cups, saucepan, blender or food processor, 8-inch flat-bottomed square baking pan

PER 5.5 OZ SERVING: 209 CALS, .3 G TOT FAT, 0 G MONO FAT, .1 G SAT FAT, 0 MG CHOL

Creamy Rice Pudding

When fragrant basmati rice simmers in a long, gentle baking, slowly absorbing the milk and spices while the raisins are busy plumping up, the result is an exceptionally creamy, soft pudding studded with sweet juicy raisins. A quick stir every half hour during the two-hour baking is all the work involved.

 PREHEAT THE OVEN to 350°. Butter the baking dish.

IN THE PREPARED baking dish, stir together the rice, milk, sugar, salt, and cinnamon sticks. Place the dish in the oven and bake for 1½ hours, stirring every 30 minutes.

MEANWHILE, IN A small bowl, combine the raisins or currants, vanilla, and spices, if using (see Note), and set aside. When the rice has baked for 1½ hours, remove it from the oven and stir in the raisin mixture.

RETURN THE PUDDING to the oven and bake for 30 minutes more. Don't be tempted to bake it longer even if it still looks slightly soupy. The rice will continue to absorb the milk and will produce a much thicker pudding upon cooling. Remove from the oven and let cool at room temperature for at least an hour, stirring occasionally to speed the cooling process.

SERVE WARM OR chilled. Store covered and refrigerated.

 NOTE If you choose not to add any spices except cinnamon, 1 to 2 teaspoons of freshly grated lemon or orange peel adds a lovely fragrant touch.

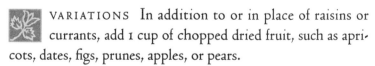 VARIATIONS In addition to or in place of raisins or currants, add 1 cup of chopped dried fruit, such as apricots, dates, figs, prunes, apples, or pears.

- ½ cup white basmati rice
- 8 cups milk
- ½ cup sugar
- ½ teaspoon salt
- 3 cinnamon sticks
- 1 cup raisins or currants
- 1 tablespoon pure vanilla extract
- ½ teaspoon freshly grated nutmeg (optional)
- ½ teaspoon freshly ground cardamom (optional)
- ⅛ teaspoon ground cloves (optional)

■ **PREPARATION TIME:** 10 minutes
■ **BAKING TIME:** 2 hours
■ **COOLING TIME:** at least 1 hour
■ **EQUIPMENT:** 3- or 4-quart ovenproof baking dish, the deeper the better

Everyday Rice Pudding

This nutritious and easy-to-make pudding is a convenient way to use up leftover rice. You can make it with either dairy or soy milk. Serve it with fresh fruit or whipped cream—or both!

■ **SERVES 8**

1 quart milk or soy milk

1½ cups cooked rice, such as white, brown, basmati (page 355), or arborio (page 213)

½ cup sugar or ⅓ cup honey

½ teaspoon ground cinnamon

¼ teaspoon ground nutmeg

3 tablespoons cornstarch

freshly grated peel of 1 lemon (optional)

2 teaspoons pure vanilla extract

½ cup currants or raisins

COMBINE THE MILK, rice, sugar or honey, cinnamon, nutmeg, cornstarch, and lemon peel, if using, in the saucepan. Bring to a simmer on medium heat, stirring often to avoid scorching. If the pudding starts to stick to the bottom of the pan, place the pan on a heat diffuser.

SIMMER THE PUDDING, stirring often, for about 20 minutes, until it thickens enough to coat the spoon. Remove the pudding from the heat, add the vanilla and currants or raisins, and refrigerate. The pudding will thicken more as it cools.

■ **TOTAL TIME:** 30 minutes

■ **EQUIPMENT:** 2-quart nonreactive saucepan, heat diffuser (optional)

Budini di Riso

Literally "little rice cakes," this Italian take on baked rice pudding is best made with arborio rice, which slowly absorbs the milk and becomes creamy as it cooks. This version, made with low-fat milk and one egg, is low in calories and fat. Golden raisins or dried cherries are equally delicious. If you use golden raisins, serve with Chunky Winter Fruit Sauce (page 305); serve the dried cherry variation with Cherry Sauce (page 304).

 PREHEAT THE OVEN to 325°.

IN A SMALL bowl, combine the cherries or raisins with the rum or orange juice and set aside. In the saucepan, bring the milk to a boil on low heat. Add the sugar and rice and simmer for about 40 minutes, stirring occasionally, until the rice is tender and the starch from the rice has thickened the milk a bit. Stir in the soaked cherries or raisins with their soaking liquid.

LIGHTLY OIL THE baking cups. In a medium bowl, beat the egg, orange peel, and vanilla lightly with a whisk or fork. Beat a little of the hot rice into the egg mixture and then stir the egg mixture back into the rice. Spoon the rice mixture into the prepared cups. Place the filled cups in the baking pan and add boiling water to reach about halfway up the sides of the cups.

BAKE THE CUSTARDS for 25 to 30 minutes, until the centers are set. Remove from the water bath and cool. Serve warm or chilled.

- **PREPARATION TIME:** 45 minutes
- **BAKING TIME:** 25 to 30 minutes
- **EQUIPMENT:** medium saucepan, six 6-ounce ovenproof custard cups, flat-bottomed baking pan

SERVES 6

- ½ cup dried cherries or golden raisins
- 1 tablespoon rum or orange juice
- 4 cups low-fat milk
- ½ cup sugar
- ½ cup arborio rice* or medium-grain white rice
- 1 large egg
- 1 teaspoon freshly grated orange peel
- 1 teaspoon pure vanilla extract

* Arborio rice is an Italian short-grain rice especially used in making risottos. This high-starch rice can absorb large quantities of liquid very rapidly to make a creamy, velvety-textured dish, yet the centers of the rice kernels remain firm and chewy.

Savannah Banana Pudding

On a recent trip to Savannah, Moosewood cooks Penny Condon and Jenny Wang were lucky to sample some banana pudding from Mrs. Wilkes' Boarding House, where strangers share tables and stupendous southern meals. The memories inspired Jenny to create this luscious version, an instant Moosewood favorite, that has our Yankee patrons swooning with delight.

About half of our Poundcake Loaf (page 123) is enough poundcake for this recipe.

■ **SERVES 6**

4 cups milk
1 cup sugar
¼ teaspoon salt
¾ cup unbleached white flour
4 eggs
2 teaspoons pure vanilla extract
3 to 4 ripe bananas
4 cups cubed poundcake
1 cup heavy cream

IN THE SAUCEPAN, bring 3½ cups of the milk to a near boil on medium heat.

WHILE THE MILK heats, in a bowl whisk together the sugar, salt, and flour with the remaining ½ cup of milk and set aside.

WHEN THE HEATED milk is very hot, whisk in the flour mixture. Cook on medium heat, whisking constantly until thickened, 5 to 10 minutes. Remove from the heat. In a bowl, lightly beat the eggs; then briskly whisk about a cup of the hot milk mixture into the eggs. Stir the eggs back into the hot milk mixture and return it to medium-low heat.

CONTINUE TO COOK the custard, stirring constantly and keeping it just under a boil, until very thick and pudding-like, 5 to 10 minutes. Remove from the heat and stir in the vanilla. Let cool to room temperature or cooler. Slice the bananas into the pudding and stir in the poundcake cubes. Just before serving, whip the cream and gently fold it into the pudding.

■ **TOTAL TIME:** 25 minutes
■ **EQUIPMENT:** 2-quart saucepan

Couscous Date Pudding

The Moroccan cousin of rice pudding, this soothing and enticing dessert is easily made. Serve it to conclude a North African or Middle Eastern meal with a cup of Spiced Ethiopian-style Coffee (page 297). One could even be tempted to eat it for breakfast and not feel too terribly decadent.

We prefer this pudding with dates, but raisins, dried currants, or chopped dried apricots are fine—probably with a little additional sweetening. Honey or maple syrup to taste can replace the sugar and soy milk can replace the milk for those who follow a dairyless diet.

Serve garnished with orange slices or a dollop of whipped cream dusted with cinnamon.

IN THE SAUCEPAN, place the milk on medium-low heat. Stir in the sugar, orange peel, vanilla, cinnamon, salt, and couscous and continue to heat for about 5 minutes, stirring often to prevent sticking. If the pudding begins to stick, reduce the heat. After about 5 minutes, add the dates and continue to cook at a gentle simmer until the pudding has thickened but is not stiff, about 5 to 10 minutes. Chill in the refrigerator in a large serving bowl or in dessert cups, or right in the pan. The pudding will continue to thicken as it cools.

- **PREPARATION TIME:** 20 minutes
- **CHILLING TIME:** 1 hour
- **EQUIPMENT:** heavy nonreactive saucepan, large serving bowl or six 6-ounce dessert cups

PER 7 OZ SERVING: 254 CALS, 3.2 G TOT FAT, .9 G MONO FAT, 1.8 G SAT FAT, 11 MG CHOL

- **SERVES 6**

4 cups milk
¼ cup sugar
1½ teaspoons freshly grated orange peel
1 teaspoon pure vanilla extract
½ teaspoon ground cinnamon
¼ teaspoon salt
¾ cup couscous*
⅔ cup chopped pitted dates

Couscous, a finely milled semolina wheat originally from North Africa, is quick cooking and mildly flavored. It is available in well-stocked supermarkets and natural food stores.

Indian Pudding

This warming New England harvest-time dessert is soft and creamy, with spicing reminiscent of pumpkin pie. The pudding can be baked in one large casserole, but the texture is silkier when it's baked in individual custard cups.

Serve Indian Pudding warm or chilled, plain or topped with whipped cream, vanilla ice cream, or frozen yogurt.

■ **SERVES 6**

4 cups milk

½ cup cornmeal

2 tablespoons butter

½ cup packed brown sugar

¼ cup unsulphured molasses

1 teaspoon ground cinnamon

½ teaspoon ground ginger

⅛ teaspoon ground cloves

¼ teaspoon salt

2 large eggs, lightly beaten

2 teaspoons fresh lemon juice

PREHEAT THE OVEN to 325°. Butter the custard cups or casserole dish.

IN A HEAVY saucepan, whisk together the milk and cornmeal until smooth. Bring to a low boil, reduce the heat, and simmer, stirring often, for 10 minutes, until somewhat thickened. Remove from the heat and stir in the butter, brown sugar, molasses, cinnamon, ginger, cloves, salt, eggs, and lemon juice.

POUR THE PUDDING into the prepared custard cups or casserole dish, place the filled cups or dish in the baking pan, and fill the pan with about 1 inch of very hot water. Bake until the pudding is fairly firm around the edges but still slightly soft in the middle. The baking time varies, depending upon the size and shape of the dishes used. Begin to check the pudding after 50 minutes and do not bake longer than 1¼ hours. Overbaking results in a rubbery texture.

VARIATION For a Vegan Indian Pudding, replace the milk with vanilla soy milk and the butter with soy margarine; omit the eggs. The pudding will be quite thin when hot from the oven, but it will set up nicely as it cools.

■ **PREPARATION TIME:** 15 to 20 minutes
■ **BAKING TIME:** about 50 minutes in custard cups, 1¼ hours in a casserole dish
■ **EQUIPMENT:** six 8-ounce ovenproof custard cups or one 2-quart ovenproof casserole dish, 2-inch-deep flat-bottomed baking pan

PER 7 OZ SERVING (VARIATION ONLY): 218 CALS, 5 G TOT FAT, 1.3 G MONO FAT, .7 G SAT FAT, 0 MG CHOL

Low-fat Sweet Potato Pudding

Although rich with flavors we find appealing in fall and winter, this pudding complements Mexican or Caribbean foods any time of year. It is surprisingly fresh and light and is especially good with a last-minute caramelized sugar topping.

PREHEAT THE OVEN to 400°. Lightly oil the custard cups or baking dish and place in the baking pan.

COMBINE THE MASHED potatoes or pumpkin purée, sugar, ginger root, orange peel, orange juice, cinnamon, salt, milk, and vanilla in a blender and purée until smooth. In a separate bowl, beat the egg whites until stiff. Gently fold the sweet potato mixture into the egg whites.

SPOON THE PUDDING into the baking cups or dish and fill the larger baking pan with an inch or two of boiling water. Bake for about 25 minutes, until puffed and golden.

SERVE CHILLED.

VARIATION If you'd like to serve this pudding with a caramelized brown sugar topping, preheat the broiler just before serving. Evenly sprinkle the chilled pudding with a light layer of brown sugar and place under the broiler for about a minute, until the brown sugar melts and is slightly caramelized. Be sure your baking cups are broilerproof.

- **PREPARATION TIME:** 20 minutes with already mashed sweet potatoes
- **BAKING TIME:** 25 minutes
- **EQUIPMENT:** four 8-ounce ovenproof custard cups or a 1-quart baking dish, flat-bottomed baking pan, blender, electric mixer

PER 6 OZ SERVING: 225 CALS, .6 G TOT FAT, .1 G MONO FAT, .2 G SAT FAT, 1 MG CHOL

- **SERVES 4**

1½ cups cooled mashed sweet potatoes* or pumpkin purée

½ cup sugar, or to taste*

1 tablespoon grated fresh ginger root

1 teaspoon freshly grated orange peel

⅓ cup orange juice

1 teaspoon ground cinnamon

¼ teaspoon salt

¼ cup milk

1 teaspoon pure vanilla extract

3 egg whites

Sweet potatoes vary in sweetness, so add sugar to taste. Taste the pudding before adding the egg whites and remember that the baked pudding will taste a little sweeter than it does unbaked.

Crème Brûlée

The crunchy, hot, caramelized sugar topping on these flans contrasts nicely with the cool, creamy custard. Crème Brûlée is the French name for this standard Latin American dessert, which has become quite popular in the United States.

Be sure to use sturdy ovenproof custard cups that can withstand the heat of the broiler.

■ **SERVES 4**

1 cup milk

1 cup half-and-half

4 large egg yolks

1 tablespoon cornstarch

½ cup sugar

1 teaspoon pure vanilla extract

3 tablespoons packed brown sugar

slices of fresh fruit

 PREHEAT THE OVEN to 350°.

HEAT THE MILK and half-and-half in the saucepan just to the boiling point, then remove from the heat and set aside. In a bowl, beat together the egg yolks, cornstarch, sugar, and vanilla with a wooden spoon to make a smooth paste. Ladle about ½ cup of the hot milk into the egg mixture and combine well. Stir the egg mixture back into the saucepan. Cook the custard on medium-low heat for about 15 minutes, stirring gently and continuously, until thick enough to coat the spoon.

POUR THE CUSTARD into the baking cups, place the filled cups in the baking pan, and fill the pan with about 2 inches of boiling water. Bake for 20 minutes, until set, then remove the cups from the pan and chill for 2 to 3 hours.

WHEN THE FLANS are chilled and ready to serve, preheat the broiler. Sprinkle about 2 teaspoons of brown sugar on top of each flan. Place the custard cups in a baking dish and surround the cups with about an inch of crushed ice. This will keep the custard cool while the sugar topping melts. Place the pan on the top rack of the broiler and broil for 2 to 5 minutes, until the sugar has just caramelized. Be sure to watch closely, since the topping can easily burn. Garnish with fruit slices and serve.

■ **PREPARATION TIME:** 25 to 30 minutes
■ **BAKING TIME:** 20 minutes
■ **CHILLING TIME:** 2 to 3 hours
■ **EQUIPMENT:** small saucepan, four 6-ounce ovenproof custard cups, 8-inch square flat-bottomed baking pan

Pots de Crème à l'Orange

This sophisticated dessert is simple to prepare and is so creamy and smooth that it melts away on your tongue. Our pots de crème represent the perfect marriage of chocolate and orange.

IN THE DOUBLE boiler, heat the cream, half-and-half, and chocolate until the chocolate melts. Stir with a whisk until all of the ingredients are well blended and remove from the heat.

IN A BLENDER, whirl the egg yolks, liqueur, and orange peel. With the machine running, slowly pour in the hot chocolate mixture. Return the mixture to the double boiler and continue to cook until it thickens to a lightly set pudding.

DIVIDE AMONG THE dessert cups and chill for 2 hours. Serve garnished with whipped cream and orange slices or kumquat halves.

- **PREPARATION TIME:** 25 minutes
- **CHILLING TIME:** 2 hours
- **EQUIPMENT:** double boiler (page 370), blender, six 6-ounce dessert cups

■ **SERVES 6**

- 1 cup heavy cream
- 1 cup half-and-half
- 12 ounces semi-sweet chocolate, broken into pieces
- 6 egg yolks
- 3 tablespoons orange-flavored liqueur, such as Grand Marnier
- ¼ teaspoon freshly grated orange peel

  fresh whipped cream

  a few orange slices and/or kumquat halves

Coeur à la Crème

Coeur à la Crème, a very romantic dessert, is sweetened soft white cheese surrounded by straw-
berry or raspberry sauce or by fresh strawberries or raspberries. Coeur à la Crème is usually
molded in a heart shape and the surface bears the textured impression of cheesecloth or the criss-
crossed pattern of the wicker baskets traditionally used. Often a single Coeur à la Crème is
shared by two people, presumably sweethearts.

Traditional Coeur à la Crème is one of the richest desserts we know of—made with
cream cheese and crème fraîche, whipped cream, or sour cream—and it's a bit too much for us.
Our recipe is less rich than the traditional, but tastes very similar, and the low-fat version,
made with cottage cheese and yogurt, is lighter yet. We've added a bit more sugar and some
vanilla to our low-fat Coeur à la Crème to compensate for the tartness of yogurt. Some of us
like our regular version with the additional sugar and vanilla, too.

If you don't want to bother making a cooked fruit sauce for the Coeur à la Crème, just
purée a pint of fresh raspberries or strawberries (or 8 ounces thawed frozen berries) and sweeten
to taste with confectioners' sugar.

■ **SERVES 4 TO 8**

COEUR À LA CRÈME

1 cup cottage cheese

¾ cup cream cheese

¼ cup heavy cream

1 tablespoon sugar

Fresh Strawberry Sauce
(page 255) or Raspberry
Sauce (page 310)

fresh strawberries or
raspberries

WHIRL ALL OF the Coeur à la Crème ingredients in a food processor bowl or blender until very smooth (see Note).

LINE EACH MOLD with a single layer of dampened cheesecloth or with paper coffee filters. Spoon the cheese mixture into the molds, pressing with the back of the spoon to fill the mold completely and remove any air pockets. Smooth the tops. Place the molds in a shallow pan to catch the liquid that drains out and refrigerate for at least 6 hours or up to 48 hours.

WHEN READY TO serve, turn the molds out onto serving plates and remove the cheesecloth. Spoon the berry sauce of your choice around each Coeur à la Crème and garnish with whole or sliced berries.

NOTE If using a blender, you will need to stop and scrape down the sides several times. Or press the cottage cheese through a sieve, and then place all of the ingredients in a bowl and beat with an electric mixer until very smooth. This method works best when the ingredients are at room temperature.

VARIATION For a delicious lower-fat Coeur à la Crème, use 1½ cups cottage cheese, ¾ cup low-fat or nonfat yogurt, 3 tablespoons sugar, and ½ teaspoon pure vanilla extract. This version will set up more quickly—in a mere 4 to 4½ hours.

- **PREPARATION TIME:** 20 to 30 minutes
- **DRAINING TIME:** 6 hours to 2 days
- **ASSEMBLING TIME:** 20 minutes
- **EQUIPMENT:** food processor (preferably) or blender or electric mixer, four 4-ounce Coeur à la Crème molds or a 1-pint mold with drainage holes, cheesecloth or paper coffee filters

Ceramic heart-shaped Coeur à la Crème molds are available in cookware and department stores. We've sometimes used metal heart-shaped gelatin molds after punching a few drainage holes in the bottoms with a hammer and nail. But any shape mold works—either small 4-ounce individual molds or a larger mold—even a sieve lined with paper coffee filters.

Coffee Flan

Silky smooth flans appear in cuisines around the globe. With the creamy, strong taste of ever-popular caffe latté, this custard is perfect for any time of day, any time of year.

■ **SERVES 6**

5 large eggs

¾ cup sugar

12 ounces evaporated milk

1 cup half-and-half

3 tablespoons instant coffee granules

1 teaspoon pure vanilla extract

fresh whipped cream

dash of ground cinnamon or unsweetened cocoa powder

 PREHEAT THE OVEN to 325°.

WHIRL THE EGGS, sugar, milk, half-and-half, coffee granules, and vanilla in the blender until well combined. Divide the mixture among the custard cups. Place the filled cups in the baking pan and add hot water to the pan to reach about halfway up the sides of the cups.

BAKE THE FLANS for 45 to 60 minutes, until the centers are just firm (see Note). Chill for 1 to 2 hours before serving.

GARNISH WITH A dollop of whipped cream and a sprinkling of cinnamon or cocoa.

 NOTE Be careful not to overbake flan. When shaken in the cup, flan should still jiggle a little. It's ready when a knife inserted in the center comes out *almost* clean.

- **PREPARATION TIME:** 10 minutes
- **BAKING TIME:** 45 to 60 minutes
- **CHILLING TIME:** 1 to 2 hours
- **EQUIPMENT:** blender, six 6-ounce ovenproof custard cups, flat-bottomed baking pan

Flan de Piña y Lima

Pineapple, lime, and rum brighten this festive Cuban flan. Garnish it with whipped cream, lime peel, a fresh pineapple spear, and a paper parasol, if desired. Cuba, si!

PREHEAT THE OVEN to 350°.

COMBINE ALL OF the ingredients in the blender and whirl until thoroughly mixed. Pour the mixture into the custard cups. Place the cups in the baking pan and pour boiling water into the pan to reach about halfway up the sides of the cups. Bake for 40 to 45 minutes, until the custard is just set and a knife inserted in the center of a flan comes out almost clean.

REMOVE THE CUPS from the pan to cool. Serve chilled.

- **PREPARATION TIME:** 15 minutes
- **BAKING TIME:** 40 to 45 minutes
- **CHILLING TIME:** at least 30 minutes
- **EQUIPMENT:** blender, six 8-ounce or eight 6-ounce ovenproof custard cups, flat-bottomed baking pan

- **SERVES 6 TO 8**

6 eggs

2 egg yolks

1 cup pineapple juice

1 cup whole milk or half-and-half

½ cup sugar

1 tablespoon fresh lime juice

1 teaspoon freshly grated lime peel

2 tablespoons dark rum (optional)

Lemon Raspberry Flan

Eliana Parra was a Chilean refugee when she came to Ithaca in 1979. She learned English in Moosewood's kitchen, and we learned some choice words in Spanish, such as "Mas flan, Nana, por favor." She's always been a model of speed and efficiency for all of us. This classic lemon flan couldn't be easier to make and has raspberries added for a tart-sweet contrast.

■ **SERVES 4**

1 cup milk

1 cup half-and-half

⅓ cup sugar
   freshly grated peel
   of 1 lemon

2 large eggs

2 egg yolks

¾ cup fresh or frozen
   raspberries*

* If using frozen berries, thaw and drain them for this recipe.

 PREHEAT THE OVEN to 325°.

IN THE SAUCEPAN, combine the milk, half-and-half, sugar, and lemon peel and heat until the mixture reaches the simmering point. Remove from the heat and allow the lemon peel to steep for 10 to 15 minutes. Break the eggs and egg yolks into the blender. While the blender whirls, pour the hot milk mixture through a strainer into the eggs and blend for a few seconds.

POUR THE MIXTURE into the custard cups. Place 6 to 8 raspberries in each cup on top of the custard and set the cups in the baking pan. Pour boiling water into the pan to reach about halfway up the sides of the cups. Bake the flans for 50 to 60 minutes, until the center is just set; the center shouldn't jiggle when you shake a cup. Cool the flans on a wire rack and then refrigerate until cold. Serve chilled.

■ **PREPARATION TIME:** 20 minutes
■ **BAKING TIME:** 50 to 60 minutes
■ **CHILLING TIME:** at least 30 minutes
■ **EQUIPMENT:** saucepan, blender, four 6-ounce ovenproof custard cups, large flat-bottomed baking pan

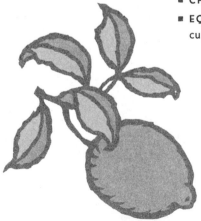

Orange and Ginger Islands

Inspired by the ubiquitous orange custards and creams one encounters throughout the islands of the Caribbean, we created this light, heady pudding that's bursting with the bright flavors of oranges and ginger. The first bite will instantly transport you to Barbados, Jamaica, Puerto Rico, St. John, Martinique, or Cuba.

We suggest an elegant presentation here, turning the individual servings out onto plates like a flan, but the pudding is also appealing served home-style from one large bowl and spooned into dessert cups at the table. We've served it at Moosewood as a refreshing parfait, alternating layers of the pudding with fresh orange sections soaked in Grand Marnier.

COMBINE THE ORANGE juice, milk, egg, tapioca, sugar, cinnamon, and ginger root in the saucepan. Let sit for 5 minutes, then cook for about 10 minutes on medium-low heat, stirring almost constantly, until just below the boiling point.

POUR THE PUDDING into the ramekins or dessert cups, filling each one almost to the top. Refrigerate for at least 2 hours, until chilled and set. To serve, run a knife around the inside of each ramekin and invert the pudding onto a dessert plate. Drizzle with a teaspoon of orange liqueur, garnish with orange sections, and top with a dab of whipped cream, if desired.

- **PREPARATION TIME:** 20 minutes
- **CHILLING TIME:** at least 2 hours
- **EQUIPMENT:** medium nonreactive saucepan, four 4-ounce ramekins or dessert cups

PER 7.5 OZ SERVING: 190 CALS, 2.4 G TOT FAT, .7 G MONO FAT, .6 G SAT FAT, 67 MG CHOL

- **SERVES 4**

1 cup fresh orange juice

1 cup skim milk

1 egg, beaten

3 tablespoons granulated tapioca*

¼ cup sugar

¼ teaspoon ground cinnamon

½ teaspoon grated fresh ginger root

4 teaspoons orange-flavored liqueur, such as curaçao

2 oranges, peeled and sectioned (page 372)

fresh whipped cream (optional)

* Tapioca is cassava meal that has been roasted and granulated. We call for quick-cooking or "minute" tapioca here.

Mango Mousse

The combination of yogurt cheese, whipped cream, and mangoes creates a simple dessert with complex flavors that are simultaneously light and rich, tangy and sweet. Be sure to use mangoes that are ripe and sugary.

■ **SERVES 6**

2 ripe mangoes

1 cup nonfat yogurt cheese (page 366)

¼ cup pineapple juice concentrate

2 tablespoons rum (optional)

1 cup heavy cream

¼ cup confectioners' sugar

¼ cup toasted unsweetened coconut (optional)

sliced strawberries or orange slices

PEEL THE MANGOES. Cut the flesh away from the pit of one of the mangos and purée it in a blender or food processor. Set aside. Chop the flesh of the other mango into small pieces (page 372) and set aside. In a medium bowl, combine the yogurt cheese, puréed mango, pineapple juice concentrate, and rum, if using, until smooth. Stir in the mango chunks.

IN A SMALL, deep bowl, combine the cream and confectioners' sugar and whip until stiff. Fold the whipped cream into the mango mixture. Spoon the mousse into six parfait glasses. Top with toasted coconut, if using, and an orange or strawberry slice and serve.

■ **TOTAL TIME:** 25 minutes

■ **EQUIPMENT:** blender or food processor, electric mixer, 6 parfait glasses

Summer Berry Pudding

While it is true that berries are at their best in the summer, the availability of frozen berries year-round makes them an elegant option in the depths of winter as well. The garnet red color of the fruit in this pudding not only evokes thoughts of summertime berry-stained fingers but also makes for a festive dessert during the winter holiday season. Homemade crème fraîche, which—like the pudding—needs to be made in advance, is a perfect accompaniment.

This pudding varies a bit from the traditional English berry pudding. Instead of lining the bowl with bread, we simply layer the bread and berry sauce. When the pudding is inverted, the berries are visible while the bread "disappears" into the structure of the pudding.

■ **SERVES 8 TO 10**

COMBINE THE BERRIES in the bowl. In the saucepan on low heat, melt the jelly together with the lemon juice. Add the fruit and cook on medium heat, stirring occasionally, until the berries are soft, about 10 minutes. Taste for sweetness and add sugar, if needed.

POUR ABOUT A cup of the berry mixture into the bottom of the bowl. Lay a slice or two of bread in a single layer on top. Continue layering the berries and bread until all of the berries are used. The last layer of berries should cover the bread completely.

COOL THE PUDDING, uncovered, in the refrigerator for about 2 hours. Cover the pudding with plastic wrap and weight it down with a few plates that just fit inside of the bowl. Refrigerate for at least 2 hours or overnight, if possible.

WHEN READY TO serve, remove the plates and plastic wrap, run a spatula around the edge of the bowl, and invert the pudding onto a pie pan or a rimmed platter.

- 8 cups mixed fresh or frozen berries, such as sliced strawberries, raspberries, blueberries, or blackberries
- 12 ounces currant jelly
- 2 tablespoons fresh lemon juice
- 2 to 6 tablespoons sugar, depending on the sweetness of the berries
- ½ loaf fine-textured white bread, such as challah (page 357), cut into ¼-inch slices

■ **PREPARATION TIME:** 25 minutes

■ **CHILLING TIME:** at least 4 hours

■ **EQUIPMENT:** 2-quart bowl (nicely shaped to mold the pudding, which will be inverted), 3-quart nonreactive saucepan, 10-inch pie pan or a deep-rimmed platter

PER 6 OZ SERVING: 250 CALS, 1.7 G TOT FAT, .6 G MONO FAT, .3 G SAT FAT, 0 MG CHOL

White Chocolate and Raspberry Fool

A fool is a mousse or parfait usually made with whipped cream. Here fluffy whipped cream flavored with melted white chocolate is layered with red or black raspberries, creating a beautiful, elegant dessert served in parfait glasses. For a smooth, delicate consistency, it is important to use a good-quality white chocolate made with cocoa butter, not coconut or palm oil.

■ **SERVES 6**

1 cup well-chilled heavy cream

¼ cup confectioners' sugar

1 teaspoon pure vanilla extract

1 cup chopped white chocolate

1 to 2 tablespoons sugar (optional)

4 cups fresh or frozen raspberries

IN A BOWL, combine ¾ cup of the heavy cream, the confectioners' sugar, and the vanilla. Using an electric mixer, whip until stiff and then chill.

IN A DOUBLE boiler, gently melt the white chocolate with the remaining ¼ cup of cream, stirring frequently. Remove the melted white chocolate from the heat, cool for 2 or 3 minutes, and then gently fold it into the whipped cream. In a separate bowl, stir the sugar into the raspberries, if they require sweetening. Refrigerate the flavored whipped cream and the berries for about 30 minutes.

WHEN EVERYTHING IS well chilled, and you are ready to serve—or no more than 2 hours before serving—spoon alternating layers of the raspberries and the whipped cream into large wine glasses or parfait glasses, beginning with raspberries and ending with whipped cream. Chill the assembled fool until ready to serve.

 VARIATION Replace the raspberries with fresh peach slices and/or blueberries.

■ **PREPARATION TIME:** 15 minutes
■ **CHILLING TIME:** 30 minutes
■ **EQUIPMENT:** electric mixer, double boiler (page 370), six 8-ounce parfait or wine glasses

Chocolate Bread Pudding

This recipe was inspired by the European classic snack, bread and chocolate, and the thrifty American colonial classic, bread pudding. Use fresh bread crumbs, not cubes, made from a good-quality French or Italian bread or an eggy challah.

 PREHEAT THE OVEN to 350°. Butter the casserole dish.

IN THE SAUCEPAN, heat the milk, chocolate, and butter until the chocolate has melted, about 5 minutes. Stir in the sugar and vanilla and set aside. In a medium bowl, whisk the cream and eggs until evenly colored. Add the melted chocolate and the bread crumbs and mix well.

POUR THE PUDDING into the prepared baking dish and bake until puffed and set, about 1 hour. The center may jiggle a little but a knife inserted in the center should come out almost clean. Serve warm or chilled, with a dollop of whipped cream and garnished with fresh berries, if desired.

 VARIATION   Add ¼ cup orange or coffee liqueur to the mixture before baking.

- **PREPARATION TIME:** 30 minutes
- **BAKING TIME:** 1 hour
- **EQUIPMENT:** large heavy saucepan, 2- to 3-quart round casserole dish

SERVES 6 TO 8

3 cups milk

4 ounces unsweetened chocolate

2 tablespoons butter

1 cup sugar

2 teaspoons pure vanilla extract

1 cup heavy cream

4 large eggs

4 cups coarse fresh bread crumbs*

dollop of fresh whipped cream (optional)

a few fresh berries (optional)

* You can easily make bread crumbs in the bowl of a food processor.

Lemon Bread Pudding

A tangy lemon custard combined with buttery toasted bread cubes is a fabulously moist, spongy pudding.

■ **SERVES 8**

1 thin baguette or ½ a fat French loaf (to make 8 cups of 1-inch cubes)

5 eggs

1 tablespoon freshly grated lemon peel

6 tablespoons fresh lemon juice

1 cup sugar

3 cups buttermilk

¼ teaspoon salt

½ cup butter, melted

PREHEAT THE OVEN to 350°. Generously butter the cake pan.

CUT THE BREAD into 1-inch cubes and toast them lightly in the oven for 5 to 10 minutes.

MEANWHILE, LIGHTLY BEAT the eggs and then whisk in the lemon peel, lemon juice, sugar, buttermilk, and salt. When the bread cubes are toasted, toss them lightly with the melted butter. Add the buttered bread cubes to the egg custard and set aside for about 15 minutes.

POUR THE CUSTARD and bread cubes into the prepared pan and bake for about 1 hour, until the top is brown and crusty and the custard still jiggles a bit. Serve warm or at room temperature.

■ **PREPARATION TIME:** 20 minutes
■ **SITTING TIME:** 15 minutes
■ **BAKING TIME:** 1 hour
■ **EQUIPMENT:** 8-inch square or 9-inch round nonreactive cake pan, preferably glass or ceramic

Peach Bread Pudding

This old-fashioned American classic is the perfect vehicle for peaches and sweet spices. For a special treat, make it with cinnamon raisin bread. Warm from the oven, it is heavenly served plain, with Raspberry Sauce (page 310), or with a dollop of whipped cream. For a New Orleans touch, serve the pudding in a pool of Rum Custard Sauce (page 317).

■ SERVES 8 TO 10

 PREHEAT THE OVEN to 350°.

PLACE THE BREAD cubes in a large mixing bowl. Whisk together the milk, eggs, vanilla, and 1 cup of the brown sugar. Pour over the bread cubes, stir lightly, and set aside.

IN A SEPARATE bowl, toss the peaches with the remaining ¼ cup of brown sugar and the cinnamon, nutmeg, and rum, if desired. Stir into the bread mixture. Melt the butter right in the baking pan in the oven and when the butter has melted, tilt the pan to coat.

POUR THE BREAD and peach mixture evenly into the buttered baking pan and bake until puffed and golden, about 50 min‑ utes. Serve warm or cold.

- **PREPARATION TIME:** 25 minutes with frozen peaches, 40 minutes with fresh
- **BAKING TIME:** 50 minutes
- **EQUIPMENT:** 9 × 13-inch baking pan

5 cups French or Italian bread or challah (page 357), cut into small cubes

4 cups milk

4 large eggs

1 tablespoon pure vanilla extract

1¼ cups packed brown sugar

3 cups chopped, peeled fresh or frozen peaches

½ teaspoon ground cinnamon

¼ teaspoon ground nutmeg

2 tablespoons rum (optional)

2 tablespoons butter

Low-fat Pineapple Pudding Cake

This delightful low-fat pudding cake separates into layers: a sweet, fruity pudding on the bottom and a light meringue cake on the top.

■ **SERVES 8**

20 ounces undrained canned crushed unsweetened pineapple

1 tablespoon cornstarch

1 tablespoon packed brown sugar

½ cup unbleached white flour

½ teaspoon baking powder

1 cup sugar

1 cup buttermilk

2 tablespoons fresh lemon juice

2 egg yolks

4 egg whites

pinch of salt

 PREHEAT THE OVEN to 350°. Very lightly oil or spray the baking cups. Place the cups in the baking pan.

DRAIN THE PINEAPPLE, reserving the juice (see Note). In a small bowl, combine the drained pineapple with the cornstarch and brown sugar. Mix well and divide evenly among the prepared custard cups.

IN A LARGE bowl, combine the flour, baking powder, ½ cup of the sugar, the buttermilk, pineapple juice, lemon juice, and egg yolks. Beat well. In a separate bowl, beat the egg whites and salt until stiff. Beat in the remaining ½ cup sugar. Gently fold the egg whites into the batter.

SPOON THE BATTER into the prepared custard cups. Pour boiling water into the pan to reach about halfway up the sides of the cups. Bake for 35 to 45 minutes, until puffy and golden. Remove the cups from the pan to cool. Serve warm or chilled.

NOTE You should get about 1 cup of pineapple and 1 cup of juice.

■ **PREPARATION TIME:** 15 to 20 minutes
■ **BAKING TIME:** 35 to 45 minutes
■ **EQUIPMENT:** eight 8-ounce ramekins or ovenproof dessert cups, flat-bottomed baking pan, electric mixer

PER 5.75 OZ SERVING: 221 CALS, 2.2 G TOT FAT, .8 G MONO FAT, .7 G SAT FAT, 76 MG CHOL

Russian Apple Bread Pudding

We've lightened up a recipe for apple charlotte that we found in an old Russian cookbook, but we've kept the distinctive flavorings of cherry preserves and lemon for an old-fashioned, homey dessert with Russian character.

 PREHEAT THE OVEN to 325°. Butter the baking pan.

PLACE THE DRY bread cubes in a mixing bowl. Beat together the eggs, milk, vanilla, and sugar. Pour this custard mixture over the bread and allow it to soak while you peel, core, and thinly slice the apples. Gently stir the lemon peel and the apple slices into the custard-soaked bread.

POUR THE MIXTURE evenly into the prepared baking dish. Dot the top with spoonfuls of preserves and bake for about 1 hour, or until the custard is set and the top is slightly crusty. Serve warm or cold.

 NOTE If the bread cubes are not stale and hard, dry them on a baking sheet for about 10 minutes in a 350° oven.

- **PREPARATION TIME:** 30 minutes
- **BAKING TIME:** 1 hour
- **EQUIPMENT:** 8-inch square baking pan

■ **SERVES 6**

- 3 cups stale bread cubes from challah (page 357) or French or Italian bread
- 2 large eggs
- 2 cups milk
- 1 teaspoon pure vanilla extract
- ⅓ cup sugar
- 2 or 3 apples (about 3 cups, thinly sliced)
- 2 teaspoons freshly grated lemon peel
- ½ cup preserves, preferably cherry or currant*

Although we usually use unsweetened fruit spreads, the preserves in this recipe should have larger or whole pieces of fruit—not blended like in the spreads. These kinds of preserves are usually sweetened.

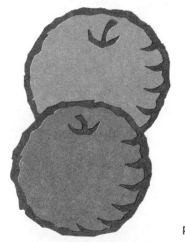

FROZEN DESSERTS

Frozen Desserts

FROZEN DESSERTS CAN SATISFY A MULTITUDE OF CULINARY NEEDS.
An invigorating granita refreshes the palate at the end of a hearty meal. An elegant dinner
is complemented by a luxurious semi-freddo. Fruit sorbets or nonfat frozen yogurt offer
the illusion of richness with no compromise in flavor. And besides being a vehicle for a
seemingly infinite variety of flavors, ice cream is a great comfort food. Those of
us old-timers at Moosewood who grew up in urban or suburban settings were less likely
to experience homemade frozen desserts than the stuff we bought in stores or from white
trucks that cruised the neighborhood with jingling bells. On the other hand, for special
occasions, our country cousins had the real thing freshly made with cream, sugar, fresh
fruit, or cocoa and nuts. Everybody took turns cranking the ice cream freezer on the front
porch. This chapter presents frozen desserts that allow anybody, anywhere, to appreciate the difference homemade ice cream can make, as well as offering an engaging
pastime. Most of the recipes require only equipment that is readily at hand in the
typical household. Good examples are refreshing, thirst-quenching granitas, ices, and
slushes made from juice or fruit as well as flavorful liquids like coffee or spirits. Granita di

Caffé is stirred as it freezes to achieve a pleasantly grainy texture. Ices, on the other hand, are made by shaving the frozen liquid with a fork or sharp-edged spoon, resulting in a mound of ice crystals. Both look beautiful in champagne glasses; eat the slivers of flavored ice with a spoon and sip the cool liquid as it melts. To make smoother, fluffier slushes, freeze the liquid and then churn it in a food processor. Both the Melon Midori Slush and the Grapefruit Tequila Slush achieve their distinctive texture because of the presence of alcohol, which doesn't freeze as hard as other liquids. Other frozen desserts will require the use of an ice cream maker or machine. Electric ice cream machines effortlessly turn out a batch of ice cream, sherbet, frozen yogurt, or sorbet while you tend to other things. Some ice cream makers don't require electricity but use supercooled cylinders (stored in the freezer) that are turned by hand every few minutes for up to half an hour. Ice cream machines are a worthwhile investment for creative cooks who love to invent their own flavors. Making homemade ice cream or sorbet from freshly picked summer peaches, raspberries, strawberries, or blueberries is a treat that could become a seasonal ritual. In this chapter, you'll also find tips for creating both plain and fancy ice cream treats by enhancing commercial ice cream. A little softened ice cream or frozen yogurt between two cookies makes an instant ice cream sandwich. A banana and a few favorite toppings will create a new version of the traditional banana split. For a more elegant dessert, swirl a sauce into softened ice cream, drizzle on a liqueur, layer sauces and fruits in tall parfait glasses, or design an elaborate "strata" using layers of cake, fruit, liqueur, nuts, and ice cream. Fill puffy little profiteroles with ice cream and top with a sauce to make another quick but fancy and tempting treat. We hope this chapter will inspire you to take a whirl with your own frozen dessert creations.

Apple Ice

This is a bright and refreshing confection, and one that's oh-so-easy to make. Finish a rich dinner with this granita-style ice, use it to cleanse the palate during a multicourse meal, or serve it to your children as an after-school treat.

Granitas freeze most quickly in nonreactive metal baking pans, but freezerproof glass pans or casseroles will also work. If you like, you can freeze this recipe in an ice cube tray; then just before serving, let the cubes sit at room temperature for about 5 minutes and whirl in a food processor. The result will be a slightly softer ice than the granita texture produced by the freeze-and-stir method we describe below.

■ **SERVES 4 TO 8**

1½ cups unsweetened applesauce

1 cup fruit juice, such as raspberry, apple-cranberry, or cranberry-orange*

¼ to ½ cup sugar, to taste*

dash of salt

* The juice adds both color and flavor—we recommend raspberry or one of the blends, but plain apple juice works, too. The amount of sugar needed will depend upon the sweetness of the applesauce and juice. Remember that once frozen, the mixture will taste less sweet than when cool or at room temperature.

IN A BLENDER, combine all of the ingredients and purée for 2 or 3 minutes until very smooth. Pour into the pan and place on a level surface in the freezer. Freeze for at least 2 hours, stirring every 30 minutes until no liquid is left. Be sure to scrape the sides of the dish. If lumps form, crush them with a table fork to maintain the texture of a soft ice slush. Store well covered.

NOTE   If the granita freezes solid, remove it from the freezer for about 15 minutes, break it up with a sturdy fork, and whirl the pieces in a food processor for a somewhat different—but still good—texture.

■ **YIELD:** 1 quart
■ **PREPARATION TIME:** 10 minutes
■ **FREEZING TIME:** 2 hours
■ **EQUIPMENT:** blender, 1- or 1½-quart nonreactive metal or freezerproof glass pan or dish

PER 5.75 OZ SERVING: 147 CALS, 0 G TOT FAT, 0 G MONO FAT, 0 G SAT FAT, 0 MG CHOL

Tropical Fruit Ice

Tropical Fruit Ice, a cross between a slush and a granita, is effortless to make—and what a pleasure it is to come home on a hot sultry day, open the freezer, pop the already made ice cubes in the food processor, and, mmm, *relax and enjoy.*

Make this drink over and over again trying all of the tropical juices you've never tasted before and mixing and matching flavors to find just the perfect blend for the moment. Guava juice will give a transluscent pink cast to the drink that can be mesmerizing, with or without rum.

Remember, if you do add the rum, the fruit juice mixture will take longer to freeze.

COMBINE ALL OF the ingredients well. If you add sugar, whirl in a blender for better dissolving. Pour into two ice cube trays and freeze solid. Store the cubes in a tightly sealed plastic bag.

WHEN READY TO serve, whirl in batches in a food processor until smooth and "creamy." Serve immediately.

- **PREPARATION TIME:** 5 minutes
- **FREEZING TIME:** 2½ to 3 hours
- **EQUIPMENT:** blender, 2 ice cube trays, food processor

PER 8 OZ SERVING: 198 CALS, .3 G TOT FAT, 0 G MONO FAT, 0 G SAT FAT, 0 MG CHOL

- **SERVES 2**

3 cups tropical fruit juice or a mixture*

1 teaspoon pure vanilla extract

sugar or honey to taste**

1 ounce rum, or to taste (optional)

* *Try mango, pineapple, passion fruit, coconut, guava, papaya, orange, or tangerine. The combination of mango, pineapple, and guava is very nice, too.*

** *When you add sugar or honey to taste, remember that it will taste less sweet when frozen. Try a tablespoon of sugar and ½ ounce of rum to start.*

Pear Sorbet

This sorbet has a bright, lemony flavor and a voluptuous "mouth feel."

We think that pears provide a particularly appealing texture, but the same basic method can be used with almost any pulpy fruit to make other great sorbets. A pairing of plums and pears is nice. Strawberries and peaches, too. If you use raspberries or blackberries, strain and discard the seeds (page 127) and add a poached pear or two for substance.

Sorbets come out best if the sorbet mix is cold when you pour it into the ice cream machine.

■ SERVES 4 TO 6

3 large fresh pears
²⁄₃ cup sugar
¹⁄₃ cup water
freshly grated peel of 1 lemon
juice of 1 lemon

PEEL THE PEARS and then poach them by gently simmering in water to cover for 30 to 40 minutes, until easily pierced with the tip of a paring knife. Drain and refrigerate until cold.

IN THE SMALL saucepan, stir together the sugar and water. Bring to a boil, stirring occasionally, until the sugar is dissolved. Refrigerate until cold.

SLICE THE PEARS in half and remove the stems, seeds, and cores. In a food processor or blender, whirl the pears for 2 or 3 minutes until very smooth. Add the sugar syrup, lemon peel, and lemon juice and purée until smooth.

POUR INTO AN ice cream machine and freeze according to the manufacturer's directions. Store in a covered container in the freezer. If your freezer is very cold, let the sorbet sit at room temperature for a few minutes before serving.

- **YIELD:** 3 cups
- **PREPARATION TIME:** about 1½ hours
- **FREEZING TIME:** 20 to 30 minutes in most ice cream machines
- **EQUIPMENT:** 2-quart saucepan, small saucepan, food processor or blender, ice cream machine

PER 3.5 OZ SERVING: 120 CALS, .2 G TOT FAT, 0 G MONO FAT, 0 G SAT FAT, 0 MG CHOL

Granita di Caffé

The most popular granita flavoring in Italy is surely coffee. It is an icy treat that, spoonful by spoonful, chills your mouth and refreshes your spirit. It can be flavored with ½ teaspoon of unsweetened cocoa powder per cup of coffee, stirred in with the sugar while the coffee is hot.

We give you two methods for making granita. The traditional stirring method results in a granular, icy concoction, with flakes of ice resembling transparent mica. The food processor method produces a softer, smoother, slushier texture. If you have the patience to use a blender, stopping often to push the ice down into the blade area, you can make a very smooth coffee ice that's whipped so much that you'd swear it contained cream. Because it doesn't, however, it has a clean, clear mouth appeal, without cream's cloying aftertaste.

This recipe can easily be doubled or tripled.

WHILE THE COFFEE or espresso is hot, add the sugar and stir for about 15 seconds, or until completely dissolved.

FOR THE TRADITIONAL method, pour the coffee into the nonreactive freezerproof pan and place it on a flat surface in the freezer. After 30 minutes, stir the ice crystals around the edges into the center. Freeze for 1 to 3 hours longer, stirring every 20 to 30 minutes. If chunks of ice form, crush them with a fork.

TO MAKE GRANITA in a food processor or blender, freeze the sweetened coffee in ice cube trays or in a bowl or pan until solid. When ready to serve, whirl in a food processor or blender to a crunchy or soft consistency, as you prefer. Spoon the granita into goblets, glasses, or bowls and serve plain or topped with whipped cream, if desired.

- **PREPARATION TIME:** 5 to 10 minutes
- **FREEZING (AND STIRRING) TIME:** 1 to 3 hours
- **EQUIPMENT:** nonreactive freezerproof container (a flat-bottomed stainless steel pan is best), food processor or blender (optional)

PER 8 OZ SERVING: 78 CALS, 0 G TOT FAT, 0 G MONO FAT, 0 G SAT FAT, 0 MG CHOL

■ **SERVES 2**

2 cups freshly brewed hot coffee (or espresso for a stronger granita)

2 to 4 tablespoons sugar

fresh whipped cream (optional)

Grapefruit Tequila Slush

The combination of grapefruit and tequila is wonderfully bracing. Try this tropical delight as a palate-cleansing "pause" during a hearty meal or as a finish for a holiday celebration.

■ **SERVES 4**

12 ounces frozen unsweetened grapefruit concentrate

⅓ cup tequila

¼ cup sugar

1½ cups water

MIX ALL OF the ingredients well either by hand or in a blender. Pour the mixture into two ice cube trays and freeze until almost solid, at least 3 hours. In a food processor or blender, pulse small batches of the frozen cubes until you get a granular "slush."

POUR INTO PRETTY glasses and serve with a spoon and a straw.

■ **PREPARATION TIME:** 5 minutes
■ **FREEZING TIME:** 3 hours
■ **PULSING TIME:** 5 minutes
■ **EQUIPMENT:** blender, 2 ice cube trays, food processor (optional)

PER 6 OZ SERVING: 191 CALS, .4 G TOT FAT, 0 G MONO FAT, 0 G SAT FAT, 0 MG CHOL

Melon Midori Slush

This icy, airy sweet is a welcome refresher with hot spicy cuisines, such as Szechuan, Mexican, or Thai, or at the end of a hot humid day. Choose a melon that is fully ripe and sweet.

 SPREAD THE MELON cubes on a baking sheet, cover with plastic wrap or wax paper, and place in the freezer for at least 2 hours (see Note).

COMBINE THE FROZEN melon cubes, Midori, and frozen limeade concentrate in a food processor or blender and purée for about 2 minutes until smooth, stopping to scrape the sides if necessary.

SERVE IMMEDIATELY, TOPPED with kiwi or strawberry slices, or return to the freezer for up to an hour. Should the slush become too icy or hard, simply reprocess for a few seconds before serving.

NOTE Once frozen, melon cubes will keep for several days in the freezer in a tightly covered container.

- **YIELD:** about 3 cups
- **PREPARATION TIME:** 5 minutes
- **FREEZING TIME:** 2 hours
- **EQUIPMENT:** baking sheet, food processor or blender

PER 5.5 OZ SERVING: 119 CALS, .4 G TOT FAT, 0 G MONO FAT, 0 G SAT FAT, 0 MG CHOL

- **SERVES 4**

- 3 cups cantaloupe or honeydew melon, cut into 1-inch cubes (about ½ melon)
- ¼ cup melon-flavored liqueur, such as Midori
- ¼ cup frozen limeade concentrate

a few kiwi or strawberry slices

Easiest Peach Ice Cream

Philadelphia-style ice creams are made without eggs and are uncooked, so preparation is quite simple. The emulsifying action of the peaches gives the ice cream its smoothness.

This ice cream is soft and delectable when it's first made. If you're not going to serve it right away, store it in a covered container in the freezer. Depending upon the conditions in your freezer, it may be best to let it soften for a few minutes before serving.

■ **SERVES 6 TO 8**

3 cups peeled chopped
  fresh peaches or
  1 pound thawed
  frozen peaches

1¼ to 1½ cups sugar*

⅛ teaspoon salt

1 cup peach juice

1 cup half-and-half

2 teaspoons pure
  vanilla extract

* The riper the peaches, the less sugar you'll need.

IN A BLENDER or food processor, combine the peaches with ½ to ¾ cup of the sugar and the salt and whirl until fairly smooth. In a separate bowl, combine the peach juice, half-and-half, ¾ cup of the sugar, and the vanilla. Stir until the sugar dissolves. Add the peaches.

POUR THE MIXTURE into an ice cream machine and freeze according to the manufacturer's directions.

VARIATION   Replace the peaches with 3 cups of chopped fresh mangoes—another fruit that will produce a velvety smooth ice cream.

■ **YIELD:** 1 quart
■ **PREPARATION TIME:** 25 minutes
■ **FREEZING TIME:** about 30 minutes
■ **EQUIPMENT:** blender or
  food processor,
  ice cream machine

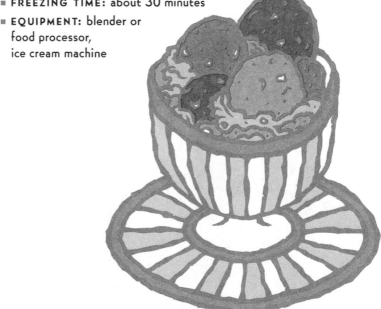

Low-fat Blueberry Buttermilk Ice

This simple yet elegant dessert is the perfect solution when no one wants to cook but the summer fruits are inviting and abundant. Vary the amount of sugar in the recipe depending upon the sweetness of the fruit—you will almost certainly want to reduce the sugar when making the banana variation.

Fruit ices can be stored in a sealed container in the freezer for at least a week.

■ **SERVES 6 TO 8**

3 cups fresh or frozen blueberries

½ cup sugar

1 cup buttermilk

1 teaspoon pure vanilla extract

COMBINE ALL OF the ingredients in a blender and purée until smooth. Pour the sauce into the pan and freeze for 2½ to 3 hours until frozen solid. Using a large, heavy spoon, scrape the "ice" from one side of the pan to the other.

SPOON INTO BOWLS and serve immediately.

VARIATIONS Replace the blueberries with 3 cups of any of the following fruits: hulled and sliced strawberries, sliced ripe bananas, peeled sliced peaches, pitted sweet cherries, or sliced mango.

To make raspberry or blackberry ices, you may wish to remove the seeds for a smoother texture. Simply cook 3½ cups of berries on medium heat for 3 to 5 minutes until juicy, purée them in a blender, and force through a fine-mesh strainer to remove the seeds. Proceed with the recipe as above.

■ **YIELD:** 1 quart
■ **PREPARATION TIME:** 5 minutes
■ **FREEZING TIME:** 2½ to 3 hours
■ **EQUIPMENT:** blender, nonreactive 9-inch square or 10-inch round freezerproof pan

PER 3.5 OZ SERVING: 91 CALS, .6 G TOT FAT, .1 G MONO FAT, .2 G SAT FAT, 1 MG CHOL

Strawberry Sour Cream Sherbet

We no longer make our own ice cream or sherbet at Moosewood, but many of us love to prepare fresh frozen desserts at home. When longtime cook Nancy Lazarus began developing recipes for this chapter, she aimed for full fresh fruit flavor and easy preparation (no fussy custards). This sherbet is one of her many successes.

Nancy is now the happy owner of an electric ice cream maker that regularly churns out frozen treats year-round—from hot summer days to winter nights by a sizzling fireplace. When something so good is so easy, why resist?

■ **SERVES 6 TO 8**

1 pint fresh strawberries, hulled and rinsed

¾ cup sugar

1 cup sour cream (see Note)

½ teaspoon pure vanilla extract

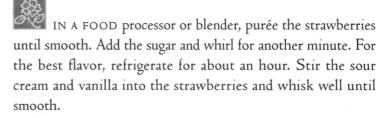 IN A FOOD processor or blender, purée the strawberries until smooth. Add the sugar and whirl for another minute. For the best flavor, refrigerate for about an hour. Stir the sour cream and vanilla into the strawberries and whisk well until smooth.

TRANSFER TO AN ice cream machine and freeze according to the manufacturer's directions. Store in the freezer in a covered container until ready to serve.

NOTE This sherbet can be served straight out of the ice cream maker, but it keeps well in the freezer, too. If your freezer is particularly cold, let the sherbet soften a little, at room temperature or in the refrigerator, before scooping it.

We prefer the flavor and texture of regular sour cream, but you can use yogurt, nonfat yogurt, or nonfat sour cream with very good results.

■ **YIELD:** about 1 quart
■ **PREPARATION TIME:** 10 to 15 minutes
■ **CHILLING TIME:** 1 hour
■ **FREEZING TIME:** 20 to 30 minutes in most ice cream machines
■ **EQUIPMENT:** food processor or blender, ice cream machine

Chocolate Hazelnut Semi-Freddo

Italians seem to have a particular finesse with frozen desserts. "Semi-freddo," which means partially cold or frozen, is not at all hard and icy—instead it's a luxuriantly smooth and rich frozen custard. It is customarily made in a loaf shape to be sliced. The sublime flavor produced by combining chocolate and hazelnuts lingers without a trace of cloying sweetness.

 LINE THE LOAF pan with plastic wrap and set aside.

IN A 325° oven, toast the hazelnuts for about 10 minutes. Cool, then rub in a towel to remove as many of the skins as possible. In a blender or food processor, whirl the nuts until finely ground. Combine the ground nuts and the milk in a saucepan and heat until almost boiling. Set aside for about 1 hour to allow the hazelnuts to infuse the milk with flavor.

STRAIN THE MILK through a fine sieve into the top of a double boiler and discard the nuts. Add the egg yolks, sugar, and liqueur and cook, stirring continuously, for about 10 minutes, or until the mixture reaches a custard-like consistency; the custard should be thick enough to coat a spoon. Whisk in the melted chocolate and the vanilla. Chill for at least 30 minutes.

WHIP THE CREAM until stiff, then fold it into the cooled custard. Pour the custard into the prepared pan and fold the plastic wrap loosely over the top. Freeze for at least 8 hours.

TO SERVE, UNCOVER the top of the semi-freddo, dip the loaf pan in warm water for 30 seconds, and invert the semi-freddo onto a plate. Remove the plastic wrap. Slice portions onto individual plates and garnish with fruit slices or berries, if desired.

- **PREPARATION TIME:** 30 minutes
- **STEEPING TIME:** 1 hour
- **CUSTARD CHILLING TIME:** 30 minutes
- **FREEZING TIME:** 8 hours or overnight
- **EQUIPMENT:** 9 × 5-inch loaf pan, blender or food processor, small saucepan, sieve, double boiler (page 370)

- **SERVES 6 TO 8**

½ cup whole hazelnuts

1 cup milk

5 egg yolks

½ cup sugar

¼ cup hazelnut-flavored liqueur, such as Fra Angelico

2 ounces semi-sweet chocolate, melted

1 teaspoon pure vanilla extract

1 cup heavy cream

a few fruit slices or berries

Apricot Amaretto Tortoni

This rich, decadent dessert is similar to a semi-freddo—not quite ice cream, not quite custard. Tortoni would make an elegant filling for melon or ripe peach halves. Or layer tortoni with fresh fruit in a parfait glass. Or serve plain, garnished with chopped toasted almonds, fresh grapes, peaches, apricots, or cantaloupe.

■ **SERVES 8**

1 cup heavy cream

1 cup dried apricots

2 tablespoons almond-flavored liqueur, such as amaretto

1 cup whole almonds

10 amaretti (page 354) (about 1 cup, crushed)

⅓ cup confectioners' sugar

CHILL THE CREAM and refrigerate the beaters and bowl.

CHOP THE APRICOTS into small pieces, place in a small bowl, sprinkle with the amaretto, and set aside. Toast and chop the almonds (page 364). Using a blender, food processor, or rolling pin, crush the amaretti into fine crumbs.

USING THE CHILLED beaters and bowl, beat the chilled cream and the confectioners' sugar until stiff peaks form. Fold in the apricots and amaretto, the chopped almonds, and crushed amaretti. Fill the custard cups, glasses, or pan with the mixture, cover with foil, and place in the freezer for 20 minutes. Remove from the freezer and refrigerate for at least 20 minutes longer before serving.

■ **TOTAL TIME:** 1 hour
■ **PREPARATION TIME:** 25 minutes
■ **CHILLING TIME:** 40 minutes
■ **EQUIPMENT:** electric mixer; blender, food processor, or rolling pin; eight 6-ounce custard cups or parfait glasses or a 9-inch square pan

Boardwalk Bananas

This treat is reminiscent of the Jersey Shore in the '50s, when all along the boardwalk you could purchase a frozen chocolate-covered banana to eat while riding a bicycle-built-for-two. We find this is a perfect dessert-on-a-stick for children, and it's so easy to make that they can help with preparation, too.

IN THE DOUBLE boiler, melt the chocolate with the milk, stirring until smooth.

CUT EACH BANANA into 3 or 4 pieces and insert a skewer or ice cream stick into each piece. Place the peanuts on a small plate. Dip each banana piece into the melted chocolate, roll in the peanuts, and place on the wax paper-lined baking sheet. Place the bananas in the freezer for 1½ to 2 hours, until icy but not hard. If the bananas harden, allow them to thaw for about 15 minutes before serving.

VARIATION   Substitute ⅔ cup shredded unsweetened or sweetened coconut or coarsely ground toasted almonds, cashews, or hazelnuts for the peanuts.

- **PREPARATION TIME:** 25 minutes
- **FREEZING TIME:** 1½ to 2 hours
- **EQUIPMENT:** double boiler (page 370), bamboo skewers or wooden ice cream sticks, wax paper–lined baking sheet

- **SERVES 6 TO 8**

½ cup semi-sweet chocolate chips

¼ cup milk

2 large firm bananas

⅔ cup crushed roasted unsalted peanuts

Dairyless Peanut Butter Fudge Pops

You can't buy these fudge pops from the seasonal ice cream truck, but they're delicious and have that tongue-tingling "lick-fast-before-they-drip" quality.

This recipe can also be used for making "ice milk" in an ice cream maker. It's a bit more "icy," melts a little faster, and has a cleaner, fresher aftertaste than its dairy-laden cousin.

See our variations for other frozen confections and experiment with some of your own ideas.

■ SERVES 4 TO 6

2 cups chilled soy milk or rice milk*

1½ tablespoons smooth peanut butter

2 tablespoons unsweetened cocoa powder

½ teaspoon pure vanilla extract

¼ teaspoon pure almond extract

sugar to taste*

* Different brands of soy milk and rice milk vary greatly in taste and sweetness. After you've blended everything but the sugar, add sugar to taste, keeping in mind that when frozen it will taste somewhat less sweet.

IN A BLENDER, whirl all of the ingredients except the sugar until smooth. (Omit the vanilla if using vanilla-flavored soy or rice milk.) Add sugar to taste and blend well.

TO MAKE ICE milk, pour the mixture into an ice cream maker and freeze according to the manufacturer's directions. Store covered in the freezer.

TO MAKE THE pops, use one of these methods:

■ Pour the mixture into an ice cream maker and freeze until slushy and soft. Spoon into ice pop molds or small paper cups, pressing out any air pockets. Place a stick in the center of each pop and freeze until firm.

■ Pour the mixture into a shallow pan, place it in the freezer, and freeze until firm, but not ice-hard. Scoop into a food processor or blender and whirl until smooth. Immediately spoon into ice pop molds or small paper cups and proceed as above.

■ Pour the unfrozen mixture directly from the blender into ice pop molds or small paper cups, insert the sticks, and freeze until firm. This method makes icier pops.

WHEN READY TO serve, run hot water over the mold to free the pops. If you want to reuse the molds before you're ready to eat the pops, unmold the pops, wrap them tightly in plastic wrap, seal the end with a twist tie around the stick, and store in the freezer.

 VARIATIONS For Fruit Ice Pops, combine ½ cup of fruit juice, 1 cup of soy milk or rice milk, and 1 cup of fresh, frozen, or canned fruit. Add sugar, vanilla, or almond extract to taste and purée everything until smooth. Some good fruit and juice combinations are bananas and pineapple juice, canned peaches and peach juice with almond or vanilla extract, and strawberries with orange juice and vanilla extract.

Try flavored soy milks with different combinations of fruit and fruit juices.

- **YIELD:** ten 2-ounce ice pops or a generous pint of ice milk
- **PREPARATION TIME:** 5 minutes
- **FREEZING TIME:** varies
- **EQUIPMENT:** blender, ice cream maker (optional), ice pop molds (optional), wooden ice cream sticks

Spumoni

Start with your favorite store-bought vanilla ice cream or frozen yogurt, pack it full of good things, and you'll have a delectable gourmet adults-only treat that will close any pasta dinner in style.

Ice cream this good can't be found in the freezer case. Made without any any liqueur, this Spumoni still tastes good.

■ **SERVES 6 TO 8**

1 quart vanilla ice cream or frozen yogurt, slightly softened

½ cup chopped toasted almonds (page 364)

½ cup finely chopped frozen or canned sweet cherries

½ cup chopped toasted shelled pistachio nuts (page 364)

1 tablespoon fresh coarsely grated orange peel

2 ounces semi-sweet chocolate, finely chopped

2 tablespoons almond-flavored liqueur, such as amaretto

2 tablespoons orange-flavored liqueur, such as cointreau

IN A LARGE bowl, mix together all of the ingredients. Pour into a freezerproof container, cover the surface with plastic wrap, and freeze until firm, at least 2 hours.

SERVE PLAIN OR topped with chocolate sauce or liqueur.

■ **YIELD:** 1½ quarts
■ **PREPARATION TIME:** 20 minutes
■ **FREEZING TIME:** 2 to 4 hours
■ **EQUIPMENT:** 1½- or 2-quart freezerproof container

Pumpkin Ice Cream Strata

The strong flavors of pumpkin and chocolate are unusually good in combination. Made ahead and frozen, Pumpkin Ice Cream Strata is great for unexpected guests, sweet tooth cravings, or a Halloween party. The moist loaf cake, layered with ice cream, slices into attractive servings.

To really take this dessert over the top, drizzle each slice with chocolate sauce (pages 312 to 313). If it's Halloween, plastic spiders are a fetching embellishment.

PREHEAT THE OVEN to 350°. Butter the loaf pan and dust it lightly with flour.

IN A LARGE bowl, cream the butter and sugar together until well mixed. Add the eggs and beat for about 2 minutes, until smooth and lightened in color. Stir in the pumpkin. In a separate bowl, sift together the flour, baking soda, cinnamon, nutmeg, and salt. Add the flour mixture to the pumpkin mixture and stir until the batter is very smooth. Fold in the chocolate chips.

POUR THE BATTER into the prepared loaf pan and bake for about 1 hour, until the top is firm but not crusty and a knife tests clean. Remove from the pan and cool on a rack.

WHEN THE CAKE is completely cool, slice it horizontally into 3 layers. Spread half of the ice cream on the bottom layer, gently press the middle layer in place, spread on the rest of the ice cream, and press the top layer in place. Wrap tightly with plastic wrap and freeze for about 1 hour. Remove from the freezer 5 to 10 minutes before slicing. Serve in 1-inch-thick slices.

VARIATION For a quicker unlayered version that doesn't require freezing, simply cool the cake to room temperature and serve it à la mode.

- **CAKE PREPARATION TIME:** 20 minutes
- **BAKING TIME:** about 1 hour
- **ASSEMBLING TIME:** 10 minutes
- **EQUIPMENT:** 9 × 5-inch loaf pan

■ **SERVES 8**

½ cup butter,
   at room temperature

¾ cup sugar

2 eggs

¾ cup unsweetened
   pumpkin purée
   (6-ounce can)

1¾ cups unbleached
   white flour

1 teaspoon baking soda

1 teaspoon
   ground cinnamon

½ teaspoon
   ground nutmeg

½ teaspoon salt

1 cup semi-sweet
   chocolate chips

1 pint ice cream or
   frozen yogurt, such
   as vanilla, chocolate
   chip, chocolate,
   cinnamon, or pumpkin

Strawberry Ice Cream Torte

Although this fancy dessert looks complicated to prepare, it really isn't, because each step is easy. The cake can be baked ahead of time, filled with ice cream, and stored in the freezer. When you're ready to serve it, just top it with sauce, fresh strawberries, and whipped cream and voilà!

The simple, light cake has no leavening except eggs, so it requires a lot of beating. But there's something especially satisfying about making this cake—it feels somehow like being linked to earlier generations of bakers who worked magic with a few simple ingredients.

The Fresh Strawberry Sauce is one that we bet you'll turn to again and again, to serve on ice cream, poundcakes, Profiteroles (page 256), oatmeal. . . . It is smooth and clear and retains the flavor of fresh strawberries. Serve it warm, at room temperature, or chilled. The sauce recipe makes 1 cup.

■ **SERVES 8 TO 10**

CAKE
- 4 eggs
- ⅔ cup sugar
- 2 teaspoons pure vanilla extract
- ¼ cup butter, melted
- ¾ cup unbleached white flour

FILLING
- 1 quart vanilla ice cream

PREHEAT THE OVEN to 350°. Generously butter the cake pan and dust it with flour.

IN A LARGE bowl, beat the eggs and sugar with an electric mixer at high speed until well blended, thick, and foamy, about 5 minutes. Stir the vanilla and ¼ cup of the whipped eggs into the melted butter and set aside. Working quickly but gently, gradually fold ½ cup of the flour into the bowl of whipped eggs. Fold in the butter mixture and then the rest of the flour.

POUR THE BATTER evenly into the prepared cake pan and bake for 25 to 30 minutes, until the top is golden and springs back when touched. Run a knife around the edges of the pan to loosen the cake. Remove the cake from the pan, turn right side up, and cool completely on a rack.

ALLOW THE ICE cream to soften in the refrigerator until it can be spread but is not soupy. Slice the cooled cake in half horizontally with a serrated knife. Spread the bottom layer with the softened ice cream. Replace the top layer, gently pressing it down. Wrap tightly with plastic wrap and freeze.

MEANWHILE, MAKE THE sauce. Combine the strawberries, sugar, and ¼ cup of the water in the saucepan and bring to a simmer. Cook, stirring frequently for about 3 minutes, until the strawberries are foaming, swollen, and easily mashed with a fork. Dissolve the cornstarch in the remaining ¼ cup of water and stir it into the strawberries. Simmer, stirring constantly, just until the juice is clear and thickened. Stir in the orange juice, and if you prefer a perfectly smooth sauce, whirl briefly in the blender. Refrigerate until ready to use.

TO SERVE, UNWRAP the cake, place it on a serving plate, and defrost it at room temperature for 10 to 15 minutes. Top the cake with the strawberry sauce, allowing it to drizzle down the sides. Decorate with sliced strawberries and whipped cream and serve.

VARIATION Try a Chocolate Sponge Cake for the torte. Replace ¼ cup flour with ¼ cup of sifted unsweetened cocoa powder. Fill the cake with vanilla, peppermint, or peanut butter ice cream, Strawberry Sour Cream Sherbet (page 246), or Easiest Peach Ice Cream (page 244) and top with Bittersweet Chocolate Sauce (page 312) or Summer Berry Sauce (page 309) and fresh whipped cream topped with chopped nuts or sliced fresh fruit.

- CAKE PREPARATION TIME: 25 minutes
- BAKING TIME: 25 to 30 minutes
- TORTE ASSEMBLY TIME: 45 minutes
- EQUIPMENT: 9-inch round cake pan, electric mixer, small nonreactive saucepan

FRESH STRAWBERRY SAUCE

- 2 cups stemmed chopped fresh strawberries
- ¼ cup sugar
- ½ cup water
- 2 teaspoons cornstarch
- ⅓ to ½ cup fresh orange juice

TOPPINGS

- 1 pint fresh strawberries, sliced
- ½ pint heavy cream, whipped

Profiteroles (Cream Puffs)

An impressive, yet not difficult, dessert, Profiteroles are a versatile cream puff pastry shell. At Moosewood, one of our favorite ways to serve them is also one of the easiest: fill the puffs with ice cream and top them with Bittersweet Chocolate Sauce (page 312). Other good sauce combos with ice cream filling are Cherry Sauce (page 304), Dried Fruit and Vanilla Sauce (page 307), or Fresh Mango Sauce (page 308).

Be sure to have the oven preheated to 400° when the puffs go in; the high heat quickly expands the egg-rich dough.

■ **SERVES 4 TO 8**

1 cup water

5 tablespoons butter

1 cup unbleached white flour

¼ teaspoon salt

2 teaspoons sugar

4 large eggs

 PREHEAT THE OVEN to 400°.

IN THE SAUCEPAN, bring the water and butter to a boil. Combine the flour, salt, and sugar in a small bowl and add to the saucepan all at once, stirring vigorously with a wooden spoon. Continue stirring until the mixture forms a ball and pulls away from the sides of the pan. Remove from the heat and allow to cool for 2 or 3 minutes. Beat in the eggs one at a time. As each egg is beaten in, the dough will go from a slippery, clumpy texture to a smooth mass.

LIGHTLY OIL A baking sheet. Using the wooden spoon, place mounds of dough 2 inches apart on the baking sheet. Use about ¼ cup of dough for each large puff or about 2½ tablespoons for smaller puffs. Bake for 10 minutes at 400°, then reduce the temperature to 350° and bake for 20 minutes more for smaller puffs or 25 minutes more for larger puffs.

IF YOU WANT the puffs to rise properly, restrain yourself from peeking into the oven until the baking time is almost over. When the puffs are firm, turn off the oven, remove the puffs, and using a small sharp knife, score a horizontal cut about ⅔ of the way up each puff. Return the puffs to the still warm oven for about 15 minutes to let the residual heat dry them a bit. Remove and cool completely.

FILL AS DESIRED by cutting the top from each puff at its scored mark, mounding the filling inside, and replacing the top.

- **YIELD:** 4 large or 8 smaller puffs
- **PREPARATION TIME:** 15 minutes
- **BAKING TIME:** 30 to 35 minutes
- **COOLING TIME:** about 30 minutes
- **EQUIPMENT:** heavy saucepan, baking sheet

FILLING SUGGESTIONS

Sautéed Apples (page 12)

summer berries with Flavored Whipped Cream (page 318)

gingered mango, melon, and peaches

frozen yogurt

ice cream

White Chocolate and Raspberry Fool (page 228)

Peanut Butter Ice Cream Pie

It's always fun to watch mature, sophisticated, discriminating gourmet diners go gaga over this like little kids at a birthday party.

Soften the ice cream just until you can stir it. Don't let it get soupy. This filling is good in just about any no-bake or prebaked pie shell. For an excellent chocolate pie, fill the Chocolate Graham Cracker Crust with Chocolate Ricotta Mousse (page 340) and top with whipped cream.

■ **SERVES 8 TO 10**

CHOCOLATE GRAHAM CRACKER CRUST

8 plain or chocolate graham crackers (1 cup crumbs)*

2 tablespoons butter, melted

½ cup semi-sweet chocolate or chocolate chips, melted

FILLING

1 cup roasted peanuts

1 quart vanilla ice cream or frozen yogurt, softened**

½ cup peanut butter, at room temperature

1 tablespoon pure vanilla extract

chocolate sauce (optional)

* *Or use crumbs made from crisp chocolate wafers, if you like.*

** *Allow to sit at room temperature for about 10 minutes.*

TO PREPARE THE crust, crumble the graham crackers into a food processor or blender and whirl to make a cup of fine crumbs. Or place the graham crackers in a plastic bag and crush them with a rolling pin. Place the crumbs in a bowl, drizzle the melted butter and melted chocolate over them, and stir until well mixed. With your fingers or the back of a spoon, press the mixture into the bottom and up the sides of the pie pan. Cover with plastic wrap and chill for about 1 hour until cold.

FOR THE FILLING, coarsely chop the peanuts by hand or by whirling them in a food processor. In a bowl, briskly stir together the softened ice cream, peanut butter, vanilla, and half of the chopped peanuts. Pour the filling into the chilled pie crust, smooth the top, and sprinkle with the remaining chopped peanuts. Wrap the pie with plastic wrap and freeze until firm.

REMOVE THE PIE from the freezer a few minutes before serving. Offer chocolate sauce on the side, if you wish.

■ **PREPARATION TIME (CRUST):** 10 minutes
■ **CHILLING TIME (CRUST):** 45 to 60 minutes
■ **PREPARATION TIME (FILLING):** 10 minutes
■ **FREEZING TIME:** at least 2 hours
■ **EQUIPMENT:** food processor, blender, or rolling pin; 9-inch freezerproof pie pan

Things to Do with Ice Cream

Everyone loves a festive dessert, but not everyone loves the work required to prepare one. Ice cream by itself is a simple treat, but with just a bit of enhancement, it can be easily transformed into a fancier dessert with a presentation as plain or as elaborate as you choose. There are some fine store-bought ice creams and frozen yogurts, and using purchased items, you can assemble an elegant parfait, make unusual ice cream sandwiches, or create your own "flavor" of ice cream.

Please note that every place we say ice cream here you can substitute frozen yogurt, and you can always omit the liquor or liqueur, although the final texture of the ice cream will be somewhat different.

Enhanced Store-bought Ice Cream

Start with your favorite plain flavor of ice cream, add bits of your favorite goodies, and you've got something really delicious, better than any commercially prepared "premium" ice cream. Spumoni (page 252) is an example of what we're talking about. Add nuts, shaved or chopped chocolate, fresh fruit, liqueur-soaked dried fruit, rum-soaked raisins, crushed candies, or crumbled cookies. Some of our favorite combinations are:

■ toasted hazelnuts, dark rum, and chopped semisweet chocolate in vanilla, chocolate, coconut, or pineapple ice cream

■ crumbled amaretti (page 354), amaretto, and chopped toasted almonds in vanilla or peach ice cream

■ rum-soaked raisins, chopped cherries, and caramel sauce in vanilla or chocolate ice cream

Soften the ice cream in a plastic bag in the refrigerator for 10 to 20 minutes. Don't let it get soupy or it won't refreeze well. Stir in the "enhancements," spoon the ice cream into a freezerproof container, cover it, and return it to the freezer for about an hour, until firm.

Ice Cream Swirls

When you make your own swirled ice cream, you control how little or how much "swirl" is added, the flavor combination, and the quality of the swirled-in sauce. Swirl in any smooth sauce with a thick consistency; fruit preserves, jams, and spreads work well. Try:

■ strawberry sauce with vanilla ice cream

■ raspberry sauce with chocolate ice cream

■ mango sauce with vanilla or ginger ice cream

■ puréed sweetened canned fruits with a complementary ice cream

■ sauces on pages 303 to 319 with any ice cream you like

Soften the ice cream for 10 to 20 minutes in the refrigerator. Stir it well. In a freezerproof container, layer an inch of ice cream, cover that with a thin layer of sauce, and alternate layers of ice cream and sauce until the container is full. With a sturdy wooden spoon held vertically, push straight down into the center of the ice cream all the way to the bottom. Pull the spoon from one side to the other, ending in the center. Rotate the container a couple of inches and pull the spoon to the left, to the right, and back to center. Repeat once or twice more to create an asterisk-like pattern from above. Pull the spoon straight up to remove it. Cover and return to the freezer to harden.

Ice Cream Cordials

Scoops of ice cream drizzled with liqueur and maybe topped with a few raspberries, a nasturtium, or shaved chocolate—what could be more simple? Yet, ice cream cordials, elegantly presented, are perfectly suited to both a quiet evening at home and a formal dinner party. Stick to classic combinations or go wild—we've even seen (but don't necessarily recommend) root beer-flavored and cookies 'n' cream-flavored liqueurs.

- Pear Sorbet (page 240) with raspberry- or plum-flavored liqueur and fresh fruit, or anisette and slices of kiwi
- vanilla ice cream with Fra Angelico (hazelnut-flavored liqueur) and whole roasted hazelnuts, or Grand Marnier and fresh orange sections
- chocolate ice cream with raspberry-flavored liqueur and fresh raspberries, or peppermint schnapps and shaved chocolate, or coffee-flavored liqueur, such as Kahlúa, and a sprinkling of cinnamon or grated coconut
- coffee ice cream with Scotch whiskey and finely ground espresso, or crème de cacao and chocolate wafers or chocolate-covered coffee beans
- peach ice cream with almond-flavored liqueur, such as amaretto, and amaretti (page 354)
- Strawberry Sour Cream Sherbet (page 246) with crème de cacao and fresh mint leaves

Ice Cream Sundaes and Parfaits

A sundae can be as simple as a scoop of ice cream topped with a sauce and whipped cream or it can be several different flavors of ice cream smothered with sauces, nuts, fruit, candies, cookie crumbles, and whipped cream with a cherry on top.

Ice cream parfaits are layered sundaes served in clear, tall glasses. Just alternate layers of ice cream and sundae-type toppings:

- vanilla and/or peach ice cream with amaretto and/or chocolate sauce, crumbled amaretti (page 354), slivered almonds

- strawberry and/or vanilla ice cream with Fresh Strawberry Sauce (page 255), crumbled brownies, fresh sliced strawberries, and whipped cream
- peach or cherry ice cream with peach or cherry sauce or liqueur and fresh peaches or cherries
- sorbets with rum- or liqueur-soaked ladyfingers and chocolate sauce
- pumpkin ice cream, crumbled gingersnaps, pure maple syrup, fresh whipped cream
- vanilla ice cream, sautéed apples, chopped toasted walnuts (page 364), pure maple syrup

Banana Splits

Build a complex sundae on top of a banana and you have a banana split:

- Traditional Banana Split: three ice cream flavors, three sauces, nuts, whipped cream, and cherries
- Low-fat Sorbet Banana Split: various flavors of sorbet, crushed pineapple and sliced fruits or fruit sauces, Light Chocolate Sauce (page 312), toasted wheat germ
- Tropical Banana Split: coffee, coconut, and chocolate ice creams; rum; crushed pineapple, mango sauce, and chocolate sauce; grated coconut; and peanuts or chopped macadamia nuts

Ice Cream Sandwiches

Ice cream sandwiches can be made with many types and sizes of flat cookies, from big, chewy oatmeal cookies to small vanilla wafers. Try:

- pumpkin ice cream and gingersnaps
- lemony Cornmeal Cookies (page 181) and raspberry ice cream or sorbet
- Chocolate Sugar Cookies (page 180) and cherry, strawberry, peanut butter, coffee, or mocha chip ice cream

■ Peanut Butter Cookies (page 186) and chocolate, butter pecan, or banana ice cream

■ oatmeal, molasses, or chocolate chip cookies and vanilla ice cream

Soften the ice cream in the refrigerator for 10 to 20 minutes. Cover the flat bottom of a cookie with ice cream 1 to 2 inches thick. Press the flat side of a second cookie onto the ice cream and smooth the edges with a table knife. If you wish, roll the edges in chopped nuts, cookie crumbs, coconut, or mini chocolate chips. Freeze until hard, then tightly wrap each sandwich in plastic and return to the freezer until ready to serve.

Ice Cream Stratas

Stratas are made up of cake sprinkled with liqueur and layered with fruit and ice cream:

■ Blueberry-Peach Strata: amaretto or peach-flavored liqueur, vanilla or peach ice cream, fresh blueberries

■ Banana Strata: dark rum or maple syrup, vanilla ice cream, sliced bananas, and toasted walnuts. Top each serving with chocolate sauce.

■ Melba Strata: raspberry liqueur, peach ice cream, fresh raspberries

■ Strawberry Strata: kirsch, strawberry or vanilla ice cream, fresh strawberries, and sliced almonds

Start with a freezerproof bowl, dish, or pan. Cover the bottom with a thin layer of poundcake or ladyfingers moistened with liqueur or a thin fruit sauce. Spread a layer of softened ice cream to cover the cake all the way to the edges. Sprinkle with fresh berries or sliced fruit. Repeat the layers, ending with ice cream. Cover and freeze until firm. To serve, turn the strata out of the bowl

onto a plate, slice, and top with dollops of whipped cream and perhaps more sauce on the side. See also page 253.

Ice Cream Pies

Fill just about any prebaked or no-bake pie crust with softened ice cream. Cover and freeze until firm. When ready to serve, top with sauce and nuts, fruit, candies, or crumbled cookies . . . and whipped cream.

Ice Cream Sodas

A generous glass, a long-handled spoon, and a fat straw are important ingredients. Add about an inch of flavoring, a carbonated liquid, and a scoop of ice cream and you have a good old-fashioned soda fountain treat. Our favorites are:

■ Black and White Soda: an inch of chocolate syrup plus an inch of cream or nonfat condensed skim milk, sparkling water, vanilla ice cream

■ Cream Pop (vanilla and orange in one of these combinations): vanilla ice cream with Orangina or sparkling water and orange juice concentrate, or orange sherbet with sparkling water and sweetened cream or half-and-half with a drop of vanilla extract

■ Raspberry Fizz: ginger ale with raspberry sherbet or sorbet and a raspberry on top

■ Maple Medley: maple syrup, cream, sparkling water, and vanilla or maple walnut ice cream

■ Tropical Cooler: pineapple juice, sparkling water or ginger ale, rainbow sherbet or coconut ice cream

■ Peaches and Cream: puréed fresh, frozen, or canned peaches, cream soda, and vanilla ice cream

MUFFINS CUPCAKES BREADS AND COFFEECAKES

Muffins, Cupcakes, Breads, and Coffeecakes

YOU'LL RETURN OFTEN TO THE RECIPES IN THIS CHAPTER BECAUSE they are so tasty and making them is no big production. These pastries are appealing whether you have a sweet tooth or not. We expect a fancy layer cake to be sweet, but you can easily vary the sweetness of a muffin or nut bread. We've included a wonderful variety of quick bread, muffin, and cupcake recipes that can be served for dessert, at breakfast or brunch, or as a delightful snack at any time. Many of us prefer this sort of simple treat to richer fare. The thought of baking from scratch can be intimidating for those who are inexperienced or just venturing beyond commercial mixes. Although the rising process of a yeasted dough may seem mysterious, in fact, it mostly takes care of itself, and quick breads (those without yeast) are some of the easiest baked goods to try. Quick bread dough is distinguished from yeasted dough by the leavening and has a very different texture. Quick breads are leavened with baking powder and/or baking soda. The wet and dry ingredients are mixed together gently and quickly and placed immediately in a preheated oven—the batter will rise while baking. There is something about the moist, crumbly texture of quick breads that makes them very satisfying. Their crumb tends to be light and tender, and they are the perfect vehicle for chopped nuts, fruit, and spices. Viennese Cupcakes, with apricot and chocolate, are a nod to fancy tortes, but with vastly simplified preparation. Lemon Loaf, with its sweet-and-sour glaze, is an always welcome dessert. Breakfast or brunch becomes a special event when warm Pumpkin Cranberry Muffins and Maple Walnut Bread are served. Children love Gingerbread Cupcakes, Peanut Butter Cupcakes, Banana Muffins, and Frosted Apple Spice Cupcakes, and older folks can't resist Chocolate Swirled Bread and Ruth's Sour Cream Coffeecake. Remember, you don't need a certificate from a culinary academy to tackle a yeasted dough, although it usually requires additional preparation time to produce its wonderful, springy, elastic texture. It is usually kneaded or beaten to bring out the gluten in the flour, covered, and left to rise in a warm place before baking. But two of our yeasted recipes don't require any kneading, and one uses a cool-rise method in which the dough rests overnight in the refrigerator. When you're planning an affair to remember, New York Chocolate Babka and Cinnamon Honey Coffeecake are luscious and well worth the effort, and they can be frozen for quick reheating. Pear and Almond Pizza is a sweet twist on pizza that no one can resist. These foolproof recipes will give you the confidence to experiment with the whole spectrum of dessert breads.

Lemon Loaf

We were introduced to this delightful sweet bread at the home of Pat Cerretani, friend, caterer, and former Moosewood worker. Pat heeded the siren call and flew off to the island paradise of Maui. In Ithaca, we love this bread still warm from the oven, but Pat is probably on her lanai, wearing her sarong, serving chilled Lemon Loaf and herbal iced tea beneath the palm trees.

■ **SERVES 10**

LOAF

½ cup butter, at room temperature

¾ cup packed brown sugar

2 large eggs

freshly grated lemon peel of 1 large lemon (about 1 tablespoon)

1½ cups unbleached white flour

1 teaspoon baking powder

¼ teaspoon salt

½ cup milk

½ cup chopped walnuts or ¼ cup poppy seeds (optional)

LEMON GLAZE

½ cup sugar

¼ cup fresh lemon juice (about 2 lemons)

 PREHEAT THE OVEN to 350°. Butter the loaf pan and lightly dust it with flour.

IN A LARGE bowl, cream together the butter and brown sugar by hand or with an electric mixer until light and blended. Beat in the eggs one at a time. Add the lemon peel. In a separate bowl, sift together the flour, baking powder, and salt. Alternately add the flour mixture and the milk to the creamed mixture, beating just enough to combine after each addition. Stir in the walnuts or poppy seeds, if using.

POUR THE BATTER into the prepared loaf pan and bake for about 45 to 60 minutes, until puffed and golden and a knife inserted in the center comes out clean. Cool for 10 to 15 minutes.

IN THE SAUCEPAN, combine the sugar and lemon juice for the glaze. Heat, stirring constantly, until the sugar dissolves. Lemon Loaf is most easily served directly from its baking pan. However, if you wish to serve it on a plate, remove it from the pan before topping with the lemon glaze. Poke holes in the top of the loaf with a toothpick or small sharp knife and slowly pour the lemon glaze over it.

■ **PREPARATION TIME:** 30 minutes
■ **BAKING TIME:** 45 to 60 minutes
■ **COOLING TIME:** 10 to 15 minutes
■ **EQUIPMENT:** nonreactive 4½ × 8 ½-inch loaf pan, small nonreactive saucepan

Chocolate Swirled Bread

Impress your guests with a quick bread that easily surpasses its simple, descriptive name. Swirls of chocolate will delight the palate and the loaf's regal streusel crown is a treat to behold.

PREHEAT THE OVEN to 350°. Butter or oil the loaf pan and dust it with flour.

SEPARATE ONE OF the eggs, placing the yolk in a large bowl and the white in a smaller bowl. Coarsely chop the chocolate into pea-sized or smaller pieces. Mix with the egg white and set aside. To the egg yolk, add the second egg, buttermilk, oil, and vanilla and beat for about a minute, until well blended. Sift together the dry ingredients and set aside.

USING A PASTRY blender, two knives, or a food processor, combine the streusel ingredients until crumbly but not too finely textured. Spread ⅓ of the streusel mixture over the bottom of the prepared loaf pan. Combine the wet and dry ingredients and mix until just blended. Add the chocolate, folding or swirling it into the batter with a rubber spatula or butter knife; don't overmix it or the cake will not be as nicely marbled.

POUR THE BATTER into the loaf pan and top with the remaining streusel. Bake for about 1 hour, until the bread is firm and pulls away from the sides of the pan. Allow it to cool before removing from the pan.

NOTE We usually use block or bar semi-sweet chocolate, which is harder and doesn't melt and disappear into the bread the way chocolate chips do. We enjoy the "little explosions" of chocolate chunks in the bread. Our preferences aside, though, chocolate chips can be used quite successfully.

- **PREPARATION TIME:** 40 minutes
- **BAKING TIME:** 1 hour
- **EQUIPMENT:** 8½ × 4 ½-inch loaf pan (a 9 × 5-inch baking pan is okay, too), pastry blender or food processor

- **SERVES 8 TO 10**

WET INGREDIENTS

- 2 eggs
- 5 ounces semi-sweet chocolate (see Note)
- ⅔ cup buttermilk
- ¼ cup vegetable oil
- 1 teaspoon pure vanilla extract

DRY INGREDIENTS

- 2 cups unbleached white flour
- 1 teaspoon baking powder
- ½ teaspoon baking soda
- ¼ teaspoon salt
- ½ cup sugar
- ¼ teaspoon ground cinnamon

STREUSEL

- 2 tablespoons unbleached white flour
- 2 tablespoons butter
- 3 tablespoons sugar
- ¼ teaspoon ground cinnamon, or more to taste

Maple Walnut Bread

The delicate sweetness of maple syrup and the nutty tastes of toasted walnuts and wheat germ flavor a pleasant loaf with a cake-like texture.

■ **SERVES 10**

½ cup butter, at room temperature

½ cup packed brown sugar

½ cup pure maple syrup

1 large egg

¾ cup buttermilk

½ teaspoon pure maple extract

2 cups unbleached white flour

1½ teaspoons baking powder

¼ teaspoon baking soda

¼ teaspoon salt

⅓ cup wheat germ

¾ cup chopped toasted walnuts (page 364)

MAPLE GLAZE

⅓ cup confectioners' sugar

2 tablespoons pure maple syrup

¼ teaspoon pure maple extract

PREHEAT THE OVEN to 350°. Butter and lightly flour the loaf pan.

IN A LARGE bowl using an electric mixer, cream together the butter and brown sugar. Add the maple syrup, egg, buttermilk, and maple extract, beating well after each addition. In a separate bowl, sift together the flour, baking powder, baking soda, and salt. Stir in the wheat germ. In two or three batches, stir the dry ingredients into the wet ingredients, mixing until well blended. Fold in the walnuts.

POUR THE BATTER into the prepared pan and bake for 50 to 60 minutes, until a knife inserted in the center comes out clean. Cool in the pan for about 15 minutes, then turn the bread out onto a serving plate.

IN A SMALL bowl, whisk together the confectioners' sugar, maple syrup, and maple extract—the glaze will be thick but pourable. Spread it on top of the warm loaf and drizzle it down the sides. Cool thoroughly before cutting.

■ **PREPARATION TIME:** 20 to 25 minutes
■ **BAKING TIME:** 50 to 60 minutes
■ **COOLING TIME:** 15 minutes
■ **EQUIPMENT:** 5 × 9-inch loaf pan, electric mixer

Cinnamon Honey Coffeecake

Here is a yeasted coffeecake that is neither labor-intensive nor overly time-consuming. Because the dough is actually a batter, there's no kneading involved and it rises right in the baking pan.

The light whole wheat pastry is gently spiced with cinnamon, orange peel, and cardamom to taste, giving this coffeecake a heavenly scent reminiscent of Finnish baked goods. It's filled with a layer of orange marmalade or fruit preserves to make each and every slice flavor packed.

HEAT THE MILK until slightly warm to the touch, about 105°. Add the yeast and stir to dissolve. Set aside to proof for 5 minutes until bubbles rise to the surface. Stir the butter into the beaten eggs. Add the honey, salt, orange peel, cinnamon, cardamom, and yeast mixture and stir to combine. Mix in the whole wheat and white flours with a wooden spoon and beat vigorously for 1 minute to develop the gluten.

FOR THE FILLING, cut the butter into the flour with two knives, a pastry fork, or a food processor. When the mixture resembles coarse meal, fold in the orange marmalade or fruit preserves.

BUTTER THE BUNDT or loaf pans and fill with half of the dough. Spread the fruit filling evenly over the bottom layer of dough and spoon the remaining dough on top. Cover the pan(s) loosely with plastic wrap and set in a warm, draft-free place. Let rise until doubled, about 1 hour.

PREHEAT THE OVEN to 350° when 45 minutes of the rising time have elapsed. After rising for an hour, the dough should fill the pan(s) by at least ¾. Bake for 1 hour and cool in the pan(s) for 15 minutes before transferring to a serving plate to cool completely.

- **PREPARATION TIME:** 30 minutes
- **RISING TIME:** 1 hour
- **BAKING TIME:** 1 hour
- **COOLING TIME:** 15 minutes
- **EQUIPMENT:** food processor or pastry fork (optional), one 10-inch bundt pan or two 8½ × 4 ½-inch loaf pans

■ **SERVES 6 TO 8**

DOUGH

- ½ cup milk
- 1 ounce yeast (2 packages)
- ¾ cup butter, melted
- 4 eggs, beaten
- ½ cup honey
- ½ teaspoon salt
- 1 tablespoon freshly grated orange peel
- 1 teaspoon ground cinnamon
- ¼ teaspoon ground cardamom
- 1 cup whole wheat flour
- 2 cups unbleached white flour

FILLING

- ¼ cup butter
- ½ cup unbleached white flour
- ¾ cup orange marmalade or other fruit preserves

Cranberry Orange Coffeecake

The flavors of cranberries and oranges combine to create a brightly flavored, unusual topping for this coffeecake. Since fresh cranberries are available only seasonally, we like to keep cranberries in the freezer for year-round use.

■ **SERVES 4 TO 6**

CAKE BATTER

½ cup butter, at room temperature

¾ cup packed brown sugar

1 egg

1½ cups unbleached white flour

½ teaspoon baking soda

¼ teaspoon salt

¼ cup milk

¼ cup orange juice

½ teaspoon pure vanilla extract

TOPPING

2 cups cranberries, rinsed and picked over

¼ cup butter

¾ to 1 cup lightly packed brown sugar

1½ teaspoons freshly grated orange peel

dash of salt

PREHEAT THE OVEN to 350°. Lightly butter and flour the cake pan.

CREAM TOGETHER THE butter and brown sugar with an electric mixer until light and fluffy. Add the egg and beat until well blended. Sift together the flour, baking soda, and salt. Add the sifted ingredients alternately with the milk and orange juice. Stir in the vanilla. Pour the batter into the prepared pan and bake for 40 minutes, or until a knife inserted in the center comes out clean.

WHILE THE CAKE is baking, combine all of the topping ingredients in the saucepan and cook on medium heat, stirring often, until the cranberries soften, about 10 minutes. Set aside to cool.

WHEN THE CAKE is done and has cooled 10 minutes, top with the cranberry topping, or invert the cake on a platter and then top with the topping.

■ **PREPARATION TIME:** 15 to 20 minutes
■ **BAKING TIME:** 40 minutes
■ **COOLING TIME:** 10 minutes
■ **EQUIPMENT:** 8-inch square or 9-inch round cake pan, electric mixer, nonreactive saucepan

Ruth's Sour Cream Coffeecake

Our Penny Condon's Aunt Ruth Rosenthal is a third-generation Jewish baker from Newport, Rhode Island, whose ancestors came from Romania and Hungary. An octogenarian who is still a world-class athlete, Ruth has been making and eating this coffeecake for over fifty years. And now, when she's not on the golf course, she's still selling her baked goods on the wharves of Newport.

PREHEAT THE OVEN to 350°. Butter and flour the bundt pan or cake pan.

CREAM THE BUTTER with 1½ cups of the sugar. Beat in the eggs until thoroughly blended. Beat in the sour cream, vanilla, baking powder, baking soda, and salt. Finally, stir in the flour by hand until completely incorporated.

IN A FOOD processor or by hand, coarsely chop the pecans. Toss the chopped nuts with the remaining tablespoon of sugar, the cinnamon, and the nutmeg, if using.

SPOON HALF OF the batter into the prepared pan. Sprinkle all of the nut mixture evenly over the batter in the pan. Spoon the rest of the batter into the pan and bake the coffeecake until a knife inserted in the center comes out clean, about 50 minutes for a bundt cake and 55 to 70 minutes for a square cake. Cool in the pan on a rack. If making the bundt cake, turn it out onto a plate after 10 minutes. Serve warm or at room temperature.

- **PREPARATION TIME:** 20 minutes
- **BAKING TIME:** 50 minutes for the bundt cake, 55 to 70 minutes for the square cake
- **COOLING TIME:** 10 minutes
- **EQUIPMENT:** 8-inch square baking pan or 10-inch bundt pan, electric mixer, food processor (optional)

■ **SERVES 8 TO 10**

- 1 cup butter, at room temperature
- 1½ cups plus 1 tablespoon sugar
- 2 eggs
- ¾ cup sour cream
- 1 teaspoon pure vanilla extract
- ½ teaspoon baking powder
- ½ teaspoon baking soda
- ½ teaspoon salt
- 2 cups unbleached white flour
- 1 cup toasted pecans (page 364)
- 1 teaspoon ground cinnamon
- ¼ teaspoon ground nutmeg (optional)

New York Chocolate Babka

"Babka," the diminuitive form of "Baba," is a Polish word for an elderly woman. But you don't have to be a babka to appreciate this fabulous coffeecake. When David Hirsch was growing up in Bayside, Queens, favorites like this one, filled with walnuts, raisins, and semisweet chocolate, made him think being a baker would be an enjoyable profession. Now, many years and a few pounds later, his boyhood vision has been partially realized by developing pastries for this book.

This recipe requires less attention than most yeasted cakes; no kneading or multiple rising is required—just a little patience. The batter is mixed and refrigerated overnight, or 8 to 12 hours before baking time.

We like to serve this for special brunches or as an anytime dessert with coffee.

■ SERVES 8 TO 10

DOUGH

- 1 cup butter
- ½ cup milk
- 2 tablespoons yeast (2 packages)
- ¼ cup warm water
- 3 egg yolks
- 2½ cups unbleached white flour
- ½ teaspoon salt
- 2 tablespoons sugar

AT LEAST 8 hours before you plan to bake the babka, prepare the dough. Heat the butter and milk together until the butter has just melted. Set aside to cool. In a small bowl, dissolve the yeast in the warm water. Separate 3 eggs and mix the egg yolks into the dissolved yeast. Refrigerate the egg whites until you make the filling.

IN A SEPARATE bowl, sift together the flour, salt, and sugar. Stir the cooled milk (105° to 115°) into the flour, then add the yeast mixture. Mix the ingredients until a smooth batter is formed. Cover and refrigerate overnight, or for at least 8 hours or up to 2 days.

FOR THE FILLING, combine the water and ⅓ cup of sugar in a saucepan and bring to a boil. Add the walnuts, raisins, and cinnamon and simmer for about 10 minutes, until thickened. When cool, stir the chocolate into the walnut mixture. Refrigerate the walnut mixture if preparing it more than 2 hours before you plan to bake the babka.

JUST BEFORE ASSEMBLING the babka, bring the reserved egg whites to room temperature and beat until foamy, using an electric mixer. Gradually add ½ cup of sugar and beat until soft peaks form.

PREHEAT THE OVEN to 350°. Butter the bundt or tube pan.

DIVIDE THE CHILLED dough into 4 equal pieces. On a well-floured surface and with a floured rolling pin (preferably chilled), roll one of the pieces into a 12-inch square. Work quickly because the dough softens and becomes more difficult to handle as it warms. It may help to refrigerate the pieces of dough waiting to be rolled.

SPREAD ¼ OF THE egg whites and then ¼ of the filling over the square to within 1 inch of the edges. Roll up like a jelly roll and pinch to seal the ends. Using one or two long spatulas, carefully lift the roll and place it in the bundt or tube pan so that the ends meet. Repeat with the remaining three pieces of dough—stacking the rolls one on top of each other.

BAKE FOR 50 to 60 minutes, until firm, lightly browned, and bread-like on top. Cool the babka in the pan on a rack for 20 minutes and then turn it out onto a plate to cool further.

- **PREPARATION TIME:** 1 hour
- **CHILLING TIME:** at least 8 hours and up to 2 days
- **BAKING TIME:** 50 to 60 minutes
- **COOLING TIME:** 30 minutes
- **EQUIPMENT:** medium saucepan, electric mixer, 10-inch bundt or tube pan, rolling pin

FILLING

⅔ cup water

⅓ cup sugar

¾ cup chopped walnuts

¾ cup raisins

1 teaspoon ground cinnamon

¾ cup chopped semi-sweet chocolate or chocolate chips

3 egg whites, at room temperature

½ cup sugar

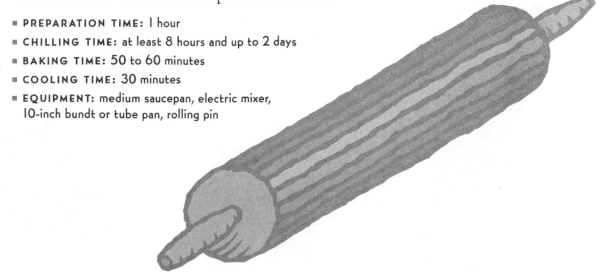

Banana Muffins

Banana muffins are one delicious solution to the problem of too many bananas. The chocolate chips, raisins, and nuts are all optional, and depending on your mood, you can choose any of the seven possible combinations. If all of your bananas ripen at once and you don't have time to bake that week, you can peel the ripe bananas and store them in a plastic bag in the freezer until ready to use.

■ **YIELDS 12**

½ cup vegetable oil

1 cup packed
   brown sugar

2 eggs

3 large ripe bananas
   (about 3 cups
   mashed)

2 cups unbleached
   white flour

1 teaspoon
   baking powder

1 teaspoon baking soda

½ teaspoon salt

2 teaspoons pure
   vanilla extract

½ cup chocolate chips
   (optional)

½ cup raisins (optional)

½ cup chopped almonds,
   walnuts, or pecans
   (optional)

PREHEAT THE OVEN to 350°. Oil or spray the muffin tin or use paper liners.

IN A LARGE bowl, with an electric mixer or by hand, beat the oil, sugar, eggs, and mashed bananas until well blended. Sift together the flour, baking powder, baking soda, and salt. Fold the dry ingredients into the wet ingredients with quick strokes —be careful not to overmix. Fold in the vanilla and, if using, the chocolate chips, raisins, and/or nuts.

SPOON THE BATTER into the prepared muffin tin and bake for 20 minutes, until a knife inserted in the center of a muffin comes out clean. Turn the muffins out of the tin and cool on a rack.

■ **PREPARATION TIME:** 10 minutes
■ **BAKING TIME:** 20 minutes
■ **EQUIPMENT:** standard 12-cup muffin tin, paper liners, electric mixer

Pumpkin Cranberry Muffins

With the spicy flavor and moist texture of gingerbread, these pumkin muffins are crowned by a tangy, crunchy cranberry-walnut topping. They are pretty enough to become a perennial favorite at Thanksgiving or a special Halloween treat.

PREHEAT THE OVEN to 375°. Oil the muffin tin or line it with paper cups.

RINSE AND SORT the cranberries. Coarsely chop the cranberries and walnuts by hand or in a food processor. Add the brown sugar, ginger, and cinnamon; mix well and set aside.

WHISK TOGETHER THE pumpkin, eggs, oil, buttermilk, molasses, grated ginger root, cinnamon, and brown sugar in a mixing bowl. Sift together the flour, baking powder, baking soda, and salt in a separate bowl. Combine the wet and dry mixtures, stirring until just blended; the batter will not be completely smooth.

FILL THE PREPARED muffin cups about ¾ full and top each muffin with about 2 tablespoons of the cranberry-nut mixture. Bake for about 30 minutes, until a knife inserted in the center of a muffin comes out clean.

- **PREPARATION TIME:** 20 minutes
- **BAKING TIME:** 30 minutes
- **EQUIPMENT:** standard 12-cup muffin tin, paper liners, food processor (optional)

■ **YIELDS 12**

TOPPING

- 1 cup fresh cranberries
- ½ cup walnuts
- ¼ cup packed brown sugar
- ¼ teaspoon ground ginger
- ¼ teaspoon ground cinnamon

MUFFIN BATTER

- 1 cup cooked pumpkin purée (15-ounce can)
- 2 eggs
- ¼ cup vegetable oil
- ¼ cup buttermilk
- ¼ cup unsulphured molasses
- 2 teaspoons grated fresh ginger root
- ¼ teaspoon round cinnamon
- ¼ cup packed brown sugar
- 1½ cups unbleached white flour
- 1 teaspoon baking powder
- ½ teaspoon baking soda
- ½ teaspoon salt

Frosted Apple Spice Cupcakes

Cupcakes are both quicker to make and quicker to bake than most cakes. Here the grated apples make these little cakes moist and flavorful.

■ **YIELDS 12**

CUPCAKES

1 apple

2 cups unbleached white flour

1½ teaspoons baking powder

1 teaspoon ground cinnamon

½ teaspoon ground nutmeg

¼ teaspoon salt

⅔ cup butter, softened

1 cup packed brown sugar

2 large eggs

1 teaspoon pure vanilla extract

¾ cup unsweetened apple juice

APPLE FROSTING

2 tablespoons butter, at room temperature

2 ounces cream cheese (generous ¼ cup), at room temperature

1 tablespoon frozen apple juice concentrate

¼ teaspoon ground cinnamon

⅔ cup confectioners' sugar

PREHEAT THE OVEN to 350°. Butter the muffin tin or use paper liners. Peel, core, and grate the apple to make about 1 cup of grated apple and set aside.

SIFT TOGETHER THE flour, baking powder, cinnamon, nutmeg, and salt and set aside. With an electric mixer, cream the butter and sugar until fluffy. Beat in the eggs one at a time; add the vanilla. Alternate adding the juice and the flour mixture, beating well after each addition. Fold in the grated apple.

SPOON THE BATTER into the prepared muffin tin (the cups will be quite full). Bake for 25 to 30 minutes, until a knife inserted in the center of the largest cupcake comes out clean. Turn the cupcakes out of the tin and cool on a rack before frosting.

IN A SMALL bowl, beat together the butter, cream cheese, and apple juice concentrate with an electric mixer. Add the cinnamon to the confectioners' sugar and gradually beat it into the butter mixture until the frosting is smooth and spreadable. Frost the cupcakes and serve.

VARIATION Our frosting adds a perfect finishing touch, but a simple dusting of confectioners' sugar is also good on these spiced treats.

■ **PREPARATION TIME:** 20 to 25 minutes
■ **BAKING TIME:** 25 to 30 minutes
■ **EQUIPMENT:** standard 12-cup muffin tin, paper liners, electric mixer

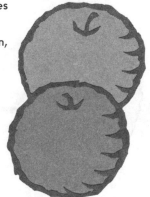

Gingerbread Cupcakes

Easy to whip together, these dark, full-bodied cupcakes are moist and tender and especially nice topped with a creamy lemon frosting.

PREHEAT THE OVEN to 350°. Generously butter the muffin tin or use paper liners.

WITH AN ELECTRIC mixer, cream the butter or oil and sugar until light. Add the molasses and egg and beat until smooth. Add the ginger, cinnamon, allspice, nutmeg, and flour and beat until well blended. In a separate cup, dissolve the baking soda in the boiling water. Add it to the batter and mix until smooth.

POUR THE BATTER into the prepared muffin tin. Bake for 20 minutes, until the cupcakes are slightly springy to the touch. Cool for 2 or 3 minutes, and then remove the cupcakes from the tin and cool on racks.

TO MAKE THE frosting, cream the butter and cream cheese with an electric mixer. Beat in the confectioners' sugar until fluffy. Add the lemon extract and beat until smooth. When the cupcakes are cool, frost them.

VARIATION   For a low-fat version, replace the oil or butter with ¼ cup of applesauce, replace the whole egg with 2 egg whites, and top with the bright counterpoint of a lemon glaze or simply dust with confectioners' sugar.

TO MAKE LEMON GLAZE, heat ¼ cup of sugar and 2 tablespoons of fresh lemon juice in a small nonreactive saucepan on medium heat, stirring constantly, just until the sugar dissolves, about 1 minute. Brush the tops of the cupcakes with the glaze.

- **PREPARATION TIME:** 15 to 20 minutes
- **BAKING TIME:** 20 minutes
- **EQUIPMENT:** standard 12-cup muffin tin, paper liners, electric mixer, small nonreactive saucepan

PER 2 OZ SERVING (VARIATION ONLY): 134 CALS, .2 G TOT FAT, 0 G MONO FAT, .1 G SAT FAT, 0 MG CHOL

- **YIELDS 12**

CUPCAKES

- ¼ cup butter or oil
- ½ cup sugar
- ½ cup unsulphured molasses
- 1 large egg
- 1½ teaspoons ground ginger
- 1 teaspoon ground cinnamon
- ½ teaspoon ground allspice
- ½ teaspoon ground nutmeg
- 1¼ cups unbleached white flour
- 1 teaspoon baking soda
- ½ cup boiling water

LEMON CREAM CHEESE FROSTING

- 2 tablespoons butter, at room temperature
- 2 ounces cream cheese (generous ¼ cup), at room temperature
- ⅔ cup confectioners' sugar
- ¼ teaspoon pure lemon extract

Peanut Butter Cupcakes

These big, generous cupcakes are delicious warm from the oven while the chocolate chips are still molten. To make them even better, you might top them with Chocolate Vegan Glaze (page 349), Cream Cheese Frosting (page 89), Hot Fudge Sauce (page 313), or just a bit of fresh whipped cream.

■ YIELDS 12

1 cup unbleached
  white flour

1 teaspoon
  baking powder

½ teaspoon salt

⅔ cup smooth
  peanut butter

⅓ cup butter

⅓ cup sugar

½ cup packed
  brown sugar

2 eggs

1 teaspoon pure
  vanilla extract

⅓ cup milk

1 cup semi-sweet
  chocolate chips

PREHEAT THE OVEN to 350°. Line the muffin tin with paper liners.

SIFT TOGETHER THE flour, baking powder, and salt and set aside. Cream together the peanut butter, butter, sugar, and brown sugar until smooth and well blended. Add the eggs one at a time, beating well after each addition, until the mixture is thick and glossy. Stir in the vanilla. Alternately fold in the flour mixture and the milk by thirds, until well blended. Fold in the chocolate chips.

FILL THE PREPARED muffin cups ¾ full and bake for 25 minutes, until a knife inserted in the center comes out clean.

AFTER THE CUPCAKES are cool, frost them, if desired.

■ PREPARATION TIME: 15 to 20 minutes

■ BAKING TIME: 25 minutes

■ EQUIPMENT: standard 12-cup muffin tin, paper liners

Viennese Cupcakes

Apricot jam, almond extract, and a simple chocolate glaze create a special cupcake that's quick and easy to make. The glaze reminds us of one of our favorite candies in the Whitman's Sampler: the chocolate-covered fruit creams. At Moosewood, we prefer to use unsweetened fruit spread.

PREHEAT THE OVEN to 350°. Butter the muffin tin or use paper liners.

USING AN ELECTRIC mixer, cream together the butter, brown sugar, and preserves or jam until smooth. Add the almond extract and the egg and beat well. In a separate bowl, sift together the flour, baking powder, baking soda, and salt. Add the flour mixture to the creamed mixture in two batches alternating with the buttermilk; beat well after each addition. Stir in the chocolate chips and mix well.

SPOON THE BATTER into the prepared muffin cups, filling them about ⅔ full. Bake for 15 to 20 minutes, until a knife inserted in the center comes out clean and the cupcakes are golden. Remove the muffins from the tin to cool.

IN THE SAUCEPAN on very low heat, melt the chocolate for the glaze. Stir in the apricot preserves or jam. While the glaze is still warm, brush some on top of each cooled cupcake. The glaze will become firmer and shinier as it cools.

- **PREPARATION TIME:** 30 minutes
- **BAKING TIME:** 15 to 20 minutes
- **COOLING TIME:** 20 to 30 minutes
- **EQUIPMENT:** standard 12-cup muffin tin, paper liners, electric mixer, small heavy saucepan, pastry brush

■ **YIELDS 12**

½ cup butter, at room temperature

½ cup packed brown sugar

¼ cup apricot preserves or jam (preferably unsweetened)

1½ teaspoons pure almond extract

1 large egg

1½ cups unbleached white flour

1 teaspoon baking powder

½ teaspoon baking soda

¼ teaspoon salt

¾ cup buttermilk

½ cup semi-sweet chocolate chips

CHOCOLATE APRICOT GLAZE

⅓ cup semi-sweet chocolate chips

3 tablespoons apricot preserves or jam

Pear and Almond Pizza

Here is a most unusual and festive dessert—decorative and delicious. The idea for it just popped into Moosewood cook Nancy Lazarus's head one day, and we're glad it did. Like many of Nancy's creative ideas over the years, the real thing is every bit as good as what she envisioned. Fresh sliced pears and almonds are bound together by luscious almond-flavored cream cheese atop a yeasted dough. Golden, sweet, and studded with slivered almonds, this pizza is excellent for a buffet or large dinner party and perfect for an elegant brunch.

Use commercial slivered almonds to save time, if you like. For a change of pace, try substituting fresh apricots for the pears and garnish the finished pizza with shaved chocolate curls.

■ **SERVES 8 TO 12**

DOUGH

2¼ teaspoons active dry
    yeast (1 package)

⅓ cup warm water

2 tablespoons sugar

2 cups unbleached
    white flour

½ teaspoon salt

2 tablespoons butter,
    melted

1 egg, beaten

TOPPING

8 ounces cream cheese

1 egg

2 teaspoons pure
    vanilla extract

1 teaspoon pure
    almond extract

½ cup sugar

⅓ cup whole almonds
    (about ½ cup
    slivered)

4 pears

IN A LARGE bowl, stir together the yeast, warm water, sugar, and 1 tablespoon of the flour. Set aside in a warm place for 10 to 15 minutes, until foamy. Add the salt, butter, and egg and mix briefly. Stir in the remaining flour to form a soft dough. If the dough is too dry, add a tablespoon of water. Knead the dough for 5 minutes, until smooth and elastic. Place the dough in a lightly oiled bowl, cover with a clean cloth, and let rise in a warm place for about 1 hour, until doubled in size.

WHILE THE DOUGH rises, whirl the cream cheese, egg, vanilla, almond extract, and sugar in a blender or food processor until smooth and set aside. Slice the almonds lengthwise into slivers. Peel and core the pears and cut them lengthwise into ¼-inch slices (to make about 4 cups of sliced pears).

PREHEAT THE OVEN to 400°. Lightly oil the pizza pan.

WHEN THE DOUGH has risen, punch and flatten it with your hands or roll it out to approximately the size of the pan. Place the dough on the pan and stretch it with your fingers to cover the pan, forming a ridge around the outside edge.

ARRANGE THE PEAR slices in a decorative pattern evenly over the dough, slightly pressing each one into the dough. Sprinkle half of the almonds evenly over the pizza. Drop the cheese mixture by large spoonfuls onto the pizza. Use the back of the spoon to spread the cheese smoothly over the pear slices, so that it fills the gaps between the slices and moistens the tops of all the pears. Sprinkle the remaining almond slivers over the pizza.

BAKE FOR 25 to 30 minutes, until the dough is cooked and the top is golden brown. Serve warm or at room temperature.

- **PREPARATION TIME:** 30 minutes
- **RISING TIME:** 1 hour
- **BAKING TIME:** 25 to 30 minutes
- **EQUIPMENT:** blender or food processor, 14-inch round pizza pan, rolling pin (optional), pizza cutter (for serving)

DESSERT BEVERAGES

Spiced Cranberry Punch

Apricot Lassi

Strawberry Mango Lassi

Sweet Fruit Milks

Creamy Coffee Shake

Pineapple Coconut Smoothie

Avocado Lime Shake

California Date Shake

Sunset Punch

Bellini

Tropical Fruit Colada

Manhattan Papaya Frappe

Watermelon Licuado

Coffee Breeze

Spiced Tea

Spiced Ethiopian-style Coffee (Bunna)

Hot Chocolate

Cocoa

Mulled Cider

Dessert Beverages

A LIGHT, SLOWLY SIPPED DESSERT BEVERAGE IS OFTEN JUST THE right way to cap a meal, sometimes more appealing than a sweet cake or pudding. On a sultry evening, a tall, cold Watermelon Licuado is most welcome. On a wintry night, a cup of smooth Hot Chocolate can be perfect. We love that all of the recipes in this chapter are quickly prepared and can be made at the last minute. It only takes a few minutes to put together an Apricot Lassi. You can whip up just one to satisfy your own sweet tooth or make a bunch to please a crowd. While your guests retreat to more com-fortable chairs after their meal, you can disappear and moments later reappear with stemmed glasses of beautiful Sunset Punch or cups of fragrant and tempting Spiced Tea. You might want to add a cookie or two, or some spiced nuts, but these drinks can stand on their own. The beverages in this chapter have names to pique your curiosity: breeze, colada, punch, fruit milk, licuado, shake, smoothie, lassi, and frappe. Ranging from steaming hot Spiced Ethiopian-style Coffee to frosty and fresh Tropical Fruit Colada, from a sophisticated peach and champagne Bellini to the sweet innocence of Cocoa, from a familiar drink like Mulled Cider to an unexpected one like Avocado Lime Shake, and from rich, thick Creamy Coffee Shake to fruity and low-fat Manhattan Papaya Frappe, these beverages should satisfy a yen for something light and delicious. See page 261 for a number of dessert beverages that include ice cream or sorbet.

Spiced Cranberry Punch

In Ithaca, the snow sometimes falls from late November until early April. We warm our hands and brighten our spirits with steaming mugs of this fragrant, garnet-colored spiced punch.

We find that a blended cranberry-raspberry juice makes for a sweeter punch, and the raspberry flavor nicely offsets the flavors of the spices and tart cranberries. Choose your own favorite combination of juices. The punch is especially pretty served in glass mugs garnished with thin lime slices.

COMBINE ALL OF the ingredients except the cranberries in the saucepan and bring to a boil on high heat.

WHILE THE PUNCH is heating, coarsely chop the cranberries and add them to the punch. Cover the saucepan and simmer the punch on low heat for about 20 minutes, or longer for a more intense flavor. Strain to remove the spices, lime peel, and cranberry solids. Cool for about 10 minutes and serve warm.

- **PREPARATION TIME:** 10 minutes
- **COOKING TIME:** 20 minutes
- **COOLING TIME:** 10 minutes
- **EQUIPMENT:** medium nonreactive saucepan

PER 4 OZ SERVING: 79 CALS, 0 G TOT FAT, 0 G MONO FAT, 0 G SAT FAT, 0 MG CHOL

- **SERVES 6**

- 1 quart cranberry-raspberry juice
  peel of 1 lime
- 2 tablespoons fresh lime juice (about 1 lime)
- 2 quarter-sized slices of peeled fresh ginger root
- 5 whole allspice berries
- 1 cinnamon stick
- 3 whole cloves
  honey to taste (optional)
- 3 or 4 whole peppercorns (optional)
- 1 cup fresh or frozen cranberries, rinsed and sorted

Apricot Lassi

This creamy refreshing drink is our version of the Indian yogurt and fruit drink called lassi. A little cardamom and orange enliven the mild flavors of vanilla and apricot.

■ **SERVES 2**

½ cup unsweetened canned apricots

½ cup vanilla yogurt

½ cup milk

⅛ teaspoon ground cardamom

⅛ teaspoon freshly grated orange peel

 WHIRL ALL OF the ingredients in a blender until smooth and foamy. Pour into two 8-ounce glasses and serve garnished with fresh mint, if desired.

NOTE If you wish to use plain yogurt, add ¼ teaspoon of vanilla and 1 tablespoon of honey.

■ **TOTAL TIME:** 10 minutes
■ **EQUIPMENT:** blender

Strawberry Mango Lassi

Lassi is a healthful, refreshing yogurt drink from India. Cool and pastel pretty, it's a lovely way to finish a spicy hot meal. It is easy to vary the flavors according to fruits that happen to be in season. Use raspberries and peaches for a delicious variation.

■ **SERVES 3**

1 ripe mango

1 cup nonfat or low-fat yogurt

½ cup milk

¼ cup coconut milk (page 358) (optional)

½ cup strawberries, hulled and sliced in half

2 tablespoons honey

PEEL THE MANGO and cut it into chunks (page 372). In a blender, whip the mango chunks, yogurt, milk, coconut milk, if using, sliced strawberries, and honey until smooth.

POUR THE LASSI into tall glasses. Garnish each serving with a whole strawberry and a sprig of mint, if desired.

■ **TOTAL TIME:** 10 minutes
■ **EQUIPMENT:** blender

Sweet Fruit Milks

These sweet milks are light, satisfying treats that are not too sweet, too rich, or too complicated. Enjoy them as snacks or after a summer lunch or supper, when you want to linger over a little something more. Licuado de Leche y Fruta, a favorite Mexican drink, is very similar to our fruit milks—try other fruits such as papayas, mangoes, persimmons, strawberries, peaches, and guavas. Serve chilled or over crushed ice or ice cubes. Or, just before serving, whirl the fruit milk in the blender with a cup of crushed ice until very smooth.

The amount of sugar needed depends on the sweetness of the fruit and type of milk used. In place of sugar, try sweetening with honey, rice syrup, maple syrup, or fruit juice concentrate. For a richer treat, use half-and-half in place of milk.

■ SERVES 2 OR 3

PINEAPPLE SURPRISE

- 1⅓ cups unsweetened pineapple juice
- ⅔ cup milk, soy milk, or rice milk
- ½ teaspoon freshly grated nutmeg
- 2 tablespoons sugar (or to taste)
- rum to taste (optional)

CANTALOUPE ALMOND DRINK

- ½ cantaloupe, seeded, peeled, and cubed
- ½ cup milk, soy milk, rice milk, or almond milk
- 2 tablespoons sugar (or to taste)
- ¼ to ½ teaspoon almond extract

BANANA MILK

- 1 large or 2 small very ripe bananas (about ¾ cup, mashed)
- 1½ cups milk, soy milk, or rice milk
- 2 tablespoons brown sugar
- ½ to 1 teaspoon pure vanilla extract

 IN A BLENDER, whirl all of the ingredients for the fruit milk of your choice until very smooth. Serve immediately over ice.

- **■ TOTAL TIME:** 5 minutes
- **■ EQUIPMENT:** blender

Creamy Coffee Shake

Leftover coffee gets a new lease on life in this simple but rich coffee shake that requires only a few basic ingredients. Just chill the coffee and the shake is practically made.

For a real indulgence, fortify this frosty drink with a dash of Kahlúa and embellish with a dollop of fresh whipped cream and delicate shavings of chocolate.

■ **SERVES 4**

2 cups chilled
   strong regular
   or decaffeinated
   coffee

2 cups vanilla ice cream

IN A BLENDER or food processor, whirl the coffee and ice cream (and Kahlúa, if using) for a few seconds until smooth. Pour into tall glasses, garnish with whipped cream and chocolate shavings, if you like. Serve immediately.

■ **TOTAL TIME:** 5 minutes
■ **EQUIPMENT:** blender or food processor

Pineapple Coconut Smoothie

Serve an intoxicating indulgence that leaves everyone a designated driver. The nonfat yogurt and light coconut milk reduce the fat in this piña colada-style shake. Serve with a Caribbean, African, or Indian meal, or with any cuisine that evokes a tropical clime.

■ **SERVES 2 OR 3**

1 cup canned pineapple
   with juice

1 cup nonfat vanilla
   frozen yogurt

1 cup reduced fat
   coconut milk (page
   358)

½ cup pineapple juice

2 teaspoons fresh
   lemon juice

COMBINE ALL OF the ingredients in a blender and whirl until smooth and creamy. Serve immediately (see Note).

NOTE Although we prefer this smoothie served right away, chilling it for 15 to 20 minutes in the refrigerator will produce a creamier drink. Or you may like to put it in the freezer for 30 minutes to make a Pineapple Coconut Slush.

■ **TOTAL TIME:** 5 minutes
■ **EQUIPMENT:** blender

Avocado Lime Shake

Avocado is a creamy fruit with an affinity for limes, so what could be more natural than a smooth, lime-green avocado shake?

COMBINE THE AVOCADO, lime juice, cold water, sugar, and salt, if using, in a blender and whirl until completely smooth. Pour the shake over crushed ice into two 8-ounce glasses. Garnish the drinks with thin slices of lime and fresh mint leaves.

- **TOTAL TIME:** 10 minutes
- **EQUIPMENT:** blender

- **SERVES 2**

½ ripe avocado

¼ cup fresh lime juice (about 2 limes)

¾ cup cold water

2 tablespoons sugar

dash of salt (optional)

thin slices of lime and fresh mint leaves

California Date Shake

This is a delectable beverage—tropical fruit flavors that belong together in a dreamy yet dairy-less shake. Allowing the puréed dates to sit and soften in the liquid makes a smoother-textured drink. Decorate the glass rims with orange slices, if desired.

COMBINE THE DATES, orange peel, orange juice, and soy milk in a blender and whirl for 30 seconds. Let sit for at least 15 minutes. Whirl again for 15 seconds. Add the banana and ice cubes and blend until smooth. Serve immediately.

- **PREPARATION TIME:** 10 minutes
- **SITTING TIME:** 15 minutes
- **EQUIPMENT:** blender

- **SERVES 2**

½ cup coarsely chopped pitted dates

1 teaspoon freshly grated orange peel

¼ to ⅓ cup fresh orange juice

1 cup soy milk

1 ripe banana

6 ice cubes

Sunset Punch

It is easy to increase the quantities of this beautiful rosy-hued punch for parties. Create a marvelous-looking punch bowl by floating strawberries, orange rounds, or pineapple slices on top. You can also freeze blueberries or other small pieces of fruit in ice cubes and float them in the punch along with a few edible flower blossoms. It can be made with or without the alcohol.

- **SERVES 3 OR 4**

  1 cup fresh or frozen strawberries

  1 cup orange juice

  1 cup unsweetened pineapple juice

  2 tablespoons sugar, or to taste

  rum to taste (optional)

PLACE THE STRAWBERRIES in a blender with about half of the orange juice and whirl until smooth. Add the rest of the orange juice, the pineapple juice, and the sugar and blend briefly. Stir in rum to taste, if desired. Serve well chilled.

- **TOTAL TIME:** 5 minutes
- **EQUIPMENT:** blender

PER 5.5 OZ SERVING: 95 CALS, .3 G TOT FAT, 0 G MONO FAT, 0 G SAT FAT, 0 MG CHOL

Bellini

The Bellini originated at Harry's Bar in Venice and became so popular there that it has almost become a symbol for that serene and beautiful city. Imbibe or indulge in this bubbly and festive Champagne punch when you want to celebrate a special occasion. Use fresh, ripe peaches for the best flavor, but if they're not available, use thawed, frozen ones.

- **SERVES 4**

  2 cups fresh or frozen ripe, peeled peach slices, chilled

  3 tablespoons sugar

  1 teaspoon fresh lemon juice

  2 cups chilled medium-dry sparkling wine or Champagne

IN A BLENDER, purée the peaches, sugar, and lemon juice until smooth. Pour the peach purée into the glasses. Pour ½ cup of sparkling wine into each glass. If you like, garnish with fresh mint leaves and slices of fresh strawberry.

- **TOTAL TIME:** 5 minutes
- **EQUIPMENT:** blender, 4 stemmed glasses

Tropical Fruit Colada

Eliza Leineweber grew up in Hawaii and trained as a dessert chef there. Now living in Ithaca, where it is often cool and cloudy, Liza still retains a warm, sunny aura and so do many of her Moosewood dessert creations. The color of this elegant refresher reminds us of a pastel sunset. It's a delectable slow-sipping drink to savor on a hot summer day or evening or to enjoy while sitting next to the fire on a snowy winter night, reading stories of tropical lands or a book filled with photos of turquoise waters, lush foliage, and pristine beaches.

Serve in graceful glasses garnished, if you like, with mint leaves.

IN A BLENDER, whirl the pineapple juice, coconut milk, and fruit juice or nectar for about a minute until smooth. Add sugar to taste. Stir in the rum, if desired. Serve on ice cubes and sprinkle with nutmeg.

- **TOTAL TIME:** 10 minutes
- **EQUIPMENT:** blender

■ **SERVES 1**

FOR EACH SERVING

⅓ cup chilled pineapple juice

⅓ cup chilled reduced-fat coconut milk (page 358) or nectar*

⅓ cup tropical fruit juice or nectar*

sugar to taste

1 ounce rum (optional)

ice cubes

freshly grated nutmeg

* Goya makes good tropical fruit nectars in a variety of flavors, including coconut, papaya, guanabana, mango, passion fruit, guava, and tamarind.

Manhattan Papaya Frappe

Most of us like to make periodic forays from bucolic Ithaca into New York City to visit friends and family, soak up a little big city life, and, of course, check out the great food. One of our favorite street foods is the papaya drink dispensed from the Papaya King hot dog stands. On a frenetic Manhattan street a paper cup of this fruity concoction is a soothing tropical tonic.

Our healthful version of this exotic treat is a frosty sweet frappe with the tang of papaya that is just right for a humid summer night. Decorate with fresh fruit slices, if desired, or maybe those little paper umbrellas, if you have some on hand.

Spiced Nuts (page 324) or a light cookie, such as Butterscotch Oatmeal Lace Crisps (page 175) or Chocolate Meringue Cookies (page 189), are a nice accompaniment.

■ **SERVES 3 OR 4**

1 papaya, seeded, peeled, and sliced

1 banana

¼ cup fresh lime juice

1 cup fresh or frozen strawberries

1 cup papaya nectar (see Note), or pineapple or orange juice

6 or 7 ice cubes

sugar to taste

IN A BLENDER, purée the papaya, banana, lime juice, strawberries, and papaya nectar or other juice until smooth. Add the ice cubes and whirl until the ice is completely broken up. Taste and add sugar, if desired.

POUR INTO STEMMED glasses and serve.

NOTE We have found several good brands of papaya nectar in the juice aisle of health food stores and well-stocked supermarkets or in the Latin American section of ethnic grocery stores. The bonus for seeking out papaya is that it acts as a natural aid to digestion.

 VARIATIONS Add a little rum or campari, if the spirit moves you.

Add a little yogurt for a pleasant and nutritious breakfast drink.

If you can't find a good ripe papaya, use about ¼ of a cantaloupe instead. The frappe will be a little thinner and sweeter.

■ **TOTAL TIME:** 5 minutes
■ **EQUIPMENT:** blender, 3 or 4 stemmed glasses

PER 7 OZ SERVING: 101 CALS, .5 G TOT FAT, .1 G MONO FAT, .1 G SAT FAT, 0 MG CHOL

Watermelon Licuado

In Mexico, licuados are refreshing and easily prepared hot-weather drinks made from puréed seasonal fruits. Our favorites are watermelon and strawberries. At the peak of their summer ripeness, watermelons may be so sweet and delicious that this recipe will not require fruit juice or sugar. Let taste be your guide.

Although we were skeptical about whirling unseeded watermelon in a blender, we thought it was worth a try. Amazingly enough, it works! As long as some liquid is added to the blender and you only blend for a minute or two, the seeds quite magically are not pulverized and can be easily strained out.

■ **SERVES 2**

2 cups unseeded watermelon cubes

½ cup water or fruit juice, such as orange, pineapple, or apple

fresh lemon juice to taste

sugar to taste

PLACE THE WATERMELON and water or juice in a blender in two batches and whirl just until the cubes of watermelon are smooth—don't blend for too long or you'll grind up the seeds. Pour through a strainer and discard the seeds. Add lemon juice and sugar to taste. Serve very cold.

VARIATIONS Return the strained, seedless licuado to the blender and add ½ cup of fresh or frozen strawberries. Whirl until smooth and add lemon juice and sugar to taste. Frozen strawberries work very well and eliminate the need to chill the licuado before serving.

ADD A TEASPOON of amaretto or a splash of rum or vodka to each serving, if desired.

■ **TOTAL TIME:** 5 minutes
■ **EQUIPMENT:** blender

PER 8 OZ SERVING: 77 CALS, .8 G TOT FAT, 0 G MONO FAT, 0 G SAT FAT, 0 MG CHOL

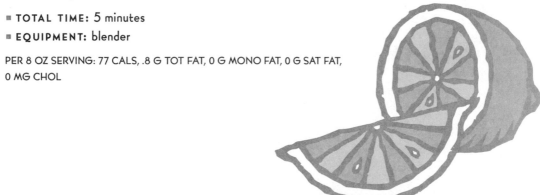

Coffee Breeze

Cooling as a summer breeze, quick and refreshing as a summer shower, this low-fat beverage is an easy, elegant treat to sip from a tall iced glass while lounging on a lawn chair.

Serve it with straws and long-handled parfait spoons, garnished with fresh raspberries, shaved chocolate, or a sprinkling of ground cinnamon.

■ **SERVES 4 TO 6**

3 tablespoons instant coffee granules or espresso powder

½ cup boiling water

2 to 3 tablespoons sugar, to taste

1 cup nonfat vanilla ice cream* or vanilla frozen yogurt

½ cup 1% milk

½ cup evaporated skim milk

2 tablespoons coffee-flavored liqueur, such as Kahlúa (optional)

12 ice cubes

* When we investigated nonfat ice cream, we found that Breyers has the purest ingredients, with 100 calories and 0 grams fat per ½ cup serving—almost too good to be true.

DISSOLVE THE COFFEE granules in the boiling water and pour into the blender. Add the sugar, ice cream or frozen yogurt, milk, evaporated milk, liqueur, if using, and the ice cubes. Using the ice breaker button, whirl for 5 to 10 seconds, or until the ice is coarsely crushed. Taste for sweetness and add more sugar if you like.

SERVE IMMEDIATELY. Store any leftover beverage in the freezer and reblend as needed.

■ **TOTAL TIME:** 5 minutes
■ **EQUIPMENT:** blender

PER 8 OZ SERVING: 113 CALS, .4 G TOT FAT, .1 G MONO FAT, .2 G SAT FAT, 2 MG CHOL

Spiced Tea

Known as "chai masala" in India, this flavorful beverage has as many versions as there are teapots. Newly popular in coffee bars in this country, spiced tea is even better as a cozy repast at home. Sip it as a subtly sweet, lively dessert or as a restorative—a sort of steamy aroma therapy.

Use a rich, full-bodied tea to match the strength of the spices. Adjust the proportions or the spice mixture to suit yourself.

COMBINE THE COLD water, ginger root, orange slices, fennel seeds, cloves, and peppercorns in the saucepan. Bring to a boil, reduce the heat, cover, and simmer for 10 to 12 minutes.

POUR THROUGH A strainer into 2 cups and add the teabag of your choice to each cup. Steep for 1 to 3 minutes and add honey or sugar to taste. Garnish with additional orange slices, if desired.

- **TOTAL TIME:** 20 minutes
- **EQUIPMENT:** small saucepan, strainer

PER 8 OZ SERVING: 21 CALS, .3 G TOT FAT, .1 G MONO FAT, 0 G SAT FAT, 0 MG CHOL

- **SERVES 2**

2½ cups cold water

4 slices of fresh ginger root, about ¼ inch thick and the size of a quarter

3 orange slices, about ½ inch thick

½ teaspoon fennel seeds

½ teaspoon whole cloves

¼ teaspoon whole black peppercorns

2 teabags (black, green, or mint tea work well)

honey or sugar to taste

orange slices (optional)

ABOUT COFFEE

Coffee originated in Ethiopia and spread through Arabia to the rest of the world. The word coffee itself is derived from Kaffa, a province in southwestern Ethiopia. The coffee shrub, with its glossy evergreen leaves and berries that turn red when ripe, grows wild in parts of Ethiopia. Legend has it that goatherds first discovered coffee—their curiosity piqued when they noticed the energetic behavior of goats who grazed on the coffee plants.

Coffee does more than provide the stereotypical wake-up jolt in the morning and the afternoon pick-me-up. In many parts of the world, coffee drinking is an important part of business and social transactions. In many countries, coffee shops have traditionally been a focal point of any public gathering place. From about 1650 to 1850, they were considered the center of business, cultural, and political life in London.

Coffee houses or shops bring to mind images of intense conversation, heated political debate, and exchanges among artists and intellectuals. The increasing number and widespread popularity of good coffee shops in American cities may eventually reduce the predominance of bars as meeting places in the United States.

In some Ethiopian and Eritrean homes, serving coffee takes on a ceremonial quality. Coffee beans are roasted by the hostess, treating everyone to the wonderful aroma. The coffee is brewed with spices in a special clay vessel over a charcoal stove, then sweetened. In a leisurely, relaxed fashion, three successive cups are offered to guests, each one slightly weaker than the previous one. Although it's hard to replicate the ambience of this unique experience here, we can give you a version of the coffee itself.

Spiced Ethiopian-style Coffee (Bunna)

Freshly brewed coffee can serve as the backdrop for many of the desserts in this book. Served alone, or embellished with whipped cream or ice cream, it can be the perfect light end to a robust meal.

COMBINE ALL OF the ingredients in the saucepan and bring just to a boil. Reduce the heat and simmer gently for 5 to 10 minutes, depending upon how strong you like your coffee. Strain through a fine-mesh sieve and serve hot in small cups or demitasse cups.

VARIATIONS Add 1 tablespoon of unsweetened cocoa for every 3 rounded tablespoons of finely ground coffee. Add 1 tablespoon of coffee-flavored liqueur, such as Kahlúa, to the brewed coffee and serve with milk and sugar to taste.

ADD ½ TEASPOON of ground cinnamon for every 3 rounded tablespoons of finely ground coffee. Top each coffee cup with a dollop of fresh whipped cream and dust with ground cardamom, if desired. Add a little almond-flavored liqueur, such as amaretto, to taste.

- **YIELD:** 2 demitasse-sized cups
- **TOTAL TIME:** 5 to 10 minutes
- **EQUIPMENT:** small saucepan, sieve

PER 4 OZ SERVING: 40 CALS, .6 G TOT FAT, .1 G MONO FAT, 0 G SAT FAT, 0 MG CHOL

- **SERVES 2**

1 cup cold water

6 whole cloves

6 to 12 whole cardamoms

1 slice of fresh ginger root, about the size and thickness of a nickel

3 heaping tablespoons finely ground coffee beans

1 tablespoon sugar, more or less to taste

Hot Chocolate

For many of us, a steaming cup of hot chocolate has a taste full of childhood associations, memories of sweet solace and warm comfort offered on bitter cold days. But hot chocolate is not just for kids. If chocolate is an aphrodisiac (and surely it is), then hot, liquid chocolate may serve as a love potion, a rich, sensual pleasure to end an intimate dinner and perhaps provide a lightly stimulating prelude to the rest of the evening.

■ **SERVES 2**

2 cups milk

3 ounces fine-quality semi-sweet chocolate

fresh whipped cream (optional)

 HEAT THE MILK in the saucepan on low heat, stirring occasionally. Break the chocolate into small pieces. One easy way to do this is to leave the chocolate in its paper wrapper or put it into a sturdy plastic bag. Place it on a cutting board or well-supported countertop and give it a couple of good whacks with a hammer. Drop the chocolate pieces into the milk and continue to heat, stirring until the chocolate melts.

SERVE HOT IN large mugs and top with a dollop of whipped cream, if desired.

VARIATIONS Add 1 teaspoon of instant espresso or instant coffee granules.

ADD 2 TEASPOONS of orange-flavored liqueur, such as Grand Marnier, or 4 teaspoons of almond-flavored liqueur, such as amaretto, just before serving.

ADD 1 TABLESPOON of brandy, rum, or chocolate- or coffee-flavored liqueur just before serving.

SPRINKLE WITH A little cinnamon or freshly grated nutmeg, or garnish with a cinnamon stick.

■ **TOTAL TIME:** 10 to 15 minutes
■ **EQUIPMENT:** saucepan

Cocoa

Cocoa is not quite as smooth and voluptuous a drink as hot chocolate, although it delivers a brisk enjoyment all its own. Cocoa is lower in fat than chocolate, is cheaper, and is easier to store in the pantry. Our recipe is less sweet and (believe it or not) a bit simpler to make than the ones found on the back of a cocoa box.

All of our variations for hot chocolate can be used for cocoa, too. Skim milk can be used in either drink, if you wish. Use whole milk for a thicker, richer beverage.

MIX THE COCOA powder, sugar, and salt in the saucepan. Stir in just enough milk to make a smooth paste, then gradually stir in the rest of the milk. Heat, stirring occasionally, until steaming hot. Add the vanilla and serve immediately.

- **TOTAL TIME:** 5 minutes
- **EQUIPMENT:** heavy saucepan

- **SERVES 2**

- 2 tablespoons unsweetened cocoa powder
- 4 teaspoons sugar
  dash of salt
- 2 cups milk
- ½ teaspoon pure vanilla extract

Mulled Cider

Cold nights in midautumn, when the house is filled with the aroma of apples and spice, are the perfect time to curl up with a good novel and a mug of hot cider. This recipe may be doubled or tripled. Leftovers can be stored in the refrigerator and reheated.

PLACE ALL OF the ingredients in the saucepan. Using a heat diffuser on medium heat, bring the cider to a simmer—but don't let it boil or it will curdle. Reduce the heat to low; steep the spices at a very low simmer for 20 minutes.

POUR THE CIDER into mugs and garnish with slices of apple.

- **TOTAL TIME:** 30 minutes
- **EQUIPMENT:** small heavy saucepan, heat diffuser

PER 8 OZ SERVING: 127 CALS, .4 G TOT FAT, 0 G MONO FAT, .I G SAT FAT, 0 MG CHOL

- **SERVES 2**

- 2 cups apple cider
- 2 slices of lemon
- I cinnamon stick
- I teaspoon grated fresh ginger root
- ½ teaspoon ground cardamom

a few apple slices

SAUCES AND TOPPINGS

Blueberry Peach Sauce

Cherry Sauce

Chunky Winter Fruit Sauce

Cranberry Apricot Pear Sauce

Orange Sauce

Dried Fruit and Vanilla Sauce

Fresh Mango Sauce

Summer Berry Sauce

Raspberry Sauce

Warm Apple Walnut Sauce

Bittersweet Chocolate Sauce

Light Chocolate Sauce

Hot Fudge Sauce

Chocolate Ganache

Maple Cinnamon Coffee Sauce

Champagne Zabaglione

Rum Sabayon Sauce

Rum Custard Sauce

Flavored Whipped Creams

Low-fat Creamy Toppings

Sauces and Toppings

THE SAUCES AND TOPPINGS IN THIS CHAPTER ARE INTENDED TO BE served over, under, or in between cakes, pies, custards, sliced fruit, or frozen desserts. Our sauces, are generally quickly and easily prepared, yet one of these fabulous sauces can transform a simple dessert into a great one. Vanilla ice cream is marvelous with Summer Berry Sauce, and poundcake approaches the sublime when topped with Raspberry Sauce and Flavored Whipped Creams. Whereas full-flavored fresh fruit sauces are delightful companions to ice cream, frozen yogurt, or cake, other sauces are intended to dress up fruit desserts. We like to top ripe pears with Champagne Zabaglione and serve Rum Custard Sauce or Rum Sabayon Sauce over tropical fruits such as pineapple, mango, or papaya. This chapter has a sauce for everyone. Bittersweet Chocolate Sauce, Fresh Mango Sauce, and Low-fat Creamy Toppings are indulgent yet low in fat. Anxious bakers may find redemption for a fallen cake in a tasty topping like Hot Fudge Sauce or Warm Apple Walnut Sauce. Throughout the book, we've suggested many uses for our sauces, but perhaps the most irresistibly tempting is simply "sampling" the sauce by the spoonful.

Blueberry Peach Sauce

It takes only five minutes to whip up this vividly colored sauce, which is luscious made with fresh or frozen fruit. It's a lovely way to dress up a simple poundcake, ice cream, sweet hot biscuits, or waffles. In summer, when fresh blueberries and peaches are in season, be sure to remember this delightful use for ripe, freshly picked fruit. Fresh fruit may require an extra 5 minutes for washing and peeling, and depending on the degree of natural sweetness, you might want to add a little additional sugar.

COMBINE THE PEACHES, lemon peel, lemon juice, sugar, cinnamon, and salt in the saucepan and cook on medium heat, stirring, for about 2 minutes. Add the blueberries and continue to cook and stir for another minute. Add the cornstarch mixture and cook for about 2 minutes longer, stirring frequently, until the sauce is thick and bubbly.

REMOVE FROM THE heat and add more sugar, if necessary. Serve warm or chilled.

- **TOTAL TIME:** 5 to 10 minutes
- **EQUIPMENT:** medium saucepan

PER 2 OZ SERVING: 90 CALS, .2 G TOT FAT, 0 G MONO FAT, 0 G SAT FAT, 0 MG CHOL

- **YIELDS 2 CUPS**

1½ cups chopped frozen peaches or peeled and chopped fresh peaches

1 teaspoon freshly grated lemon peel

1 tablespoon fresh lemon juice

2 tablespoons sugar

¼ to ½ teaspoon ground cinnamon

pinch of salt

1 cup fresh or frozen blueberries

1 tablespoon cornstarch dissolved in ½ cup water

more sugar to taste (optional)

Cherry Sauce

Dried cherries are now commonly available in supermarkets. We wanted to create something to make the most of this concentrated essence of cherry—and this delicious sauce is it. Serve warm or chilled, over Poundcake Loaf (page 123), Very Low-fat Vanilla Cheesecake (page 161), or on your favorite ice cream.

■ **YIELDS 1½ CUPS**

2 cups cherry juice*

1 cup dried pitted sweet cherries

1 to 2 tablespoons sugar

½ teaspoon fresh lemon juice

pinch of salt

1 tablespoon cornstarch dissolved in 1 tablespoon cherry juice

½ teaspoon pure vanilla extract (optional)

* *We recommend Lakewood cherry juice, which is pure cherry juice without any apple juice added.*

IN THE SAUCEPAN, combine the cherry juice and the dried cherries and bring to a boil. Add the sugar, lemon juice, and salt and simmer for 3 to 5 minutes. Add the dissolved corn-starch to the sauce and continue to stir until the sauce begins to thicken and coats a metal spoon. Remove the sauce from the heat and stir in the vanilla, if using. The sauce will thicken a bit more as it cools.

■ **TOTAL TIME:** 10 minutes
■ **EQUIPMENT:** small nonreactive saucepan

PER 2 OZ SERVING: 156 CALS, .2 G TOT FAT, .1 G MONO FAT, 0 G SAT FAT, 0 MG CHOL

Chunky Winter Fruit Sauce

We've created a golden fruit sauce to brighten the long nights of late autumn and early winter. Winter Fruit Sauce is the perfect companion for Honey Cake (page 139), Polenta Poundcake (page 122), Poundcake Loaf (page 123), Pear Sorbet (page 240), or your favorite ice cream or frozen yogurt.

PEEL, CORE, AND chop the pears and apples into bite-sized pieces and place them in a medium bowl. Add the canned pineapple chunks or, if using fresh pineapple, peel, core, and chop the pineapple into bite-sized pieces (page 372). Then add them to the bowl. You should have about 6 cups of fruit. Sprinkle the lemon juice over the fruit and toss gently.

MELT THE BUTTER in the saucepan. Add the fruit and cook on medium heat for about 5 minutes, just until the fruit becomes soft and juicy.

IN A SMALL bowl, dissolve the cornstarch in the juice and add it to the saucepan. Stir in the salt and raisins. Continue to cook on medium heat, stirring occasionally, until the sauce thickens and the fruit is tender. Stir in the honey and remove the sauce from the heat.

SERVE WARM OR chilled.

- **TOTAL TIME:** 30 minutes
- **EQUIPMENT:** nonreactive saucepan or skillet

■ **YIELDS 4 1/2 CUPS**

2 or 3 ripe pears

2 or 3 apples

2 cups canned unsweetened pineapple chunks* or 1/2 medium-sized pineapple

1 tablespoon fresh lemon juice

1 tablespoon butter

2 teaspoons cornstarch

1 cup pineapple juice* or unsweetened apple juice

pinch of salt

1/2 cup golden raisins

2 tablespoons honey

If using canned pineapple, reserve a cup of the juice to use later in the recipe.

Cranberry Apricot Pear Sauce

The fruits of fall are showcased in this crimson-colored, refreshing topping. You can create a decorative effect by swirling this sauce onto a cake that has been iced with cream cheese frosting.

- **YIELDS 2 CUPS**

½ cup dried apricots

2 cups fresh whole cranberries, sorted and washed

2 cups peeled sliced pears

I cup water

¼ cup sugar

COMBINE ALL OF the ingredients in the saucepan. Simmer for 10 to 15 minutes, or until the fruit is tender. Purée in a food processor or blender and strain through a wire mesh strainer, or pass through a food mill; discard the pulp. Serve warm or at room temperature.

- **TOTAL TIME:** 40 minutes
- **EQUIPMENT:** heavy nonreactive saucepan, blender or food processor, wire mesh strainer or food mill

PER 2.5 OZ SERVING: 77 CALS, .I G TOT FAT, 0 G MONO FAT, 0 G SAT FAT, 0 MG CHOL

Orange Sauce

It's fast, it's easy, it's even fat-free. Use this sauce to perk up a plain cake, to fill Orange Meringues (page 75), or as a topping for Orange Coconut Angelfood Cake (page 140).

- **YIELDS I ³/₄ CUPS**

2 cups orange juice

¼ cup sugar

I orange, sectioned and cut into bite-sized pieces (page 372)

2 tablespoons cornstarch

COMBINE THE ORANGE juice, sugar, orange sections, and cornstarch in the saucepan. Bring to a simmer on medium heat, stirring constantly as soon as the sauce begins to thicken. When smooth and thick, remove from the heat. Chill.

VARIATION For a Pineapple Orange Sauce, simmer 1 cup of orange juice, ¼ cup of brown sugar, and 2 tablespoons of cornstarch until thickened. Stir in 20 ounces of undrained canned unsweetened pineapple. Chill.

- **TOTAL TIME:** 15 minutes
- **EQUIPMENT:** nonreactive saucepan

PER I OZ SERVING: 39 CALS, .I G TOT FAT, 0 G MONO FAT, 0 G SAT FAT, 0 MG CHOL

Dried Fruit and Vanilla Sauce

The mellow essence of vanilla balances the intense sweetness of dried fruit in this handsome sauce. The fruit is simmered just long enough to infuse it with a hint of vanilla and each glistening little piece holds its shape nicely. Choose fruits with contrasting colors as well as flavors. If you use unsulphured fruit, the color variation will be more subtle but still pleasing.

This sauce is at its fragrant best when it's freshly made and served warm over vanilla ice cream or poundcake, but it can be served at room temperature as well, and it will keep for up to a week in the refrigerator. Some of us admit to using a dab on our morning oatmeal.

IN THE SAUCEPAN, soak the split vanilla bean in the water for 30 minutes. Meanwhile, cut the dried fruit into neat, uniform shapes about the size of dried cherries.

AFTER THE VANILLA bean has soaked, add the sugar to the water and bring it to a boil, stirring occasionally. Remove the vanilla bean (see Note) and add the dried fruit. Return the mixture to a boil, then reduce the heat and simmer for 5 minutes, until the pieces of fruit have softened but have not lost their distinct colors and shapes.

STIR THE DISSOLVED cornstarch mixture into the fruit and simmer for about 1 minute, stirring constantly, until the syrup is thick, glossy, and translucent.

NOTE The bean can be rinsed, dried, and stored to use again. Although a vanilla bean is more subtle and fragrant, it is quicker and considerably less expensive to use pure vanilla extract. Simply remove the thickened finished sauce from the heat and stir in 1 teaspoon of vanilla.

- **PREPARATION TIME:** 15 minutes
- **SOAKING TIME:** 30 minutes
- **EQUIPMENT:** heavy nonreactive saucepan

PER 3.5 OZ SERVING: 161 CALS, .2 G TOT FAT,
.1 G MONO FAT, 0 G SAT FAT, 0 MG CHOL

- **YIELDS 2 CUPS**

  1 vanilla bean,
    split lengthwise

  1½ cups water

  2 cups mixed
    dried fruit*

  ½ cup sugar

  1 teaspoon cornstarch
    dissolved in 2
    tablespoons water

* Our favorite combination is equal amounts of dried cherries, peaches, pears, and prunes—about ½ cup of each.

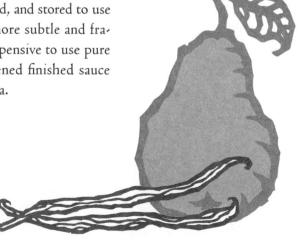

Fresh Mango Sauce

We like this luscious sauce on vanilla frozen yogurt, pineapple or lemon sorbet, pineapple chunks, or on bright red sliced fresh strawberries, which make its interesting flavor and gorgeous color even more evident. It is also a delightful dressing for a fruit salad.

Fresh Mango Sauce is quick to make, but the mangoes must be really ripe for the sauce to be at its best. For this sauce we do not recommend the mango slices available in jars.

■ **YIELDS 1 1/2 CUPS**

3 ripe mangoes, peeled, pitted, and cubed (page 372) (about 2 cups)

1 tablespoon sugar

2 tablespoons fresh lime or lemon juice

1/8 teaspoon ground ginger

pinch of salt

1 tablespoon rum (optional)

IN A BLENDER or food processor, combine the mangoes, sugar, lime or lemon juice, ginger, salt, and rum, if desired, and purée until smooth. Serve immediately or chill. Stored in a sealed container in the refrigerator, this mango sauce will keep for 3 or 4 days. Stir well before serving.

■ **TOTAL TIME:** 20 minutes
■ **EQUIPMENT:** blender or food processor

PER 2 OZ SERVING: 46 CALS, .2 G TOT FAT, .1 G MONO FAT, 0 G SAT FAT, 0 MG CHOL

Summer Berry Sauce

This not-too-sweet, uncooked sauce is easy, breezy, and beautiful. While the strawberries should be fresh, the blueberries and raspberries can be either fresh or frozen, but use frozen fruit that has no added sugar or syrup.

Serve over ice cream or frozen yogurt, or try this sauce as a topping for Fluffy Sweet Biscuits (page 33) or slices of Poundcake Loaf (page 123).

IN A BOWL, combine 1 cup of the strawberries with the blueberries and raspberries. In a blender, purée the remaining cup of strawberries with the sugar and pour over the other berries. Mix well. Add a couple of drops of balsamic vinegar, if desired, as a flavor booster.

VARIATION Doubling this recipe will make just the right amount of filling for a double-crust 10-inch pie. Just one small change—add ¼ cup quick-cooking tapioca to the strawberries and sugar that are puréed in the blender. Use our Best All-Purpose Pie Crust (page 64) and bake at 375° for 50 to 60 minutes, until golden brown.

■ **TOTAL TIME:** 15 minutes
■ **EQUIPMENT:** blender

PER 3.75 OZ SERVING: 70 CALS, .4 G TOT FAT, 0 G MONO FAT, 0 G SAT FAT, 0 MG CHOL

■ **YIELDS 3 CUPS**

2 cups fresh strawberries, hulled and cut in half

1 cup fresh or frozen blueberries

1 cup fresh or frozen raspberries

¼ cup sugar

2 or 3 drops balsamic vinegar (optional)

Raspberry Sauce

In this simple sauce, raspberries are the main event—as they should be. Smooth or chunky, this vivid sauce will both beautify and enhance plain poundcakes, custards, and frozen desserts.

To make a seedless sauce, omit the cornstarch, heat the berries and juice briefly, whirl them in a blender, and strain the sauce through a sieve, pressing it through with the back of a spoon. The sauce is delicious on Peach Bread Pudding (page 231).

■ **YIELDS 1³/₄ CUPS**

½ cup orange juice

2 teaspoons cornstarch

2 cups fresh or frozen raspberries

2 tablespoons sugar, or to taste

IN THE SAUCEPAN, whisk together the orange juice and the cornstarch until the cornstarch has dissolved. Add the raspberries and cook on low heat, stirring constantly, until the sauce thickens. Stir in the sugar and remove from the heat.

SERVE WARM, AT room temperature, or chilled. Refrigerated, the sauce will keep for about 2 weeks.

■ **TOTAL TIME:** 5 minutes
■ **EQUIPMENT:** small saucepan

PER 1 OZ SERVING: 21 CALS, .1 G TOT FAT, 0 G MONO FAT, 0 G SAT FAT, 0 MG CHOL

Warm Apple Walnut Sauce

Any time of year, evoke the sensations of crisp autumns, steamy kitchens, woodstoves, rustling leaves, hot cider . . . with a sauce that flatters poundcake or vanilla ice cream and makes a special breakfast or brunch with pancakes, waffles, or Fluffy Sweet Biscuits (page 33).

IN THE SKILLET, sauté the apples in the butter and brown sugar, stirring constantly on medium heat, for 5 to 10 minutes, until tender. Transfer to a bowl and set aside.

WHISK TOGETHER THE apple juice and cornstarch until smooth and dissolved.

ADD THE CINNAMON, and the cloves and lemon juice, if using. Pour the juice mixture into the unrinsed skillet and cook for 3 to 5 minutes, stirring to deglaze the pan, until thick and clear.

POUR THE THICKENED sauce over the cooked apples and stir in the walnuts and maple syrup. Serve warm; store refrigerated.

- **TOTAL TIME:** 15 minutes
- **EQUIPMENT:** heavy nonreactive skillet (preferably nonstick)

■ YIELDS 4 CUPS

- 3 cups thinly sliced peeled apples
- ¼ cup butter
- ¼ cup packed brown sugar
- 1 cup unsweetened apple juice or apple cider
- 1 tablespoon cornstarch
- ½ teaspoon ground cinnamon
- pinch of cloves (optional)
- 1 tablespoon fresh lemon juice (optional)
- 1 cup coarsely chopped toasted walnuts (page 364)
- ¼ cup pure maple syrup

Bittersweet Chocolate Sauce

Try this dark, rich, velvety chocolate sauce on ice cream or frozen yogurt, or use it to quickly dress up simple cakes like Poundcake Loaf (page 123).

- **YIELDS 1 CUP**

  4 ounces semi-sweet chocolate

  ½ cup half-and-half

  2 tablespoons sugar

  ¼ teaspoon pure orange extract (optional)

 IN THE DOUBLE boiler, heat the chocolate, half-and-half, and sugar. As the chocolate melts, whisk the sauce until perfectly smooth. Remove from the heat and whisk in the orange extract, if desired. Serve the sauce warm.

VARIATION Whisk ¼ cup of peanut, hazelnut, or almond butter into the hot sauce. Serve warm.

- **TOTAL TIME:** 15 minutes
- **EQUIPMENT:** double boiler (page 370)

Light Chocolate Sauce

Hurray—a low-fat alternative to hot fudge! Dark, thick, and rich-tasting without the usual amount of fat, this sauce is delicious served hot over your favorite ice cream, frozen yogurt, or sorbet. When chilled, it thickens to the perfect texture for spreading on a layer cake or pound-cake and will hold its own even at room temperature. It's quick, easy, and really good.

- **YIELDS 1½ CUPS**

  2 ounces unsweetened chocolate

  1 tablespoon unsweetened cocoa powder

  14 ounces canned nonfat sweetened condensed milk

  ¼ cup skim milk

  1 teaspoon pure vanilla extract

COMBINE ALL OF the ingredients in a double boiler and heat, whisking occasionally, until the chocolate melts and the sauce is a uniform dark color.

USE WARM AS a sauce or chill until the sauce thickens to a frosting consistency.

 NOTE Borden's Eagle Brand makes both a low-fat and a nonfat condensed milk.

- **PREPARATION TIME:** 15 minutes
- **EQUIPMENT:** double boiler (page 370)

PER 1 OZ SERVING: 36 CALS, 1.2 G TOT FAT, 0 G MONO FAT, .7 G SAT FAT, 1 MG CHOL

Hot Fudge Sauce

Our classic hot fudge sauce thickens to a soft taffy-like texture once it's drizzled over cold ice cream or frozen yogurt. Chilled, this sauce can also be used as a spread or will frost about 2 dozen cupcakes. Try it on our Peanut Butter Cupcakes (page 278).

IN THE SAUCEPAN on very low heat, carefully melt the chocolate and butter, stirring constantly. Add the corn syrup, sugar, and milk. Increase the heat to medium-high, bring to a boil, and cook for 5 to 8 minutes, until the mixture becomes a candy-like, gooey fudge. Stirring while it cooks is not necessary —the chocolate sauce will not burn! Remove from the heat and stir in the vanilla.

THIS SAUCE WILL keep refrigerated for 2 weeks. Reheat in a double boiler or microwave oven.

- **TOTAL TIME:** 20 to 25 minutes
- **EQUIPMENT:** saucepan

■ **YIELDS 1 CUP**

- 3 ounces unsweetened baking chocolate
- 2 tablespoons butter
- ½ cup light corn syrup
- ½ cup sugar
- ¼ cup milk
- 1 teaspoon pure vanilla extract

Chocolate Ganache

A rich, indulgent frosting or filling for special cakes, this ganache is a day trip to chocolate cream heaven. You can make it ahead of time and refrigerate it until you're ready to use it. If it becomes too stiff, just stir it every 15 minutes as it warms to room temperature until it becomes easy to spread.

It can be used to frost or fill cakes, to fill truffles, or to sandwich between two cookies; heated, the ganache makes a good ice cream topping or sauce for poached pears. Or use it European-style as a spread for bread. Any baked goods frosted or filled with ganache should be stored refrigerated until shortly before serving time, especially in warm weather.

■ **YIELDS 2½ CUPS**

1½ cups heavy (or whipping) cream

9 ounces semi-sweet chocolate

1 tablespoon hazelnut-flavored liqueur, such as Fra Angelico (optional)

 IN THE SAUCEPAN, bring the cream to a simmer. Melt the chocolate or chop it into small pieces. Whisk the melted chocolate or chocolate pieces into the simmering cream and continue to heat gently, if necessary, to fully melt the chocolate. Stir in the liqueur, if using. Pour the chocolate cream into a bowl, using a rubber spatula to get every last drop into the bowl.

CHILL THE GANACHE for about an hour, stirring every 10 to 15 minutes until it has thickened enough to spread. Store in the refrigerator until needed.

NOTE This recipe yields just enough to fill and frost a 9-inch 2-layer cake.

■ **PREPARATION TIME:** 10 minutes
■ **CHILLING TIME:** 1½ to 2 hours
■ **EQUIPMENT:** small saucepan

Maple Cinnamon Coffee Sauce

The flavor of this sauce is almost like a combination of caramel and cappuccino. It is a wonderfully quick ice cream topping and all-purpose dessert sauce. We like it on everything from ice cream to fresh bananas to fruit-filled crêpes. In fact, why not fresh bananas and vanilla ice cream wrapped in a crêpe and topped with the sauce? Mmmm . . .

IN THE SAUCEPAN, combine all of the ingredients and bring to a boil on medium heat, stirring frequently. Cook for about 3 minutes, until the coffee and sugar have dissolved.

REMOVE FROM THE heat and serve warm or at room temperature.

- **TOTAL TIME:** 10 minutes
- **EQUIPMENT:** small saucepan

■ **YIELDS ³⁄₄ CUP**

½ cup heavy cream

2 teaspoons instant coffee granules

3 tablespoons packed brown sugar

3 tablespoons pure maple syrup

½ teaspoon ground cinnamon

½ teaspoon pure vanilla extract

pinch of salt

Champagne Zabaglione

A luscious, velvety sauce, this zabaglione is a bit lighter than the classic Italian version, which is made with marsala wine. Serve it with fresh fruit in glass goblets or in dessert dishes for a stunning presentation, or create a sophisticated parfait by alternating layers of fresh fruit, ladyfinger pieces, and zabaglione.

We suggest the ripest fruits at their peak. Try raspberries, strawberries, blueberries, pineapple, melon, peaches, cherries, oranges, or kiwi. Champagne Zabaglione will also dress up frozen fruit for desserts when your seasonal favorites are unavailable. As with wine in cooking, don't use any Champagne that you wouldn't consider drinking.

■ **YIELDS 2 CUPS**

2 eggs

3 egg yolks

⅔ cup sugar

1 cup dry sparkling wine or Champagne

1½ tablespoons fresh lemon juice

1½ teaspoons freshly grated lemon peel

IN A DOUBLE boiler, whisk the whole eggs, egg yolks, and sugar for about 5 minutes, until the mixture thickens slightly. Add the Champagne, lemon juice, and lemon peel; the mixture will foam up. Continue to simmer gently, whisking constantly for 5 to 10 minutes, until the sauce thickens to the consistency of a custard sauce. Remove from the heat. Stir occasionally as the zabaglione cools. Chill for at least 30 minutes and serve.

■ **PREPARATION TIME:** 15 minutes
■ **CHILLING TIME:** 30 minutes
■ **EQUIPMENT:** double boiler (page 370) or equivalent

Rum Sabayon Sauce

For a happy ending to a Caribbean or Polynesian meal, this is the perfect complement for tropical fruits such as pineapple, mango, banana, or papaya. It is also an impressive custard sauce that will brighten bread puddings or trifles. The quantity of rum in the sauce can be varied depending upon how prominent you'd like its flavor to be.

WHISK TOGETHER ALL of the ingredients in a double boiler. Heat the sauce, whisking continuously, for about 5 minutes, just until it thickens; don't let it boil. Remove from the heat. Serve warm or chilled.

- **TOTAL TIME:** 10 minutes
- **EQUIPMENT:** double boiler (page 370)

- **YIELDS 1½ CUPS**

  2 eggs
  3 egg yolks
  2 to 4 tablespoons rum
  ½ cup sugar
  2 tablespoons fresh lemon juice

Rum Custard Sauce

This sweet, creamy sauce takes minutes to prepare, and its rich sophisticated flavor enhances the simplest dessert of fresh fruit, such as pineapple and bananas. Spoon it warm over Peach Bread Pudding (page 231) for a fancier, heartier dessert.

COMBINE THE MILK, cream, and brown sugar in the saucepan. Whisk in the flour. Cook on low heat, stirring constantly, until the sauce thickens. Remove from the heat and stir in the rum. Cool slightly before using. Serve warm.

THIS SAUCE WILL keep, refrigerated, for 1 week. Reheat in a double boiler (page 370) or microwave oven.

- **TOTAL TIME:** 15 minutes
- **EQUIPMENT:** small heavy saucepan

- **YIELDS 1 CUP**

  ½ cup milk
  ½ cup heavy cream
  ½ cup packed brown sugar
  1 tablespoon unbleached white flour
  2 tablespoons rum

Flavored Whipped Creams

Admittedly, this high-butterfat item should be an occasional treat, but nothing surpasses whipped cream for luxurious smoothness and delicate sweetness. This topping is good on, in, or between layers of just about any dessert.

When you're going to indulge, get the best-tasting heavy or whipping cream, which is pasteurized—but not ultrapasteurized. Ultrapasteurized cream has a longer shelf life but is decidedly lacking in flavor. You may have to shop around to find fresh cream. Unfortunately, it is becoming increasingly scarce. For sweetening, we use confectioners' sugar because it dissolves rapidly and contains a small amount of cornstarch, which helps to stabilize the cream.

■ **YIELDS 2 CUPS**

BASIC VANILLA

- 1 cup heavy cream
- 1 teaspoon pure vanilla extract
- 3 tablespoons confectioners' sugar or 2 tablespoons pure maple syrup

ORANGE

- 1 cup heavy cream
- 3 tablespoons undiluted orange juice concentrate, thawed
- 2 tablespoons confectioners' sugar

MOCHA

- 1 tablespoon instant coffee granules dissolved in 1 cup heavy cream*
- ¼ cup confectioners' sugar
- 1 tablespoon unsweetened cocoa powder

ALMOND OR HAZELNUT

- 1 cup heavy cream
- 2 tablespoons confectioners' sugar
- 2 tablespoons amaretto (almond) or Fra Angelico (hazelnut) liqueur

GINGER

- 1 cup heavy cream
- 2 tablespoons confectioners' sugar
- 2 tablespoons minced crystallized ginger (page 363)
- 1 teaspoon ground ginger or finely grated fresh ginger root

* Be sure to stir instant coffee granules into the cream until the coffee crystals are thoroughly dissolved before whipping.

WHIP THE CREAM in a mixing bowl with an electric mixer or a whisk until soft peaks form. Add the sugar or syrup and flavorings and continue to whip until stiff peaks begin to form. Do not overbeat or you risk making sweetened flavored butter. Serve at once or refrigerate for up to 2 days, until ready to serve.

■ **TOTAL TIME:** 5 minutes
■ **EQUIPMENT:** whisk or electric mixer

Low-fat Creamy Toppings

Here are two excellent replacements for whipped cream or sour cream that are much lower in fat. Either topping can be combined with fresh fruit for easy summer desserts or spooned over cobblers, parfaits, crumbles, or unfrosted cakes. For a wonderfully pink and subtly flavored topping, add two fresh strawberries to the processor.

The recipes are easily multiplied to serve more people and they will keep for a week if well chilled. Try both versions to see which you prefer; we think either turns simple ingredients into satisfying toppings.

COMBINE ALL OF the topping ingredients in the bowl of a food processor and purée for about 1 minute until very smooth, stopping the machine once or twice to scrape down the sides of the bowl with a rubber spatula.

FOR THE BEST flavor, chill the topping for at least an hour.

NOTE A food processor is best for making these toppings, but a blender will work. Just add the ingredients gradually—not all at once—to ensure complete blending.

VARIATION For Creamy Grapes and Strawberries, combine 1 cup of sliced seedless grapes, 1 cup of sliced strawberries, and 1½ cups of the creamy topping of your choice. Chill for 30 minutes. Mound in pretty dessert cups. Serves 4.

- **TOTAL TIME:** 5 minutes
- **CHILLING TIME:** 1 hour (optional)
- **EQUIPMENT:** food processor or blender (see Note)

PER 1 OZ SERVING (COTTAGE CHEESE): 31 CALS, .4 G TOT FAT, .1 G MONO FAT, .3 G SAT FAT, 2 MG CHOL

PER 1 OZ SERVING (RICOTTA): 40 CALS, 1.5 G TOT FAT, .4 G MONO FAT, .9 G SAT FAT, 6 MG CHOL

- **YIELDS 1 CUP**

COTTAGE CHEESE TOPPING

- 1 cup regular or low-fat cottage cheese
- 2 tablespoons sugar
- 1 tablespoon fresh lemon juice

RICOTTA TOPPING

- 1 cup ricotta cheese
- ½ cup plain nonfat yogurt
- 2 to 3 tablespoons pure maple syrup, sugar, or honey*

* If using sugar or honey, 2 tablespoons should be plenty. If using maple syrup, start with 2 tablespoons and add the additional tablespoon only if desired.

CONFECTIONS

Panforte

Spiced Nuts

Chocolate-Dipped Fresh Fruit

Fruit and Nut Truffles

Mocha Grappa Truffles

Nutty Fruit Nuggets

Stuffed Dried Fruit

Candied Citrus Zest

Confections

EVERY CULINARY TRADITION CONTAINS A FEW TIDBITS OF CONCENTRATED sweetness that conjure visions of luxury and heaven on earth for sweet tooths of all ages. Indulging in good-quality imported or domestic candies can be an expensive proposition, while making your own can be fun and relatively inexpensive. Don't limit yourself to the realm of Christmas candy, fudge, taffy pulls, and nut brittle, but browse here as well. We hope that our recipes will delight your palate and impress you with their relative ease of preparation. Stuffed Dried Fruit, simple confections on the lighter side, are certainly easy and fun when made by several people working together around a table. Another healthful treat is Nutty Fruit Nuggets; some of us have made these with kids in school to rave reviews. Making Chocolate-Dipped Fresh Fruit is a simple, engaging activity that falls into our "what could be bad?" category. An adult treat, truffles embody the ultimate in intensity of richness, flavor, and silken texture. Spiced Nuts make a nice nibble before or after dinner or can dress up a simple dessert, such as fruit salad, sorbet, Mango Mousse (page 226), or Raspberry Poached Apricots (page 7). Try decorating sherbets, ice cream, or frosted cakes with delicate but intensely flavored Candied Citrus Zest. Dense with chocolate, fruits, and nuts, Panforte, the Italian classic, combines all the best a sweet has to offer. Our homemade candies are like sweet sentiments, the very thing to give as a Valentine to someone special.

Panforte

"Panforte" means "strong bread" and is a classic Italian dish associated with Siena. This cross between a fruitcake and a candy keeps well when stored in a sealed container, and it makes an energy-rich snack or a nice after-dinner confection.

PREHEAT THE OVEN to 300°. Lightly oil the baking pan and line it with parchment paper.

IN A FOOD processor, whirl the orange juice, honey, brown sugar, cocoa, flour, cinnamon, cloves, ginger, coriander, dates, figs, and raisins until well mixed. Scrape into to a mixing bowl and stir in the nuts.

SPREAD THE VERY thick batter evenly into the prepared pan and bake for 1 hour, until the Panforte has a dull sheen and is fairly dry. Turn off the heat and leave the Panforte in the warm oven for 15 minutes.

INVERT ONTO A serving platter and remove the parchment paper. When cool, dust with confectioners' sugar and cut into 24 pieces (6 columns by 4 rows).

- **PREPARATION TIME:** 35 minutes
- **BAKING TIME:** 1 hour
- **SITTING TIME:** 15 minutes
- **EQUIPMENT:** 8-inch nonreactive square baking pan, parchment paper, food processor

- **SERVES 8 TO 12**

½ cup fresh orange juice

½ cup honey

½ cup packed brown sugar

¼ cup unsweetened cocoa powder

½ cup unbleached white flour

2 teaspoons ground cinnamon

½ teaspoon ground cloves

½ teaspoon ground ginger

½ teaspoon ground coriander

1 cup lightly packed coarsely chopped dates

1 cup lightly packed coarsely chopped figs

1 cup raisins

1 cup toasted hazelnuts, coarsely chopped (page 364)

1 cup toasted almonds, coarsely chopped

dusting of confectioners' sugar

Spiced Nuts

These tasty treats are wonderful for nibbling on as you enjoy a glass of dessert wine or an unadorned piece of fresh fruit. They're the perfect accompaniment to a dessert beverage such as Manhattan Papaya Frappe (page 292) or Spiced Cranberry Punch (page 285).

We like to serve them on a platter along with a couple of other confections, such as Mocha Grappa Truffles (page 327) and Stuffed Dried Fruit (page 329). Spiced Nuts also make good appetizers and snacks.

■ **YIELDS 2 CUPS**

2 cups cashews, pecans, almonds, or walnuts, or a mixture

2 tablespoons butter, melted

2 tablespoons sugar or honey

½ teaspoon freshly grated orange peel

½ teaspoon ground cardamom

⅛ teaspoon salt

⅛ teaspoon ground cayenne (optional)

 PREHEAT THE OVEN to 325°. Lightly oil a baking sheet.

PLACE THE NUTS in a bowl, pour the melted butter over them, and stir to coat. Sprinkle the sugar, orange peel, cardamom, salt, and cayenne, if using, over the nuts and toss until well mixed. Spread on the prepared baking sheet and bake for 15 to 20 minutes, until the nuts are golden and fragrant.

LET COOL, THEN serve or store in a sealed container. Spiced Nuts are best when used within 2 days.

■ **PREPARATION TIME:** 5 to 10 minutes
■ **BAKING TIME:** 15 to 20 minutes
■ **EQUIPMENT:** baking sheet

Chocolate-Dipped Fresh Fruit

Dazzling to look at and succulent and sweet to eat, these jewel-like sweets are the perfect offering for a fancy reception or dessert tasting. Use chunks of fresh pineapple, strawberries with their stems intact, slices of star fruit, or tangerine sections.

MELT THE CHOCOLATE in a double boiler, stirring with a fork as it softens. Turn off the heat and leave the bowl of melted chocolate over the hot water.

LINE A BAKING sheet with wax paper. Dip each chunk of fruit into the chocolate, coating one side, and then place on the baking sheet uncoated side down. Refrigerate the dipped fruit.

TRANSFER TO AN elegant serving plate or tray when ready to serve.

■ **TOTAL TIME:** 20 to 30 minutes
■ **EQUIPMENT:** double boiler (page 370), baking sheet, wax paper

4 ounces semi-sweet chocolate*

20 to 25 pineapple chunks, whole strawberries, slices of star fruit, or tangerine sections

We recommend Tobler, Suchard, and Callebaut brand chocolate.

Fruit and Nut Truffles

These delectable nuggets are wildly popular with adults and children. They're fun to make with a few like-minded people who have visions of sugarplums in their heads and don't mind getting their hands messy. Their preparation is astonishingly quick—a mere 15 minutes—when the fruit and nuts are chopped with a food processor.

■ YIELDS 35 TO 40

16 ounces semi-sweet chocolate

1 cup heavy cream or evaporated milk

1 tablespoon cognac, rum, brandy, or espresso, or to taste (optional)

1 cup walnuts, finely chopped

½ cup dried apricots, finely chopped

½ cup raisins or dried cranberries

½ cup unsweetened cocoa powder

IN A DOUBLE boiler over barely simmering water, melt the chocolate with the cream, stirring occasionally until smooth. Stir in the Cognac or other liqueur, if desired, and the walnuts, apricots, and raisins or dried cranberries. Spread evenly in the pan. Cover and refrigerate for several hours or overnight, until well chilled and firm.

SPREAD THE COCOA on a plate. Cut the chilled mixture into 35 to 40 equal squares. Remove a square from the pan with a spatula, quickly roll it between your palms into a walnut-sized ball, and evenly coat each ball in the cocoa.

PLACE EACH TRUFFLE in a paper candy cup or arrange them in layers, separating the layers with wax paper to keep the truffles from sticking together. Stored in an airtight container and refrigerated, these truffles will keep for at least 2 weeks. They can also be frozen indefinitely.

■ TOTAL TIME: 15 to 25 minutes
■ EQUIPMENT: double boiler (page 370), 9 × 13-inch nonreactive baking pan, paper candy cups or wax paper

Mocha Grappa Truffles

Truffles are the ultimate adult confection. These unbelievably alluring spheres of flavored chocolate are smooth and sophisticated and should be savored with a mug of freshly brewed coffee or with a small glass of grappa.

We recommend using unsalted butter and the finest chocolate you can find.

IN A DOUBLE boiler or in a bowl in a microwave oven, melt the chocolate with the butter, stirring occasionally, until smooth. Stir in the grappa and espresso and set aside to cool for 10 minutes.

POUR THE MIXTURE into the pan, cover, and refrigerate until well chilled and firm, for a couple of hours or overnight. If, after an hour or so, streaks of butter rise to the surface, stir the truffle mixture with a fork and return to the refrigerator.

WHEN THE CHOCOLATE is chilled and firm, spread the cocoa powder on a plate. Scoop up rounded spoonfuls of the chilled chocolate mixture and shape into balls about an inch in diameter by rolling briefly between your palms. (If you've used a rectangular pan, cut the chocolate into squares and then roll each square into a ball.) Roll each ball in the cocoa powder until well coated. Place each truffle in a paper candy cup or arrange them in layers, separating each layer with wax paper to prevent them from sticking together. Well sealed and refrigerated, these truffles will keep for at least 2 weeks. They can also be frozen.

VARIATIONS Try other liqueurs in place of grappa. A sweet, milder liqueur, such as Kahlúa, makes a very different but also delicious truffle. You can omit the liqueur altogether and increase the amount of espresso to ½ cup.

- **PREPARATION TIME: 20 minutes**
- **CHILLING TIME: several hours to overnight**
- **EQUIPMENT: double boiler (page 370), 9 × 13-inch nonreactive baking pan, paper candy cups or wax paper**

■ **YIELDS 35 TO 40**

12 ounces semi-sweet chocolate

¼ cup butter

¼ cup grappa*

¼ cup strong brewed espresso

⅓ cup unsweetened cocoa powder

* Grappa, an Italian (or Californian) brandy with a tingling bite, is distilled from the pomace (pulpy remains) of wine grape pressings. Traditionally, grappas are a fiery, somewhat harsh spirit, but today, with their resurgence in popularity, many grappas, especially those produced for an American market, are mellower and softer but retain the characteristic potent, fruity essence.

Nutty Fruit Nuggets

These easy-to-make dried fruit confections have all the virtues of candy without the vices—the recipe uses only a tablespoon of brown sugar! And the fruit nuggets are tasty, crunchy, sweet, chewy, healthful, energy-packed snacks. What more could you want? The wheat germ provides a concentrated source of vitamins to boot.

■ **YIELDS 20 TO 24**

1 cup packed mixed dried fruit*

½ cup toasted cashews or walnuts

1 teaspoon freshly grated lemon peel

1 tablespoon fresh lemon juice

1 tablespoon packed brown sugar

¼ cup toasted wheat germ

⅓ cup wheat germ, confectioners' sugar, or toasted unsweetened grated coconut

* Choose two or three of the following: raisins, apricots, prunes, dates, or sweet cherries.

IN A VEGETABLE steamer basket over boiling water, steam the dried fruit for about 10 minutes, until soft. Combine the softened fruit with the remaining ingredients in a food processor and whirl until well blended.

ROLL SPOONFULS OF the mixture between the palms of your hands to shape into balls about the size of walnuts, 1 to 1¼ inches in diameter. Roll each ball in wheat germ, confectioners' sugar, or grated coconut until evenly coated all around.

STORED IN A sealed container and refrigerated, these will keep for at least a week.

■ **TOTAL TIME:** 15 to 20 minutes
■ **EQUIPMENT:** food processor

PER .6 OZ SERVING: 48 CALS, 1.5 G TOT FAT, .1 G MONO FAT, .2 G SAT FAT, 0 MG CHOL

Stuffed Dried Fruit

All over the Mediterranean, dried fruits become a confection when stuffed with a tempting filling. In southern Italy, little pieces of chocolate, almond, and orange peel are stuffed into dried figs in preparation for festive occasions. In Morocco, children might have the task of stuffing almond paste into dates to make a huge mound of sweets for a holiday.

Use only one fruit or a variety with any combination of filling ingredients. Make just a few or dozens—the whole family can help. Arranged in an attractive tin, by themselves or with an assortment of cookies or truffles, they are a perfect holiday gift.

CUT A SLIT in the side of each piece of dried fruit. Stuff each piece with one or more of the following: a chocolate piece, a nut, a pinch of orange peel, or about ½ teaspoon almond paste. Press the fruit around the filling to hold it in place—some of the filling will most likely peek out. For a frosted look, sprinkle them with confectioners' sugar.

TO SERVE, ARRANGE the stuffed fruits on a platter lined with a paper doily or place them in fluted paper liners. Just before serving chocolate-stuffed fruits, you might like to melt the chocolate by baking the sweets at 325° for 5 to 10 minutes or by putting them in the microwave for 10 to 20 seconds. Stored in a sealed container, the stuffed fruits will keep for a week at room temperature or for 3 to 4 weeks refrigerated.

whole pitted dried soft fruit (dates, prunes, apricots, and/or figs)*

semi-sweet chocolate (chips or squares broken into pieces)

toasted almonds or walnut or pecan halves (page 364)

freshly grated or candied orange peel

almond paste

* If the fruit you have is not moist enough to be handled easily, steam it over boiling water until softened.

Candied Citrus Zest

Making candied citrus peel is for many cooks a facet of decorative culinary art that transforms everyday fruits into elegant, edible, jewel-like garnishes for a myriad of desserts.

Especially for this recipe, we recommend organically grown fruits.

Make these candy garnishes during dry weather, so the peel will crystallize more quickly. When the humidity is high, the drying time can be as long as 24 hours. While it is important that the candied peel be thoroughly dry before it is packed for storage, slightly wet peel is fine for immediate use.

■ **YIELDS 1 CUP**

- 5 quarts plus ⅓ cup water
- 2 grapefruits
- 4 oranges
- 3 lemons
- 3 limes
- 1 cup sugar

IN THE SAUCEPAN, bring 4 cups of the water to a boil (see Note). Using a vegetable peeler, remove the thin outer rind of the citrus fruit, avoiding the white pith. You may peel long, curly tendrils, julienne-type strips, or a combination of both. Simmer the strips in the water for 5 to 6 minutes and drain well.

REFILL THE PAN with fresh water and simmer the peeled strips again for 5 to 6 minutes. Repeat this process three more times to remove all bitterness from the peel. Drain the peel and remove it from the saucepan.

IN THE SAME saucepan, bring the sugar and the remaining ⅓ cup of water to a simmer. Continue to simmer until the sugar dissolves completely. Cover the pan and boil for about 3 minutes. When, as you stir the syrup, the last drops that fall from the spoon form a thread, the syrup has reached the right consistency.

REMOVE FROM THE heat, stir in the citrus peel, and steep for 1 hour. Drain the peel in a colander. Spread the peel on a wax paper–lined baking sheet and allow the peel to thoroughly dry. This may take up to 24 hours in humid weather.

WHEN THE PEEL is dry, carefully remove it from the wax paper and store it in a tightly covered jar. It will keep for up to a month. Use candied citrus peel to garnish frosted cakes, cheese-cakes, and flans.

NOTE Keeping about 4 cups of water simmering in a teakettle ready for each water change is more efficient and quicker than bringing fresh tap water to a boil four times.

- **PREPARATION TIME:** 1 hour
- **STEEPING TIME:** 1 hour
- **DRYING TIME:** usually 8 to 12 hours
- **EQUIPMENT:** medium saucepan, sharp vegetable peeler, wax paper, baking sheet

MOOSEWOOD CLASSICS

Amaretto Peach Parfait

Apricot Baklava

Double Pear Crisp

Fresh Fruit Trifle

Chocolate Ricotta Mousse

Fruit Ricotta Mousse

Gingered Plum Sauce

Low-fat Lemon Pudding Cake

Our Favorite Poundcake

Prune and Armagnac Cake

Six-Minute Chocolate Cake

Tiramisù di Ithaca

Southern Nut Pie Eudora

Moosewood Fudge Brownies

Moosewood Classics

WHAT MAKES SOMETHING A "CLASSIC"? A CLASSIC WITHSTANDS
the test of time, never goes out of style, and inspires imitation, adaptation, and descriptive phrases such as "ever-popular," "memorable," "timeless," and . . . where is Alistair Cooke when we need him? All of the recipes in this chapter have been published previously in other books from Moosewood Restaurant, but we simply couldn't conceive of a book celebrating our best-loved desserts without including some that have been among our most popular. Admittedly, we argued and pleaded with one another about which ones to include. We were torn between our own personal favorites, Moosewood Restaurant's greatest hits, and the wish not to exclude those suggested by our family members and loyal customers. Not every contender made it, but we'ved done our best to be fair. Our customers go crazy for Moosewood's Fudge Brownies à la mode, Our Favorite Poundcake, luscious Amaretto Peach Parfait, luxurious Chocolate Ricotta Mousse, and moist Six Minute Chocolate Cake, because they are so delicious. These recipes are also our dessert chefs' favorites because they're so easy and dependable. "Greatest hits," including Apricot Baklava, Southern Nut Pie Eudora, Tiramisù di Ithaca, and Low-fat Lemon Pudding Cake, have never failed to please, over and over, year after year. We think you'll be happy to have them all in one place to return to time and time again.

Amaretto Peach Parfait

This easy dessert glorifies fresh peaches at their peak, but strawberries or pitted fresh sweet cherries can stand in for the peaches. Crisp sugar cookies or gingersnaps can replace the amaretti, in which case you may wish to substitute 1 teaspoon of vanilla for the amaretto when whipping the cream. The peaches can be prepared and the cream whipped several hours ahead of serving time, covered, and chilled, but the parfaits should be assembled at the last minute.

■ SERVES 4

WHIP THE CREAM, amaretto, and confectioners' sugar with an electric mixer until stiff. Peel and slice the peaches. In individual dessert cups or parfait glasses, layer half of the peach slices, top with half of the cookie crumbs, and spoon in half of the whipped cream. Repeat with a second layer of each, then serve immediately.

NOTE To crumble amaretti quickly and neatly, place them in a resealable plastic bag and crush with a rolling pin.

- 1 cup heavy cream, well chilled
- 2 tablespoons almond-flavored liqueur, such as amaretto
- 2 tablespoons confectioners' sugar
- 4 ripe fresh peaches
- 8 amaretti, crumbled (page 354)

■ TOTAL TIME: 10 minutes
■ EQUIPMENT: electric mixer, rolling pin

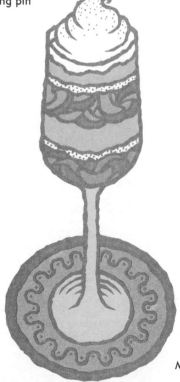

Apricot Baklava

Baklava is a traditional pastry of the Near East, enjoyed from North Africa to the mountains of Armenia and Georgia. This unorthodox version contains almonds and apricot custard.

■ **SERVES 18**

1 cup dried apricots

1 cup apple or apricot juice or water

2 eggs

½ cup butter, melted

½ pound filo dough

1½ cups almonds, toasted and finely chopped (page 364)

½ cup honey, gently heated until warm

2 tablespoons water (or replace 1 tablespoon water with fresh lemon juice)

SIMMER THE DRIED apricots in the cup of juice or water for about 30 minutes. Set aside to cool. Purée the cooled cooked apricots with the eggs in a blender or food processor.

PREHEAT THE OVEN to 350°.

USING A PASTRY brush or a small paintbrush, butter the baking pan. Unroll the filo dough. Fold a filo sheet in half and place it in the baking pan. It should be flat and unwrinkled. Brush the top with butter and sprinkle with chopped almonds. Work quickly, keeping the remaining filo dough covered with a damp towel or it will dry out and become difficult to use. Repeat this process until about half of the filo is used. Spread the apricot purée evenly on the top layer of filo, then continue layering filo, butter, and almonds. End with a buttered sheet of filo and top with chopped almonds.

BEFORE BAKING THE baklava, score it with a sharp knife into 3 columns by 6 rows to form eighteen 3 × 2-inch pieces. Cut through the top few layers, but not as deep as the custard layer. Bake for about 30 minutes, until the top is golden.

WHEN THE BAKLAVA has cooled for about 20 minutes but is still warm, cut all the way through the scoring. Combine the heated honey and the water (and lemon juice, if using) and warm gently. Drizzle evenly over the baklava. Store refrigerated and well covered. Serve chilled.

- **COOKING TIME FOR APRICOTS:** 30 minutes
- **PREPARATION TIME:** 45 minutes
- **BAKING TIME:** 30 minutes
- **COOLING TIME:** 20 minutes
- **EQUIPMENT:** blender or food processor, pastry brush, 9 × 13-inch baking pan

Double Pear Crisp

The taste of juicy, fresh pears is intensified by the concentrated flavor of dried pears in this simple, wholesome dessert. Our Moosewood customers are always happy to see it on our dessert menu.

 PREHEAT THE OVEN to 375°.

CUT OUT AND discard any stems and hard cores from the dried pears and chop into ½-inch pieces. In the small saucepan, cover the dried pear pieces with the pear juice and bring to a boil. Reduce the heat and simmer until the pears are tender, about 10 minutes. Meanwhile, core and chop the fresh pears into bite-sized pieces and spread them in the baking dish.

IN THE MEDIUM saucepan, melt the butter. Add the brown sugar or maple syrup, the oats, cinnamon, and nutmeg. Stir to evenly coat the oats and set aside. When the dried pears are tender, pour them and their cooking liquid over the fresh pears in the baking dish. Spoon the oat mixture evenly over the top and bake, uncovered, for 35 to 45 minutes, or until the topping is browned and crisp.

SERVE WARM OR cool, topped with ice cream or fresh whipped cream, if desired.

- **PREPARATION TIME:** 25 to 30 minutes
- **BAKING TIME:** 35 to 45 minutes
- **EQUIPMENT:** small saucepan, 2-quart baking dish, medium saucepan

■ **SERVES 6 TO 8**

6 ounces dried pears

1 cup pear juice

4 or 5 medium pears (about 4 cups chopped)

½ cup butter

½ cup packed brown sugar or ⅓ cup pure maple syrup

2 cups rolled oats

1 teaspoon ground cinnamon

½ teaspoon ground nutmeg

ice cream or whipped cream (optional)

Fresh Fruit Trifle

English trifle is traditionally served in a large clear glass bowl, so that all the colorful layers can be admired. We use fresh fruit, rather than the customary jam, but our trifle still evokes images of Victorian English holidays. We've offered suggestions for several combinations of different fruits, liqueurs, and custard. You could use fruit juice in place of liqueur.

Our blender method for making Vanilla Custard Sauce is so quick that you may decide to serve it immediately while it's warm and fragrant, but it's equally delicious cold. Well covered and refrigerated, it keeps for several days. The recipe makes about 2½ cups of this homey, versatile sauce, so you'll have a little left over for another dessert later in the week.

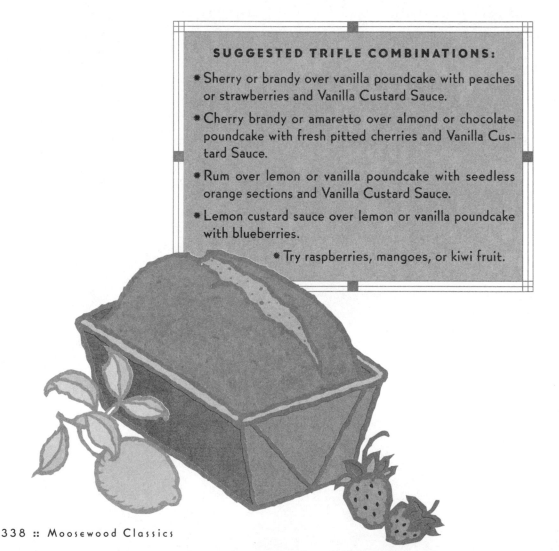

SUGGESTED TRIFLE COMBINATIONS:

* Sherry or brandy over vanilla poundcake with peaches or strawberries and Vanilla Custard Sauce.

* Cherry brandy or amaretto over almond or chocolate poundcake with fresh pitted cherries and Vanilla Custard Sauce.

* Rum over lemon or vanilla poundcake with seedless orange sections and Vanilla Custard Sauce.

* Lemon custard sauce over lemon or vanilla poundcake with blueberries.

* Try raspberries, mangoes, or kiwi fruit.

IN THE SAUCEPAN, heat the milk and sugar almost to a boil. While whirling the eggs in the blender, gradually add the hot milk in a thin stream to cook the eggs. Add the vanilla and set aside (see Note).

PREPARE THE FRESH fruit of your choice. Peel, pit, and slice peaches. Peel, seed, and section oranges (page 372). Pit cherries. Gaze fondly upon labor-free berries. Combine the prepared fruit in a bowl and set aside.

ARRANGE A LAYER of poundcake chunks on the bottom of a large bowl or individual dessert cups. Pour about half of the liqueur over the cake and allow it to soak in for several minutes. Spoon half of the custard onto the liqueured cake and then sprinkle on the fresh fruit. Layer everything again in order, using the rest of the poundcake, liqueur, and custard, and most of the fruit. Top with the sweetened whipped cream and decorate with the last of the fruit. Chill.

NOTE Usually the custard is ready at this stage, but if it hasn't thickened enough to coat a spoon, pour the mixture back into the saucepan and cook gently, stirring, until it thickens. If the custard should then overcook and become lumpy, whirl it in the blender once more.

- **TOTAL TIME:** 25 to 30 minutes
- **EQUIPMENT:** heavy saucepan, blender, 8 to 10 dessert cups or a large serving bowl

- **SERVES 8 TO 10**

VANILLA CUSTARD SAUCE

- 2 cups milk
- ¼ cup sugar
- 4 eggs
- 1 teaspoon pure vanilla extract

TRIFLE

- 3 cups fresh fruit, such as peaches, oranges, cherries, or berries
- 4 cups plain or flavored poundcake, broken into bite-sized chunks*
- 3 tablespoons liqueur, such as brandy, sherry, or rum
- 2 cups heavy cream, whipped with ½ teaspoon pure vanilla extract and pure maple syrup, honey, or confectioners' sugar to taste

* This is a good use for leftover poundcake (pages 119 to 124, or 344), but you can also use a purchased poundcake.

Chocolate Ricotta Mousse

This is one of our most often requested recipes. It makes a foolproof, almost instant, rich, and velvety dessert.

■ **SERVES 6**

3 ounces unsweetened chocolate, melted

1 pound ricotta cheese

1½ teaspoons pure vanilla extract

⅓ cup honey, or other sweetener to taste

1 cup heavy cream

1 tablespoon pure maple syrup

fresh fruit or shaved chocolate

COMBINE THE MELTED chocolate, ricotta cheese, 1 teaspoon of vanilla, and the honey in a blender or food processor bowl and whirl until very smooth. Pour into dessert cups and chill.

JUST BEFORE SERVING, combine the heavy cream, the remaining ½ teaspoon of vanilla, and the maple syrup, and whip until stiff.

SERVE THE MOUSSE topped with whipped cream and garnished with a fresh ripe strawberry, a few raspberries, an orange or kiwi fruit slice, or shaved chocolate.

■ **PREPARATION TIME:** 15 to 20 minutes
■ **CHILLING TIME:** at least 1 hour
■ **EQUIPMENT:** blender or food processor

Fruit Ricotta Mousse

This fluffy pudding is a perennial favorite at Moosewood. In the summer, it's an easy way to show off fresh ripe cherries and berries at their peak. In winter, we might use frozen, pitted, whole sweet cherries, blueberries, or raspberries. We don't recommend frozen strawberries in this recipe because they don't retain their texture well. Look for frozen fruit that contains no added sugar or syrup.

We think this mousse is most welcome after a light, dairy-free meal. Fruit Ricotta Mousse is also wonderful served in a melon half for brunch. It's surprisingly light and refreshing.

When choice fruit is plentiful, you might freeze some for an out-of-season treat. To prevent soft fruits such as berries, pitted cherries, or sliced peaches from sticking or clumping together, spread them onto trays with each piece separate and not touching its neighbor. Freeze for 24 hours; then, working quickly, pack the fruit in resealable bags.

IN THE BOWL of a food processor or with an electric mixer, whip the ricotta for about 2 minutes, or until very smooth and slightly fluffed up. Rinse and stem the fresh fruit. Cut large strawberries into smaller pieces and pit cherries. Set aside several pieces of fruit for garnishing the finished mousse. Fold the fresh fruit and the fruit spread into the ricotta. Just before serving, whip the cream until quite stiff and then fold in. (see Note)

SERVE CHILLED IN individual dessert cups, topped with the reserved fruit garnish.

NOTE The mousse (without the whipped cream) can be made well in advance of serving. Whip the cream and fold it in just before serving. The finished mousse will keep refrigerated and well-covered for about two days.

- **TOTAL TIME:** 10 minutes
- **EQUIPMENT:** food processor or electric mixer

■ **SERVES 8**

- 1 pound ricotta cheese
- 1 pint fresh strawberries, or fresh or frozen cherries, blueberries, or raspberries
- ½ cup fruit spread or preserves*
- 1 cup heavy cream

* Use fruit spread made of the same fruit as the fresh fruit you are using. By "fruit spread," we mean no-sugar-added fruit spreads, conserves, or jams, such as Sorrel Ridge, Polaner's All Fruit, Woodstock, Just Fruit, or Knudsen's.

Gingered Plum Sauce

This chunky, tart-sweet sauce is a brilliant burgundy color. Serve it warm or cold on vanilla ice cream, frozen yogurt, or lemon sherbet, or present it as a kissel topped with whipped cream.

Gingered Plum Sauce is a wonderful autumn harvest dessert topping and has an affinity for many cuisines—Eastern European, New England, Chinese, and Scandinavian, to name a few. It is also an excellent breakfast topping for oatmeal or pancakes.

■ **YIELDS 2 CUPS**

1 pound firm fresh plums (6 or 7 large purple plums, or 10 to 12 prune plums)

¼ cup pure maple syrup

¼ teaspoon ground ginger

1 teaspoon cornstarch

2 tablespoons fresh lemon juice

CUT THE PLUMS along the midlines, twist apart, and remove the pits. Slice each half into 3 or 4 wedges. In the saucepan, combine the plums, maple syrup, and ginger and cook on medium-low heat, stirring frequently. In a small bowl or cup, stir the cornstarch into the lemon juice until dissolved. When the plums begin to release juice but are still firm, add the lemon juice mixture and bring to a boil. Cook, stirring frequently, until the liquid is thickened and clear.

SERVE WARM OR cold.

■ **TOTAL TIME:** 15 minutes
■ **EQUIPMENT:** nonreactive saucepan

Low-fat Lemon Pudding Cake

This favorite old-fashioned dessert separates into layers during baking—a tart-sweet pudding on the bottom and a light spongy cake on top. You'd never guess it was so low in fat from the luscious taste. Serve it warm or chilled, plain or with fresh berries. Or, for a more extravagant treat, top it with Summer Berry Sauce (page 309) or Orange Sauce (page 306).

Tightly sealed and refrigerated, this cake will keep for about 5 days.

■ **SERVES 8**

 PREHEAT THE OVEN to 350°. Lightly oil the baking cups and place them in the baking pan.

IN A LARGE BOWL, combine the flour, baking powder, and ¾ cup of the sugar (see Note). Stir in the buttermilk, lemon juice, the grated lemon peel, if using, and the egg yolks and set aside.

WITH AN ELECTRIC mixer, beat the egg whites and salt until the whites are stiff. Beat in the remaining ½ cup of sugar. Gently fold the egg whites into the batter. Spoon the batter evenly into the prepared cups. Pour boiling water into the baking pan to reach halfway up the sides of the cups.

BAKE FOR 35 to 45 minutes, until puffy and golden.

NOTE If you want a very sweet confection, add an extra ¼ cup of sugar at this step.

- ½ cup unbleached white flour
- ½ teaspoon baking powder
- 1¼ cups sugar
- 1½ cups buttermilk
- ½ cup fresh lemon juice (about 3 lemons)
- 2 teaspoons freshly grated lemon peel (optional)
- 2 egg yolks, lightly beaten
- 4 egg whites
- pinch of salt

■ **PREPARATION TIME:** 20 minutes
■ **BAKING TIME:** 35 to 45 minutes
■ **EQUIPMENT:** eight 8-ounce ramekins or ovenproof dessert cups, flat-bottomed baking pan, electric mixer

PER SERVING: 229 CALS, 2.6 G TOT FAT, .9 G MONO FAT, .9 G SAT FAT, 87 MG CHOL

Our Favorite Poundcake

At Moosewood, we've served poundcakes based on this recipe for most of our history. Pound-cake is a surefire customer pleaser—it's hard to beat its fine texture and rich, buttery flavor. Our dessert chefs love it because it's reliable and versatile and lends itself to invention.

For instance, you can use brown sugar instead of white. Any flavor of extract will work. We sometimes replace the milk with yogurt, sour cream, fruit juice, coconut milk, wine, or even whiskey. You can eliminate the liquid altogether if you fold in a juicy fruit. Add nuts, dried fruit, coconut, or chocolate chips. The cake can also be glazed, frosted, dusted with confection-ers' sugar, soaked with a liqueur, or served with sliced fruit, whipped cream, or lemon curd.

It's fun to dream up new variations, but there's really nothing better than a slice of dense, plain poundcake, served with a cup of tea or a glass of cold milk.

■ SERVES 16

2 cups butter, softened

3 cups sugar

6 eggs

4 cups unbleached white pastry flour (page 361)

½ cup milk

2 teaspoons pure vanilla or lemon extract

2 teaspoons baking powder

PREHEAT THE OVEN to 350°. Generously butter and flour the bundt pan.

IN A LARGE bowl, cream the butter and sugar with an electric mixer on high speed. Beat in the eggs. Lower the mixer speed to medium and add 2 cups of the flour, mixing thoroughly. Blend in the milk and extract. In a separate bowl, combine the baking powder with the remaining 2 cups of flour. Add to the batter and beat well, until the batter is smooth and thick.

POUR THE BATTER evenly into the bundt pan. Bake for 1 hour to 1 hour and 20 minutes, or until the cake pulls away from the sides of the pan and a knife inserted in the center comes out clean. Cool in the pan on a rack for 20 minutes and then invert onto a serving plate to cool, leaving the pan on top of the cake for about 20 minutes, so the cake will hold its shape nicely.

NOTE Not every 10-inch bundt pan holds the same number of cups, since there can be differences in the fluting and the slopes of the sides. Be sure that your bundt pan holds at least 12 cups for this recipe. These are substantial cakes and if your bundt pan is too small, the batter is likely to overflow during baking and make a mess in your oven.

VARIATIONS   Amaretto Poundcake: Use almond extract instead of vanilla, reduce the flour to 3½ cups, and add 1½ cups of ground toasted almonds. When you remove the cake from the oven, drizzle ½ cup of almond-flavored liqueur, such as amaretto, over it. The liqueur will soak in as the cake cools in the pan.

BLUEBERRY LEMON POUNDCAKE: Use pure lemon extract and eliminate the milk. When the batter has been beaten smooth and thick, just before pouring it into the bundt pan, fold in 1 pint of fresh blueberries or 2 cups of thawed frozen blueberries. This cake may take 20 to 25 minutes longer to bake than the basic poundcake, especially when using frozen berries.

- **PREPARATION TIME:** 15 minutes
- **BAKING TIME:** about 1 hour
- **COOLING TIME:** 40 minutes
- **EQUIPMENT:** 10-inch bundt pan (see Note), electric mixer

Prune and Armagnac Cake

This is a wonderful cake—glossy, dark, and very moist. The rich prune flavor is heightened by spices and Armagnac, a special Cognac from the Armagnac region of France. The ingredient list is long but the cake is not the least bit difficult to make.

Serve at room temperature with ice cream or whipped cream, if desired. The best tool for cutting this tender cake is a long serrated bread knife.

■ **SERVES 16**

CAKE

2 cups pitted prunes

¼ cup Armagnac or Cognac

2 cups water

¾ cup vegetable oil

1½ cups packed brown sugar

4 large eggs

2 teaspoons pure vanilla extract

3 cups unbleached white pastry flour (page 361)

2 teaspoons baking soda

1 teaspoon salt

½ teaspoon ground allspice

1 teaspoon ground nutmeg

1 teaspoon ground cloves

½ teaspoon ground cardamom

2 teaspoons ground cinnamon

1 cup buttermilk

IN THE SAUCEPAN, combine the prunes, Armagnac, and water and simmer for 20 to 25 minutes, until the prunes are tender. Drain, reserving the liquid for the glaze. Coarsely chop the prunes and set aside.

PREHEAT THE OVEN to 350°. Butter the bundt pan and dust it with flour. Tap out the excess flour. Set aside.

IN A LARGE bowl, cream together the oil and brown sugar with an electric mixer. Add the eggs and vanilla and beat well. In a separate bowl, combine the flour, baking soda, salt, allspice, nutmeg, cloves, cardamom, and cinnamon. Add the flour mixture to the batter, beating until well blended. Pour in the buttermilk and beat just until smooth. Fold in the chopped prunes.

POUR THE BATTER into the prepared pan and bake for 1 hour to 1 hour and 10 minutes, until a knife inserted in the center of the cake comes out clean. Cool the cake in the pan on a rack for 10 minutes, then invert it onto a serving platter without removing the pan. Cool the cake for 15 minutes more, then remove the pan.

COMBINE ALL OF the glaze ingredients in the saucepan and bring to a boil. Cook on medium-high heat for 2 minutes, stirring constantly. Remove from the heat. With a toothpick or skewer, pierce the top of the cake in 10 or 12 places. Slowly pour the glaze over the cake, allowing it to soak in.

- **PREPARATION TIME:** 30 to 35 minutes
- **BAKING TIME:** 1 hour to 1 hour and 10 minutes
- **COOLING TIME:** 25 minutes
- **EQUIPMENT:** 10-inch (12-cup) bundt pan, small saucepan, electric mixer

ARMAGNAC GLAZE

- 1 cup sugar
- 2 tablespoons fresh lemon juice
- ¼ cup Armagnac or Cognac
- ¼ cup reserved prune cooking liquid

Six-Minute Chocolate Cake

No one would ever suspect that this dark, elegant, scrumptious cake is both eggless and dairy-less. It's economical and low-cholesterol, and what's more, it goes into the oven in 6 minutes with no mixing bowl to clean because the batter is mixed directly in the baking pan. You may be surprised to see vinegar in the ingredient list, but it's not a mistake. The combination of vinegar and baking soda helps the cake to rise. When cool, cut and serve the cake directly from the pan using a small metal spatula or pie server; it cannot be easily turned out onto a serving plate.

However, if you have time for a 12-minute cake, you can mix the batter in a bowl, line the bottom of the cake pan with parchment paper, and generously oil the sides of the pan and dust with flour. Then the cake can be removed from the pan with no trouble at all, for a more elegant presentation or for a layer cake.

For the chocolate glaze, use a good-quality chocolate, such as Callebaut or Valrhôna. Or try it with your favorite frosting or a dusting of confectioners' sugar, or topped with whipped cream, ice cream, or sliced fruit.

■ **SERVES 8**

CAKE

1½ cups unbleached white flour (page 361)

⅓ cup unsweetened cocoa powder

1 teaspoon baking soda

½ teaspoon salt

1 cup sugar

½ cup vegetable oil

1 cup cold water or coffee

2 teaspoons pure vanilla extract

2 tablespoons cider vinegar

 PREHEAT THE OVEN to 375°.

SIFT TOGETHER THE flour, cocoa, soda, salt, and sugar directly into the cake pan. In the measuring cup, measure and mix together the oil, cold water or coffee, and vanilla. Pour the liquid ingredients into the baking pan and mix the batter with a fork or a small whisk. When the batter is smooth, add the vinegar and stir quickly. There will be pale swirls in the batter as the baking soda and the vinegar react. Stir just until the vinegar is evenly distributed throughout the batter.

BAKE FOR 25 to 30 minutes and set aside to cool.

TO MAKE THE optional glaze, melt the chocolate in a double boiler, microwave oven, or reset the oven to 300° and melt the chocolate in the oven for about 15 minutes in a small ovenproof bowl or heavy skillet. Stir the hot water and the vanilla into the melted chocolate until smooth. Spoon the glaze over the cooled cake. Refrigerate the glazed cake for at least 30 minutes before serving.

VARIATION To make a dozen cupcakes, follow the recipe directions, mixing the batter in a bowl. Pour the batter into a cupcake tin with paper liners and bake at 375° for 20 minutes. While the cupcakes bake, prepare the glaze. When the cupcakes are done, remove them from the oven and spoon on the glaze, if using. Refrigerate for at least 30 minutes before serving.

TO MAKE A FANCY Vegan Layer Cake, double the cake recipe and follow the instructions in the headnote for "12-minute cake." Spread ½ cup of raspberry or apricot preserves or Raspberry Sauce (page 310) between the layers, and ice the cake with Chocolate Vegan Glaze.

OR TRY FROSTING the cake with Mocha Frosting: Melt 8 ounces of semi-sweet chocolate in a double boiler or microwave. Add ⅔ cup of freshly brewed coffee, 1 teaspoon of pure vanilla extract, and ½ cup of confectioners' sugar. Chill the frosting for 20 to 30 minutes, stirring occasionally, until it reaches a good spreading consistency. If it overthickens, heat the bottom of the bowl until some of the frosting melts, then stir briskly until it softens again.

- **PREPARATION TIME FOR CAKE:** 6 minutes
- **BAKING TIME:** 30 minutes
- **PREPARATION TIME FOR GLAZE:** 15 minutes
- **CHILLING TIME (IF USING GLAZE):** 30 minutes
- **EQUIPMENT:** 9-inch round or 8-inch square cake pan, 2-cup measuring cup, double boiler (page 370) (optional)

CHOCOLATE VEGAN GLAZE (OPTIONAL)

½ pound semi-sweet chocolate

¾ cup hot water

½ teaspoon pure vanilla extract

Tiramisù di Ithaca

Tiramisù, Italian for "pick-me-up," is considered a fortifying treat in Italy, where it is customarily made with egg yolks, mascarpone cheese, and marsala wine. We understand that this traditional dessert has become so popular in Japan that it is even available in vending machines.

In our little town of Ithaca, tiramisù is still a novelty for many people, and it wows dinner guests every time. A couple of world-traveling tiramisù aficionados, who had tasted hundreds of other renditions, declared ours their favorite. This version is a bit lighter than usual and very easy to make. It is especially pleasing after a light vegetable meal, whether Italian or Japanese.

Tiramisù looks its best when served within a few hours after it has been assembled. This recipe gives instructions for individual servings of tiramisù, but it can also be assembled in one large dessert bowl and then spooned out into individual cups at serving time.

SUGGESTED TOPPINGS FOR TIRAMISÙ

* shaved or grated chocolate
* dusting of unsweetened cocoa powder
* sprinkling of fresh raspberries
* sprinkling of chocolate-covered coffee beans

COMBINE THE NEUFCHÂTEL or cream cheese, confectioners' sugar, vanilla, instant coffee granules, and cocoa powder, if using, in a large bowl and beat with an electric mixer for 3 or 4 minutes until evenly colored and fluffy. In a separate bowl, whip the cream until quite stiff. Gently fold the whipped cream into the Neufchâtel mixture with a spatula until smooth.

IN A WIDE, shallow bowl, combine the cool brewed coffee and the liqueur or marsala, if using. Break a ladyfinger in half and dip it into the coffee mixture just until it absorbs liquid and softens—without falling apart. Some ladyfingers require just a quick dip and others need to soak a bit. Place the 2 dipped halves of the ladyfinger in the bottom of one of the dessert cups. One at a time, break in half and moisten 5 more ladyfingers for the other dessert cups.

SPOON THE NEUFCHÂTEL mixture evenly over the ladyfingers in the dessert cups. Break and moisten the remaining 6 ladyfingers as before. Push 2 moistened halves vertically down into the mounds of Neufchâtel to stand upright along opposite sides of each dessert cup.

REFRIGERATE FOR AT least 1 hour and serve cold. Before serving, decorate each cup with one of the suggested toppings.

NOTE Ladyfingers, found in the cookie aisles of well-stocked supermarkets, are also called "savoiardi" and "boudoirs." Our favorite brand, for flavor and texture, is Bistefani. You will only need about half of a 7-ounce package for this recipe.

- **PREPARATION TIME:** 45 minutes
- **CHILLING TIME:** 1 hour
- **EQUIPMENT:** electric mixer, 6 six-ounce dessert cups or wine glasses

■ **SERVES 6**

8 ounces Neufchâtel or other low-fat cream cheese

½ cup confectioners' sugar

½ teaspoon pure vanilla extract

1 heaping tablespoon instant coffee granules or espresso powder

1½ teaspoons unsweetened cocoa powder (optional)

½ cup heavy cream

1 cup fresh strong coffee (decaffeinated or regular), cooled

¼ cup mocha- or coffee flavored liqueur, marsala, or additional coffee

12 ladyfingers (see Note)

Southern Nut Pie Eudora

Maple syrup, harvested from the wooded hillsides surrounding Ithaca, combined with the option of using walnuts, gives a northern twist to our version of a compelling southern classic, pecan pie.

This is the pie our veteran dessert chef, Susan Harville, presented to the great southern writer (and one of Susan's favorites), Eudora Welty, who came to Ithaca to give a reading. Miss Welty accepted the pie very graciously and said, ". . . the pleasure you've had from reading my work? Why, surely it couldn't add up to a whole pecan pie!"

■ **SERVES 8**

1 unbaked 9-inch pie crust (page 64)

1½ cups pecan or walnut halves

¼ cup butter, melted

1 teaspoon pure vanilla extract

2 tablespoons unbleached white flour

½ teaspoon salt

3 eggs, well beaten

1 cup pure maple syrup

1 cup heavy cream or half-and-half

apple slices

fresh whipped cream or ice cream

 PREHEAT THE OVEN to 375°.

SPREAD THE NUTS evenly in the bottom of the unbaked pie shell and set aside. In a large bowl, mix the melted butter, vanilla, and flour. Add the salt, eggs, maple syrup, and cream or half-and-half and mix thoroughly. Pour the filling over the nuts in the pie shell. The nuts will float to the top, so to prevent them from burning during baking, gently push them down into the liquid with the back of a spoon to wet them.

BAKE FOR 50 to 60 minutes, or until a knife inserted in the center comes out clean. Let the pie cool for at least 15 minutes before slicing. Serve plain or with a few crisp apple slices and a dollop of whipped cream or a scoop of ice cream.

■ **PREPARATION TIME:** 25 minutes including crust
■ **BAKING TIME:** 50 to 60 minutes
■ **COOLING TIME:** 15 minutes
■ **EQUIPMENT:** 9-inch pie pan

Moosewood Fudge Brownies

The first Moosewood fudge brownies came from a recipe found on the back of a chocolate box over twenty years ago. Over the years we've changed the recipe several times; now they're the moistest, fudgiest brownies you've ever tasted. We've served them at the restaurant almost every day, and they are the overwhelming favorite of our customers, our children, and our friends. Some things never change. And if you're not afraid to gild the lily, serve the brownie à la mode, garnished with a strawberry or cherry.

If you mix the batter by hand or use an electric hand mixer, melt the butter and chocolate in a pot large enough to hold all of the batter. You can add each ingredient directly into the pot without having to clean a mixing bowl.

We crumble leftover brownies to use as a sundae topping. The crumbs freeze very well and can go straight from the freezer to the sundae with no defrosting.

■ **SERVES 9 TO 12**

½ cup butter

3 ounces unsweetened chocolate

1 cup lightly packed brown sugar

½ teaspoon pure vanilla extract

2 eggs, lightly beaten

½ cup unbleached white flour*

* *Using pastry flour in place of the regular unbleached white flour yields a fudgier, less cake-like brownie.*

 PREHEAT THE OVEN to 350°. Butter the baking pan.

IN THE POT, melt the butter and chocolate together on low heat, stirring occasionally. Remove from the heat. Add the brown sugar and vanilla and beat by hand or with an electric mixer. Add the eggs and beat well. Stir in the flour and mix until the batter is thoroughly blended and smooth.

POUR THE BATTER into the prepared pan and bake for about 20 minutes, until the brownies are just beginning to pull away from the sides of the pan and are still fudgy in the center. If you prefer more cake-like brownies, bake an additional 5 minutes.

■ **PREPARATION TIME:** 10 minutes
■ **BAKING TIME:** 20 minutes
■ **EQUIPMENT:** 8- or 9-inch square baking pan, heavy pot, hand mixer or electric mixer (optional)

GLOSSARY OF INGREDIENTS

Almond milk

This beverage joins the growing number of milk alternatives for vegans and cholesterol-conscious or dairy-sensitive people—or for those who simply like it. Almond milk has a pleasant, slightly sweet, almond flavor. It is often made of water, brown rice syrup, almonds, lecithin, barley malt, natural vanilla, sodium citrate, sea salt, and carrageenan, a thickener derived from edible seaweed. Almond milk is delicious in shakes, cocoas, puddings, sauces, and baked goods, but remember to adjust for its sweetness and flavoring. Once opened, store in a tightly closed container in the refrigerator and it will keep for about 2 weeks.

Amaretti

Crisp, airy, Italian meringue cookies made with almonds or almond paste, sugar, and egg whites. In Italy, it is traditional to add a portion of bitter almonds to this mix. *"Amaro"* in Italian means "bitter" and so amaretti, "little bitter ones," became the name of the cookies. Amaretti can be made at home (see our recipe in *Sundays at Moosewood,* page 373) or found in Italian food stores, gourmet shops, or the ethnic section of many supermarkets. Imported amaretti are strongly flavored and very sweet. They are delicious dipped in red wine or espresso. Crushed amaretti can be a novel component of pressed pie crusts— 4 ounces of amaretti will make 1 cup of crumbs. Stored in a tightly closed container, amaretti will keep for months.

Baking powder

Without leavening, baked goods will not rise. Baking powder is a rising or leavening agent. Rising occurs when the primary ingredients, alkali baking soda and one or more acids, release carbon dioxide gas (CO_2) in the presence of liquid and/or heat. The carbon dioxide trapped in a dough or batter forms tiny bubbles in the gluten of the flour, causing the dough to rise and puff. To insure that the leavening doesn't exhaust itself before the cake is in the oven, most modern-day baking powders are "double acting." Double acting powders contain two acids, one that reacts strongly with liquid and a slower-acting acid that reacts to heat.

Flour or another type of starch is added to baking powder as a filler and moisture absorber, so the baking powder won't release CO_2 during storage. Nonetheless, an opened and recapped can of baking powder will absorb some atmospheric moisture and generally has a shelf life of 3 to 12 months. To test your baking powder for activity, mix 1 teaspoon of powder into ½ cup of warm water. If the water bubbles vigorously, you're in business. If it doesn't, a home version can be made by mixing 1 tablespoon of baking soda with 2 tablespoons of cream of tartar. Since this mixture contains only one acid (cream of tartar), it is single acting and will begin producing CO_2 as soon as moistened. It is therefore important to pop the batter into the oven as soon as possible. Homemade baking powder does not keep; mix it up only as needed.

A metallic aftertaste may be evident when baking powder that contains aluminum acid salts is used. Rumford Baking Powder is one brand that is aluminum-free.

Baking soda

Also known as bicarbonate of soda and sodium bicarbonate, baking soda neutralizes or reduces the acidity of ingredients such as citrus, cultured dairy products, sweeteners, and chocolate and, in the presence of acidic ingredients, becomes a leavener. When baking soda combines with a food acid, leavening begins immediately, so act quickly to get the batter into the oven. When recipes call for both baking soda and baking powder, the soda's purpose is to mellow an acidic ingredient. The alkalinity of baking soda deepens the color of cocoa and chocolate during

baking. Too much soda can turn a white cake yellow and affect the aroma and flavor of any baked good. Because baking soda clumps, always sift it before adding it to a batter. Baking soda keeps indefinitely.

Basmati rice

With its lovely fragrance, this long-grain rice adds a distinctive touch to desserts like rice pudding. It is available in natural food stores, well-stocked supermarkets, and Indian groceries.

Brown sugar

Lyrics have been written about it and plays named for it. Brown sugar is a mixture of white sugar and molasses, available in two varieties—light and dark—depending on the amount of molasses added. When our recipes call for brown sugar, the light, milder-tasting variety is intended, unless otherwise stated. Cup for cup, brown sugar has the same sweetening power as white sugar. However, because white sugar is more dense, brown sugar must be packed when measured. The molasses in brown sugar adds moisture and flavor to baked goods. However, brown sugar adds weight, so it is not recommended for fragile or delicate cakes.

Store brown sugar in a covered glass jar or in a tightly closed, sturdy plastic bag in the refrigerator. In a pinch, brown sugar can be made at home. For 1 cup of brown sugar, combine 2 tablespoons of unsulphured molasses with 1 cup of granulated sugar.

Butter

Good butter has a clean, fresh scent, a slightly nutty taste, and an ungreasy texture. At room temperature high-quality butter does not sweat droplets of moisture. At Moosewood, we use both salted and unsalted butter. For delicate cakes, cookies, and pastries that rely on a rich, buttery flavor for taste, we recommend unsalted butter. For baked goods in which chocolate, spices, and fruit are predominant, salted butter is generally the best choice. Whipped butter has nitrogen added to improve its spreadability; it can be used in dessert making, but must be measured by weight rather than volume.

"Light" butters with a third less fat than regular butter can be used at the table but do not work in baked goods. We never substitute margarine for butter in dessert recipes. We've developed our recipes using butter because it's delicious and it is the most wholesome shortening. Studies report that margarine (as well as solid vegetable shortening), containing transfatty acids formed during the hydrogenation process, contributes to elevated cholesterol levels and may increase the risk of heart disease and some cancers.

For lasting freshness, store butter in the coldest part of the refrigerator, rewrapped in its original wrapper. Careful rewrapping or storing in a tightly closed butter dish prevents butter from absorbing food odors. Don't wrap butter in aluminum foil, which will give it a metallic taste. Enclosed in its original wrapper and sealed in a freezer bag, it keeps frozen for up to 6 months.

Buttermilk

The sweet, rich, tangy taste of buttermilk is a boon to the discerning and health-minded dessert-maker. Buttermilk is low-fat and adds richness, flavor, and leavening to many baked goods. Its acidic quality inhibits the development of the gluten present in wheat flour and so it is a natural tenderizer. When combined with baking soda, it gives a rapid rise to quick-baking items, like biscuits, muffins, waffles, and pancakes.

Originally, buttermilk was the milky residue of the butter-making process and had the sweet tang produced by the natural bacteria that develop at room temperature. Today, buttermilk is made with skim or low-fat milk mixed with a lactic acid bacteria that gives it flavor and thickness. Powdered buttermilk, though not intended for drinking, can be reconstituted for cooking and baking and is available in the baking supplies section of many food markets. Powdered buttermilk is convenient, lasts longer than fresh buttermilk, and can be reconstituted to make exactly the amount needed.

If you'd like to substitute buttermilk for milk in a recipe, neutralize its acidity by adding $\frac{1}{8}$ teaspoon of baking soda for up to 2 cups of milk and $\frac{1}{4}$ teaspoon of baking soda for more than 2 cups. To replace buttermilk with milk in a recipe, use 1 tablespoon of white vinegar or fresh lemon juice and 1 cup of low-fat milk, or use 2 to 3 tablespoons of nonfat or low-fat plain yogurt and 1 cup of skim milk.

Cardamom

A sweet, aromatic spice, best known for its use in Indian desserts and Scandinavian breads and cakes, cardamom is an interesting and versatile spice for puddings, coffeecakes, and compotes. It is available whole, in the pod, as shelled seeds (often labeled decorticated), and ground. For best flavor and bouquet, we recommend grinding whole cardamom seeds just before using. Pods are used primarily for mulling. Cardamom is available in the spice section of most supermarkets.

Challah (hah'-luh)

A braided egg bread with a soft, yellow inside and a shiny brown crust. It is heavenly spread with unsalted butter and makes good French toast and bread puddings. Available at Jewish bakeries, delicatessens, and in many supermarkets.

Chocolate

Chocolate starts out as small beans clustered inside football-sized pods that grow from the trunks and branches of the tropical cocoa tree, *Theobroma Cacao*. The journey from beans to "chocolate kiss" is a long and awesome one. To begin, cocoa beans, composed of cocoa butter and protein- and carbohydrate-rich cocoa solids, are fermented, dried, roasted, hulled, ground, and heated into a chocolate liquor. Sugar, vanilla (or vanillin, an artificial flavoring), lecithin (an emulsifier), additional cocoa butter, and, in the case of milk chocolate, milk solids are added. This mixture is then "conched" (kongkt), a process of simultaneously reheating, mixing, grinding, and stirring for up to 4 full days.

Conching produces chocolate's satiny-smooth texture. For gloss and snap, chocolate is then "tempered" by more heating, cooling, and reheating. Finally comes the molding and shaping process.

A chocolate's type and quality depend on the amount of cocoa butter and sugar added, the mixture of cocoa beans, the roasting time, and the conching time. The types of chocolate used in our recipes are:

- UNSWEETENED OR BAKING CHOCOLATE Made with chocolate liquor from processed whole cocoa beans. No sugar is added, but sometimes vanilla is included.
- SEMI-SWEET CHOCOLATE Made with chocolate liquor, additional cocoa butter, sugar, vanilla (or vanillin), and lecithin. Available in chips and in solid blocks. European semi-sweet chocolates are usually called "bittersweet" and are somewhat less sweet than semi-sweet chocolates made in the United States.
- WHITE CHOCOLATE Made of cocoa butter, sugar, vanilla, milk solids, and lecithin, white chocolate is not a "true" chocolate because it does not contain any cocoa solids. The richest white chocolates are often European and contain large amounts of cocoa butter. (Some white chocolates use vegetable oil and a smaller proportion of cocoa butter.)

At Moosewood, we use a Belgian chocolate called Callebaut. European chocolates are available in many supermarkets, usually in the candy aisle rather than in the baking section.

To store chocolate well is to know chocolate well. It is ultrasensitive to the elements and melts at 80°, so keep it cool (50° to 60°) but not *too* cool. Low temperatures cause chocolate to "bloom"—the cocoa butter rises to the top and streaks or dusts the chocolate with white.

(Bloomed chocolate is, however, not spoiled and is completely safe to eat.) Chocolate likes it dry; humidity can also cause blooming. And it needs seclusion. Store chocolate in a well-sealed container because it absorbs odors easily. Well-stored, dark chocolate keeps for years. Milk and white chocolates are more perishable, lasting from 3 to 12 months.

Cocoa

The cocoa or cacao bean is part cocoa butter (fat) and part cocoa solids (which contain both protein and starch). In the production of cocoa and chocolate, the first stage involves roasting, grinding, and melting cocoa beans. To produce the unsweetened cocoa powder used in baking, the cocoa solids and a small amount of cocoa butter are extracted.

Dutch cocoa, sometimes called Dutch-processed or alkaline-treated cocoa, has a small amount of alkali added to neutralize cocoa's natural acidity, yielding a mellower, more deeply colored cocoa that dissolves more easily. However, the absence of acid can also affect leavening, so use Dutch-processed cocoa in baking only when specified, or when rising is not an issue.

When working with cocoa, crush lumps before measuring. Store in a tightly sealed container and keep in a cool, dry place. Cocoa is temperature-, humidity-, and odor-sensitive.

Coconut

Our recipes call for unsweetened, dried, shredded coconut, available in natural food stores and in stores where Indian, Caribbean, or Southeast Asian foods are sold. To toast shredded coconut, spread it on an unoiled baking sheet and toast at 350° in a standard oven or a toaster oven for 2 to 3 minutes, until very lightly golden brown. If your only option is the sweetened, shredded coconut found in the baking section of the supermarket, remember to reduce any other sweetener in your recipe.

Coconut milk

When our recipes call for coconut milk, we are referring to the unsweetened, thick, creamy liquid that can be purchased in cans in Indian, Asian, and Hispanic food stores or in the ethnic sections of some supermarkets. This product should not be confused with the sweetened coconut milk or cream used in tropical beverages and mixed drinks or with the milky liquid found inside a whole coconut.

Coconut milk can easily be made at home. For a generous cup of coconut milk, combine 1 cup of unsweetened, dried, shredded coconut with 1½ cups of hot tap water. Allow the coconut to soften for 5 minutes, then purée the mixture in a blender for about a minute. Pour the purée into a strainer set over a bowl and press on the pulp, squeezing it by the handful to extract as much milk as possible. Pour the milk through a fine-mesh strainer. Coconut milk will keep for about 3 days, tightly covered and refrigerated. Frozen, coconut milk keeps indefinitely.

Confectioners' sugar

Also known as powdered sugar or icing sugar, this is the sweetener of choice for uncooked sauces, frostings, and dessert toppings. Confectioners' sugar is finely pulverized granulated sugar—a small amount of cornstarch is added to it to absorb atmospheric moisture and keep it powdery. Confectioners' sugar dissolves almost instantly. It is available in three grades: 4x, 6x, and 10x, representing graduated degrees of fineness. Any grade will work fine in our recipes. Always store it in a tightly sealed container.

Cornstarch

This almost tasteless thickener has some qualities that make it superior to flour as a thickener for desserts. Unlike flour, cornstarch thickens without contributing color or film, and sauces and fruit mixtures thickened with it have a clear, translucent sheen. And, because it is gluten-free, it is less likely to form lumps. Half as much cornstarch as flour is needed to thicken a given amount of liquid.

Before stirring cornstarch into a hot liquid, dissolve it in a small amount of cool liquid (to prevent lumps and promote smooth thickening). It is usually stirred in near the end of cooking. Thickening will occur once the dissolved cornstarch has come to a boil. If it is overcooked or stirred too vigorously, however, its structure may break down, causing the thickened mixture to thin out. Cornstarch has an extended but limited shelf life; after a couple of years, cornstarch can lose its thickening power.

Corn Syrup

A sugar syrup obtained by partial hydrolysis of cornstarch. Corn syrup is solidly entrenched in the candy-making world and has a long-term relationship with pecan pie. Light corn syrup should always be used unless a recipe specifies the stronger-tasting, dark variety.

Cream (heavy cream)

Cream by itself can be a silky topping for desserts such as cobblers, fresh or cooked fruit, Indian and bread puddings, and rice puddings. It doubles in volume when whipped, and at Moosewood we fold it in to make melt-in-the-mouth mousses and trifles. Cream can also be added to sauces, custards, and puddings for mellow richness and taste.

Because cream is less dense than water, it naturally rises to the top of unhomogenized whole milk, where it can be skimmed off. Commercially, cream is separated from milk by centrifugal force. Two types of heavy cream are widely available in stores, pasteurized and ultrapasteurized. Pasteurization is a heat treatment that kills harmful microbes. Ultrapasteurization employs a higher heat to lengthen shelf life. We recommend pasteurized cream, especially for whipped cream and desserts such as ganache or trifle, in which the flavor of the cream predominates. Some of us think that pasteurized cream tastes better and describe ultrapasteurized cream as tasting boiled, but either type will work in our recipes.

Whip cream in a chilled bowl with chilled beaters or whisk for best results. Pasteurized cream will keep refrigerated for about 3 days. It can be frozen for several months, but when thawed cannot be used for whipping or in a dish where cream's smoothness is essential to the dish's texture.

Crème fraîche

This slightly tangy, thickened cream is delicious on fresh fruit and in pastry fillings. Crème fraîche can be found in the dairy section of some supermarkets and in specialty food stores, and it can easily be made at home. Mix 1 teaspoon of buttermilk into 1 cup of heavy cream, heat it to baby-bottle temperature, and let it stand, partially covered, at room temperature for about 8 hours or up to a day, until thickened. Sitting at room temperature allows the cream to "sour sweetly," as Craig Claiborne says. Once thickened, stir and refrigerate.

Cream of tartar

Also known as potassium acid tartrate, this white, slightly sour powder, synthesized from the residue of wine making, has a few discrete but notable functions in the dessert kitchen. A small quantity of cream of tartar beaten with egg whites (1 teaspoon per cup of egg whites) produces stiff but not dry peaks. It also stabilizes meringue during baking to preserve volume. Two tablespoons of cream of tartar combined with 1 tablespoon of baking soda produces homemade baking powder. Commercially, cream of tartar is used to inhibit crystallization when making sugar syrups and candy. It keeps indefinitely.

Dried fruit

Dried fruit is versatile, keeps well, and is convenient to have on hand. It can give a jeweled effect and natural sweetness to cakes, muffins, and breads and can easily be used in sugarless low-fat compotes, toppings, and pastry fillings. We have a few favorites—Smyrna and Calimyrna figs,

whole nonextruded dates, Turkish apricots—but you can't go wrong if you choose fruit that is plump, moist, and fresh. Old dried fruit looks dusty because of the crystallization of its fruit sugars and the further loss of water. We prefer unsulphured dried fruit both because it tastes better and because many people are sensitive to sulfites. Store dried fruit in the refrigerator, tightly sealed in a container or plastic bag.

Eggs

Whites and yolks, apart or together, are a gift to the dessert chef. Eggs are a natural leavener, colorer, and thickener, and give custards and sauces a velvety texture and mellow richness.

Eggs overcook and curdle easily. Before adding to a warm sauce or other hot ingredients, raise the temperature of the eggs by blending a small amount of the hot base mixture into them. To avoid curdling, add eggs at the end of cooking, use low heat, stir often, and remove from the heat as soon as the mixture thickens. Custards, puddings, and flans are baked in a hot water bath (the baking cups are placed in a baking pan filled with a couple inches of very hot water) to keep the level of heat surrounding them steady. Eggs will continue to cook even after they are removed from a direct heat source, so remove custards from the oven before they are completely set, while their centers jiggle. A custard that completely sets in the oven will be overcooked and will lack that satiny creaminess that pretty much defines a good custard or flan.

You may have noticed that many recipes often instruct you to lightly beat eggs; this is because overbeating whole eggs can weaken their thickening power.

Egg whites whip up glossy and smooth, providing lightness and loft to a host of baked goods. Egg whites do best when brought to room temperature before beating. Keep them free of any yolk or fat, and beat with clean, dry beaters. Overbeating egg whites, until they are dry and begin to clump, reduces their water content and therefore volume. To guard against the effects of overbeating and to help stabilize egg whites during baking, add cream of tartar, lemon juice, vinegar, sugar, or salt.

The eggs called for in our recipes are large eggs, about 2 ounces each. Egg weight seems to climb by $\frac{1}{4}$-ounce increments. Here's a chart to help you with substitutions:

SMALL	$1\frac{1}{2}$ ounces
MEDIUM	$1\frac{3}{4}$ ounces
LARGE	2 ounces
EXTRA LARGE	$2\frac{1}{4}$ ounces
JUMBO	$2\frac{1}{2}$ ounces
4 TO 6 WHOLE EGGS	1 cup
10 TO 12 WHITES	1 cup
13 TO 14 YOLKS	1 cup

Extracts and flavorings

The methods for making extracts and for making flavorings differ—the goal is to produce the truest, most intense flavor. Extracts are created by soaking the most flavorful part of the plant (usually the bean, rind, or pith) in alcohol. The alcohol is then cooked off, which leaves a thick, syrup-like oleoresin. Alcohol is then reintroduced in a ratio of one part oleoresin to four parts alcohol. When making flavorings, glycerin is added to the oleoresin instead of alcohol. Pure extracts and flavorings taste far better than artificial ones, and we recommend Frontier as a reliable source for pure ingredients. Frontier's extracts and flavorings are available in natural food stores and many supermarkets. They can also be ordered from Frontier Cooperative Herbs, Norway, Iowa 52318.

Filo (phyllo)

Filo is the Greek word for leaf, an apt description for a dough so thin and paper-like. Making filo by hand is an art requiring the highest order of dexterity; thankfully, filo is available in the refrigerator or freezer cases of many supermarkets. When exposed to air, filo dries out quickly, so work rapidly and brush it liberally with butter or oil to keep it moist and pliant. During baking, the filo leaves separate, puff up, and turn golden.

Frozen filo should be thawed for about 2 hours in its box before using. If you have filo left over, wrap it tightly in plastic, return it to the box, and refrigerate.

Flour

Wheat grown in North America is usually one of two types: hard or soft. Most hard wheat, which is high in protein, is grown in the western plains. Soft wheat, which is lower in protein, is grown in milder climates. Gluten is produced when wheat proteins combine with water. It gives elasticity and chewiness to bread doughs and structure to cakes. Baked goods are best when made with the most appropriate wheat flour:

■ BREAD FLOUR is highest in protein (at least 12 percent), and should be avoided when a high-gluten-content dough is undesirable (such as in dessert baking).

■ ALL-PURPOSE FLOUR is the most versatile and widely available wheat flour. Usually a blend of hard and soft wheats, all-purpose flour's protein content ranges from 8 percent to 12 percent. We prefer to use unbleached flour without preservatives or bromates. Unbleached flours are naturally aged and matured without the use of chemical bleaching agents. Most of the recipes in this book can be made with all-purpose flour. To substitute for pastry flour, use 1 cup minus a generous tablespoon of all-purpose flour per cup of pastry flour.

■ PASTRY FLOUR is our choice for pie and tart doughs, biscuits, muffins, and some cookies and cakes. The lower protein content of the soft wheat used in pastry flour helps to create baked goods with a more tender crumb. But in some cakes, pastry flour may make a dense cake with less "rise." Cookies made with pastry flour tend to be flatter and crisper; all-purpose flour is better for softer cookies. Pastry flour is often used in low-fat baking to achieve a more tender texture than all-purpose flour, which relies upon the presence of fats to tenderize its flour protein. To substitute for all-purpose flour, use 1 cup plus 2 tablespoons of pastry flour for each cup of all-purpose.

■ CAKE FLOUR is a low-protein, soft wheat flour that is heavily chlorinated or bleached to inhibit its ability to form gluten with liquids. It bonds more readily with fats and absorbs liquids faster than other flours, making for especially light, delicate cakes. At Moosewood, we don't use cake flour because we believe the fewer chemicals in our food and environment, the better. To substitute cake flour for all-purpose flour, use 2 tablespoons more cake flour per cup of all-purpose flour. To approximate cake flour, replace 2 tablespoons of bleached all-purpose flour with 2 tablespoons of cornstarch per each cup of bleached all-purpose flour.

■ WHOLE WHEAT FLOUR contains all of the nutrients available in wheat, including fiber, vitamins, and minerals. The fat content of wheat germ shortens the shelf life of whole wheat flour, so store it in the refrigerator.

■ WHOLE WHEAT PASTRY FLOUR is the best type of whole wheat flour to use for desserts. Its lower gluten content creates a more tender product than regular whole wheat flour. Whole wheat pastry flour can be substituted cup for cup for all-purpose flour. It will produce baked goods that have a higher nutritional value, but are denser, less lofty, and coarser in texture. Instead of sifting whole wheat pastry flour, which would remove the fiber-rich bran, stir the flour to fluff it before measuring.

■ SELF-RISING FLOUR is common in the American South and should not be substituted for all-purpose or pastry flour. It contains baking powder and salt and may wreak havoc with the texture of a baked dessert.

Store flour in a cool, dry location in airtight containers. Whole wheat pastry flours should be refrigerated. Flours kept in paper bags or the original sack can absorb odors from other foods.

Fromage blanc

Fromage blanc is a type of unripened cheese made from different kinds of milk that are naturally fermented by the addition of lactic acid bacteria. Once the milk thickens, it is slowly strained. Fromage blanc can be curded or smooth. It can be low-fat or not, depending on the fat content of the milk used and whether other soft cheeses or cream are added. It can be formless or shaped. Fromage blanc can be made at home or purchased in cheese stores and in markets with specialty cheese departments. When we call for fromage blanc in our recipes, we are referring to a soft, smooth, mellow variety.

Fruit conserves and spreads

We enjoy the rich, concentrated fruit flavors of all-fruit (no sugar added) spreads. They can be used in any recipe that calls for jam or preserves. They are available in natural food stores and many supermarkets.

Fruit juice concentrates

Our lime and tangerine cheesecakes couldn't be so creamy and dense without fruit juice concentrates. Besides adding flavor, concentrates add natural fruit sugars and reduce the amount of other sweeteners needed in desserts. In addition to the ubiquitous orange juice, you can find tangerine, lime, cherry, and berry frozen concentrated juices and blends in many supermarkets.

Ginger

A highly aromatic, lively seasoning, ginger is the root-like stem of a tropical plant. Dried ginger is a distinctive dessert spice familiar to anyone who has eaten gingersnaps or gingerbread. But do not substitute it in recipes that call for the fresh root.

In baking, fresh ginger root has traditionally taken a back seat to dried ginger. However, its refreshing taste and slight pungency can give an extra sparkle to baked or fresh desserts. Fresh ginger is easily grated with a handheld grater with round holes a little smaller than 1/8 inch in diameter. Much bigger or smaller holes just don't grate the ginger as well. Ginger root can be stored for several months in a plastic bag in the freezer. Frozen roots grate easily; prepare as much as needed for a given recipe, then return the root to the freezer. Fresh ginger is found in the produce section of well-stocked supermarkets.

Crystallized ginger is ginger root preserved dry in sugar; ginger preserves are similar to marmalade. Both date back to a time before refrigeration and air freight made the widespread use of the perishable fresh root possible. Crystallized ginger is available with Chinese or Asian products in supermarkets or ethnic markets. Ginger preserves can be found with preserves or imported marmalades.

Half-and-half

As you might have guessed, this dairy product is half milk and half cream with an average butterfat content of 11.7 percent. It is lower in fat than light cream (20 percent), which seems to have disappeared from the dairy scene in most places. We use half-and-half in recipes such as custards and ice creams where a rich, smooth texture and taste are desirable.

Honey

If you wish to try substituting honey for sugar in our recipes, keep the following in mind:
1. Honey is sweeter than sugar. Use 7/8 cup of honey for each cup of sugar called for in a recipe.
2. Honey is a liquid. Reduce another liquid in the recipe by 3 tablespoons for each 7/8 cup of honey added.

3. Honey caramelizes quickly and adds a brown color to baked goods. Therefore, it may work best in darker baked goods, such as ginger-breads, bran muffins, and banana breads.

4. Honey is acidic. A pinch of baking soda will help to neutralize its acidity.

5. Honeys vary in strength and flavor. Avoid strong, dark honeys and look for a honey without too distinctive a flavor.

Maple syrup

This intensely flavored, caramel-colored concentrate of maple tree sap is best in its pure, undiluted form. It takes about 40 gallons of sugar maple sap to produce 1 gallon of syrup, a fact reflected in the price tag. We realize this is an expensive product, but we consider it a worthwhile luxury because of its incomparable flavor.

Milk

Recipes in this book were tested with 2 percent milk, except for some of our low-fat desserts, which specify either (nonfat) skim or 1 percent milk. In most cases, whatever milk you have on hand will work fine. However, some desserts such as flans and puddings may have a less velvety texture if you use skim milk.

■ EVAPORATED MILK is a canned milk whose moisture content is 60 percent less than that of regular milk. Processing cooks the natural milk sugars and results in a somewhat sweet flavor. Evaporated skimmed milk can add a rich, creamy quality to low-fat desserts without the butterfat.

■ CONDENSED MILK is a highly sweetened, concentrated canned milk that is also available skimmed for use in low-fat desserts.

Molasses

This sugarcane product provides sweetness and rich flavor and is a good source of B vitamins and iron. Some producers add sulphur to lighten the color of the syrup, but the sulphur has an unpleasant aftertaste, so we use unsulphured molasses. We seldom use blackstrap molasses because it has a strong flavor that can overwhelm the other flavors in a dessert. Baked goods made with molasses retain moisture and keep well.

Nuts and seeds

Nuts and seeds lend their flavor, richness, and sometimes (when whole or coarsely chopped) an appealing crunchiness to desserts. We recommend the use of whole shelled nuts. They're less expensive than prepackaged chopped or sliced ones, and their flavor is far superior if they're chopped, ground, or sliced just before using. Nuts should be kept refrigerated for short-term storage or can be frozen in airtight containers for up to a year.

Light toasting brings out the natural flavor of nuts and seeds. Preheat a conventional oven (or set a toaster oven) to 350° and roast the nuts in a single layer on a shallow pan for 5 to 10 minutes, until the nuts or seeds are fragrant and slightly browned. Cool before chopping.

To make 1 cup of ground nuts, start with 1¼ to 1½ cups of whole nuts. Nuts exude oil when ground in a food processor, so add a couple of tablespoons of flour or sugar from the recipe being worked on and avoid overprocessing, which might result in "pasty" nuts. Blenders effectively grind small batches of nuts (about ½ cup) at high speed. (For more information, see page 373.)

Oats

Oats add flavor and texture to baked goods and retain moisture for good keeping quality. Both regular and quick-cooking oats are available; unless otherwise stated, our recipes call for regular rolled oats.

Oil

For desserts, we use bland vegetable oils, such as canola, soy, or safflower, all without preservatives.

Peanut butter

Our peanut butter of choice is made from just peanuts with no added sweeteners, stabilizers, or hydrogenated fats. Unhomogenized peanut butter should be thoroughly stirred to distribute the peanut oil, then stored in the refrigerator.

Puff pastry

Commercially prepared puff pastry makes an impressive presentation for occasions when the dessertmaker is especially pressed for time. Frozen, unbaked puff pastry dough usually comes in 16-ounce packages containing two sheets. The appropriate quantity for a given recipe should be thawed for several hours (or overnight) in the refrigerator or for 20 minutes at room temperature. Puff pastry is available in the frozen pastry section of most supermarkets.

Ricotta cheese

Traditionally used in Italian cooking for both sweet and savory dishes, soft, fresh, mild-tasting ricotta is extremely versatile in dessert cooking. Its creamy texture makes it suitable for light cheesecakes or fresh fruit combinations. Ricotta cheese is available as a whole milk, reduced fat, or nonfat product.

Sour cream

Baked goods made with sour cream have a particularly tender, light crumb thanks to the lactic acid present in cultured sour cream. Conventional sour cream has a butterfat content of 18 to 20 percent, light sour cream about 10 percent, and, of course, nonfat has none. Nonfat sour cream achieves its creamy texture by the addition of thickeners and starches.

Soy drinks

Sometimes called soy "milk," soy drinks can substitute for milk in almost any dessert recipe. With a base of soybeans and water, soy drinks may contain other ingredients, flavorings, or sweeteners such as rice syrup or malt extracts, although some are unsweetened. Fat content varies from low-fat to nonfat. Soy drinks are available in natural food stores and well-stocked supermarkets.

Sugar (granulated, cane)

White sugar is no doubt the most frequently used sweetener. Sugar sweetens without competing with other flavors. Many recipes for baked goods begin with the thorough creaming of butter and sugar because the sharp-edged sugar crystals facilitate the incorporation of air into fats such as butter. Confectioners' sugar, also called powdered sugar, is very finely milled, lacks sharp-edged crystals, and shouldn't be substituted for granulated sugar in delicately textured baked goods.

There has been much debate about the relative merits of one sweetener over another. Some nutritionists believe that all sugars, including molasses, honey, and natural fruit sugars, are metabolized by the body in a similar fashion. Others disagree. We use all of these kinds of sugar in our cooking at Moosewood, but we never use sugar substitutes like saccharin and aspartame.

Tofu

Also called bean curd, tofu is a high protein soy product with a creamy, soft, cheese-like texture. "Silken" and soft tofu are the best types for dessert making because of their particularly smooth, custard-like consistency. Available in natural food stores, Asian markets, and supermarkets, fresh tofu is found in the refrigerator section; vacuum-packed tofu is found on the shelf and can remain at room temperature until it is opened.

Yeast

A live organism that feeds on starch and sugar and produces carbon dioxide, which causes breads, cakes, and pastries to rise. Yeast is available both fresh and dried; both types should be refrigerated after purchase. Fresh yeast has a relatively short life span (up to two weeks if kept properly chilled), while dried or powdered yeast can last for up to a year. One package (a scant tablespoon) of dried yeast granules is equivalent to a standard ⅗ ounce of fresh yeast.

Yogurt

Cultured with live, beneficial bacteria, yogurt is a familiar dairy product made from whole, low-fat, or skim milk. Like many "soured" dairy products, it creates a very tender crumb in baked goods.

Yogurt cheese

A soft and creamy cheese easily made at home. If prepared with nonfat or low-fat yogurt, it can serve as a lighter replacement for cream cheese or sour cream.

To make yogurt cheese in the traditional way, line a colander or large sieve with overlapping paper coffee filters or several layers of cheesecloth. Place the colander or sieve in a large bowl. Spoon in 2 quarts of yogurt and cover with plastic wrap. Refrigerate for 12 to 24 hours. After 3 or 4 hours or overnight, discard the liquid collected in the bowl. The yogurt will thicken to a consistency similar to soft cream cheese and should yield about 3 cups.

For our Quick Yogurt Cheese Method, reduce the amount of yogurt to between 1¼ and 1½ quarts. Set up the yogurt to drain as in the traditional method above, but weight the top of the covered yogurt with a plate and a heavy can or other object. Refrigerate for about 2 hours. The added weight will speed the draining process and will produce 3 to 4 cups of yogurt cheese firm enough for most recipes.

Beating

Mixing by hand or with an electric mixer to blend a batter until smooth, or to make lighter by incorporating air. Beating is more vigorous than stirring. When beating by hand, use a circular motion of the wrist—direction doesn't matter. Use medium or high speed on an electric mixer. Beating until an ingredient (such as egg whites or cream) expands greatly in volume is usually referred to as whipping.

Blending

Stirring or mixing until ingredients are well combined and smooth in texture. Because incorporating air is not a goal of blending, it is less energetic than beating. Blend just until smooth to avoid overbeating.

Cake pans, preparing

Except for angelfood cakes, all cakes should be baked in pans that have been buttered (or oiled) and floured to ensure a clean release from the pan. For further insurance, when using a flat-bottomed pan, cut a piece of parchment paper, wax paper, or aluminum foil to fit the bottom and butter and flour it as well.

Cakes, cutting

Most cakes can be easily cut with a long-bladed knife. But for sticky or soft cakes, such as cheesecakes, use fishing line or household thread. Hold the line or thread tautly above the cake and pass it down through the center to cut the cake in half. Let go of one end and pull the line out. Repeat the process, making as many wedges as you wish. Very little cake will stick to the line and the cuts will be very straight. One drawback is that sometimes you may not be able to cut all the way through to the bottom. Still, the cuts are good guidelines and you'll only need to cut the last half inch or so by knife.

Cakes, frosting and decorating

Most frostings become thinner if heated, so in most cases cakes should be completely cool or even chilled before frosting. But for a very quick icing, as soon as a cake comes out of the oven, sprinkle the top with chocolate chips, or with white chocolate, milk chocolate, peanut butter, butterscotch, or carob chips. Wait about 5 minutes for the chips to melt and then spread gently in a thin layer. While the icing is still warm, decorate with fruits or nuts, if desired.

Sifted confectioners' sugar beautifully contrasts with almost any baked cake and is a nice alternative to frosting. The bright white of the sugar is especially pleasing against golden brown or dark chocolate cakes. A doily or a simple paper cutout (such as the snowflakes we made as children) can make a great stencil for decorative patterns.

Gussy up a plain or frosted cake by sprinkling with chopped nuts, shaved chocolate, dragées, or toasted coconut. Don't forget the wonderful flavors and colors provided by all sorts of berries or cherries, and peaches, pears, or apples dipped in lemon juice to prevent discoloring. Gummy candies, small candy hearts, dried fruits (raisins or apricots cut into slivers), and fruit leathers (cut into designs or shapes) can spell out words or fantasies. Theme cakes can be created with nonedible decorations such as small plastic toys. Just be sure to remove them before serving!

Semi-sweet or white chocolate melted with a little butter can be drizzled or piped onto cakes in random, swirled, or geometric patterns to great effect. For a wider range of colors, royal icing, made with a ratio of 1 egg white to 1½ cups confectioners' sugar and a few drops of lemon juice, can be tinted and then piped.

If you don't have a pastry bag and decorating tips, small plastic bags with a small snip at the corner or handmade paper cones make very good substitutes. Paper cones can be made by cutting a square of parchment or wax paper into two triangles. With the longest side of the triangle nearest to you, curl the lower right-hand point up and around until it meets the top point, forming a cone shape. Holding those two points together, wrap the remaining flap around the cone shape until all three points of the triangle meet. You should have a cone with a very sharp tip. Staple the three points together. Snip off the tip to create a small hole. Fill the paper cone with frosting and use it as you would a pastry bag to make polka dots, stripes, concentric circles, or any other design you wish.

For more ideas see Decorating a Fancy or Tiered Cake, page 83.

Cakes, troubleshooting

Every now and then, when a cake comes out of the oven, it's clear that something went wrong. If the cake is coarse and dense, it may have begun baking in too cool an oven, it may not have been beaten enough, or it may have too little baking powder or other leavening. If the cake is sunken, it may have been overbeaten or it may have too much sugar, baking powder, or liquid. Using a high-gluten flour may cause the top of a cake to peak too much, or the gluten may have been overdeveloped by too much beating after the flour was added, so be sure to cream and beat the ingredients well before the flour is added. Be sure your oven is preheated thoroughly and invest in an oven thermometer to make sure the thermostat is accurate. Too hot an oven can cause an unshapely, uneven, and/or overly browned top. Most ovens have hot spots, so rotate cakes during baking unless instructed otherwise. Sometimes turning the pan around on the same oven rack is enough, but in some ovens you may need to move the pan to a different rack midway through baking.

Caramelizing

See Sugar Syrups and Caramel, page 374.

Chocolate, chopping and melting

The melting temperature of chocolate is lower than body temperature, which is why it melts in your hand and separates or burns easily when precautions are not taken. Chocolate melts best at 100° and melts most quickly when chopped into small, uniform pieces about the size of chocolate chips. When chocolate is cold, it is brittle, but at room temperature, it is softer and can be cut more easily. When melting chocolate on the stove, use a double boiler or very low heat and stir constantly to prevent scorching. Chocolate can also be melted in a covered pan set into a larger pot of boiling water that has just been removed from the heat. Or it can be melted in a 100° oven. Melting chocolate in a microwave prevents scorching, but the chocolate must be stirred often to distribute the heat evenly and prevent graininess. Whichever method you use, don't try to melt every last piece of chocolate. As long as the melted chocolate is warm to the touch, there will be enough residual heat to melt any remaining lumps. If the chocolate reaches 120°, it will begin to separate and become grainy, and although it may look lumpy, as if it needs to melt more, the damage is already done.

Don't let any water or nonfat liquid get into melting chocolate, or the satiny smooth chocolate will turn into a muddy mess. Although this "seized" chocolate may no longer be suitable for the recipe you're working on, it can be salvaged for some other use, such as in a cake or brownie batter. To smooth it out, add 1 teaspoon of vegetable oil per ounce of chocolate. Or you can add even more liquid, such as hot water, coffee, milk, cream, or, when appropriate, fruit juice. Because it will not harden completely when cooled, this "soft" chocolate is a better choice for cake toppings than plain melted chocolate, which hardens as it cools and might crack when cut. For information on choosing and storing chocolate, see page 357.

Citrus, getting the most out of

Rinse lemons, limes, and oranges before grating their peels. Grate only the thin, flavorful, outer colored peel and avoid the bitter white pith. We never use graters with rough punctured holes, but prefer open-holed graters (actually shredders) because they work better and are much easier to clean. Sometimes we use a vegetable peeler to peel off larger strips and then chop the strips finely with a knife or whirl them with some sugar in the food processor. There are also hand tools called citrus zesters, each with a five-holed blade that produces thin threads when the blade is drawn against the peel.

Remember to grate the peels before juicing the citrus. Let citrus come to room temperature before juicing it to get the most juice.

Cooling, baked goods

In general, baked goods (with the exception of pies) should be removed from the pan when they have become slightly cool and more firm, because steam trapped between a cake and its pan may eventually make the cake soggy. Most cakes shrink away from the sides of the pan somewhat as they cool, so running a dull knife around the edges to loosen the cake will help keep it from cracking as it cools and shrinks. This is especially true for cheesecakes, which are baked in springform pans that aren't removed until the cheesecake is completely chilled. Some cookies become very brittle when cool, so remove them from the baking pan while they are still warm and slightly pliable.

For all types of baked goods, cooling racks allow for better air circulation, resulting in better and more even cooling.

Creaming

When a recipe instructs you to "cream" the fat, usually butter, by itself or with sugar, the purpose is to lighten it with air so that additional ingredients, such as eggs, can be blended in more easily. Butter at room temperature and a sturdy wooden spoon or an electric mixer (initially at low speed) are essential for easy and complete creaming. If you are trying to bring cold butter to room temperature in a hurry, don't melt it. Cut it into small pieces, place it on a plate, and set the plate on top of a bowl of very warm water or in your unlit oven (a pilot light usually provides enough warmth to soften the butter within 10 minutes). You can also use the defrost mode on a microwave for 10 to 15 seconds at a time.

Custards, stovetop cooking and water bath baking

To create a smooth and velvety custard and prevent curdling, always slowly beat hot liquid into the eggs to warm them gradually. If you were to add cool eggs to hot liquid, there is a good chance the eggs would curdle—actually scrambling from the heat of the liquid. When baking custards, a water bath, or "bain marie," acts as an insulator, keeping the temperature at 212° and preventing

the custard from baking too fast. The hot (not boiling) water bath may increase the baking time but it also reduces the risk of overcooking the custard. Remove baked custards from the oven while the centers still jiggle slightly; overbaking causes the proteins to coagulate further and wring out liquid, which results in a broken, curdled, and watery custard. Stovetop custards don't set as firmly as baked custards due to the constant stirring that is necessary to insure they cook evenly.

Double boiler

A piece of standard cookware consisting of one pan nesting neatly inside a slightly larger one. The lower section is filled with a few inches of water and placed on the heat source. The ingredient(s) placed in the top section are then heated via a hot water bath, which ensures a gentle, constant, indirect heat that minimizes chances of scorching and overcooking. Often used for melting chocolate and for cooking delicate sauces or puddings.

You can simulate a double boiler by setting a covered pan over a larger pot of boiling or simmering water. Be sure the pot and pan are compatible sizes and together form a safe, stable unit. Or fit a metal or ovenproof stoneware bowl into a saucepan. In a pinch, a small saucepan placed into a larger saucepan will work, even though there are gaps between the sides of the two pans; just be sure to check occasionally that the level of the boiling water doesn't get too low through evaporation.

Eggs, separating and storing leftover

Separating eggs is best done while they are cold. Crack the egg on the rim of a bowl and gently break the shell in two, keeping the yolk in one half of the shell. Let the white drain off into the bowl by slipping the yolk from one half shell to the other. Some people prefer to gently pour the egg into their hand and let the white run out between their fingers. If the yolk breaks and runs into the whites, use an egg shell to scoop it out. A useful precautionary step is to separate one egg at a time into a cup and transfer the white to a bowl, so that any broken yolks or shells won't contaminate a large batch of egg whites.

Extra yolks and whites can be stored in the refrigerator for later use in custards and cakes. Eggs are prone to absorbing odors, so place the yolks or whites in a sealed container (or cover them tightly with plastic). Stored in the refrigerator they will keep for three or four days. To prevent stored yolks from forming a skin, cover them with a layer of water before sealing; then simply pour off the water before using.

Separated whites and yolks can be frozen for several months and sometimes up to a year. Store in a well-sealed container with room for expansion. Thaw frozen egg whites in the refrigerator. Be sure to thaw them completely for use in batters or meringues; then whip them up just like fresh whites. Egg yolks and whole eggs must be stabilized before freezing. Add about 1½ teaspoons of salt or sugar per cup of eggs or yolks to prevent them from thickening. An ice cube tray wrapped in a plastic bag is handy for freezing small quantities so you can take out what you need without thawing all of your eggs at once. In case you forget to mark your container with the number of whites or yolks stored, one egg white is about 2 tablespoons and one egg yolk equals about 1 tablespoon.

Folding

A technique for gently incorporating one ingredient into another while keeping the batter light and airy. Although both *The Joy of Cooking* and *The Fannie Farmer Cookbook* recommend using one's hand (giving a twist to the phrase "mix by hand"), we use a rubber spatula to cut down through the mixture in a scooping motion. The U-shaped motion of the spatula brings the heavier mixture up and around the ingredient to be folded in. Rotate the bowl as you repeat the same motion. Ingredients are well folded in when there are very few or no streaks left. To lighten a batter with beaten egg whites, stir about a third of the egg whites into the heavier batter and then fold in the remaining whites. When beaten egg whites are to be combined with flour (as in an angelfood cake), sift the flour over the egg whites and fold it into the whites.

Freezing, baked goods

Whether stored at room temperature, refrigerated, or frozen, the higher the proportion of fat in a given baked good, the longer it will keep. A butter cake with a buttercream frosting will freeze and thaw much better than a sponge cake with a whipped cream frosting. Most baked goods should be completely cool and well wrapped before freezing. The exception is a frosted cake, which should be put in the freezer unwrapped until the frosting has hardened. Then wrap it well for longer storage. When ready to thaw, remove the wrapping to keep the frosting unmarred and beautiful.

Some cake batters can be frozen and then baked later. This works best with batters leavened with baking powder—don't try it with cakes leavened with egg whites or baking soda. Freeze the unbaked cake batter in a pan (or pans) lined with aluminum foil. Once frozen, lift out the disk of batter, wrap well, and return it to the freezer. When ready to bake, remove the foil, set the frozen disk of batter in a buttered and floured pan (the pan in which it was frozen), and bake at the temperature called for in the recipe for 10 to 15 minutes longer than the original baking time.

Most cookies and cookie doughs freeze well. For baked cookies, allow ample thawing time and warm them in a slow oven for a few minutes. Freeze unbaked dough in cookie-sized portions on a baking sheet. When frozen, transfer to a plastic bag. This provides you with quick access to freshly baked goodies—just arrange the frozen cookie dough on sheets and pop into the oven, allowing a few extra minutes of baking time.

Pies can be frozen at any stage. The dough, rolled out as a crust or not, may be frozen for up to 2 months. A baked pie shell will keep for about 3 months. Frozen unbaked, filled double-crusted pies need not be thawed before baking. Cut vent holes in the top crust just prior to baking. When using cornstarch as a pie filling's main thickener, add an extra tablespoon if you plan to freeze the unbaked pie.

Fresh fruits, preparing

To ripen most fruits, put them in a paper bag at room temperature (with a banana if you really want to hurry the process) until the flesh softens a bit and the fruit smells ripe and sweet.

■ BERRIES Don't wash berries until ready to use. To freeze a summer's bounty of berries for wintertime use, freeze them on a tray until hard, then gather them in a freezer bag. Presto! your own IQF (individually quick frozen) fruit!

■ MANGOES Locate the alignment of the pit by feeling for a slight ridge located along the length of the mango. Cut along each side of this ridge, curving the knife slightly as necessary to maneuver around the pit. Score through the flesh—but not the skin—of each half both lengthwise and crosswise. With your fingers, pop the mango half inside out so the fruit protrudes and carve off the cubes of fruit. Pare the remaining flesh from the pit.

■ ORANGES AND GRAPEFRUIT To peel and section, cut both the ends from the fruit, cutting down to the flesh, and place the fruit cut side down on a cutting board. Slice down the sides of the fruit with wide strokes, just deep enough to remove the peel and all of the bitter pith. Hold the peeled fruit over a bowl to catch any dripping juice and, with a paring knife, carefully cut between the membrane on one side of each section and back out the other side to release it from the membrane. This can be done with one smooth in-and-out motion.

■ PEACHES Drop peaches into boiling water for about a minute, then plunge them into ice water to stop the cooking. The peel should slip off easily. To cut a peach into wedges, cut out a single wedge at a time, working it free from the stone. It is more difficult to cut the peach in half and work each half from the stone.

■ PINEAPPLES Cut off the spiky top, then slice off the thick, thorny skin in long vertical strokes. Cut out any deep eyes with the tip of a knife or with diagonal slices. Remove the tough center core. If you don't need pineapple rings, removing the core is easy. Cut the peeled pineapple lengthwise in half and then cut each half lengthwise in half again. Carve out the hard, fibrous core from each quarter. For rings, cut the peeled pineapple crosswise into quarters, core each section, and slice into rings.

Measuring

Most of the time, baking is more like chemistry than art, so measure ingredients accurately. Use dry measuring cups without spouts for dry ingredients.

When one of our recipes calls for a "packed" ingredient, such as brown sugar, lightly press it into the measuring cup with the back of a spoon.

Some dry ingredients, such as flour, cocoa, and cornstarch, may settle and pack, so fluff them up before spooning them into the measuring cup. Level the top by scraping off the excess with a dinner knife—don't tap the cup because it will settle the contents. Some cooks prefer to scoop flour directly from its container with a measuring cup and not quite fill it—to approximate a fluffed, spooned, and leveled cup. This method requires a practiced eye and some experience but can work fine. What is most important is for the cook to develop a consistent and accurate way to measure flour, whatever the method. We recommend choosing your favorite method, sticking to it, and perfecting it.

Mixing

Mixing by hand and mixing by machine are not necessarily interchangeable. For example, when mixing a butter cake or cheesecake by hand, it is important to begin with softened butter and then to cream it very well. Otherwise the cake may be heavy, coarse grained, or lumpy. With a heavy duty stand mixer, however, a pound of cold butter can be creamed in a matter of minutes. For recipes without butter, cream cheese, or whipped eggs, mixing by hand is more economical (and perhaps more enjoyable) than mixing by machine.

Whether mixing by hand or machine, always begin slowly so that ingredients like flour aren't tossed out of the bowl in a cloud. Alternating the addition of wet and dry ingredients originated as a hand-mixing technique, a way to thoroughly incorporate large amounts of flour or liquid. When mixing by machine, alternating additions may not be necessary. But when using a mixer, it is important to turn off the machine now and then to scrape down the sides and bottom of the bowl. This will help to ensure a smooth batter. Be careful when mixing by machine not to overbeat, which can lead to clumpy egg whites, butter instead of whipped cream, and tough cakes.

Nuts, toasting, chopping, and grinding

Nuts, especially ones that have been stored for a while, almost always benefit from toasting. The exception is nuts used for crusts or toppings, which should *not* be toasted because they may burn more easily. Toasting nuts on a baking sheet in the oven (page 364) is often the most convenient method, but toasting them in a heavy unoiled skillet on the stove may bring out more flavor. Cool toasted nuts before chopping or adding to a batter. To grind nuts in a food processor, thoroughly cool them and grind them with some of the flour or sugar in the recipe to prevent clumping. Overprocessing nuts, especially hot nuts, results in nut butter. Nuts, especially those with a high fat content, such as pecans, macadamia, and pine nuts, should be stored in the refrigerator or freezer to prevent rancidity.

Ovens

The hottest part of the oven is generally the top, making the upper rack ideal for browning the tops of baked goods. The lower rack is best for setting custards, cooking pastry crusts, or crisping the bottoms of some kinds of cookies. If you are baking several things at once, stagger them on the racks, leaving a little space between the pans and the oven wall. Avoid arranging pans directly over one another. During baking, rotate them top to bottom and front to back. If your oven is too hot on the bottom, try placing your cake and cookie pans on an additional baking sheet to shield them from direct heat. If the tops of your baked goods brown too quickly, lightly cover them with a sheet of foil to prevent further browning.

The set temperature of electric ovens is usually more accurate than that of gas ovens. Gas ovens tend to fluctuate as much as 25° hotter or cooler than the set temperature; use an oven thermometer to check the accuracy of your oven for best results. Electric ovens may be more energy-efficient because they reach the set temperature more quickly.

Pie crust

Making pie crust is a bugaboo for many people. There are endless caveats about overworking the dough while blending in the butter, adding too much liquid or flour, and overhandling the dough and ending up with a greasy, sticky mess, flour all over your face, and a tough crust. With the advent of food processors, many people who *never* made pie crust in the past have overcome their fears. Food processors cut the flour and butter perfectly and distribute the ice water evenly. The trick is to use cold ingredients and not to overprocess the dough.

If you are going to chill a dough, divide it into single-crust portions and flatten it into disks. When you are ready to roll out the chilled dough, let it soften for 5 to 10 minutes at room temperature to help prevent cracking. Keep the rolling pin, dough, and rolling surface well dusted with flour. Regularly lift and turn the dough to roll more evenly and to make sure it is not sticking. Always roll from the center to the edge, never from the edge to the center. Take care not to tear the dough by catching a sticky edge with the rolling pin. If the dough is impos-

sibly sticky, put the mess on a baking sheet and chill—both you and the dough. Roll a too-crumbly dough between two pieces of plastic wrap or wax paper well dusted with flour.

Sugar syrups and caramel

Sugar syrups are made by melting and cooking sugar, with or without water. When the sugar has just dissolved and the syrup is clear, the syrup can be used on filo pastries, in sorbets, or to sweeten cold drinks. Cooked further, sugar syrup can be used to cook the egg yolks in a classic Buttercream Frosting (page 84). Baked goods absorb flavored syrups or sugar syrups best when both are still hot (or quite warm).

Caramelization occurs when sugar syrup is cooked to an amber brown, acquiring a depth of flavor and color that accents butter, cream, or fruit, as in Caramel Apple Tarte Tatin (page 67). Successful caramelizing requires that all the sugar crystals be completely melted before the syrup is allowed to boil. Any undissolved crystals will set off a chain of crystallization that will ruin the syrup. The following tips may help in your fight against crystallization:

1. Wash down the sides of the pan with a pastry brush dipped in water and/or cover the pot with a tight-fitting lid, which causes steam to wash down the sides of the pot.

2. Do not stir once the syrup has begun to boil.

3. Add a bit of lemon juice to the syrup and/or replace some of the sugar with corn syrup.

A candy thermometer is ideal for monitoring temperature. Otherwise you will need to have a bowl of ice water handy and know your "thread" stage from your "hard crack" stage. Briefly, these are the stages of the syrup when a drop of it is placed in ice water: thread (230° to 236°), soft-ball (234° to 240°), firm-ball (244° to 248°), hard-ball (250° to 265°), soft-crack (270° to 290°), hard-crack (300° to 310°), light-caramel (320° to 338°), dark-caramel (350°).

Whipping

A rigorous circular beating motion with a wire whisk, whip, or electric mixer in order to incorporate air into cream or egg whites.

Heavy cream or whipping cream should be beaten with cold beaters and in a cold bowl. At 45° or higher, cream is less viscous and can be accidentally beaten into butter more easily. Any flavoring or sugar should be added just before the desired consistency is reached.

When whipping egg whites, use warm (not hot) egg whites for the greatest volume. The bowl and beaters must be impeccably clean and dry with no trace of fat from egg yolk or anything else. Stabilize whipped whites with a small amount of acid, such as cream of tartar, which should be added when the whites are still frothy. Other ingredients, such as salt and sugar, should be added when the whites are almost the desired consistency. Added earlier, these ingredients may increase beating time and/or reduce the potential volume of the whipped egg whites.

Pan Sizes by Volume

Below is a chart of the pan sizes used throughout this book and a list of the approximate amounts each pan will hold if filled to capacity with fluid. When filling a pan with batter, never fill it to capacity—always leave ample room for the batter to expand and rise during baking.

At Moosewood we most frequently use standard-sized pans to ensure a reliable baking time and finished baked good. Commercial pan sizes do vary, however, and a variation in the depth of a pan will significantly change its capacity. Our best advice is to know your own pans well. We have especially noticed a difference in the capacities of 10-inch bundt pans, which (depending upon their shape and depth) hold anywhere from 10 to 15 cups of liquid when filled to capacity. When we call for a 10-inch bundt pan, we mean one that will hold 12 cups when full.

Pans with identical volumes but different shapes are not always perfectly interchangeable, since the change in surface area might cause a difference in how the item bakes. In some cases, a substitute pan works fine with a simple adjustment in baking time. In other cases, the particular pan called for is the only answer. We recommend using the specified pan whenever possible. Substituting different pans is always an experiment in which you are taking a chance.

Type	Volume*	Type	Volume*
9-inch round cake pan	6½ cups	10-inch tube pan	12 cups
10-inch round cake pan	10 cups	10 × 3½-inch bundt pan	12 cups
8-inch square baking pan	7 to 8 cups	10 × 4-inch angelfood cake pan	16 cups
9 × 13-inch baking pan	15 to 16 cups	8½ × 4½-inch loaf pan	6 cups
7 × 11-inch baking pan	9 to 10 cups	9 × 5-inch loaf pan (large)	8 to 9 cups
9 × 2-inch springform tube	9 to 10 cups	15½ × 10½ × 1-inch jelly roll pan	10 cups
*Volume equals the pan filled to capacity with fluid.			

Equipment List

THERE ARE FEW THINGS more frustrating than being all set to bake something delicious only to discover you don't have the right pan. Below is a list of all of the equipment you'll need to create the recipes in this book. Using the exact pan size specified in a recipe is not always necessary, but it can spare you possible disappointment. We recommend glass, ceramic, stainless steel, and other nonreactive cooking and baking pans. Aluminum and cast iron interact with citrus and other acidic ingredients and can give your dessert a metallic taste. Having appropriate utensils and equipment increases the ease and enjoyment of cooking and baking, so acquiring them is a worthwhile investment.

Baking sheets

Blender

Bowls, a range: small (3 cups), medium (2 quarts), and large (6 to 8 quarts)

Cake pans

Bundt (10-inch or 12 cups)

Drop bottom:

springform (9 ½-inch or 10-inch)

tube pan (10-inch)

tart pan (9 ¼-inch)

Jelly roll (10½ × 15½ × 1-inch)

Loaf, regular (4½ × 8½ × 2¾-inch)

large (5 × 9 × 3-inch)

Rectangular (7 × 11-inch, 9 × 13-inch, 11 × 15-inch)

Round (9-inch)

Square (8-inch)

Candy thermometer

Cheesecloth

Custard cups (6- or 8-ounce)

Double boiler

Electric mixer

Food processor

Graters (cheese grater or box grater for citrus peels, nutmeg, and ginger root)

Ice cream maker

Measuring cups:

liquid (glass with ounce markings)

dry (cups usually sized in ¼- and ⅓-cup increments)

Measuring spoons

Muffin tin (standard 12-cup)

Nonreactive sauce and sauté pans (glass, stainless steel, ceramic)

Paper cupcake liners

Parchment paper or wax paper

Paring knife

Pastry bag with decorating tips

Pastry brush (1-inch or 2-inch)

Pastry cutter

Pie plates (9-inch and 10-inch)

Pie weights, aluminum or ceramic (or dried beans)

Rolling pin

Rubber spatula

Spice grinder or coffee grinder, or a mortar and pestle

Strainers, small- and medium-sized mesh

Wire cooling racks

Wire whisk

Wooden spoons

Zester

Pantry List

WHEREAS DESSERTS WITH special and/or perishable ingredients will probably require a shopping trip, many of the recipes in this book can be made with ingredients commonly kept on hand. Keeping a well-stocked pantry allows for spontaneity and for baking up a storm on bad weather days.

Chocolate

chocolate chips
cocoa
semi-sweet or bittersweet
unsweetened

Coconut

unsweetened dried grated
unsweetened coconut milk

Dairy products

butter
eggs
heavy cream
powdered buttermilk
sour cream

Extracts and flavorings

(look for "pure" or "natural")

almond extract
coconut flavoring
instant coffee granules, espresso
   powder, or ground espresso
   beans
lemon extract
maple flavoring
orange extract
vanilla extract

Flours, grains, and thickeners

cornmeal
cornstarch
oats (regular rolled)
rice (white, brown, basmati)

wheat flours:
   unbleached all-purpose
   unbleached pastry
   whole wheat pastry

Fruits and vegetables

canned applesauce, apricots,
   pumpkin purée
conserves or all-fruit spreads
dried apples, apricots, cherries,
   cranberries, currants, dates,
   figs, peaches, pears, prunes,
   raisins (look for unsulphured)
frozen juice concentrates: apple,
   orange, raspberry, white grape,
   lemonade or limeade
frozen berries, cherries, peaches,
   rhubarb
juices: apple, pear

Leavenings

baking powder
baking soda
cream of tartar
dry yeast
eggs

Liqueurs, wines, spirits

almond liqueur
brandy
coffee liqueur
hazelnut liqueur
orange liqueur
red and white dry table wines
rum
sherry, dry

Nuts and seeds

almonds
cashews
hazelnuts (filberts)
peanuts
peanut butter
pecans
poppy seeds
sesame seeds
walnuts

Oils

canola
soy or other mildly flavored oil
vegetable oil spray

Pastry, commercially prepared

filo dough (frozen)
puff pastry (frozen)

Soy drinks

Spices

allspice	cloves
anise seed	fennel seed
black pepper	fresh ginger root
cardamom	ground ginger
cayenne	nutmeg
cinnamon	

Sweeteners

brown sugar
confectioners' sugar
granulated sugar
honey
maple syrup, pure
molasses

Mix-and-Match List

Here is a handy list of all of the crusts, fillings, frostings, and glazes in this book to help you experiment to your heart's content. Dress up your most often made cake with a new frosting or filling, try a well-loved pie filling in a new crust, or discover a new sauce or glaze that perfectly complements your favorite fruit, pudding, ice cream, or cupcake.

We have also listed six sauces that are not in the Sauces and Toppings chapter but can be found on particular recipes. You may find other uses for these sauces, so we include them here for your convenience. While some people might enjoy the excuse to browse through the book searching for these "hidden" sauces, others may appreciate this quicker reference.

Pie Crusts

Amaretti Crust (page 159)
Best All-Purpose Pie Crust (page 64)
Chocolate Graham Cracker Crust (page 258)
Cream Cheese Crust (page 65)
Gingerbread Crust (page 58)
Graham Cracker Butter Crust (page 165)
Graham Cracker Coconut Crust (page 162)
Lime Crust (page 62)
Meringue Crust (page 63)
Nutty Oat Crust (page 160)
Shredded Wheat Crust (page 157)
Sour Cream Crust (page 59)
Sweet Lemon Crust (page 65)
Sweet Pastry Crust (page 66)

Fillings

Cherry Cream Cheese Filling (page 92)
Chocolate Almond Filling (page 110)
Chocolate Ganache (page 314)
Coffee Whipped Cream Filling (page 103)
Lemon Curd Filling (page 94)
Lime Curd Filling (page 104)
Ricotta Cheese Filling (page 90)

Frostings

Apple Frosting (page 276)
Bourbon Whipped Cream Frosting (page 86)
Buttercream Frosting (page 84)
Butterscotch Frosting (page 100)
Chocolate Almond Frosting (page 110)
Coffee Frosting (page 109)
Cream Cheese Frosting (page 89)
German Chocolate Cake Frosting (page 147)
Lemon Cream Cheese Frosting (page 277)
Maple Buttercream Frosting (page 101)
Mocha Frosting (page 349)
Orange Frosting (page 98)
Whipped Cream Frosting (page 108)

Glazes

Armagnac Glaze (page 347)
Banana Glaze (page 87)
Bittersweet Chocolate Glaze (page 197)
Chocolate Apricot Glaze (page 279)
Chocolate Cherry Glaze (page 93)
Chocolate Cream Glaze (page 198)
Chocolate Glaze (page 185)
Chocolate Orange Glaze (page 144)
Chocolate Vegan Glaze (page 349)
Coffee Glaze (page 121)
Lemon Glaze (page 266)
Maple Glaze (page 268)
Orange Glaze (page 129)
Spiced Spiked Glaze (page 35)

Sauces

Fresh Strawberry Sauce (page 255)
Gingered Plum Sauce (page 342)
Zesty Orange Sauce* (page 132)
Peanut Coconut Lime Sauce (page 43)
Strawberry Sauce (page 127)
Vanilla Custard Sauce (page 339)

This is a thin but flavorful sauce meant to soak into a cake and disappear.

Easy for Beginning Cooks

MANY BEGINNING COOKS like to begin their culinary explorations with desserts. The recipes in this list are more foolproof than others and require no particular expertise or previous cooking experience to produce good—or even excellent—results.

August Plum Toast
Banana Muffins
Banana Sour Cream Parfait
Black Mocha Cake
Blueberry Peach Sauce
Butterscotch Tapioca
Cherry Almond Crumble
Chocolate Cherry Clafouti
Chocolate Ricotta Mousse
Chocolate Swirled Bread
Couscous Date Pudding
Cowboy Cookies
Creamy Apricot Dip
Creamy Coffee Shake
Dark Chocolate Pudding
   with Bananas
Double Pear Crisp

Frosted Apple Spice
   Cupcakes
Fruit with Cardamom Yogurt
Fruit Ricotta Mousse
Guava Pinwheels
Jewish Holiday Compote
Lemon Loaf
Low-fat Blueberry
   Buttermilk Ice
Maple Cinnamon
   Coffee Sauce
Maple Walnut Bread
Midsummer Fruit in Wine
Moosewood Fudge Brownies
Navajo Peach Crumble
Nut Macaroons
Nutty Fruit Nuggets
Old-Fashioned
   Fresh Apple Cake

Peach Bread Pudding
Peanut Butter Cookies
Peanut Butter Cupcakes
Sautéed Apples
Sour Cream Fruit Dip
Spumoni
Strawberries and Rhubarb
Stuffed Dried Fruit
Summer Berry Sauce
Sunset Punch
Triple Ginger Apple Crisp
Viennese Cupcakes
Warm Apple Walnut Sauce
Yogurt Cream Cheese Parfaits
Zucchini Spice Cake

Entertaining Made Easy
(Desserts to Feed a Crowd)

THESE RECIPES ARE almost as easy to make in multiple batches as in a single batch. The ingredients are not too unusual nor are they costly. None of these dishes requires last-minute attention.

Black Mocha Cake
Buttermilk Spice Cake
Chocolate Date
  Walnut Baklava
Cowboy Cookies
Dark Chocolate Layer Cake
Festive Celebrations Cake
Frosted Orange Layer Cake
Guava Pinwheels
Moosewood Fudge Brownies

Pear and Almond Pizza
Polenta Poundcake
Pumpkin Raisin Poundcake
Savannah Banana Pudding

Stuffed Dried Fruit
Sunset Punch
Texas Italian Cream Cake
Tiramisù di Ithaca

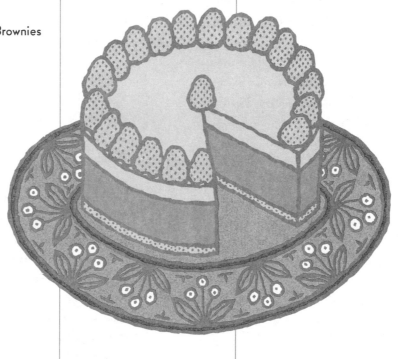

Fun for Kids

CHILDREN HAVE MORE numerous and more sensitive receptors to sweet tastes on their tongues than do adults, yet children's preferences can be just as individual and quirky as adults and maybe harder to categorize. The items on this list were chosen because they're fun to make with children, are proven school bake sale favorites, or are wholesome enough that we would choose them for kids' lunch boxes—or *all* of the above.

Apple Raspberry Crisp
Apricot Lassi
Banana Muffins
Blueberry Cobbler
Boardwalk Bananas
Butter Cookies Three Ways
Butterscotch Banana Cream Pie
Butterscotch Tapioca
Chocolate-Dipped Fresh Fruit
Chocolate Sugar Cookies
Chocolate Swirled Bread
Cocoa
Cowboy Cookies
Dairyless Peanut Butter
   Fudge Pops
Dark Chocolate Layer Cake
Everyday Rice Pudding
Fat-Free Carrot Cake
Flavored Whipped Creams
Frosted Apple Spice Cupcakes
Frosted Orange Layer Cake
Fruit and Nut Truffles
Gingerbread Cookies
Gingerbread Cupcakes

Hot Fudge Sauce
Irish Oatmeal Cake
Low-fat Pineapple Pudding Cake
Mulled Cider
Nut Butter Granola Bars
Nutty Fruit Nuggets
Old-Fashioned Fresh Apple Cake
Our Favorite Poundcake
   (Blueberry Lemon variation)
Peanut Butter Cookies
Peanut Butter Cupcakes
Polenta Poundcake
Profiteroles
Raspberry Poached Apricots
Sautéed Apples
Savannah Banana Pudding
Spiced Pumpkin Squares
Strawberry Mango Lassi
Strawberry Ice Cream Torte
Summer Berry Sauce
Sunset Punch
Sweet Fruit Milks
Things to Do with Ice Cream
   (especially Ice Cream Sandwiches)

Guiltless Low-fat Treats

Anise Almond Biscotti

Apple Ice

Apricot Poached Pears

Blueberry Peach Sauce

Broiled Figs

Butterscotch Tapioca (variation)

California Spa Salad

Caribbean Baked Pineapple

Carriacou Island Fruit Salad

Carrot Pudding

Cherry Sauce

Chocolate Cherry Clafouti
  (low-fat variation)

Chocolate Crispy Rice Macaroons

Chocolate Meringue Cookies

Coffee Breeze

Couscous Date Pudding

Cranberry Apricot Pear Sauce

Dried Fruit and Vanilla Sauce

Fat-Free Carrot Cake

Fig, Pear, and Orange Compote

Fresh Mango Sauce

Fruit with Cardamom Yogurt

Gingerbread Cupcakes (variation)

Gingerbread with Pears

Granita di Caffé

Grapefruit Tequila Slush

Indian Pudding (variation)

Jewish Holiday Compote

Light Chocolate Sauce

Low-fat Blueberry Buttermilk Ice

Low-fat Creamy Toppings

Low-fat Lemon Pudding Cake

Low-fat Pineapple Pudding Cake

Low-fat Sweet Potato Pudding

Manhattan Papaya Frappe

Melon Midori Slush

Midsummer Fruit in Wine

Mulled Cider

Nutty Fruit Nuggets

Orange and Ginger Islands

Orange Coconut Angelfood Cake

Orange Merringues

Orange Sauce

Pear Meringue Tart

Pear Sorbet

Pecan Currant Biscotti

Plum Strudel

Raspberry Poached Apricots

Raspberry Sauce

Southern Compote

Spiced Cranberry Punch

Spiced Ethiopian-style Coffee

Spiced Tea

Strawberries and Rhubarb

Summer Berry Pudding

Summer Berry Sauce

Sunset Punch

Tropical Fruit Ice

Vanilla Poached Apples

Very Low-fat Vanilla Cheesecake

Watermelon Licuado

Winter Fruit Strudel

Impressive Eye-Catchers

THESE ARE ELEGANT DESSERTS, sure to win "oohs" and "ahs" when you are entertaining guests.

Amaretto Peach Parfait

Apple Dumplings

Bellini

Big Banana Bourbon Cake

Broiled Figs

Cassata

Champagne Zabaglione

Chocolate Almond
    Meringue Torte

Chocolate Cherry
    Angelfood Cake

Chocolate Date
    Walnut Baklava

Chocolate Espresso Roll

Chocolate Fruit Purses

Chocolate Grand
    Marnier Cake

Coconut Lemon Layer Cake

Crème Brûlée

Filo Pastry Cups

Fresh Fruit Trifle

Frosted Orange Layer Cake

Fruit and Nut Truffles

Irish Whiskey Cake

Jammy Cake Shortbread

Katie's Orange Cookies

Lemon Jelly Roll

Mocha Grappa Truffles

Mocha Walnut Torte

Pear and Almond Pizza

Pizza di Grano

Profiteroles

Prune and Armagnac Cake

Pumpkin Ice Cream Strata

Raspberry Chocolate
    Cheesecake

Scandinavian Berry Pie

Southern Nut Pie Eudora

Summer Berry Pudding

Tangerine Cheesecake

Three Nut Tart

Tiramisù di Ithaca

White Chocolate and
    Raspberry Fool

Winter Fruit Strudel

Zuccotto

Last-Minute Desserts in a Pinch

THESE DESSERTS DON'T HAVE many ingredients and none of the ingredients are difficult to track down. They can be whipped together and ready to serve in a half hour or less.

Amaretto Peach Parfait
Apricot Lassi
Avocado Lime Shake
Banana Muffins
Bittersweet Chocolate Sauce
Blueberry Peach Sauce
California Date Shake
Caribbean Baked Pineapple
Cherry Sauce
Chocolate-Dipped Fresh Fruit
Cocoa
Coffee Breeze
Creamy Coffee Shake
Dried Fruit and Vanilla Sauce
Filo Pastry Cups
Flavored Whipped Creams
Fruit and Cheese
Fruit Ricotta Mousse
Gingered Plum Sauce
Hot Chocolate
Hot Fudge Sauce
Light Chocolate Sauce

Low-fat Creamy Toppings
Maple Cinnamon Coffee Sauce
Moosewood Fudge Brownies
Nutty Fruit Nuggets
Orange Sauce
Pineapple Coconut Smoothie
Raspberry Sauce
Rum Custard Sauce
Rum Sabayon Sauce
Sautéed Apples
Southern Compote
Spiced Ethiopian-style Coffee
Spiced Nuts
Spiced Tea
Strawberry Mango Lassi
Stuffed Dried Fruit
Summer Berry Sauce
Sunset Punch
Sweet Fruit Milks
Things to Do with Ice Cream
Tropical Fruit Colada
Warm Apple Walnut Sauce

Prepared in No Time

THESE DESSERTS MAY NEED to bake, chill, or freeze, but the actual hands-on work time is very short.

Amaretto Peach Parfait
Apple Ice
Apple Raspberry Crisp
Apricot Amaretto Tortoni
Apricot Lassi
August Plum Toast
Avocado Lime Shake
Banana Muffins
Banana Sour Cream Parfait
Bellini
Besbusa
Bittersweet Chocolate Sauce
Black and White Brownies
Black Mocha Cake
Blackberry Slump with Orange
    Dumplings
Blueberry Cobbler
Blueberry Peach Sauce
Boardwalk Bananas
Brandied Raisin Sour Cream
    Poundcake
Broiled Figs
Butterscotch Tapioca
California Date Shake
Cappuccino Cheesecake
Caramel Apple Tarte Tatin
Caribbean Baked Pineapple
Carriacou Island Fruit Salad

Carrot Pudding
Champagne Zabaglione
Cherry Almond Crumble
Cherry Sauce
Chocolate Cherry Clafouti
Chocolate-Dipped Fresh Fruit
Chocolate Fruit Purses
Chocolate Ginger Cake
Chocolate Ricotta Mousse
Cocoa
Coffee Breeze
Coffee Flan
Couscous Date Pudding
Cranberry Orange Coffeecake
Creamy Apricot Dip
Creamy Coffee Shake
Creamy Rice Pudding
Dairyless Peanut Butter
    Fudge Pops
Dark Chocolate Pudding
    with Bananas
Dried Fruit and Vanilla Sauce
Easiest Peach Ice Cream
Filo Pastry Cups
Flan de Piña y Lima
Flavored Whipped Creams
Flourless Chocolate Cake
Fluffy Sweet Biscuits
Fresh Mango Sauce

Frosted Apple Spice
    Cupcakes
Fruit and Cheese
Fruit and Nut Truffles
Fruit with Cardamom Yogurt
Fruit Ricotta Mousse
Ginger Pear Puff
Gingerbread Cupcakes
Gingerbread with Pears
Gingered Plum Sauce
Granita di Caffé
Grapefruit Tequila Slush
Honey Cake
Hot Chocolate
Hot Fudge Sauce
Indian Pudding
Lemon Raspberry Flan
Light Chocolate Sauce
Low-fat Blueberry
    Buttermilk Ice
Low-fat Creamy Toppings
Low-fat Lemon Pudding Cake
Low-fat Pineapple
    Pudding Cake
Mango Mousse
Manhattan Papaya Frappe
Maple Cinnamon
    Coffee Sauce
Maple Walnut Baked Apples

Maple Walnut Bread
Melon Midori Slush
Midsummer Fruit in Wine
Mocha Grappa Truffles
Moosewood Fudge
    Brownies
Mulled Cider
Navajo Peach Crumble
Nut Macaroons
Nutty Fruit Nuggets
Olive Oil and Citrus Cake
Orange and Ginger Islands
Orange Sauce
Our Favorite Poundcake
Peanut Butter Cupcakes
Pineapple Banana
    Upside-Down Cake

Pineapple Coconut Smoothie
Plum Upside-Down Cake
Pots de Crème à l'Orange
Poundcake Loaf
Profiteroles
Pumpkin Cranberry Muffins
Raspberry Poached Apricots
Raspberry Sauce
Red Devil Cake
Rum Custard Sauce
Rum Sabayon Sauce
Ruth's Sour Cream
    Coffee Cake
Sautéed Apples
Six Minute Chocolate Cake
Sour Cream Fruit Dip
Southern Compote
Southern Nut Pie Eudora

Spiced Cranberry Punch
Spiced Ethiopian-style Coffee
Spiced Nuts
Spiced Pumpkin Squares
Spiced Tea
Strawberries and Rhubarb
Strawberry Mango Lassi
Stuffed Dried Fruit
Summer Berry Pudding
Summer Berry Sauce
Sunset Punch
Sweet Fruit Milks
Tangerine Cheesecake
Things to Do with Ice Cream
Torta di Ricotta
Triple Ginger Apple Crisp
Tropical Fruit Colada
Tropical Fruit Ice
Tropical Fruit Crêpes
Vanilla Poached Apples
Viennese Cupcakes
Warm Apple Walnut Sauce
Watermelon Licuado

Vegan Desserts

VEGAN DESSERTS CONTAIN no foodstuffs of animal origin—no meat, fish, dairy products, eggs, or honey.

Apple Ice
Apricot Poached Pears
Avocado Lime Shake
Bellini
Blueberry Peach Sauce
Broiled Figs
California Date Shake
Candied Citrus Zest
Caribbean Baked Pineapple
Carriacou Island Fruit Salad
Cherry Sauce
Chocolate-Dipped Fresh Fruit
Couscous Date Pudding
Cranberry Apricot Pear Sauce
Dairyless Peanut Butter Fudge
   Pops
Dried Fruit and Vanilla Sauce
Everyday Rice Pudding
Fat-Free Carrot Cake
Fig, Pear, and Orange Compote
Fresh Mango Sauce
Gingered Plum Sauce
Granita di Caffé
Grapefruit Tequila Slush
Indian Pudding (soy variation)
Jewish Holiday Compote

Manhattan Papaya Frappe
Maple Walnut Baked Apples
Melon Midori Slush
Midsummer Fruit in Wine
Mulled Cider
Nutty Fruit Nuggets
Orange Sauce
Pear Sorbet
Raspberry Poached Apricots
Raspberry Sauce
Six Minute Chocolate Cake
Spiced Cranberry Punch
Spiced Ethiopian-style Coffee
Spiced Tea
Strawberries and Rhubarb
Stuffed Dried Fruit
Summer Berry Pudding
Summer Berry Sauce
Sunset Punch
Southern Compote
Tropical Fruit Colada
Tropical Fruit Ice
Tropical Tofu "Cheesecake" (variation)
Vanilla Poached Apples (variation)
Watermelon Licuado

ACKNOWLEDGMENTS

As time goes on and we grow a bit older, those of us in the Moosewood Collective realize more and more that we are a lucky bunch. Yes, we work hard. But the good fortune and stellar supporters that buoy us during the challenging times are gifts we can only smile at with a mixture of wonder and gratitude.

People write to us from all over the world, and we never tire of receiving the mail, whether it contains unconditional praise, thanks, suggestions, favorite recipes, or criticism. We tack this correspondence on the kitchen bulletin board for everyone to read, and we thank all of you who take the time and effort to contact us. When the dishwasher breaks or the produce delivery is delayed by icy roads, a cheery note or card delivered by the mailman can make all the difference.

With twenty collective members and almost as many loyal, energetic employees, our extended family looms large, including friends, family, business associates, and our faithful regular customers. A few people offered us recipes or recipe ideas for this book and when we used a donated recipe, we made the person's name part of the recipe title to acknowledge the contribution. Many more people tasted our new desserts-in-progress and gave helpful advice or an emphatic thumbs-up. We thank you for all of your encouragement, appetite, camaraderie, and laughter.

We feel especially fortunate to have our exceptionally talented editor, Pam Krauss, and the staff at Clarkson Potter collaborating with us on our cookbook projects. Never before have we experienced such a mountain of level-headed, good-natured, coordinated, creative, and enthusiastic support packed into a publishing house. We suspect Pam may have been lacing the coffee breaks at work with samples of our chocolate desserts. But whatever the reason, we thrive on the energy of the connection.

To our agents, Elise and Arnold Goodman, we can only say that we were under a lucky star when we found you. You simply can't be beat and that's it in a nutshell. Thanks for all the interest you've shown in getting to know us, both as a group and as individuals, over these last dozen years. You have demonstrated a commitment and way of caring all too often absent in the professional world. All of us at Moosewood appreciate your efforts on our behalf. And we savor your advice (and your jokes)—why . . . like mocha truffles!

And last but not least, to the readers and cooks who use our books, a big heartfelt thank you. And thank goodness for food!

INDEX

Conversion Chart
EQUIVALENT IMPERIAL AND METRIC MEASUREMENTS

American cooks use standard containers, the 8-ounce cup and a tablespoon that takes exactly 16 level fillings to fill that cup level. (It is possible to buy a set of American cup measures in major stores around the world.) Measuring by cup makes it very difficult to give weight equivalents, as a cup of densely packed butter will weigh considerably more than a cup of flour. The easiest way therefore to deal with cup measurements in recipes is to take the amount by volume rather than by weight. Thus the equation reads:

1 cup = 240 ml = 8 fl. oz.   ½ cup = 120 ml = 4 fl. oz.

In the States, butter is often measured in sticks. One stick is the equivalent of 8 tablespoons. One tablespoon of butter is therefore the equivalent to ½ ounce/ 15 grams.

Solid Measures

U.S. AND IMPERIAL MEASURES		METRIC MEASURES	
Ounces	Pounds	Grams	Kilos
1		28	
2		56	
3½		100	
4	¼	112	
5		140	
6		168	
8	½	225	
9		250	¼
12	¾	340	
16	1	450	
18		500	½
20	1¼	560	
24	1½	675	
27		750	¾
32	2	900	
36	2¼	1000	1

Oven Temperature Equivalents

FAHRENHEIT	CELSIUS	GAS MARK	DESCRIPTION
225	110	¼	Cool
250	130	½	
275	140	1	Very Slow
300	150	2	
325	170	3	Slow
350	180	4	Moderate
375	190	5	
400	200	6	Moderately Hot
425	220	7	Fairly Hot
450	230	8	Hot
475	240	9	Very Hot
500	250	10	Extremely Hot

Liquid Measures

FLUID OUNCES	U.S.	IMPERIAL	MILLILITERS
	1 teasp.	1 teasp.	5
¼	2 teasp.	1 dessertsp.	10
½	1 tablesp.	1 tablesp.	14
1	2 tablesp.	2 tablesp.	28
2	¼ cup	4 tablesp.	56
4	½ cup		110
5		¼ pint/1 gill	140
8	1 cup		225
9			250, ¼ liter
10	1¼ cups	½ pint	280
15		¾ pint	420
16	2 cups		450
20	2½ cups	1 pint	560
24	3 cups		675
27	3½ cups		750
30	3¾ cups	1½ pints	840

Ingredient Equivalents

all-purpose flour—plain flour

beet—beetroot

coarse salt—kitchen salt

confectioner's sugar—icing sugar

cornstarch—cornflour

granulated sugar—caster sugar

half and half—12% fat milk

heavy cream—double cream

light cream—single cream

shortening—white fat

unbleached flour—strong, white flour

vanilla bean—vanilla pod

zest—rind

zucchini—courgettes